TUNISIA

TUNISIA

An Arab Anomaly

SAFWAN M. MASRI

FOREWORD BY LISA ANDERSON

Columbia University Press
New York

Columbia University Press
Publishers Since 1893
New York   Chichester, West Sussex
cup.columbia.edu

Library of Congress Cataloging-in-Publication Data
Names: Masri, Safwan M., author.
Title: Tunisia : an Arab anomaly / Safwan M. Masri.
Description: New York : Columbia University Press, 2017. | Includes
   bibliographical references and index.
Identifiers: LCCN 2017009826 (print) | LCCN 2017011385 (ebook) |
   ISBN 9780231545020 | ISBN 9780231179508 (alk. paper)
Subjects: LCSH: Tunisia—History—Demonstrations, 2010– | Tunisia—Politics
   and government—20th century. | Tunisia—Politics and government—21st
   century. | Tunisia—History. | Tunisia—Social conditions—20th century. |
   Tunisia—Social conditions—21st century.
Classification: LCC DT266.94 (ebook) | LCC DT266.94 .M378 2017 (print) |
   DDC 961.1053—dc23
LC record available at https://lccn.loc.gov/2017009826

Columbia University Press books are printed on permanent
and durable acid-free paper.
Printed in the United States of America

Cover design: Jordan Wannemacher
Cover image: © lantapix / Alamy Stock Photo

To the loving memory of my parents:
my mother, Inam, who was, and is, my best friend,
inspiration, and role model of a learner, teacher, and woman;
and my father, Malek, who embraced difference, rejected dogma,
and lived and loved by his own rules.

Contents

Political Map of Tunisia, 2016

Drawn by Martin Hinze. Map data © 2017 Google, Inst. Geogr. Nacional.

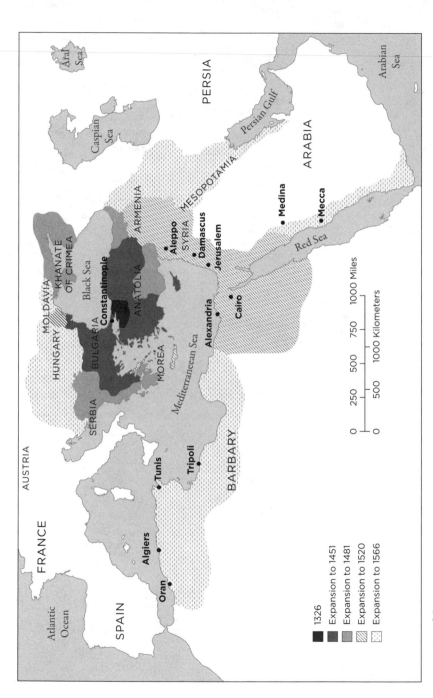

Expansion of the Ottoman Empire, 1326–1566

Drawn by Martin Hinze. Adapted from "Map: The Growth of the Ottoman Empire," from *Western Civilizations: Their History & Their Culture*, sixteenth edition, by Judith G. Coffin and Robert C. Stacey. Copyright © 2008, 2005, 2002, 1998, 1993, 1988, 1984, 1980, 1973, 1968, 1958, 1954, 1947, 1941 by W. W. Norton & Company, Inc.

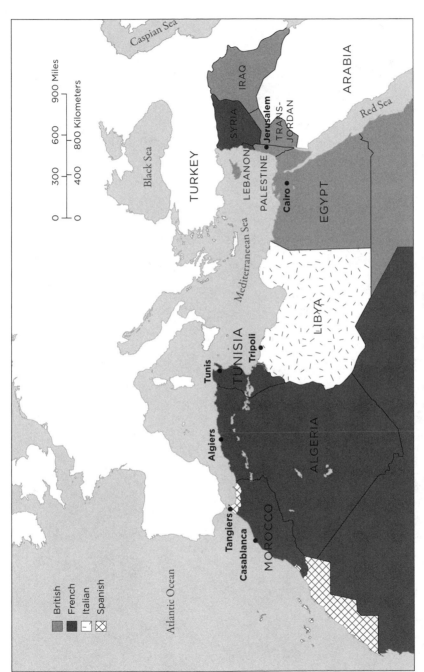

European Colonies and Spheres of Influence in North Africa and the Middle East, 1930

Drawn by Martin Hinze. Adapted from Royal Geographic Society maps, "Political Map of Africa Showing International Boundaries and Railways" (War Office, 1921) and "The Country Between the Balkans and Mesopotamia" (Edward Stanford, 1921).

Foreword

T unisia is enchanting. A country of pleasant coastal sea breezes, gentle winter rains in the north and warm, bright sun in the interior plains and southern desert, it has long entranced visitors. From the ancient Phoenician colonists who founded Carthage to the Moorish traveler Leo Africanus to European travelers, artists, and adventurers like Alexandre Dumas, Guy de Maupassant, Isabelle Eberhardt, Oscar Wilde, Aldous Huxley, Paul Klee, André Gide, Jean-Paul Sartre, and Simone de Beauvoir, Tunisia has been hospitable, engaging, and captivating.

Small wonder that Safwan Masri, too, is taken with Tunisia.

For Safwan—I use his given name here both because he and I have been colleagues at Columbia University for many years and because such easy familiarity befits the distinctive spirit of this book—Tunisia is more than a lovely interlude, and more than striking scenery for a painting or the colorful setting of a story or even, as it once was for me, a promising site in which to conduct social science research. No, for Safwan, it is a compelling personal puzzle, and this book is the result of his determination to solve that puzzle.

Tunisia: An Arab Anomaly is not a formal academic work of social science, as Safwan readily acknowledges. Indeed, it is the outcome of a deeply subjective quest to understand both himself and his society as they are reflected in the promise and mystery of Tunisia, a place at once familiar and foreign to him. Because he is not alone in this quest, the book represents a contribution to the debates about tradition and modernity, about cultural authenticity and civilizational unease, that shape contemporary life in much of the Arab world in our time.

Safwan was born and reared in Jordan. His parents were Muslim, Arabic is his mother tongue, and he is still deeply loyal to his family and friends there. Indeed, he has worked closely with the government of the Hashemite Kingdom for many years to enhance educational opportunities for the youth of the country. Yet his life in the United States, as a student, professor, and university administrator, afforded him astonishing opportunity. Steeped in American culture, he has been allowed—indeed, expected—to be professionally ambitious and successful, and he has certainly met that expectation. But he also found that he was permitted—indeed expected—to be personally fulfilled as an individual as well, and this expectation was, perhaps, an unanticipated and deeply affecting feature of American life. He has been profoundly shaped by classic American liberalism, with its emphasis on individual freedom, social equality, moral universalism, and underlying optimism. He has become what President John Kennedy characterized in 1960 as a "liberal":

> . . . someone who looks ahead and not behind, someone who welcomes new ideas without rigid reactions, someone who cares about the welfare of the people—their health, their housing, their schools, their jobs, their civil rights, and their civil liberties—someone who believes we can break through the stalemate and suspicions that grip us in our policies abroad.[1]

Those values have unleashed what seems to be a natural confidence and enthusiasm in Safwan, but they are in short supply in the Arab world today, which is fraught instead with anxiety and doubt, and suffused with the timidity and conservatism that so often accompany such trepidation.

Except, perhaps, in Tunisia.

Tunisia inaugurated the upheavals that came to be known as the Arab Spring, and it is the only country in the region that seems to be weathering the winter that followed—the periods of violence and counterrevolution that have convulsed Egypt, Libya, Syria and Yemen. Why? Why did the revolt start there? Why does it seem to have had more lasting power there? Why, when the other countries that had joined Tunisia in shaking off tyranny collapsed into civil war or renewed military rule, did Tunisia itself seem to manage to reform its state institutions, to resort to debate and dialogue—often heated but very rarely violent—to air difference and come to compromise?

It is not yet clear that the Tunisian experience is the success that both Tunisians and the rest of the world hope it will be. As the Chinese premier, Zhou Enlai, is famously reported to have observed in 1972, when asked about the impact of the French Revolution, it may be "too early to say."[2] Certainly, Tunisian hopes for civil, competitive politics and for accountable government have been raised and dashed before, not least when Zine al-Abidine Ben Ali, the despot overthrown in the revolt of 2010–11, first came into office nearly twenty-five years earlier.

But the style and spirit with which Tunisians took to the street, brought down their ruler, and then debated among themselves about the kind of government and the sort of leaders they wanted are remarkable enough to raise the sort of questions that preoccupy Safwan in this book. How is it that Tunisia seems to combine the Arab habits and routines he remembers so fondly from his youth with the liberal traditions of his liberating American adulthood? This synthetic character has long been a signal feature of Tunisia. Indeed, the first president of Tunisia, Habib Bourguiba, made much of the hybrid "Mediterranean personality" of the country in his nationalist discourses: Tunisia as a crossroads, a hybrid, a synthesis.

For Safwan, as for many others, the sources of this magic are myriad and, in what may best be read as a series of essays strung on a cord of affection and fascination, he explores various answers. He turns to Tunisia's unique geography at the edge of the Sahara and ninety miles from Sicily and to the march of empires that made Tunisia their home and left their mark: Carthaginian, Roman, Byzantine, Berber, Arab, Ottoman, and French. He examines the local character of Islam in Tunisian history and practice, the nineteenth-century encounters with the eastern Ottoman world and with Europe, and the legacy of the twentieth-century nationalist movement. He examines the stubbornly pro-Western leadership of post-independence Tunisia under President Bourguiba and Bourguiba's determined efforts to ensure that religious obscurantism did not inhibit economic development or prevent enlargement of women's rights or the expansion of education. Perhaps naturally, having spent much of his life in universities, Safwan finds Tunisia's modern history of educational reform, from the nineteenth century to today, a particularly important ingredient in the Tunisian recipe for success.

Safwan's conviction that Tunisia is an "Arab anomaly" is hardly unique. Commenting on the elections of 2014, the *Washington Post* called Tunisia an "apparent anomaly in [the] Middle East."[3] The next year, the press release for the Nobel Peace Prize, which was awarded to the Tunisian National Dialogue Quartet, observed that "[t]he course that events have taken in Tunisia since the fall of the authoritarian Ben Ali regime in January 2011 is unique and remarkable for several reasons," and then rehearsed those reasons:

> Firstly, it shows that Islamist and secular political movements can work together to achieve significant results in the country's best interests. The example of Tunisia thus underscores the value of dialogue and a sense of national belonging in a region marked by conflict. Secondly, the transition in Tunisia shows that civil society institutions and organizations can play a crucial role in a country's democratization, and that such a process, even under difficult circumstances, can lead to free elections and the peaceful transfer of power. The National Dialogue Quartet must be given much of the credit for this achievement and for ensuring that the benefits of the Jasmine Revolution have not been lost.[4]

A good part of Tunisia's seductiveness is that the country invites hope. The Nobel Committee decided it was not "too early to say" that Tunisia's transition had succeeded, just as the country had raised hopes at independence and again at the beginning of Ben Ali's presidency. One hopes, of course, that the well-wishers are not wrong. I concede that I harbor a worry, a small lingering doubt, born of an earlier disappointment. Shortly after Ben Ali came to power, he orchestrated the negotiation of a National Pact that seemed to signal a commitment to democratic government. At the time, I wrote with some enthusiasm about the Pact, not least because it was the introduction of a device that had been used successfully in then-recent democratic transitions in Latin America. I concluded optimistically:

> The Tunisian National Pact constitutes an effort to reiterate and celebrate the solidarity of the Tunisian people—their fidelity to their Islamic heritage, their pride in the nationalist struggle—while admitting and,

indeed, encouraging the existence of pluralism of ideas and interests. Far from introducing a conservative bias into subsequent political relations, this pact may be better understood as an effort to foster the tolerance of dissent and opposition which is a cornerstone of democratic politics. That the Pact itself is only a first tentative step in that direction should be apparent; there are many pitfalls in any transition of a regime. What is significant is not necessarily how far the National Pact has taken the Tunisians, but the direction in which it points.[5]

That optimism, tentative as it was, proved to be entirely uncalled for: within a few years, Tunisia's government was among the most despotic kleptocracies in the world. The wishful thinking that Tunisia evokes in so many of us conspired with the then-government's remarkable public relations skill to make us believe what was not true. From the world's tourist agencies and tour operators to the too-credulous international financial institutions, all of us who love Tunisia closed our eyes to the descent into corruption and tyranny that finally provoked the uprisings of 2010–11.

Today we can only hope that the doubters are wrong and that Safwan's sanguine assessment of the current transition is more accurate and that the change is durable.

Lisa Anderson

Preface

As millions like me followed the unfolding of regional events in 2011 and after, and as hope often gave way to despair, Tunisia took us by pleasant surprise: what started as the toppling of a regime and the setting into motion of the Arab Spring ended, unlike anywhere else, with a peaceful transition to a functioning democracy.

But should Tunisia have taken us by surprise? What made Tunisia such a special case? Did the way that things evolved *make* Tunisia unusual, or did they develop the way that they did *because* Tunisia has always been exceptional?

As I thought, discussed, read, and started to write, I yearned to validate a hypothesis that a country where certain liberal conditions existed—women's rights, modern education, and religious moderation—might just have a better chance than most to transition to democracy. Trips to Tunisia since the Jasmine Revolution helped clinch that conviction and spark a journey of inquiry.

So I became a student of Tunisia, driven not only by a quest to understand Tunisia, but also to better comprehend the Arab world through Tunisia, and vice versa.

The more I delved, through interviews and secondary research sources, and the further I compared and dove into my own recollections and lived experiences, the more I became convinced that my hypothesis held some promise: there is something unique and special about Tunisia that is missing in the rest of the Arab world, to which Tunisia both belongs and does not.

My story thus developed, and I now share it in the pages of this book. This is my narrative of Tunisia and the history that has shaped it. It is also a commentary on the Arab world, told through the lens of Tunisia. It is a personal account to a large extent as I bring to it a particular prism through which I examine Tunisia and the world. But it is also personal in that I became drawn to Tunisia, mind and soul—hoping for hope. In its story, I have found the beginnings to many answers I have sought.

This book examines social, intellectual, and political factors that, I will argue, prepared the Tunisian people for a successful democracy. It is about history, and it is about the present and the future. It synthesizes existing knowledge and is also based on hundreds of hours of interviews with dozens of experts, leaders, activists, and ordinary citizens—framing things analytically, and at times counterintuitively, to help connect dots and make sense of an emergent peaceful and largely liberal democracy in a sea of turmoil.

This is not a political science book, nor does it deal with revolutionary or democratic transition political theory. The book does not presume to be an academic treatise or the work of a historian, for it is neither. I am, after all, a systems engineer by training and have taught as a business professor for much of my career. But over the past decade, I have founded educational institutions in the Middle East and have, as my primary occupation, helped to extend Columbia's global presence. Ultimately, I identify as an educator and a student of the world.

When I started the project that has culminated in this book, my objective was not, at least consciously, to write a book. An idea was born, and it evolved into the pages of this book. I have been writing this book all my life, it seems; it has crystalized for me beliefs that I have held and ideas that I have developed over many years.

It commenced with a set of hand-scribbled notes that I took on a trip to Tunisia with Columbia University president Lee C. Bollinger; his wife, the artist Jean Magnano Bollinger; and our colleague and friend Susan Glancy. The four of us have traveled extensively around the world, seeking to understand firsthand global developments and regional and local specificities. I had been accustomed to learning with and from them.

But this experience was different, and it offered more. My interpretations and impressions were formed, it seemed, by a sense of being at once on the inside and on the outside. The visit opened my eyes in a manner that I do not think would have been otherwise possible.

Notes such as the ones I took on that trip usually end up in a drawer, or if they were really going to serve as a reference, they would be compiled and transcribed. But with these notes, I found myself expanding and researching further, and before I knew it, I had a document from the development of which I knew I was gaining much satisfaction. It also helped that I had just hired a brilliant research assistant, Raina Davis, who became my partner in the endeavor. In this document, I felt that I had the nucleus of a dissertation that had Tunisia as a focal point but was about to encompass much more.

In many respects, this book is an attempt to reconcile conflicting narratives of what is right and what is wrong. It seeks to understand how an identity and a set of values may coalesce from otherwise divergent directions and sensibilities. It is about Tunisia and the Arab world, but it is also about Islam, about Arabism, and about a struggle to authenticate an acceptance, or at least an understanding, of both sides of a conflict.

Through my life and work in the Middle East, I have come into intimate contact with the pervasive dogmas that dominate in most of the Arab world. I have been particularly drawn to how education systems were developed and the role that they have had in shaping the region's societal dynamics and its Realpolitik. I have experienced the region's religious hegemony, exclusionary identity politics, stifling of individualism, and repression of attempts to search for the truth, particularly truths that challenge conventional rhetoric.

We are told in the Arab world what political values to uphold and what is wrong and what is right about how we perceive the world and the injustices it has bestowed upon us. There is little, if any, room for deviation from "absolute" truths. If we begin to question accepted doctrines about identity, religion, and conflict, we are shamed into thinking that we are betraying our heritage. If we dare question the wisdom of our ancestors or look into a mirror for causes of injustices that we might have brought onto ourselves, we are accused of having been indoctrinated by corrupt Western perspectives. If we try to bring nuance into an issue with two sides to it, we are stigmatized as "enemy-sympathizers."

We are a proud people and find it very difficult to be self-critical, especially if it exposes our weaknesses to others. But if we do not face our histories and admit our failures, we do not evolve. From Tunisia, there are perhaps a few lessons to be learned.

I grew up in Jordan and have spent my life in and out of the Arab world, navigating West and East—professionally, culturally, and personally. I have witnessed firsthand the societal changes overtaking the region with increased sectarianism, radicalization, and religiosity.

I was born into Islam. My family, of Palestinian stock, was secular and modern, but when my parents married, Islam proved handy as my father already had a wife.

My identity has been shaped by a blend of various, often divergent, norms, values, and experiences. My personal journey, as well as my relationship with religion, sexuality, and feminism, informs my perspectives and influences my analysis.

As human beings, we often spend our lives redefining ourselves and asserting our individual identities. When we are born, we are given our identities and told what characteristics we are to assume in our lives, religious and nationalistic—identifiers that are not innate and were not programmed into our DNA. In countries of the Middle East, religious identities circumscribe us, and they become our passports. There is no escaping them, even after we die. Islamic law governs our earthly and "otherworldly" existence and affairs, whether we self-identify as Muslim or not. When I complained to my attorney friend that I did not wish to have a Muslim burial upon my death, the best advice that he could conjure up was for me not to die in Jordan.

In the West, we concern ourselves with such relatively advanced notions of freedom as those of expression, the press, and academic discourse. We take for granted basic personal freedoms, such as those of conscience, belief systems, and, increasingly, sexual and gender identity.

Tunisia provided me with a window into something different and into what might be possible in the Arab world. Freedom of conscience is a fundamental right, constitutionally protected, limiting religious and state hegemony over personal lives—private and public.

Part of what I have to say in this book will make some readers uncomfortable. Tackling taboo subjects such as religion, sexuality, Arab identity, and other social dimensions challenges mainstream Arab discourses.

My attempt at a frank and nuanced treatment of overriding perspectives on, and perceptions of, what are accepted as absolute truths, including histories and attitudes toward conflict, will undoubtedly prove controversial. But my intention is not to provoke unnecessarily, and it certainly is not to offend. What I offer is my honest take on matters, as I see them.

In discussing what has distinguished Tunisia and in drawing regional comparisons, the book may seem prejudicial at times. I will also disproportionately, but naturally, focus more of my analysis on Jordan. Jordan is where I lived, was schooled, and at times worked. It is important to note that my scrutiny of Jordan is not meant to suggest that there has not been a history, and a culture, of moderation in the country. There indeed has been, and this makes the presence of negative, regional trends in Jordan especially disconcerting.

The Tunisian experience—and my experience with Tunisia—has led me on a journey of discovery of self and of the region to which I belong. How Tunisia evolves will have much to say about how we evolve and how our world develops.

In an essay for *Vanity Fair*, Christopher Hitchens pondered the future of Tunisia, painting as he did in 2007 two potential scenarios: "Will the northern littoral of Africa become a zone of tension, uneasily demarcating a watery yet fiery line between Europe and the southern continent? Or will it evolve into a meeting place of cultures, trading freely and cross-fertilizing the civilizations, as it did once before?" In considering his trip to Tunisia for the essay, Hitchens sought Edward Said's counsel. "You should go to Tunisia, Christopher," was Edward's response, "It's the gentlest country in Africa. Even the Islamists are highly civilized."[1]

Maybe there is some latent prophecy in Hitchens's pondering, and perhaps the gains that Tunisia, arguably the gentlest of Arab countries, has made not over the years, or decades, but centuries, can be consolidated.

Introduction

Very little has been written, and is thus understood, about why Tunisia, the country that gave birth to the Arab Spring, has been the only democracy to emerge from it. "Why Tunisia?" is a question that resonates among Arabs yearning for similar democratic outcomes and wondering why such freedoms remain out of their reach.

Inspired by Tunisia's example, Arab publics rose up in expectant defiance, first in solidarity with Tunisians but then for change in its own right at home, setting into motion a domino effect that became known as the "Arab Spring." But that spring quickly turned into a dark and stormy winter, crushing all hopes for better lives and representative governments for those who had challenged the repressive status quo.

Egypt takes the prize when it comes to a revolution that dashed democratic hopes almost as quickly as it had created them. Twice, "democratic" methods were used to bring down democracy—first by the Muslim Brotherhood and then by the military. The nondemocratic conduct of the popularly elected Muslim Brotherhood brought about their fall at the hands of the military, who seized power "in defense of democracy" and were subsequently "democratically" elected only to revert back to Mubarak-style military rule.

Neighboring Libya is by all accounts a failed state: ungoverned and ruptured into fiefdoms, each a playground for one Gulf monarchy or another to advance its own version of Islamic hegemony or military rule. Coveted as an Islamic state by the likes of Da'esh, it exports terrorism through its porous borders with Tunisia.

Syria's conflict has resulted in the worst humanitarian disaster of our time and the largest refugee crisis since the Second Word War. Yemen erupted in an all-out war, serving as a proxy for a broader sectarian struggle between Saudi Arabia and Iran. Iraq suffered a decade-long foreign invasion and has, for all practical purposes, collapsed from within along sectarian divides—overrun by a violent extremist group that has fed off of these very tensions. The legacy of years of instability has spread beyond the region as hundreds of migrants have tried to cross the Mediterranean each day, many perishing along the way.

By contrast, the uprisings that took place in Tunisia during December 2010 and January 2011 and culminated in the toppling of autocratic president Zine al-Abidine Ben Ali yielded a democracy that is unique in an Arab context. By 2015, less than four years after the Jasmine Revolution, the country had adopted a progressive constitution, held fair parliamentary elections, and ushered in the country's first-ever democratically elected president. For the first time in an Arab country, an Islamist party, Ennahda, dropped its Islamist label and redefined itself, in May 2016, as a party of Muslim democrats—shifting its political focus to the country's economy and banning party leadership from participating in religious and charitable organizations or preaching in mosques.

Two peaceful transitions of power bode well for Tunisia's prospects as an inveterate democracy. Following elections in 2011, a troika of divergent parties and ideologies was formed and provided transitional leadership until it was disbanded in 2013, making way for a technocratic government that oversaw the 2014 elections. The formation of a coalition government in 2015—including the choice of prime minister—depended upon close consultation and agreement between the dominant secularist party, Nidaa Tounes, and its main rival, the then-Islamist Ennahda. Such instances of cooperation underscore the consensus building and political compromise that have been characteristic of the country's Realpolitik since the revolution.

Several factors may account for the qualified success of the Tunisian experience. In contrast to the many failed states of the Middle East and North Africa, Tunisia has a small and relatively homogeneous population;

sectarian tensions are nonexistent. There is a robust tradition of civil society engagement rooted in strong labor union movements that date back to the 1920s. Tunisia is also the only nation in the Arab world—with the exception of Egypt and, to a lesser extent, Morocco and Oman—whose boundaries have historical legitimacy predating the colonial era. Moreover, Tunisia has been largely spared from international interference, not having the geopolitical importance and consequential military buildup of a country like Egypt.

Yet perhaps no ingredient has been as decisive as Tunisia's remarkable culture of reform, which dates back to the nineteenth century and is rooted in a progressive and adaptive brand of Islam. Reformism has been critical to the nation's evolution into a progressive and tolerant society. It has made it possible for Tunisia to embrace a globalized version of the world, rather than retreat into the past in self-preservation like so many Arab countries. Tunisian reformism is a way of thinking—evident in the way Tunisians interpret their history—that facilitates a sense of social cohesion and national unity. Reformism and "*tunisianité*" are inextricable, jointly embodying Tunisian specificity or exceptionalism.

Tunisia's history of reformism has led to a distinctly Tunisian sense of "modernity," which combines Western modernity with a unique national identity and a shared heritage with the Arab and Muslim worlds.

Especially revealing in understanding this Tunisian modernity is the relationship between religion, on the one hand, and society, constitutionalism, politics, and education on the other. There is a visibly respectful and tolerant coexistence of religiosity and secularism that is remarkable. This is despite extremist acts of terror—often committed in the name of religion—that have not spared any corner of the world. Religion appears to not have been politicized nor thrust upon the public sphere, as has been the case in the rest of the Arab world since the 1970s.

In Jordan, as elsewhere in the Middle East, religion and narrow interpretations of Islam have been slowly but determinedly taking over the private and public domains. What started in the 1980s with the conspicuous rise in the appearance of seemingly benign symbols, such as the wearing of the hijab—a headscarf wrapped around the head that covers the hair and neck—has morphed into ostentatious displays of "piety" and an overbearing adoption of ever more rigidly defined lifestyles. Intolerant and exclusive attitudes are increasingly adopted against Christian minorities.

As debates raged over expressions of sympathy by Muslims over the death of a young Christian during the summer of 2016, Jordan's grand mufti had to issue a statement clarifying that it is allowable for a Muslim to offer condolences for a non-Muslim. This did not use to be the case.

On the face of it, one is struck by the sharp contrast between Tunis and other Arab capitals, which almost takes you back to a city like Amman about three or four decades ago when freedom and modernity abounded. Mosques are beautifully integrated into the mosaic of the city—both architecturally and humanly speaking. They are modest and subtle in their presence. They do not scream loudly—aesthetically or otherwise—nor do they dominate the physical or social space of the city.

Religion and piety in Tunis belong almost exclusively to the private sphere, as used to be the case in much of the Arab world that I grew up in. On the streets of Tunis, you find a mix of women with and without the hijab, but you would be hard-pressed to find a woman with her face covered by a niqab, a veil that covers up the hair, face, and body—a common sight everywhere else in the Arab world. In a city like Cairo today, one can almost be guaranteed that a woman whose head is uncovered in a public place is Christian—not surprising given that it is estimated that 90 percent of Muslim women in Egypt wear the hijab.[1]

Bearded men, an increasingly common sign of religiosity, are few and far between. Women wearing the hijab seem to me to be outnumbered by those who are not, including in lower income neighborhoods of Tunis. In Sidi Bou Said, it is not uncommon to see young couples walking hand in hand, some with the woman sporting a hijab, and exchanging romantic gestures and bodily contact. Compare that to countries like Egypt or Jordan, where the scene, which was not dissimilar during my adolescent years, is now quite different. Even in the more conservative interior of Tunisia, whether in a city like Gafsa or Béja or a rural town such as El Kef, there is far less religious symbolism than one would find in Jordan, for instance.

Today, in a city like Amman, religion dominates the public space. I remember a time when the call to prayer five times a day had some, albeit orientalist-sounding, charm associated with it. It reminded one that despite the modernity and secularist lifestyles that abounded, one was indeed in a Muslim country. Fast-forward a few decades, and there are far more mosques than schools in most Arab countries. In Jordan, there are more than 6,000 mosques to the country's 5,000 schools.[2] From minarets, muezzins broadcast not only the call to prayer but recitations of the Qur'an and sermons that preach that there is only one path to heaven, which grows stricter and narrower by the day. Signs hung on lampposts and traffic lights in Amman list the ninety-nine attributes of God—one name every few meters along main thoroughfares—or remind one of an afterlife in hell lest one not live in perpetual fear of God.

In Tunis, take a stroll in the original and still standing Medina, or city, and you will find evidence of a mix of cultures, eras, and peoples. Founded in 698 CE as one of the first Arab Islamic towns in the Maghreb, the Medina was once counted among the wealthiest and greatest cities in the Arab world. The 700 historic monuments it claims are a testament to great dynasties that once ruled over Tunisia. A sojourn through the meandering alleyways of the Medina crosses fragrances that are a mixture of perfumes, spices, and a history eloquently preserved. Like the Old City of Jerusalem, it conjures images of civilizations that have been through its gates and a sense of time that has become immortalized by structures that bear witness to the past but are very much of the present.

Completely covered and offering a cool reprieve from the heat of sun-drenched summer days, the Medina's passages are decked with old houses and workshops, many of which have been converted into restaurants and pensions—like Dar al-Jeld (House of Leather) or Fondouk al-Attarine (Hotel of Perfumers). Doors of shops and houses pay homage to a blend of history, Islam, and modernity. Many are a yellow ochre or green in color, some with double rectangles in the style of the Hafsid dynasty that established Tunis as the capital of Tunisia in the thirteenth century. Some have a *khoukha*, or small under-door that is said to have been invented by a Spanish princess—the wife of Abdulaziz Ibn Moussa Ibn Noussair—to make Muslim subjects bow to their ruler. Just eighteen kilometers from the city center, the modern blue doors of Sidi Bou Said offer a contrast, invoking images of Greece and its islands, most notably Mykonos.

Traces of Tunisia's eclectic past and rich civilizational history are very present today. Kenneth Perkins points out a wonderful example in his *History of Modern Tunisia* when he describes a ride on the TGM (Tunis-Goulette-Marsa) light rail. The names of station stops include Hannibal, the great general of the Carthaginian army, and the port city of Khereddine—a reference either to Khayr al-Din Barbarossa, an Ottoman admiral of the fleet, or Khayr al-Din al-Tunisi, the nineteenth-century reformer who helped set Tunisia on its trajectory toward constitutionality, modernity, and democracy. Another stop is Byrsa, the hill where the Phoenician queen and founder of Carthage Elissa—called Dido by the Romans—is said to have entertained Aeneas. When the train arrives at the Tunis-Marine station "after a run of some fifty minutes and fifteen miles, the train has passed by sites associated with three millennia of history."[3]

Tunisian history begins with the indigenous people of Tunisia: Berbers, who also call themselves *Amazigh*. The first records of Berber history coincide with the establishment of the city of Carthage (814 BCE) by Phoenician refugees from Tyre. Carthage adjoins Tunis and is today home to the presidential palace. When one lands at Tunisia's main aviation hub, the Tunis-Carthage International Airport, one is immediately cognizant of a present that is very much tied to the country's past.

Tunisians like to boast about their proximity to Europe. They eagerly welcome any opportunity to point out on a map that the northern tip of their country is farther north into the Mediterranean than the southern tip of Sicily. They often remind a listener that the name that it had been given by the Romans, Africa—or *Ifriqiya*, the Arabic word for Africa, as the later Muslim rulers called it—lent the continent its designation.

Tunisia's religious and ethnic demographics are essentially homogeneous. The country's population, which stands at 11 million, is roughly 99 percent Sunni Muslim, with other religious groups—including Christian, Jewish, Shi'a Muslim, and Baha'i—accounting for less than 1 percent in total. Ethnically, the population is 98 percent Arab.[4] Tunisia's demographic makeup and its geographic position in the Maghreb in the western frontiers of the Arab world make it at once Arab and African, Oriental and Occidental, but most notably, Tunisian.

Tunisian identity is not defined by religion, which is more of an individual than an ethnic issue. The pull of sectarianism is absent, as is—to a large extent—tension between the governing and governed over religion. What is present instead is a proud national identity, aided by a geography that has been intact for centuries and a rich civilizational history that is not consigned to history textbooks and archeological sites but is very much alive in how Tunisians see and define themselves.

Tunisia as a modern Westphalian nation-state, which took shape in 1956 when it gained independence from the French, had its roots in nineteenth-century reformist political thought. The progressive reforms introduced by Habib Bourguiba (1903–2000), who ruled for three decades—from independence until he was ousted by Zine al-Abidine Ben Ali in 1987—were embedded in contemporaneous and earlier reformist thinking, as the pages of this book will reveal.

Bourguiba, like other autocrats, held onto power through party nepotism and a concentration of executive power in the presidency. His firm grip on the affairs of the country often meant abuses of human rights that ran the gamut from suppression of freedoms to a tyrannical police and security apparatus. But despite his abuses and authoritarian ways, Bourguiba is hailed as the father of Tunisia who led the country to independence and ushered in the emancipation of women and a more secular and moderate Tunisian society. Bourguiba was also responsible for massive reforms that he introduced into Tunisia's education system and which have had a lasting impact on generations of Tunisians. Bourguiba's reforms have had the effect of equipping generations of Tunisians with the skills of critical and analytical thinking that have been deliberately absent in the rest of the Arab world, where students were, and are, victims of regimes' acquiescence with political Islam. This alliance helped to produce obedient, unquestioning, and ultrareligious graduates who, at least until recently, toed the party line.

Bourguiba's reforms benefited immensely from intellectual influences that argued from *within* Islam and sanctioned his emancipation of women and his education policies. They were a natural progression of the work of some important individuals and institutions before him, such as the Islamic modernist Khayr al-Din al-Tunisi (c. 1822–1890), who founded the secularly oriented Sadiqi College and advocated for a constitutional government with a parliament, and Tahar Haddad (1899–1935), one of Tunisia's most important social thinkers, who argued for women's rights within the context of Islamic history and the Qur'an.

The pages of this book will reveal the interactions and shared influences among Tunisian intellectuals and their Arab contemporaries, and how their trajectories intersected and diverged. The late nineteenth century and early twentieth century witnessed considerable intellectual reform movements elsewhere in the Arab world, particularly in Egypt and Syria-Lebanon. This intellectual renaissance, which comprised a serious attempt to reform Islam and was led by the likes of Muhammad Abduh (1849–1905),

Muhammad Rashid Rida (1865–1935), and Qasim Amin (1865–1908), failed, however, to produce similar outcomes or have as lasting an impact as Tunisia's. It was interrupted and dilapidated by currents—political and religious—that ensured its demise. A would-be awakening turned instead into a deep slumber.

Meanwhile, Tunisian intellectual reformist figures influenced the development of a robust labor union movement that would play a decisive role in the country's independence movement and in the decades to follow, including, very significantly, in the revolution and its aftermath. The *Union générale tunisienne du travail* (UGTT) was the one institution in Tunisia able to fill the power void left by Ben Ali in a way similar, albeit with a different approach, to the Egyptian military. The civil society that UGTT helped to create took hold of an orphaned revolution and turned it into a democratic transition.

The awarding of the Nobel Peace Prize in 2015 to the Tunisian *Quartet du dialogue national* for "its decisive contribution to the building of a pluralistic democracy in Tunisia" highlights the role of Tunisian civil society institutions in bringing about consensus and bridging political and religious divides.[5] The Quartet was comprised of four key organizations: *Union générale tunisienne du travail* (UGTT); *Union tunisienne de l'industrie, du commerce et de l'artisanat* (UTICA); *Ligue tunisienne pour la défense des droits de l'homme*; and *Ordre national des avocats de Tunisie*—representing, respectively, workers, business owners, human rights activists, and lawyers. The Quartet was responsible for getting Tunisia out of the political deadlock that plagued the country following two political assassinations and mass protests in 2013.

The pages of this book expose the factors that led to the revolution, but more important, they reveal how decades and centuries of a uniquely Tunisian experience help explain the country's transition to democracy and its society's evolution into a progressive, modern, and tolerant one. The book endeavors to tell a story of a nation and a people, of a struggle to seek the truth, and of a trajectory that is unique, hopeful, and inspiring.

What the book attempts to reveal are the reasons why Tunisia is a democracy and why a similar outcome elsewhere in the Arab world is unlikely any time in the near future. What I propose is that Tunisia has been predisposed to democracy because of ingredients that are uniquely indigenous to it. The book makes the case that understanding the failures of the Arab world requires an understanding of the Tunisian experience.

This is not to suggest that Tunisia's transition to democracy has been fully consolidated. Major challenges lie ahead, and the path has been speckled with obstacles and doubts. Three deadly attacks in 2015—at the Bardo Museum on March 18, at a beach resort in Sousse on June 28, and on a bus carrying presidential guards on November 24—have served as a tragic and poignant reminder of the young democracy's vulnerability. Protests that started at the end of the same year and intensified at the beginning of 2016 in the internal regions of the country, where problems of unemployment and poverty have obstinately persisted since the revolution, have also served as a warning call that unless the socioeconomic twin to the political pillar of democracy is erected, all could be lost.

The first few chapters explore the factors that led to the revolution and the developments in Tunisia ever since. They build a contextual framework for understanding dynamics at play and challenges facing the young democracy. The narrative traces lines that begin to connect modern-day Tunisia to its history, particularly of reform and intellectual development.

Giving the Tunisian story a historical context, the book next takes the reader back to Tunisia's enlightened beginnings and briefly introduces its ancient civilizations and the genesis of Tunisia's rich identity. It then discusses the arrival of the Muslim Arabs and the evolution of a progressive brand of Islam and its impact on the shaping of a moderate and tolerant Tunisian Muslim identity, exploring the influences of important Islamic scholars. Of note in that history is the celebrated Tunisian fourteenth-century philosopher and reformer Ibn Khaldūn (1332–1406), who advocated critical and analytical thinking and discussed the philosophy of history, Islamic theology, and the relationship between religion and society.

The book then discusses the setting into motion of a modern reform era that continued cumulatively and that largely explains Tunisia's distinctiveness. The modern Tunisia story starts in the middle of the nineteenth century, which saw the abolishment of slavery—nineteen years ahead of the United States—and produced the first constitution of any Arab or Muslim country. Subsequent decades witnessed consequential intellectual developments that set the stage for the introduction of Bourguiba's reforms and enabled Tunisia's evolution—educationally, socially, and constitutionally.

The journey to understand contemporary Tunisia then takes us to Bourguiba and to the reforms that he introduced and that have largely endured—particularly in the spheres of education, women's suffrage, and religion. A considerable portion of the book is dedicated to a discussion of these reforms, what made them possible, and how they set the country on a progressive course that would be very difficult to reverse. A comparative analysis of education systems in other Arab countries, which developed quite differently in the postcolonial era, supports the main thesis of the book—namely, that a progressive education system that rested on a long history of reformism is what has enabled Tunisia to be where it is today. In discussing education—and religion—some comparisons are made with Turkey. Although non-Arab, Turkey offers an interesting benchmark, given somewhat similar trajectories followed by the two countries' respective founders and how the relationship between religion, the state, and education systems has evolved in each. The closing chapter discusses the strains that Tunisia's education system has experienced over the past couple of decades and its paradoxical role in the revolution, with a younger unemployed generation leading the call for change and an older Bourguiba-educated elite leading the country during the transitional phase.

TUNISIA

PART I

Tunisian Spring

Timeline of Tunisia's Revolution (2010–2016)

December 17, 2010: Mohamed Bouazizi, a twenty-four-year-old produce vendor, sets himself on fire in Sidi Bouzid, triggering the first protests of the revolution.

December 24, 2010: Security forces fire first rounds on protesters in Sidi Bouzid, killing two.

January 8, 2011: Police fire live shots at protesters in Thala and Kasserine, killing twenty-two over the next four days.

January 12, 2011: Demonstrations spread to the capital of Tunis. Protesters call for the removal of Zine al-Abidine Ben Ali.

January 14, 2011: Ben Ali flees Tunisia, and Prime Minister Mohamed Ghannouchi assumes the presidency.

January 15, 2011: President of the Chamber of Deputies Fouad Mebezaa is named "caretaker president." Ghannouchi returns to the post of prime minister.

January–February 2011: A series of demonstrations and round-the-clock sit-ins take place at Place de la Kasbah, Tunis. Protesters call for the removal of *Rassemblement constitutionnel démocratique* (RCD) members from the new cabinet and, later, abolishment of RCD.

January 27, 2011: Prime Minister Ghannouchi reshuffles government, removing all former RCD members apart from himself.

February 27, 2011: Mohamed Ghannouchi resigns, and President Mebezaa appoints Beji Caid Essebsi prime minister.

March 9, 2011: The *tribunal de première instance de Tunis* dissolves RCD, liquidating its assets and banning it from participating in future elections.

October 23, 2011: Ennahda wins a plurality of seats in elections for the Constituent Assembly.

December 2011: Hamadi Jebali, former secretary general of Ennahda, becomes prime minister; Moncef Marzouki, former president of the *Congrès pour la République* (CPR), becomes president; and Mustapha Ben Jaafar, leader of Ettakatol, becomes speaker of the Assembly.

February 6, 2013: Chokri Belaid, leader of the leftist opposition party al-Watad, is murdered.

February 19–22, 2013: Prime Minister Hamadi Jebali resigns and is replaced by Ennahda's Ali Laarayedh.

July 25, 2013: Mohamed Brahmi, founder and leader of the *Mouvement du peuple*, is assassinated.

December 2013: The *Quartet du dialogue national—Union générale tunisienne du travail* (UGTT); *Union tunisienne de l'industrie, du commerce et de l'artisanat* (UTICA); *Ligue tunisienne pour la défense des droits de l'homme*; and *Ordre national des avocats de Tunisie*—forms a roadmap to lead the country out of political deadlock. Ennahda agrees to step down.

January 26, 2014: The National Constituent Assembly approves a new constitution.

January 29, 2014: Mehdi Jomaa assumes the role of prime minister.

October 26, 2014: Tunisia's first legislative elections since the revolution are held. Ennahda wins 69 of the 217 parliamentary seats, and Nidaa Tounes achieves plurality with 86 seats.

December 31, 2014: Beji Caid Essebsi becomes Tunisia's first democratically elected president.

January 5, 2015: Habib Essid of Nidaa Tounes is appointed prime minister.

March 18, 2015: Mass shooting by three gunmen at Bardo Museum kills twenty-two, mostly foreign tourists.

June 26, 2015: Gunman kills thirty-eight foreign tourists at a beach resort in Sousse.

October 2015: The *Quartet du dialogue national* is awarded the Nobel Peace Prize.

November 24, 2015: Suicide bombing on bus carrying Tunisian presidential guards kills thirteen.

May 19, 2016: Rached Ghannouchi announces that Ennahda is "leaving political Islam behind" and redefining itself as a party of Muslim democrats.

July 30, 2016: Tunisian parliament passes a vote of no confidence in Prime Minister Habib Essid, forcing him to step down.

August 26, 2016: Youssef Chahed, a former minister for local affairs, is confirmed by the National Assembly as prime minister of Tunisia's new unity government.

1

Can Tunisia Serve as a Model?

Almost as soon as the uprisings erupted in Tunisia in December 2010, demonstrators followed suit in other Arab countries, starting with Egypt and leading to the removal from office of President Hosni Mubarak less than a month after Tunisians toppled President Zine al-Abidine Ben Ali. Inspired by the examples of Tunis and Cairo, protesters demanded reforms, if not outright regime change, in a multitude of cities throughout the Middle East and North Africa. The outcomes ran the gamut from spiraling quickly into civil wars of gargantuan proportions to achieving limited reforms in peripheral Arab Spring nations such as Morocco and Jordan.

For a while, Egypt continued to be paired with Tunisia as a beneficiary of the so-called Arab Spring. In June 2012, the Muslim Brotherhood candidate, Mohamed Morsi, became the country's first-ever democratically elected president. One year later, however, the army overthrew President Morsi amid mass demonstrations calling on him to quit. In the ensuing weeks, hundreds were killed as security forces stormed pro-Morsi protest camps in Cairo, and some forty Coptic churches were destroyed in waves of attacks.[1] Back in the grip of military authoritarianism, with the regime of President Abdelfattah al-Sisi firmly entrenched for the foreseeable future, Egypt seems to have made a swift exit, or at least a protracted detour, from the road to democracy.

The singular Arab Spring success story of Tunisia has thus become an object of fascination for policy analysts, activists, political pundits, and journalists alike. Frustrated, disillusioned, but wanting to be inspired and hopeful, they have prophesized more positive political outcomes elsewhere based on a Tunisian model. Some have even bravely declared that Tunisia may have replaced Israel as the singular functional democracy in the region—Arab and otherwise.[2] They describe Tunisia's success in lofty prose, proclaiming that "the birth of this first fully fledged Arab democracy could offer a model of hope amid the feverish voices of despair and nihilism, and the backdrop of military dictators, corrupt theocrats, and militant anarchists."[3]

Therein lies one of the most common and misguided propositions about Tunisia—namely, that its successful transition to democracy can serve as a model for the rest of the Arab world and that the factors that led to Tunisia's democracy could be, if not easily, replicated. This theory is based on a set of assumptions, some explicit and others less so, that I argue are flawed. The factors that led to Tunisia's successful transition were either indigenous to Tunisia or many generations in the making.

There is also a simplistic and reductionist assumption that identifies Tunisia as exclusively Arab and Muslim in its identity and places it squarely within the confines of the Arab world. This assumption calls into question what it means to be Arab. It is not a distinct ethnic group or race, nor does it refer to an exclusively shared religion—an estimated 5 percent of native Arabic speakers worldwide are Christians, Druze, Jews, or animists.[4] "Arab" is based on a political and linguistic identity and a commonality of some cultural norms and traditions that generally vary from one Arab country to another across geographic regions.

Prior to the spread of Islam and the Arabic language—the language of the Qur'an and the common tongue of the "Arab" people—"Arab" denoted the largely Semitic people who lived in the Arabian Peninsula, roughly modern-day Saudi Arabia and Yemen. These Bedouin desert nomads were isolated because of their harsh desert climate—very little genetic mixing with other peoples occurred until their Muslim expeditions took them to foreign lands.[5]

Most of those who were Arabized with the Muslim Arab conquests that emanated from the Arabian Peninsula were Canaanite-Phoenician, Aramaean, Assyrian, ancient Egyptian, or Berber descendants, mixed in with various minorities such as Roman and Greek, among others. Once these populations, who inhabited the lands of the Fertile Crescent—stretching from the Persian Gulf to the Sinai—and the coastal stretch of North Africa, converted to Islam, they gave up their ancestral languages and adopted Arabic instead and came to be denoted as Arabs.

Until the nineteenth century, "Arab" evoked no pride among the largely urban elite who would later go on to promote a pan-Arab ideology. The "Arab world" is a relatively new concept, advanced during the Ottoman Empire and promoted by pan-Arab political ideologies in the middle of the twentieth century that propagated the notion of an "Arab nation." Arabism is a postcolonial identity reclamation that began to experience its quick demise following the failed merger between Egypt and Syria from 1958 until 1961 and the humiliating defeat by Israel in the 1967 Six-Day War.[6]

Shared modern histories produced an Arab identity that is singular and reductionist and that does not take into account variations in nationality, ethnicity, religion, language, and individuality. Throughout this book, when the term "Arab world" is used, it is therefore in reference to the Arabic-speaking countries and does not necessarily denote a particular identity or a population defined by homogeneity.

Arab countries are diverse—geographically, culturally, and historically. But a common language, with hugely variant spoken dialects, and a shared religion connect them, somewhat artificially.

Dialects across North Africa are infused with Berber—also called *Tamazight*—and French, rendering them almost incomprehensible to a Levantine Arabic speaker. Tunisians prefer to refer to their spoken language as *Tounsi* or *Derja*—colloquial Arabic, with Berber and French mixed into it—underscoring its idiosyncratic nature. I was amused to find on a billboard, for instance, an advertisement for a popular Turkish soap opera as the first of its genre to be dubbed in *Tounsi*. The Arabic of publications and formal speech in Tunisia is Modern Standard Arabic, or *fusha*, which is used across the Arab world but only in quite formal settings. Similarly, the Islam of the Maghreb, which adheres to the Maliki jurisprudence school and is influenced by Sūfism and local traditions, is distinct from the Islam of the East (as chapter 7 will elucidate).

Tunisia is a nation that is both within and without the Arab world. The country has more characteristics that define its uniqueness, including a decidedly Mediterranean orientation, than features that link it with a broad definition of an Arab identity. The implicit assumption that places it firmly within the Arab world and reduces its identity to Arab ignores how intricately linked Tunisia is—culturally, economically, and geographically—to Europe and Africa, historically and at present.

In some respects, Tunisia is closer to Europe than it is to other Arab countries. A flight from Tunis to Paris or Rome is shorter than one to Cairo, Amman, or Riyadh. Unlike in Beirut, French is not the sole domain of the elite but is engrained in expressions that are part of daily life in the capital. Towns on the outskirts of Tunis, like the port town of La Goulette, have retained the names that they were given when they were inhabited by *colons*, mostly French and Italian, who had lived there. Neighborhoods and streets in Tunis have French names, and there is a postcolonial European texture that is reminiscent of Beirut before the Lebanese Civil War (1975–1990).

The European connection is strongest in the coastal areas where geographic proximity has played an important role and where business and economic interests have benefited from a strong European alliance. International trade accounts for roughly 50 percent of Tunisia's economy, and 80 percent of it is with Europe, not with the Arab or Muslim world.[7] More than half of Tunisian exports are low-value-added products for France and Italy; most are built from imported intermediate components.

This trade dependency is rooted in European interests dating back to the middle of the nineteenth century, before French colonialism. France, Britain, and at times Italy competed fiercely to gain economic and political influence in Tunisia as a gateway to economic integration with the Ottoman Empire.

French continued to be the language of business and commerce in Bourguiba's postcolonial Tunisia, making it easier to trade with Francophone West Africa and southern Europe but difficult to do business with much of the rest of the world. Under Bourguiba, Tunisia became an associate member of the European Economic Community in 1969, and during Ben Ali's reign, it became the first non-European, Mediterranean country to sign an association agreement with the European Union in 1995.

Bourguiba, who firmly believed that Tunisia's future was better served through a Western orientation, was blamed for the country's continued trade dependency on Europe. The independence agreement he reached with France in 1956 ensured future economic, security, and educational ties between the two countries, including the prominence of the French language. His strategy faced serious resistance by conservative elements, most notably his former friend and cofounder in 1934 of the pro-independence Neo-Destour—*Nouveau Parti libéral constitutionnel*—Salah Ben Youssef (1910–1961), who had become committed to greater integration with the Arab and Muslim world. These rivalries between, on the one hand, modernists—perceived to be associated with the Francophone elite—and those who advocated for a stronger Tunisian Arab identity, on the other, endured; they were taken up again in the new political space opened up by the revolution.

Bourguiba's Eurocentric policies served him well and won him the support of the French against his domestic adversaries. Furthermore, his insistence on a Mediterranean character—rooted in both the country's ancient past and its modern history—enabled Bourguiba to distinguish Tunisia from its neighbors and served as a potent alternative to the Arabist and Islamist option of Salah Ben Youssef and his allies.

Tunisia is also very much a part of Africa, the continent to which it lent its name. When the Arabs ruled it until the twelfth century, before it fell into the hands of successive Berber dynasties and the Ottomans after them, they did so as part of a unified North Africa. Under Bourguiba, the links to Francophone West Africa began to take on an enduring strength. Bourguiba promoted the use of the term Francophone in the 1960s, along with Léopold Senghor of Senegal. Together they formed a Francophone alliance that was deeply intertwined with Pan-African and democratic movements. Ben Ali further solidified Tunisia's integration into North Africa, specifically, and joined the *Union du Maghreb arabe* in 1989.

Beyond the coast, Tunisian identity lies somewhere between Europe, the Middle East, and Africa. The disenfranchised interior regions have been at odds with the Tunisian coast that has benefited from tourism and the majority of foreign investment. The coastal north and east of the country, known as the Sahel, was favored during Ottoman times, a situation that was further exacerbated under the French protectorate. Insurgencies erupted in the interior in protest over poor economic conditions as far back as 1864. Regional discrepancies and interior economic hardship are thus not a new phenomenon in Tunisia; it is an old Tunisian story that had just not been as well known before Tunisia grabbed world attention with its revolution. The interior region has always been more closely connected with neighboring Algeria and Libya—culturally, tribally, and economically. Growth of informal trade across the borders has meant not only stronger, if illegal, economic ties but an infiltration of certain Islamic ideologies as well as a stronger affinity with an Arab identity than in the political and commercial centers on the coast. Tensions between the coast and the interior region carry the potential of threatening the country's efforts to consolidate its democracy.

Bourguiba's attitude toward Tunisia's orientation carried over to his foreign policy, which was decisively non-Arab leaning. Bourguiba acted independently of the rest of the Arab world. As early as 1965, he took the bold step of arguing publicly that the Palestine Liberation Organization should accept the 1947 United Nations partition of Palestine. This led to a severing of relations with Gamal Abdel Nasser (1918–1970) and of diplomatic ties with Egypt in 1966. Arab isolationism continued under Ben Ali, who was scorned, especially by Saudi Arabia and Kuwait, when he refused to take sides during the Gulf War. Financial assistance from Gulf countries decreased as a result— from $100 million in 1990 to less than $3 million in 1991.[8]

The notion that Tunisia is singularly Arab and Muslim in its orientation and that it can thus serve as a model for the rest of the Arab world is, at the very least, a naïve one. Tunisians measure their progress against Western, not Arab, yardsticks. When they complain about the deteriorating state of their French-based education system over the past couple of decades, they are hardly comforted when reminded that it still significantly outpaces that of any other Arab country, including when it comes to the relatively minor and tolerant role that religion plays in it. Tunisians, at least the educated elite among them, insist that their frame of reference is European and American, not Middle Eastern.

Tunisia cannot serve as a model for the Arab world for a number of other reasons, but I argue that none stands out as much as its tradition of reformism and of progressive and secular education. I use the term "secular" in this context somewhat loosely to distinguish an education system that includes a sparse and moderate study of religion from one that is dominated by religion—as is the case across the Arab world.

With the stage having been set for him, Bourguiba's visionary reforms, particularly in the domains of education and women's rights, sustained a trajectory of reformism that started in the nineteenth century and that has been critical to the nation's evolution into a democracy.

Immediately following independence, Bourguiba introduced a contro-versial family code, *Code du statut personnel*, or *Majallat al-ahwal al-shakhsiyya*, which he cast within Islamic justification. The code abolished polygamy, required the consent of both parties prior to marriage, extended the mini-mum age of marriage to seventeen years for women and twenty years for men, and introduced reforms to divorce and custody laws, banning the pos-sibility of repudiation. The code advanced women's rights beyond where they stand today—decades later—in any other Arab country.

Tunisian women got access to birth control in 1961 with the abolish-ment of a French law dating back to 1920 that prohibited the sale of birth control pills. It would take another six years for the same law to be abro-gated in France. Abortion became legal in 1965 for Tunisian women who already had five children, and in 1973—the same year as *Roe v. Wade*—it became fully legalized, two years before France.[9]

In terms of women's political rights, they are far more advanced in Tunisia than anywhere else in the Arab world. Bourguiba granted women the right to vote and to run in elections in 1957, before any other Arab country. Women in Saudi Arabia were permitted to vote in 2015, but only in municipal elections.

President Zine al-Abidine Ben Ali's authoritarian government carried on Bourguiba's legacy and the protection of women's rights from the threat posed by Islamic fundamentalism. Ben Ali introduced electoral gender quo-tas, and by 2010 women comprised 28 percent of parliamentary deputies, more than any other Arab country and more than many Western nations.[10]

The emancipation of women meant their education and active par-ticipation in society. Tunisian women have a higher enrollment rate than men in secondary schools and universities.[11] Literacy rates among women between fifteen and twenty-four years of age are estimated at 96 percent.[12] Most important is that women have played multiple key roles in civic soci-ety and are credited for their mobilization efforts during the Jasmine Rev-olution. Tunisians insist that it is primarily women who will safeguard the consolidation of the democratic experience and prevent a rolling back of the gains they have made.

The strong education system introduced by Bourguiba in 1958, just two years after independence, stood in sharp contrast to the failed attempts to reform—and, in many cases, introduce—education in the rest of the Arab world, as will be discussed in chapters 13 and 14. The largest component of the state budget, at times reaching one-third, was dedicated to education and youth development. Bourguiba understood that if he wanted to espouse national unity and enable his people to develop the basic literacy and human capital skills that were required for his country to advance, the state had to commit substantial resources to the effort. The reforms aimed to establish a coherent, unified, and free education system that conformed to French university standards, and to expand education drastically, with the goal of achieving universal primary education by 1968. Vocational training was introduced as a track in secondary school and through terminal intermediate schools.

Much of the credit for Bourguiba's reforms in education goes to his minister of national education, Mahmoud Messaadi (1911–2004), who held that post for an entire decade, from 1958 until 1968. Bourguiba's and Messaadi's policies in education resembled the Turkish reforms of the 1920s under Kemal Ataturk (1881–1938) in that they espoused secularism. But rather than dismiss religion, Tunisian reforms redefined its role in society and education. Unlike postcolonial education reforms in neighboring countries, which quickly Arabized and Islamized curricula and textbooks, Tunisian education policy maintained French as a language of instruction, alongside Arabic, and modeled schools after the French *lycée* system.

Bourguiba and Messaadi made sure that students were taught subjects in the humanities and the liberal arts. The teaching of Islam in primary schools was brought down to one to two hours a week, and it was almost entirely eliminated in secondary schools.[13] While Islam continues to be the only religion taught in public schools, it is taught in a way that promotes equality, unity, and acceptance. In Saudi Arabia, by contrast, where the education policy remains unchanged from when it was written in 1969, elementary schoolchildren dedicate nine hours per week each to Islam and to Arabic—taught through the Qur'an—with two to three hours for science and five for mathematics.[14]

Women and men who were the beneficiaries of Bourguiba's system of education have played key roles in leading Tunisia's transition to democracy. The experience has been aided by the presence of an intellectual class transcending socioeconomic strata and engaging in civil affairs, and a population equipped with the critical thinking and creativity skills to see its country through the transition. Tunisians have demonstrated their capacity to engage in political debate, build consensus, and envision alternative futures for the nation. When the country was on the brink of disaster in the immediate aftermath of the revolution, Tunisians were able to step back from partisan political ambitions and rationalize a solution. Tunisian education helped ensure that the country's middle class understood and supported democratic processes, and that its elites were able to make such processes work.

Education policies introduced by Bourguiba were a natural extension of advancements in education that had been made in the nineteenth century. From the founding of Sadiqi College in 1875, Tunisian rulers and leading intellectuals—both secular and religious—insisted that Tunisians should receive the best education available and that it ought to be widely accessible, by boys and girls. New secular institutions taught modern sciences and mathematics and provided both an alternative and a complement to the Qur'anic and Arabic teachings of the centuries-old Zaitouna Mosque. The modern reform movement that began under the Ottomans continued uninterrupted through liberation from the French and had a significant role in both gaining independence and shaping postcolonial Tunisia at the hands of Habib Bourguiba.

Elsewhere in the Arab world, bad education has been generations in the making, just as Tunisia's good education has been, despite some recent deterioration. Just as Tunisian leaders insisted—for more than a century—on the best education for their men and women, education in the Arab world was gravely neglected.

Poor education has been partially the effect of totalitarianism and the spreading of national fervor that underscored nation building during the postcolonial era. Alliances between oppressive regimes and conservative religious leaders led to interpretations of Islam that complemented the regimes' insistence on discipline and control. Education systems have been highly politicized, divisive on sectarian issues, and persistent in the use of rote memorization and the inhibition of creativity and questioning, rendering Arab populations ill equipped for democracy. This passive mode of education is the direct result of decades of intellectual despotism intent on voiding the Arab student from any opportunity to think for herself, to question authority or religion, or to aspire to any ideas that might threaten the status quo. Regimes understood that education would be a dangerous proposition, for an educated populace would be critical of its government and supportive of the idea of democracy.

While education played a pivotal role in the democratic transition, Tunisia's ability to navigate the upheavals of the Arab Spring was also aided by the *absence* of certain factors that hinder democracy, further setting Tunisia apart from the rest of the Arab world and rendering it less of a model that can be replicated.

Tunisia did not suffer from the resource curse of Arab Gulf nations nor from a large, poor population, often cited as a major hindrance to Egypt's prospects for democracy. Taxation as a means for government expenditure meant an avenue of accountability for government actions—unlike in countries such as Saudi Arabia or the United Arab Emirates where there is no taxation but also no answerability. In the Gulf region, a resource curse has stalled societal progress and political development. The lack of oil and gas and the country's limited strategic importance also protected Tunisia from being a target of massive external intervention and of American Cold War foreign policy.

Absent from the scene has also been a strong, large, and political army. This very "weakness" turned out to be one of Tunisia's greatest strengths. Unlike in Egypt, Tunisia was spared the threat of military intervention or takeover on the heels of Ben Ali's ouster.

French influence had instilled an apolitical attitude in the Tunisian army, which was reinforced by Bourguiba in post-independence Tunisia. The republican army, which Bourguiba had built with the assistance of former French colonial troops, was limited in size and budget. In 1985, the armed forces numbered a mere 35,000. Bourguiba instead had his own security apparatus, including a national guard under the ministry of the interior. Wary of the frequent military interventions in eastern Arab countries, he purposely kept the army separate from the political realm. Military expenditures rarely exceeded 2 percent of gross domestic product (GDP) even under Ben Ali, who did expand the army but not as fast as he did the police.[15] Ben Ali continued to view military officers with suspicion and exclude them from the political arena.

In Egypt, by contrast, a strong military presence has been characteristic of the country's polity since the reign of Muhammad Ali (r. 1805–1848). Every Egyptian president since 1952, with the exception of Mohamed Morsi, has been a military officer. Eighteen generals led the Supreme Council of the Armed Forces (SCAF)—the interim government after Mubarak's fall. The Tunisian military, on the other hand, had neither the power nor the political desire to intervene in matters of governance and politics.

What Egypt had in military strength that obstructed a democratic process, Tunisia had in the potency of its labor movement, which facilitated its democratic transition. To understand Tunisia, it is essential to understand its labor movement—unparalleled in the Arab world. The Stanford historian Joel Beinin asserts that the *Union générale tunisienne du travail* (UGTT) is "the single most important reason that Tunisia is a democracy today."[16] UGTT has been intricately interwoven with, and largely shaped by, Tunisia's intellectual reform movements, particularly those of the early twentieth century, and by notable intellectuals such as Tahar Haddad.

With three-quarters of a million dues-paying members, UGTT has been critically involved at every stage of the transition. Because UGTT can mobilize thousands of members through its 150 offices across the country, it can bring the country to an economic standstill. The Sidi Bouzid branch was seen as the driving force behind the initial protests that erupted in Mohamed Bouazizi's home governorate on the day of his self-immolation. It was the activism of UGTT's local branches that forced the executive bureau to support anti–Ben Ali protests, and more local branches became involved across the country as the protests spread. The role of UGTT after the revolution should not be underestimated either. The union played a decisive political role—intervening when there were deadlocked political processes—on a number of occasions, including its anchoring of the *Quartet du dialogue national* in 2013.

A history of political pluralism, sanctioned or not, is another factor that separates Tunisia from most Arab countries. Despite the overwhelming dominance of the ruling party, the *Rassemblement constitutionnel démocratique* (RCD), opposition parties were tolerated under Ben Ali, and the parliament had approved a transition to a multiparty system in 1988. The *Mouvement des démocrates socialistes*, founded by former interior minister Ahmed Mestiri, had called for the establishment of political pluralism and the widening of the democratic arena as far back as 1976.[17] In 2007, there were six opposition parties that had legal recognition by the state.[18] These were mostly insubstantial institutions with insignificant memberships, however, and were dominated by the ruling party.

Although Tunisia's political structure was—for all practical purposes— a one-party system, there was, nonetheless, a vibrant culture of political activism that dates back to the pre-independence era. Political organization and procedural democratic processes were also rooted in the labor union movement and UGTT. While Bourguiba and Ben Ali had a checkered history with the union, often trying to bring it under their control, they nonetheless gave it some electoral autonomy, believing that the union would provide an outlet for debate and dissent.[19] UGTT was one of the few institutions that were democratically transparent.

Active political discussion and debate took place within UGTT and among consequential actors, including in the diaspora. Political parties, including some that were illegal like Ennahda, had been meeting in France in order to negotiate and agree on fundamental principles of a democratic Tunisia. These principles included that any future elected government would have to be "founded on the sovereignty of the people as the sole source of legitimacy"; that the state would provide "the guarantee of liberty of beliefs to all and the political neutralization of places of worship" while demonstrating "respect for the people's identity and its Arab-Muslim values"; and that the new democracy would guarantee "the full equality of women and men."[20]

Moncef Marzouki, a human rights activist who would later become president of the republic, and Sheikh Rached Ghannouchi, the cofounder of Ennahda who would later become a key player in Tunisia's post-revolution political arena, were among the signatories of the Call from Tunis agreement, signed in Aix-en-Provence in 2003. According to Marzouki, whose alliance with Ennahda in 2011 was criticized as opportunist by political opponents, "the Troika did not come into existence after the election, it was prepared for a very, very long time, over a period of 20 years."[21] Unlike in Egypt where there were neither prospective rivals nor allies to the Muslim Brotherhood, Tunisia had alternative political actors who were able to step in when the Ben Ali regime fell.

Even with the monopoly of power by RCD and the limited experience of political organization and activism, there was relative maturity and sophistication in the political arena that have allowed for political parties to partake in a democratic transition of power from Ben Ali in a manner that would have been difficult to implement elsewhere. While parties remained weak, they at least had a foundation of pluralism and political platforms to build upon after the revolution.

Across the region, postcolonial and largely leftist intellectual and ideological currents gave way in the 1960s and 1970s to repressive regimes that made it difficult, if not illegal, for political activists to organize.

As political pluralism declined, citizens turned increasingly to civil society, professional organizations, and religious movements. The dearth of political activity over decades made it difficult for parties to reemerge once repressive measures started being lifted—with the exception of Islamist organizations, which continued to operate throughout, often under the guise of professional bodies and charities.

Tunisia has also been upheld as a model for the Arab world on the premise that it has offered veritable evidence of how Islam and democracy can be compatible because Tunisia transitioned into a democracy and produced a modern constitution while an Islamist party was in power.

But Ennahda did not have the political backing to push its agenda unilaterally, having gotten only a plurality of seats in the October 23, 2011, parliamentary elections. The power structure of the Troika coalition left Ennahda with control over the government, the secular Ettakatol with the legislative body, and the *Congrès pour la République* (CPR) with the presidency. Ennahda's accomplishments, including the passing of the constitution, were thus the result of coordinated efforts among these three parties and between them and the rest of the Tunisian political establishment.

Further, the constitution-writing process had actually begun before Ennahda came into power, when it was led by a non-Islamist: public law expert and academician Yadh Ben Achour. The constitution that was ultimately adopted in 2014 was the result of much debate and compromise, and its writing was aided by a balance of power in politics between Islamists and secularists.

Ennahda had to *adapt* to democracy. For Ben Achour, the most important consequence of the process since the revolution has been the "democratization of the Islamist party," and that "they [Ennahda] now speak the language of democracy."[22] The dropping of its Islamist label and its redefining of itself as a party of Muslim democrats in 2016 provide credence to the argument that Ennahda has been democratized since the revolution.

The pluralistic nature of Tunisian politics during the transition, and the role played by UGTT, ensured that Ennahda could not extend its tenure the way the Muslim Brotherhood tried to do in Egypt. Supporters of the idea that there is proof in the Tunisian experience that Islam and democracy are compatible claim that Ennahda willingly gave up power to a non-Islamist party. But Ennahda did not have the political backing to stay in power in the first place; it was pushed out.

Rallies in 2013 demanding Ennahda's removal from power—on the heels of political assassinations in which it was accused of playing a role—paralleled the protests that preceded the ousting of Egypt's President Morsi. Secularists in Tunisia became as distrustful of Ennahda as Egyptians were of the Muslim Brotherhood. Survey data from the Arab Barometer revealed that the percentage of secularists in Tunisia who had "absolutely no trust" in Islamists had grown from 37.6 percent in 2011 to 64.9 percent in 2013, compared to 44.1 percent in 2011 and 76.4 percent in 2013 in Egypt.[23] Ghannouchi had no trouble confirming that Ennahda was careful not to have a repeat in Tunisia of the fate of the Muslim Brotherhood in Egypt.[24]

The one Tunisian feature that has not been claimed as a source of inspiration for the rest of the Arab world, and which has stood out as an aberration in the face of calls for Tunisia to serve as model, is the much taunted standing of Tunisia as a breeding ground for terrorists. Ironically, given Tunisia's nonsectarian and largely secular orientation, it has made headlines as the country that has exported the largest numbers of fighters to join the ranks of Da'esh and other extremist militias. Thousands of Tunisians are reported to have traveled to Syria and Iraq as combatants since 2011, and thousands of others have been stopped at the borders.

These numbers are only partially indicative, however. Even large variances can be statistically insignificant, relative to population sizes or to numbers of jihadis from other countries that have joined extremist groups. Therefore, the fact that Tunisia may have exported more fighters to Syria than any other country might have is not necessarily significant or conclusive.

Misleading as these numbers might be, this is not to suggest that there is not a serious problem of extremism. As evidenced by the terror attacks in 2015, there also exist a serious security threat and a problem of terrorism at home, facilitated by the easily penetrable borders with Libya, across which Da'esh boasts of easily smuggling weapons and men. A study by the *Centre tunisien de recherches et d'études sur le terrorisme* (CTRET) of 384 court cases from 2011 to 2015 found that 69 percent of the assessed 1,000 incarcerated Tunisian jihadis had received military training in Libya, and of those, 80 percent had gone on to fight in Syria upon completing their training.[25]

Newly found freedoms after the revolution, making it easier to recruit would-be extremists, partially explain the extent of radicalization. There was a "free-for-all democracy" born out of the revolution as a reaction to the authoritarianism, and some say forced secularization, of former regimes, especially under Ben Ali. Thousands of radical Islamists who had been released from prison after the revolution, and many who had returned from exile, exploited the new freedoms. Many may have ended up leaving Tunisia, especially those released from jail, because they felt that there was no place for their views in the country. The lifting of travel restrictions that had been imposed under Ben Ali, which had included the arbitrary banning of travel to citizens with valid passports and entry visas to their destinations, facilitated the process of exit.

An examination of how terrorist networks have operated in Tunisia points to easy targets in the form of disenfranchised youth who have felt let down by the revolution and have tried to fill the vacuum on their own terms, often by resorting to religion. The economic divide between the coastal and interior regions of the country and the marginalization of many are seen to have contributed to the rise in fundamentalism since the revolution.

But not all Tunisian jihadis are poor or socioeconomically marginalized. Many are reported to be members of the bourgeoisie who have become devoutly religious. The example of the twenty-four-year-old perpetrator of the Sousse beach resort attack in June 2015 that left thirty-eight foreign tourists dead is illustrative. Seifeddine Rezgui had graduated from a technical institute in central Tunisia and was pursuing his master's degree. According to Tunisians familiar with the case, his job prospects were promising.[26] But Rezgui had attended a mosque where extremist views were preached. The aforementioned CTRET study on incarcerated jihadis found that 40 percent of the terrorists were university graduates or had received some level of higher education. The study concluded that "mosques, where jihadis enjoy a heavy presence, played an important role in spreading influence and recruitment." More than a third of the assessed jihadis were encouraged in their pursuit of jihad—the exertion of effort on behalf of Islam, generally understood to be through violent means—by individuals, such as preachers.

It is difficult to say whether extremists had been radical before they were exposed to religious fanaticism or if they became extremist as a result of radical religious indoctrination. In the words of political Islam expert Olivier Roy, "this [phenomenon] is not so much the radicalization of Islam as the Islamicization of radicalism."[27] Although Roy's thesis is mainly concerned with European Muslim youth, the argument may very well hold true in a place like Tunisia. Youth in the interior of the country have confirmed to me that their peers who became radicalized had not been particularly religious.

Cross-examinations of Tunisian recruits to extremist organizations have revealed common attitudes of hatred toward their home country, feelings of not belonging, and eagerness for a new identity. A decline in nationalism during Ben Ali's tenure is cited as a cause. Ben Ali was envious of Bourguiba's national persona and went to great lengths to expunge his predecessor from the public domain, dismantling nationalist sentiments associated with Bourguiba without offering an "appealing alternative."[28] The recruitment success of Da'esh, which offered an alternative system, or another state, contrasts with the relative recruitment failure of al-Qaeda in the Islamic Maghreb, which did not offer the same sort of distant alternative "statehood."

Extremist ideology and acts of terror represent a real and present danger facing Tunisia. But this does not mean that the perception of Tunisia as a moderate, progressive state is incongruent. Indeed, it is rather because Tunisia has been on an enlightened and liberal path toward consolidating its democratic transition that it has come under attack by extremist ideology invested in spoiling what it deems a corrupt Western orientation. Tunisia's success as a democratic, civil, and largely secular state poses a threat to radical Islamist currents bent on steering the region in a diametrically opposite direction.

There are enough local elements to conclude that the Tunisian experience is uniquely Tunisian. Aided by certain natural assets—size, geography, and relative social homogeneity—Tunisia has primarily benefited from a century and a half of reformist thinking that led to an advanced and modern system of education, the emancipation of women, and a moderation of the role of religion in society, governance, and politics. The Tunisian tradition of civil society engagement, rooted in UGTT, is an outgrowth of this reformism and is another potent ingredient that defines Tunisia's experience. The absence from the Tunisian scene of other factors that are considered obstacles to democratization, such as a strong and political army and a resource curse, have also contributed to Tunisia's uniqueness relative to the rest of the region.

It would be misleading to suggest that Tunisia can serve as a model for the rest of the Arab world, where most ingredients present in Tunisia are missing and would take generations to reproduce. It is also a misnomer to place Tunisia squarely within the Arab world when its identity and orientation have not been exclusively Arab, thus rendering any argument that suggests commonalities that would facilitate the transfer of experiences a tenuous one at best.

2

Prelude to Revolution

A
t 6:30 A.M. on November 7, 1987, state radio broadcasted a communiqué by Prime Minister Zine al-Abidine Ben Ali in which he announced that he was assuming the presidency in the place of Habib Bourguiba. Only a month earlier, Ben Ali had been named by Bourguiba as prime minister, the third in a span of less than two years.

Bourguiba's removal was constitutionally based (Article Fifty-Seven) on the testimony of a panel of doctors and medical experts, which stated that he was no longer physically or mentally capable of carrying out his duties as president. As prime minister, Ben Ali was the legal successor to Bourguiba. Bourguiba's peaceful removal in a "doctor's coup" and his ability to retire and die in his native country, while other ousted Arab leaders faced exile or execution, followed a quintessentially Tunisian scenario.

Bourguiba's health had been gradually declining. He suffered from arteriosclerosis and had endured two heart attacks, one in 1967 and another in 1984. The last few years of his presidency were characterized by often irrational behavior, and his leadership became progressively viewed as anxious and impulsive. He was reshuffling his government and changing policy on an almost monthly basis. In January 1984, on the heels of what came to be known as the "bread riots," tanks, armored personnel carriers, and helicopters brought in to quell the protests left 150 dead at the hands of security forces.[1] In response to public outrage, Bourguiba dismissed his cabinet but kept his handpicked successor, Prime Minister Mohamed Mzali, in office, all the while accusing Mzali of raising prices without his approval. Two and a half years later, in July 1986, Bourguiba famously woke from a nap and dismissed Mzali.[2]

Family members were not spared Bourguiba's erraticism either. Anyone who became popular or dared to act independently was sidelined. The same year that he dismissed Mzali, Bourguiba ostracized and divorced his second wife, Wassila Ben Ammar, whose political influence rivaled that of the president in his old age.[3] Also in the same year, Bourguiba dismissed his son and adviser, Habib Jr., when he voiced disagreement over the arrest of *Union générale tunisienne du travail* (UGTT) leaders the year before.[4]

It was not only during the last few years of his presidency that Bourguiba's legacy was tarnished. His trademark benevolent authoritarianism had become more authoritarian and less benevolent throughout the 1970s.

Freedoms that had been experienced by the press, unions, and the judiciary since independence were gradually revoked. Free speech was curtailed through a defamation law that was reinforced in the penal and press codes, and participation in public demonstrations became punishable by imprisonment.

Detention of political opponents escalated toward the end of Bourguiba's tenure. Reports of arbitrary arrests, torture, censorship, and harassment were common. Student activists were routinely detained and brutally tortured, and their cases propagated by the state as warnings for student union activists.

The Tunisian human rights organization, the *Ligue tunisienne pour la défense des droits de l'homme*, formed in 1976 and the first of its kind in any Arab country, pushed for reforms to laws that restricted freedom of expression and association and for the end of prolonged detentions. But even the league had its hands tied behind its back. Its chairman, Khamais Chamari, was arrested and jailed in 1987 on the dubious charge of "disseminating false information and defamation of public order and public institutions" after he granted interviews to foreign journalists and international human rights organizations.[5]

The genesis of the problems of Bourguiba's presidency lay with his ineffectiveness in managing the country's economy and his inability to translate the gains he had made on the education front into economic opportunity for his people. This was happening at a time of unprecedented population growth: the number of Tunisians doubled during Bourguiba's tenure, from 4.22 million in 1960 to more than 8 million in 1990.[6] His economic failures formed the basis for his clashes with UGTT and his increasingly oppressive methods. They also provided the backdrop for the development of Islamic revival in the late 1970s and early 1980s, and his suppression thereof.

In the years following independence, university graduates were almost guaranteed employment in Tunisia because the need for skilled manpower was no longer being fulfilled by the French. This changed in the 1970s and 1980s—after nearly twenty years of universal access to education. It became difficult for well-educated graduates to find employment opportunities. The promise of modernity and prosperity through education had lost its potency. "Educated or not," students chanted in the streets of Tunis in 1970, "the future is not ours."[7]

In efforts to placate growing discontent, the government poured tens of millions of dollars on the public in the form of subsidies—mostly funded by revenue from crude oil. The subsidy program was part of a post-socialist five-year economic development plan after an experiment with a collectivist form of socialism was abandoned in 1969.

But subsidies could not go on indefinitely: by 1983, they amounted to 11 percent of the national budget.[8] In compliance with the International Monetary Fund (IMF) and the World Bank, the government ended its food subsidies that for fifteen years had left the prices of bread, pasta, and semolina unchanged. The bread riots erupted on December 29, 1983, in the southwest of the country and quickly spread from cities in the south all the way to Tunis in the north. The president experienced the anger of his people up close when demonstrators threw stones at the car he was riding in. On January 6, 1984, Bourguiba annulled price hikes for bread and dismissed his interior minister, Driss Guiga, who was then tried in absentia on charges of high treason and sentenced to fifteen years in prison.[9] The cancellation of the price hikes marked the first time since Bourguiba had assumed office that his government reversed a decision in response to popular demand and out of fear of increasing violence.

A disastrous grain harvest brought about by a severe drought in 1985 and a decline of already limited oil proceeds in 1986 resulted in further unemployment and balance-of-payments problems. In response, the government implemented new austerity measures and increased foreign borrowing.

By 1986, external debt had reached $5 billion, or nearly 60 percent of Tunisia's gross national product at the time.[10]

The economic hardships of the 1980s were made worse for Tunisians by the persistent oppression by Bourguiba of the staunchest advocates and organizers of the labor force and the poor—namely, UGTT. The 1970s had witnessed a deterioration of the relationship between Bourguiba's regime and UGTT, culminating in a 1978 general strike organized by the union in response to Bourguiba's interference in their affairs. The regime came down hard on the protesters, jailing and dispersing many union activists. The strike ended with hundreds of workers killed, injured, or arrested on January 26, 1978, remembered as "Black Thursday."[11] The entire leadership of UGTT was put on trial and subsequently replaced with partisans of the regime.

When UGTT rejected a program imposed on the Tunisian government in 1985 by the World Bank and the IMF for structural adjustment, the state again cracked down on the union and imprisoned, for the third time, its secretary general, Habib Achour.[12] A year later, student and labor unrest again resulted in a severe clampdown on UGTT leadership and its replacement with regime loyalists. Zine al-Abidine Ben Ali, who as head of national security had led the crackdown against UGTT in 1978 and had since gained a reputation as a regime hard-liner, was promoted to the position of interior minister to help bring the union under control.

The union was not the only pretext for charging Ben Ali with the powerful task of controlling the state's security apparatus. Bourguiba wanted him to take an active role in rooting out the *Mouvement de la tendance islamique* (MTI), a fundamentalist group founded in 1981 by Islamists fearful of abandoning the political arena to the union and other emerging secular and leftist opposition parties.

The founding of MTI, the precursor to Ennahda, marked the culmination of Islamic revival in the late 1970s and early 1980s against a backdrop of the failure of Bourguiba to translate education into employment. Inspired by the 1979 Iranian revolution, MTI emerged concurrently with the *Front islamique du salut* in neighboring Algeria. Although MTI's party platform resembled those of other Islamist groups at the time in that it called for citizens to practice the moral creed of Islam in their daily lives, MTI differed in its focus on economic reform and more inclusive politics. It objected to the economic policies of the ruling *Parti socialiste destourien*, the new name adopted by Bourguiba's Neo-Destour party in 1964, and it attracted constituents from the poorest segments of Tunisian society, those most hurt by the economic decline of the late 1970s and the 1980s.

MTI was not legalized and could not run as a party in elections. Its founders, Rached Ghannouchi and Abdelfattah Mourou, were blamed for the growing political unrest in the country and accused of trying to instigate an Iran-style Islamic revolution in Tunisia. The party was suspected of involvement in the bread riots, and the suppression of Islamists became an obsession for Bourguiba.

When Islamist extremists within MTI conducted a series of bombings in 1987 targeting the tourism industry, including in Sousse and Bourguiba's hometown of Monastir, the president ordered mass executions of the perpetrators. The bombings coincided with the official holiday celebrating President Habib Bourguiba's eighty-fourth birthday, fueling his outrage and what was seen as a hysterical reaction of indiscriminate arrests and calls for bodies. The State Security Court concluded the four-week trial with fifty-six MTI members in jail, including Rached Ghannouchi, who received a life sentence, and two members sentenced to death.[13] Ben Ali, interior minister at the time, ignored the order for mass executions.[14] Rumors of an impending coup began to circulate around Tunis.

The coup promised much in the way of change. In a state address on the same day that Ben Ali announced he was taking the reins of the presidency from Bourguiba, he declared that the "constitution calls for a revision, which has today become imperative. The age in which we live can no longer permit a presidency for life, nor automatic succession as head of state. . . . Our people are worthy of a developed and institutionalized political life, founded in reality on a multi-party system and plurality of popular organizations."[15] This was specifically in reference to Bourguiba's having declared himself president for life in 1975, with the support of a vote by the Tunisian National Assembly.

True to his word, at least initially, Ben Ali introduced a constitutional amendment in July 1988 that limited any president to three five-year terms. Ben Ali rebranded the *Parti socialiste destourien*, which had retained its designation even after dropping its socialist agenda in the early 1970s, as the *Rassemblement constitutionnel démocratique* (RCD). He reduced the size of the political bureau, removing some of Bourguiba's old cronies, and sought to attract new, younger blood to the party. He also oversaw a transition to a multiparty system, opening the political arena to opposition. The first multiparty parliamentary elections since 1981 were held in April 1989, and 76 percent of eligible voters turned up at the ballot boxes.[16]

Ben Ali's immediate actions after assuming the presidency seemed to reflect his commitment to the start of a new era. He launched a program of national reconciliation and promised to extend civil liberties, allowing some media criticism and dissent. One of his early steps that demonstrated authenticity was a July 1988 modification to the Press Code that made it less restrictive.[17] In the same month, Tunisia became the first Arab country to ratify the United Nations Convention Against Torture and Other Cruel, Inhuman, or Degrading Treatment or Punishment. Ben Ali extended the state's protection of religious minorities, amended the *Code du statut personnel* in 1993—removing a wife's duty of obedience—and set up a fund to assist divorced women and their children.[18]

At first, Ben Ali also seemed conciliatory toward Islamists. Although he had never trusted them and had at times acted ruthlessly to crush them, once he became president, Ben Ali believed that they could be better controlled through concessions. In an effort at appeasement, he declared Islam the religion of the state in speeches, allowed radio and television stations to broadcast the call to prayer, legalized an MTI student organization, and made a well-publicized pilgrimage to Mecca just months after taking office. Ben Ali also encouraged political exiles to return to Tunisia on the promise of more open political processes. He freed thousands of political prisoners in 1988, including MTI members and the movement's cofounder, Rached Ghannouchi. Ben Ali also reinstated Zaitouna as a distinct religious institution of higher education.

But the short honeymoon period between Ben Ali and MTI was over in no time. Ben Ali never recognized the party, which was renamed Ennahda—meaning renaissance or revival—in 1988. Ennahda was thus excluded from the 1989 parliamentary elections. But the party ran independent candidates who won 14 percent of the popular vote, making it in effect the strongest opposition party.[19] When Ennahda's application for registration was again rejected despite a show of strong popular support, protests broke out and were met by police crackdowns. The regime quickly resorted to the old ways of oppression, including arbitrary arrests and torture. That same year, Ghannouchi left for Algeria and then the United Kingdom, where he remained in a state of voluntary exile until 2011.

After a deadly arson attack on an RCD office in Tunis in February 1991, Ben Ali, wary of the Islamist violence in neighboring Algeria, ordered another brutal crackdown on Ennahda. Clampdowns that ensued included the arrest, exile, torture, or disappearance of accused Islamists—men and women—and their families. In 1992, almost 300 members of Ennahda stood trial, some on charges of assassination and coup attempts, and its most prominent leaders were sentenced to life in prison, including Ghannouchi, who was sentenced in absentia; forty-eight Ennahda members were condemned to death.[20]

The 1991 attack on the RCD office became the tipping point for Ben Ali, who henceforth treated Islamists as a serious national security threat. In the 1990s, more than 20,000 Ennahda members, at the very least, were tried for their political activities. Many fled and went into exile, often passing through Algeria to exit.[21] Tunisian elites, worried that the violence going on next door in Algeria could spill over the border, welcomed Ben Ali's strong stance against Islamist groups, which they saw as a threat to the modern and Westernized lifestyles they enjoyed under a "secular" state.

Over the course of his presidency, Ben Ali broke each and every one of the promises he had made upon his ascension to power. The president paid lip service to gradual democratization and human rights. He allowed secular opposition parties to register and run for elections, but ensured that RCD was in practice the only party with any real power.

The regime used various tactics to ensure RCD's political domination, some Machiavellian and others blatantly suppressive. According to the 1988 multiparty law, political parties could gain recognition if they received approval from the ministry of interior, pledged allegiance to the constitution, and renounced religious, ethnic, or linguistic platforms. In paradoxical effect, political parties were subject to approval by RCD, the same party they were opposing.

The 1988 multiparty law also ensured RCD's monopoly over parliament through its electoral simple majority rule, which meant that the winning party would claim a totality of seats. RCD, having received around 80 percent of votes in the 1989 parliamentary elections, thus won all 141 seats. This domination was matched at all levels of government. The party got all but 6 of 4,090 seats in the municipal council elections of 1995.[22]

With the increase of support for Islamists, the regime gave secular parties more autonomy in the 1990s but never allowed them to gain real strength.

RCD, which acted as "a veritable political Goliath," erected structural barriers to the growth of opposition parties, denying civil service jobs and the distribution of resources to citizens or regions that voted for an opposition party, and discouraging donors from supporting the opposition by keeping close tabs on private contributions and reviewing financial records of all parties.[23] Leadership of the strongest and largest opposition parties—*Mouvement des démocrates socialistes* and *Parti démocrate progressiste*—were often harassed, tortured, and imprisoned.

Only the domination of Ben Ali as president matched the political domination of RCD. Ben Ali appointed his prime minister and cabinet ministers, as well as each of the provincial governors, and exercised strong influence over the judiciary. He ran unopposed in his first two presidential elections in 1989 and 1994. Although opposition candidates were allowed to run in the 1999 presidential elections, the elections revealed a growing disillusionment with the political system. Only 9.24 percent of voters participated, and Ben Ali received 99.44 percent of votes.[24]

Despite his repeated pledges not to follow in the footsteps of Bourguiba, no one seemed surprised when Ben Ali violated his own amendment to run for a third term and in 2002 introduced a constitutional amendment meant to extend his presidency for life. He abolished term limits on the presidency and extended the maximum age of eligibility from seventy to seventy-five. Ben Ali used the growth of Ennahda and Islamism as justification for his prolonged presidency, warning that Islamists would reverse the gains of secularism. The civil war between the military and Islamists in Algeria helped provide a pretext for Ben Ali's argument.

President for Life, or *Ben à vie*, as he was often sardonically referred to, Ben Ali quickly moved to amputate Bourguiba from the public sphere and erase his dominance of the Tunisian national identity, deconstructing the former president's nationalist myth. Statues of Bourguiba were toppled, and dozens of streets and parks that had been named after the former president were renamed. On Avenue Habib Bourguiba, the capital's main thoroughfare, Ben Ali erected a clock tower, representing modern Tunisia, to replace a statue of Bourguiba riding triumphantly on a horse.

Ben Ali's cult of personality began to permeate the visual space with images of the president cluttering public arenas and large posters hanging on buildings and highway billboards, sometimes stretching over two stories, often retouched to make him look younger and stronger. He usually appeared in these posters in a suit and tie, but sometimes was dressed in traditional Tunisian robes, with his hand over his heart, as if saying "from my heart." Disenchanted citizens said that what he was really saying was "genuinely, from his heart, screwing the country."[25]

Dominating the public space were also the number 7, commemorating his ascension to power on November 7, 1987, and the color purple, his favorite. Examples of this strange "cult of 7" included the national airline SevenAir, men's hair products and cafés branded Seven, and the Stade 7 Novembre soccer stadium. Streams of small purple flags lined streets and public squares, sometimes with the number 7 or pictures of the dictator, replacing the national color red of the Tunisian flag. Purple light fixtures adorned the streets during the annual anniversary celebration of Ben Ali's ascension, marked by a lavish party and public rally in the stadium.[26] So reviled did the color purple become among regular Tunisians as a result that when I complimented my driver Mohamed one day on his purple shirt, he sheepishly thanked me and explained that it had taken a while before people started feeling comfortable with the color again.

Public school textbooks were not spared the reach of Ben Ali's personality cult. History books were rewritten, consistent with state propaganda that shifted away from a strong emphasis on Tunisia's independence movement and a Bourguibian national identity toward the denial of a collective national memory that Bourguiba had created.

By the early 1990s, Ben Ali was practicing the "full Bourguiba"—cult and all—and over the next two decades, he far surpassed his predecessor's highest state of authoritarianism. Under Ben Ali, the party became defined by the president and indistinguishable from the state.[27] Whereas government ministers in Bourguiba's time played a meaningful role and generally had strong political backgrounds—in the party, or a trade or student union—Ben Ali recruited ministers on the basis of their technocratic and organizational abilities to follow and dispense orders.[28]

To ensure that he stayed in power, Ben Ali relied heavily on the police, which grew during his tenure as president to a total between 130,000 and 200,0000, or about 2 percent of the population.[29] No one knew exactly how large the security force was; its size may have been exaggerated in order to maintain the perception that the public was constantly being monitored by an omnipresent force that could suppress dissent or "suspicious activity" at any time. The main focus of the security forces was on domestic Islamic extremists—radical and hard-line opponents of the regime. Police monitored the activity of relatives of known extremists who were in jail or living abroad and of political critics and citizens who interacted with foreign visitors, journalists, or human rights monitors. Ben Ali's agents would always trail foreign reporters.

Ben Ali's police state suffocated Tunisia's intellectual and public discourse. Newspaper circulation, having peaked in the 1980s and early 1990s, steadily declined as the state apparatus became more controlling and there was a dearth of real news content; circulation levels in 2000 and 2001 were similar to those in the 1970s, when literacy rates had been much lower.[30]

The police, who were authorized to make arrests without warrants, rounded up thousands, including many whose gravest crime was membership in banned groups such as Ennahda and the Communist Workers' Party. Police also conducted searches without warrants routinely under the auspice that state security was at risk or a crime was in progress, exploiting two legal loopholes that were also used to justify telephone surveillance. In a scenario that started looking increasingly familiar in Ben Ali's era, Amnesty International's local head was arrested and imprisoned when the human rights organization reported in 1997 that approximately 2,000 political prisoners remained locked up in Tunisian jails. Political prisoners were subjected to a "blatant, grave, and systematic practice" of torture, according to a 1998 report by the International Federation of Human Rights Leagues. The report listed 500 cases of torture between 1990 and 1998, thirty of which led to death, and estimated that the total number of victims during this time was in the several thousands.[31]

Harrowing accounts of mistreatment suffered by Islamists and regime opponents during the 1990s and 2000s include a range of abuses from the "banning of prayer" to "solitary confinement that sometimes lasts for years on end" to "mistreatment and torture that have sometimes led to the death of the victims or their suicide."[32] The Office of the United Nations High Commission for Human Rights (OHCHR) conducted an investigation in the first few months after the revolution and concluded that under Ben Ali, "trade and students unions, human rights defenders, civil society actors, journalists and political activists were harassed, intimidated, detained, and subjected to torture, cruel, inhuman and degrading treatment."[33] Victims of torture also included ordinary citizens who refused to abide by bans on public displays of piety. Ben Ali's forced secularization often led to women being particularly targeted for dressing conservatively. Secularization by the state, it should be noted, meant the suppression of oppositional Islamist trends and was not ideologically based for Ben Ali the way it was for Bourguiba.

In blatant disregard for the constitution, courts ignored allegations of torture and accepted confessions obtained under duress. The president acted as the head of the Supreme Council of Judges while regime loyalists controlled the judicial system, despite the constitution's calling for an independent judiciary (Article Sixty-Five).[34] When Judge Mokhtar Yahyaoui, founder of the *Centre tunisien pour l'indépendance de la justice*, publicly denounced in July 2001 the "catastrophic" state of the judicial system for its lack of autonomy—specifically due to interference of the executive branch—he was summarily dismissed.[35]

The police state was bolstered when Tunisia established itself as a strong ally in the "war on terror" following the attacks on the United States on September 11, 2001. Ben Ali's regime then passed a new antiterrorism law on the heels of the al-Qaeda attack in 2002 on a synagogue on the Tunisian island of Djerba that killed twenty-one Europeans and Tunisians. The new law's vague definition of terrorism included acts of violence that could "disturb the public order" and "bring harm to persons or property," and allowed for prosecution for the use of terms or symbols that were seen as supportive of terrorism.[36]

Ben Ali's handling of security was perceived as a perilous success: on the one hand, it was used to curb liberties and silence dissent, but on the other, it was more effective at fending off terrorism than that of his predecessor, whose record is seen as having been dismal during his last years in power. Another area in which Ben Ali distinguished himself from Bourguiba was the economy.

Ben Ali was intent on following economic policies that were more aggressive than his predecessor's. He sought a shift in favor of a more liberal free market economy, introducing privatization and further positioning Tunisia as an export-oriented country. Ben Ali fully embraced structural adjustment plans imposed by the World Bank and the IMF—he cut government spending and promoted private investment. Economic reforms meant that Bourguiba's state-operated enterprises were dismantled and that controls over consumer goods' prices and the currency were reduced—as were import restrictions.

Aided for a number of years by better harvests, a rise in exports, and higher domestic investment, the result was that, on the whole, economic indicators moved in a positive direction. Household income doubled between 1988 and 1998.[37] Real GDP growth, which was 0.1 percent in 1988, grew to 7.9 percent in 1990, averaging around 5 percent until 2008. It then fell to 1.3 percent at the beginning of 2009 as a result of the impact of the 2008 financial crisis on Mediterranean countries, Tunisia's principal trading partners.[38]

But while Tunisia's economy seemed to be doing well on a macroeconomic level, economic indicators were masking some grave problems and inequities. Millions of Tunisians, representing a broad spectrum of economic strata, social backgrounds, and regions of the country, were aware—some intuitively—of how the seemingly successful economy had some serious underlying problems.

Whatever economic gains were made under Ben Ali, they were not evenly distributed across classes, regions, or age groups. Those who felt the greatest gains were the upper and upper-middle classes of Tunis and the coastal Sahel region, whose standards of living equaled those in eastern and southern Europe.[39] Business activity in the Sahel dwarfed that of the interior.

The interior towns of Kasserine and Gafsa, considered the epicenter of the revolution, suffered the highest unemployment and poverty rates.[40] Though poverty rates improved somewhat during the second half of Ben Ali's rule as a result of overall improvements in the economy and a trickle-down effect, they remained over 30 percent in the interior of the country at the time of the revolution.[41]

The legacy of Ben Ali's crony capitalism further hindered the distribution of resources across the country. Agriculture policies favored crops grown in the coastal regions, and skewed public investment created obvious disparities in the quality of public services and infrastructure in the west and south.

Demographically, much of the poverty was concentrated in the middle part of the population pyramid: working-age young men and women. Although universal education had been a goal for the state ever since Bourguiba introduced public education in 1958, challenges in finding employment for graduating students in the 1970s and 1980s had tempered this aim and helped maintain a focus on quality over quantity. But Ben Ali, in a populist move, decided to expand the education system, introducing compulsory education until age sixteen and making higher education more accessible. Ben Ali's reforms, introduced in 1991, had the effect of turning Tunisia's education system into factories for degrees that raised the expectations of their holders but almost guaranteed them unemployment. Many ended up financially worse off than their parents, who had experienced upward mobility, despite having better credentials and more education.

While overall unemployment averaged nearly 14 percent, unemployment among the youth hovered above 30 percent in the decade leading up to Ben Ali's ouster.[42] One-third of the unemployed were university graduates.[43] At the time of the revolution, unemployment rates reached 50 percent for holders of technical and master's degrees, 68 percent for those with a master's degree in legal studies, 31 percent for engineers, and 70 percent for technicians.[44]

The youth felt cheated. They had been told to go to school, work hard, and that they would be guaranteed a future. Armed with degrees, university graduates were ill equipped for the labor force and mismatched with the needs of the marketplace.

Regional inequalities were clearly present in the quality of education that students received. Success rates for the entrance examination for high schools increased as one approached large urban centers. In Sousse, for example, the discrepancy in admittance reached a 50 percent difference between schools in the center and those on the outskirts of the governorate.[45] A 1999 national employment survey found that more than half of the illiterate population lived in rural areas, even though the rural population comprised only 35 percent of the total number of Tunisians. Illiteracy rates were close to 41 percent in the countryside.[46]

Like some of his education reforms, particularly on the structural front, Ben Ali's economic reforms were unscrupulously cosmetic in nature and unsustainable. They produced little benefit for the average Tunisian.

Policies put in place under Ben Ali created a system that marginalized those who did not have significant social clout or political connections, inviting corruption and handouts based on privilege. Privatization landed assets in the hands of Ben Ali's family, whose mafia-like control over private business made it difficult for the country to attract direct foreign investment. Class distinctions and economic disparities increased as a result of Ben Ali's reforms, which ended up simply transferring state wealth into the hands of his family and friends.

Under Ben Ali's economic policies of patronage and coercion, 21 percent of private sector profits accrued to companies owned by Ben Ali's extended family—often confiscated and bestowed on them and generating just 1 percent of jobs.[47] Ben Ali's second wife, Leila Trabelsi, was despised by Tunisians and seen as behind much of the corruption. Twenty-one years younger than Ben Ali, she was nicknamed *La Régente de Carthage* as her influence over the regime grew. Her brother Belhassen Trabelsi helped himself to an airline company, a number of hotels, a private radio station, car assembly plants, a Ford distribution center, and a real estate development company.[48]

According to a 2014 World Bank study, Ben Ali and his relatives embezzled assets worth approximately $13 billion—equivalent to more than 25 percent of Tunisia's GDP in 2011—during his reign. The report also confirmed that public and private monopolies and oligopolies, largely controlled by Ben Ali's family, dominated most Tunisian industries.[49]

Tunisia was nonetheless brandished by the likes of the World Bank and the IMF as a middle-class economic miracle and a model of social liberalism and developing-world prosperity.

Biased statistical inferences and data manipulations helped preserve a fictional narrative. Unemployment for university graduates, for example, was manipulated into an official figure of 22.5 percent in 2009—half the actual number, which stood at 45 percent. National assessments of the rate of poverty conducted after the revolution revealed that it stood at 10 percent, considerably higher than the estimated 3.8 percent that had been disclosed by the Ben Ali regime.[50] International donor organizations judged economic performance by often misleading averages, assuming that eventually various strata would converge toward a mean. A 2014 examination of communications between the IMF and the governments of Egypt, Morocco, and Tunisia between 2006 and 2013 revealed that inclusiveness was never embedded into growth strategies until *after* the Arab uprisings.[51] The net effect has been the masking of troubling variances within a population and the worsening of regional disparities.

During the last decade of Ben Ali's regime, regions in the southern and midwestern parts of the country, where the rates of unemployment were highest, became centers of increasing UGTT activity and regime opposition. But UGTT was only starting to regain its power in the mid-2000s after it had been weakened during Ben Ali's presidency.

Along with the Islamists, UGTT represented the greatest political threat to Ben Ali's regime. He tried to neutralize the union in the 1990s by exercising direct control over the organization and recruiting it as an ally against the Islamists. Ben Ali was able to ensure the loyalty and ineffectiveness of the organization's central command by replacing the union's leadership with his own supporters. In 1989, he placed a regime loyalist, Ismail Sahbani, at the organization's helm. When Sahbani was accused of corruption and ousted in 2000, another loyalist, Abdessalem Jrad, replaced him.

Major agreements between the state, UGTT, and the business owners' association, the *Union tunisienne de l'industrie, du commerce et de l'artisanat* (UTICA), were signed in 1990 and 1993 in support of the neo-liberal economic reforms led by the regime.[52] The liberalizing economic reforms further weakened the bargaining power of the union. Leadership of UGTT aligned itself with the state, which was itself aligned with the interests of the business community. The union in effect shifted its aims from achieving economic justice to cosigning on governmental corporate projects.

But complicity with the regime by the union's top brass did not extend to its grass roots. Local and regional offices did not always support actions taken by UGTT's national leadership and, in fact, often worked against it. Command and control at the regional level were highly decentralized, and local branches exercised significant autonomy in running their business. The protection and power that union membership afforded workers vis-à-vis their employers also meant that, despite their loss of confidence in the union's leadership, they continued to pay their dues and participate in local UGTT affairs.

While Ben Ali, and Bourguiba before him, succeeded in silencing the union, the regime allowed it to exercise democracy, believing that discord could be contained within UGTT. Even at its weakest during the height of Ben Ali's control over the union in the 1990s, the depth and breadth of UGTT's reach, along with its distributive and democratic power structure, protected it from disintegrating.

By 2004, UGTT was starting to publicly break ranks with Ben Ali, with a number of regional and local branches voting against initiatives by the regime to further extend its power. Over the next couple of years, the union took a number of public stances critical of Ben Ali and in support of other civil society organizations that had clashed with the regime.

Aided by its historic legitimacy and transparent democratic processes, it would still take UGTT years before it could fully regain its credibility among its workers. The collusion with the regime during the 1990s ended up significantly compromising the union's central command and hurting its relationship with the workers it represented, a situation that came to a head with the 2008 Gafsa riots, when workers themselves protested *against* the union.

The Gafsa Basin riots erupted when the state-owned *Compagnie des phosphates de Gafsa*, the largest employer in the region, announced the results of its recruitment competition in early January 2008. Local workers and the UGTT branch accused the company of cronyism and discrimination against well-qualified and loyal employees in favor of those with connections. It was no secret that Amara Abbassi, the regional secretary-general of UGTT, owned several subcontracting companies related to the *Compagnie des phosphates de Gafsa* and was a member of RCD's central committee.[53] UGTT and the ruling RCD were thus seen as complicit with the company's fraudulent recruitment practices.

In protest, miners held a number of demonstrations, work stoppages, hunger strikes, sit-ins, and roadblocks of mining vehicles. Protests quickly spread to other mining towns and literally paralyzed the industry. Workers, the unemployed, civil servants, women, merchants, and craftsmen all joined. Ben Ali, aware of the region's history and role in previous economic and social disturbances, reacted quickly and harshly, sending in his infamous and terrifying national guard as well as the army.

The riots lasted for five months and left scores of workers dead. Police brutality in crushing the protests was so severe that the memory of it was deeply entrenched and ordinary citizens sought revenge for it.

Worsening poverty, mass unemployment, rising prices, and the nonexistence of distributive justice became the sparks that ultimately set the entire country on fire. In the minds of Tunisians—UGTT members, activists, and ordinary citizens—Gafsa marked the real beginning of the revolution that culminated in the removal of Ben Ali.

The precipitous and derisive impact of the 2008 global economic meltdown and the regime's brutal reaction to the Gafsa Basin riots earlier in the year fueled dissent that had been lurking over poor economic conditions, corruption, and human rights abuses. Youth unemployment was ultimately the fireball that caught revolutionary zeal, catapulting the country into a full rebellion that brought down the man who had replaced his predecessor with promises of change—promises that he broke, one by one.

3

If the People Will to Live

The word *jasmine* comes from the Persian word *yasmin*, or gift from God. The petals of the flower remain closed during the day and open between five and eight o'clock in the evening. Jasmine, first imported from Andalucía in the sixteenth century, is Tunisia's national flower. So it is little wonder that soon after Ben Ali left, following in the tradition of color and flower revolutions that started in Eastern Europe in the 1980s, foreign journalists began referring to the Tunisian revolution as the Jasmine Revolution.

January 14, 2011, the day that Ben Ali was finally pushed out, has been immortalized as a marker of the Jasmine Revolution. Ben Ali had arrived that morning at his office in the presidential palace at Carthage with his prime minister, Mohamed Ghannouchi—not to be confused with Ennahda leader Sheikh Rached Ghannouchi—and the ministers of interior and defense. Meanwhile, tens of thousands of protesters were gathering in Tunis along Avenue Habib Bourguiba. Security had broken down across the city, giving Ben Ali the final motivation to secure himself and his family by leaving Tunisia.

In his wake, the prime minister assumed the presidency, invoking Article Fifty-Six of the constitution, but that presidency lasted for just one day. The next day, the Constitutional Council announced that the post of president was definitively vacant and named Fouad Mebezaa, president of the Chamber of Deputies, as caretaker president—based on Article Fifty-Seven of the constitution. Mebezaa then tasked Ghannouchi with forming a new coalition government. That same day, an official statement from the Saudi Press Agency read: "Out of concern for the exceptional circumstances facing the brotherly Tunisian people and in support of the security and stability of their country . . . the Saudi government has welcomed president Zine El Abidine Ben Ali and his family to the kingdom."[1]

It all started on December 17, 2010, when Mohamed Bouazizi drenched himself with paint thinner and set himself on fire. Earlier that day, Bouazizi had been stopped from selling his fruits and vegetables in the interior city of Sidi Bouzid without a license. The police overturned and confiscated his cart and beat him up when he resisted. Publicly humiliated, he filed a complaint, which was rebuffed, and his attempts to see the governor were shunned. Bouazizi had been pushed to his limits, having been the main breadwinner for his family, and having endured harassment by the police for years—refusing to bribe them, or simply lacking the means to do so. On January 4, 2011, Mohamed Bouazizi died in hospital as a result of his burns.

The self-immolation of Bouazizi sent shock waves throughout Tunisia. There was an immediate and shared sentiment of empathy with his humiliation across the nation. Over the next few days, protests and clashes with police spread from Sidi Bouzid—where hundreds were met by police aggression around the governor's office—to the neighboring towns of Kasserine, Sfax, Gafsa, Menzel Bouzaiane, Regueb, and Meknassy, and then to Tunis. Photos and videos of the protests circulated around the country, though the national media remained silent. On December 22, as protesters gathered in Sidi Bouzid, twenty-two-year-old Houcine Falhi shouted "no to misery, no to unemployment!" and committed suicide by touching a high-voltage electric pole.[2] Two days later, security forces fired the first rounds on protesters, killing eighteen-year-old Mohamed Ammari and forty-four-year-old Chaoki Belhoussaine al-Hadri.

Bouazizi's humiliation resonated with the widest swaths of society who had simply just had it. Things had been boiling ever since the Gafsa riots of 2008, but had taken on an acute urgency in the weeks leading to the incident. Less than a month before Bouazizi's self-immolation, on November 28, whistle-blowing WikiLeaks had revealed accounts of the authoritarianism and corruption of Ben Ali's regime. Within hours of the government's censorship, a local site, TuniLeaks, emerged, and access was just as quickly blocked by the regime. But reports had already found their way to Tunisians, reaffirming their deep sense of inequity and confirming what they had known for years.

Diplomatic dispatches from United States ambassador Robert F. Godec to Washington in 2008, revealed through WikiLeaks, documented the nexus of corruption practiced by Ben Ali's regime. Sarcastic headlines of cables included "What's Yours Is Mine," "The Sky's the Limit," "Show Me Your Money," "This Land Is Your Land, This Land Is My Land," "All in the Family," and "Mob Rule?" Leaked documents chronicled Ben Ali's and his family's kleptocracy and embezzling ways. They revealed, for example, how before *Banque du Sud* was privatized in 2005, Ben Ali's son-in-law Marouane Mabrouk had purchased a 17 percent stake that he later sold for a huge profit.[3] He had also bought *Le Moteur*, which controlled the distribution of all Mercedes and Fiat vehicles in Tunisia, at a discounted price—thanks to his family connections. Another document chronicled how Ben Ali's wife, Leila Trabelsi, had received a desirable tract of land in Carthage for free as well as a $1.5 million "gift" from the government to build a for-profit school.[4] In a widely reported story in the French press, Imed and Moaz Trabelsi, Ben Ali's nephews, were alleged to have stolen the yacht of a well-connected French businessman, only to return it to its owner after it was spotted in the Sidi Bou Said harbor.[5] Leaked diplomatic cables from 2009 revealed troubled relations between Tunis and Washington and problems within Ben Ali's regime. The American ambassador's messages suggested that the end of Ben Ali's reign was nearing.

Ben Ali's days in office had been numbered since the 2008 Gafsa riots. At the time, the regime's repressive ways saw to it that any potential momentum generated by the riots could not be sustained. Opposition parties were too weak to lend meaningful support, and any hope for a nationwide movement was curtailed. For its part, the *Union générale tunisienne du travail* (UGTT) failed to turn the Gafsa incident to its advantage in an attempt to reclaim legitimate leadership. The opportunity to stimulate a grassroots movement and leverage citizens' fervent zeal was interrupted by the ferocious reaction of the regime to the riots. The union lamented the lost momentum, and Gafsa became a case study for how UGTT was to capture and promulgate the next opportunity and turn it into a sustained nationwide insurrection.

According to Mouldi Jendoubi, deputy secretary-general of UGTT for two terms, "the revolt remained in the memory of Tunisians. Freedom—union and non-union freedom—has always been an important issue for Tunisians in general, and for UGTT and unions especially."[6] The union's failure to capitalize on 2008 forced it to adopt a much-needed change of strategy. So when Bouazizi set himself on fire in defiance after the police confiscated his vegetable cart and source of livelihood, UGTT seized the opportunity to take what would become a final stand against Ben Ali.

Jendoubi animatedly narrated to me his version of how things transpired from the moment Bouazizi committed suicide on December 17 until the day that Ben Ali departed. He unabashedly paid tribute to UGTT's and his alleged role in connecting the dots between Bouazizi's emblematic rise and Ben Ali's ignominious fall.

The story goes that as soon as Jendoubi heard that Bouazizi had set himself on fire, he recognized this as the match that could light the fire and acted quickly in calling his colleague Mohamed Saad. Jendoubi agreed with Saad, who is from Sidi Bouzid, that they needed to get in touch with Abdessalem Jrad, secretary general of UGTT at the time, to urge quick mobilization and avoidance of a repeat of the lost opportunity of Gafsa in 2008.

When UGTT's executive committee held an emergency meeting at their offices in Tunis on the following day, Jendoubi and Saad were assigned the "Sidi Bouzid case." They headed to Sidi Bouzid immediately to meet with union cadres at the UGTT branch and found that the police were holding in custody more than thirty-five young men. Jendoubi and Saad arranged for the release of thirty-two of the detainees with the help of the governor. UGTT local leadership then told the duo that everything was under control and they should head back to Tunis. Jendoubi's response was: "We did not come to Sidi Bouzid to put out the fire; we came here to ignite it."[7]

Jendoubi's and Saad's next stop was Sbeitla. Jendoubi tells me that in Sbeitla, he called a meeting of all UGTT branches in the governorate of Sidi Bouzid and declared a districtwide general strike. From there, mobilization efforts spread from nearby locales to others farther out, "like a drop of oil in water that starts dispersing." Jendoubi claims that between December 18 and January 13, he presided over eight regional meetings like the one he held in Sbeitla, proclaimed a general strike in each of these areas, and signed the UGTT order for the general national strike that took place on January 14, the day that Ben Ali fled the country.

Jendoubi's story may have been somewhat exaggerated, for it was at the local and regional levels and at the secondary echelons of the organization's hierarchy that most of the active involvement originated. While the union did organize the first solidarity demonstration at its headquarters in Tunis on December 25, local branches played a key role in mobilizing efforts and providing crucial logistical support for protesters. UGTT's national leadership had not fully recovered from the loss of respect it had suffered after years of collaboration with Ben Ali's regime. UGTT's credibility was helped, however, when the union became a target of attacks by the regime, including a police raid on its offices in Gafsa in late December, and leadership at all levels spoke out in condemnation of the assaults.[8]

UGTT was not the only civil society organization behind the protests. Various trade, student, and teacher unions—some of them member organizations of UGTT—joined the protests early on and had a role in moving them from the interior to the towns and cities in the south and north. When protests reached a new city, they often first spread through working-class areas and attracted many of the disenfranchised. Youth were disproportionately represented among the protesters; 35 percent were under the age of twenty-four.[9] As youth—employed and unemployed—carried the mantle and kept the momentum going, they were joined by students who came from all over the country.

Tunisian women of all ages and from all walks of life participated in the protests. Both women and men took it as a given that women would be an integral part of the revolution, or any sociopolitical movement for that matter. Lawyer Bilel Larbi spoke about how the protests exemplified gender relationships in Tunisia: "Just look at how Tunisian women stood side-by-side with Tunisian men . . . They came out to the streets to protest in headscarves. They came out in miniskirts. It doesn't matter. They were there."[10]

The revolution was painted as a moment of victory for women, pointing to their involvement at the forefront of protests. International media outlets were emphatic that women, veiled and unveiled, were present and enthusiastic about the protests. They often pictured them—perhaps disproportionately so—at the front of protests, defying stereotypes and taking down a dictator in one fell swoop.

Protests were mostly apolitical. Ennahda was absent from the scene and did not make any official statements. Recognized parties were slow to react, and only illegal leftist parties were quick to support the protests, most notably the *Parti démocrate progressiste* and the Workers' Party—renamed from the Communist Workers' Party—whose leader, Hamma Hammami, was arrested on January 12 after he issued a statement calling for Ben Ali's removal. Hammami, who is also spokesperson of the Popular Front, a grouping of nine political parties and numerous independents, had spent twenty-two years between prison and exile and had been tortured for his political activism against the Ben Ali rule. He tells me that on November 22, 2010, almost a month before the first protests of the Jasmine Revolution, he came out of hiding upon receiving intelligence that a revolution was finally on the verge of erupting and that Ben Ali's regime was in a terminal state.[11]

Official media coverage during the revolution was minimal. On December 28, 2010, Ben Ali banned two leading opposition newspapers, *al-Tareeq al-jadid* and *al-Mawqif*.[12] But a second battleground of the revolution was being waged in cyberspace.

Social media were used extensively to help spread the word and to assist with organizing on the ground. At the time of the revolution, 20 percent of Tunisians had a Facebook profile, and 64 percent of students used Facebook as their primary source of information about the protests during the first four weeks.[13] On January 10, 2011, videos of young Tunisians tearing down a billboard depicting Ben Ali's portrait in the seaside resort town of Hammamet went viral. The videos prompted others to commit similar "criminal" acts across Tunisia, posting videos and photos of themselves slashing posters of the president or the number 7.

Ironically, it was Ben Ali himself who had pushed for affordable Internet access nationwide and the technical training of Tunisians. Tunisia was the first country in Africa and in the Arab world to connect to the Internet in 1996. Ben Ali's regime had worked hard to spread connectivity, launching "free Internet" programs that charged rates equal to the price of a phone call, and set up Internet cafés, or Publinets, in rural and urban areas across the country. The technologically savvy generation that he created led the charge in his ousting and was often able to outsmart the regime when it tried to quiet dissent and to control Internet access.

But Internet connectivity also meant that the regime could more easily monitor activities and control access when it felt threatened. The regime's surveillance of people's electronic communications was helped by the fact that none other than Ben Ali's daughter, Cyrine Ben Ali, controlled the main Internet service provider in Tunisia (GlobalNet).[14] The sole purpose of the Tunisian Internet regulating body, the *Agence tunisienne d'internet*, was to control the Internet and Domain Name System services, often supplying fake error pages when access was sought to a banned website. The guiles of the state and the limitations imposed by it caused Reporters Without Borders to label Tunisia an "enemy of the Internet" in 2006.[15]

When authorities led targeted phishing operations—stealing passwords, hacking accounts, and blocking users—Tunisians used proxies, encryption, and virtual private networks that helped to circumvent censorship. In retaliation and to flex cyber muscle during the revolution, a citizen cyber activist group, Anonymous, launched Operation Tunisia, which attacked government websites, leading to a temporary shutdown on January 2.[16] The virtual battlefield was wide open, and both sides in the fight were well armed.

Prominent among cyber activists during that initial phase was Lina ben Mhenni, who blogged as A Tunisian Girl and whose name was put forward for the 2011 Nobel Peace Prize—an honor that, along with her activism and outspokenness, made her the target of death threats by Islamists. I met the thirty-two-year-old activist and blogger at a café on Avenue Habib Bourguiba and found her with a security escort that had been assigned to her for her protection by the ministry of the interior. Speaking out for women's rights and individual freedoms has made this inconvenience necessary, Lina explained to me. An ironic sign of the revolution is that the same people who had targeted Lina with censorship during the authoritarian times of Ben Ali were now the people who afforded her protection. Before the revolution, Lina's blog, which started in 2007 and always showed her face, kept changing names—from Night Clubbers to Crazy Thoughts to A Tunisian Girl—in order to circumvent state censorship.[17]

The daughter of activists, Lina was one of the few individuals who used their real names to criticize the regime during the uprisings. She participated in protests outside of the capital and was in Sidi Bouzid during the early weeks of the revolution. She was the only blogger to take part in uprisings in Regueb and Kasserine, where police brutality was taking place. Like many others, including UGTT leadership, Lina thinks that the 2008 Gafsa revolt, when the "revolution really began," was a missed opportunity—from her perspective, because activists did not have a firm grasp of social media and failed to take advantage of the situation. By 2010, however, she and others had been working on online campaigns and had collaborated with counterparts in Lebanon and Egypt. Anger had been brewing, and corruption and nepotism were increasingly present—WikiLeaks only confirmed what everyone had already known. Still, the uprisings in 2010 were really spontaneous, and she, like others, was taken by surprise.

In addition to the crucial role played by social media, the revolution assumed an artistic and linguistic tone of its own that inspired publics elsewhere in what became known as the Arab Spring. The most common protest chant that Tunisians cried out was *"Dégage!"* or *"Dégage,* Ben Ali!" literally ordering the president to get out. It is telling that the chant was in French, not Arabic, a reflection of how the French language is not the exclusive reserve of businesses and elite households. Other popular chants and slogans, all apolitical and nonreligious, included "Rebel, my people, rebel, and quell the regime, quell" and "Game over,"[18] but the one that was mimicked most by protesters in other countries of the Arab Spring was *"Ash-sha'b yurid isqat an-nizam,"* meaning that the people demand the downfall of the regime.

No words were more poignant, however, than those of Tunisian philosopher and poet Abu al-Qasim al-Shabbi (1909–1934), whose poetry had special meaning that was evocative of a rise against tyranny. Al-Shabbi's poem "The Will to Live," written in 1933 when Tunisia was in the throes of French colonialism, became a mantra for liberation and independence from colonial powers throughout the Arab world. During the Jasmine Revolution, sections of the poem were chanted in the streets and displayed on T-shirts and banners, particularly the first four lines, which make up the final verse of the Tunisian national anthem, *"Humat al-hima"* ("Defenders of the Homeland"):

Itha al-sha'bu yawman arada al-hayat   If the people one day will to live

fa la budda an yastajeeb al-qaddar   then destiny is sure to respond

wa la budda lil-laylli an yanjali   and the night is destined to fold

wa la budda lil-qaydi an yankassiru   and the chain is certain to be broken

wa man lam yu'aniquhu shawq al-hayat   and whoever does not embrace the love of life

tabakhar fi jawihha wa indathar   will evaporate in its atmosphere and disappear

The poem's idea is that it is up to the people to determine their fate and that opportunity must be seized. It invites the people to a future that they need to create for themselves, as opposed to the one they lived in at the time. The poem speaks of youth and self-determination, of finding a purpose to fight for, of giving meaning and motivation to life, and of awakening a dormant desire for dignity and justice.

Abu al-Qasim al-Shabbi was a contemporary of the establishment of an active free press and labor and academic reforms. Neither a politician nor even a member of a political party in his short life, al-Shabbi demonstrated how the power of poetry and artistic expression could inspire a people to rise up and take action.

In the months leading to the revolution, political and cultural critiques became more daring, particularly in art form. Hip-hop and rap music videos were posted on YouTube and Facebook, and these had explosive effects. The rapper Hamada Ben Amor, better known by his stage name El Général, released popular songs with political messages on social media. His most famous was *"Rays lebled"* ("President of the Country"), which was released on November 7, 2010, the twenty-third anniversary of Ben Ali's assuming the presidency. *"Rays lebled,"* which called on the president to address the anguish and suffering of his people, then became, for all practical purposes, the anthem of the revolution.

A week after Bouazizi's self-immolation, El Général released another song, *"Tounes bledna"* ("Tunisia Our Country"), calling on Tunisian youth to not fear challenging the injustice and tyranny of the regime, for which he was arrested but then released.[19] The writer and philosopher Awlad Ahmed wrote a poem, titled "Butterfly," mourning the self-immolation of Mohamed Bouazizi and earning himself the designation of "the Poetic Central Command of the Tunisian Revolution."[20]

The role of hip-hop and rap music as a means of expression against Ben Ali's regime—before, during, and after the revolution—was so vigorous "that many can no longer imagine the cultural scene in Tunisia without it (despite the very fact that this genre is novel in Tunisia and in the Arab World in general)."[21] The release of *"Rays lebled"* in early November was a manifestation of brewing sentiments that had been waiting for the spark that ignited the revolution, confounding the idea that Tunisia just sprang into an Arab Spring and took the world by surprise.

Ben Ali at first dismissed the protests and attributed them to fringe extremism. On December 28, in a nationally televised broadcast, he warned that the demonstrations would hurt the economy, stating that the law would be enforced "in all firmness" to punish protesters.[22] Ben Ali relied heavily on his police forces to quell the populace. He could not depend on his small army, which had neither the power nor the political will to intervene on behalf of the regime.

Chief of Staff of the Armed Forces Rachid Ammar reportedly refused Ben Ali's orders to fire on protesters.[23] There are conflicting reports, however, as to whether Ben Ali had actually ordered the army to take aim. Ammar, who on January 10 issued an administrative telegram prohibiting his units from opening fire or using their weapons unless otherwise directed, may have done so on his own initiative.[24] Blogger Yassine Ayari, who was later sentenced in absentia by a military court to a three-year prison term for defaming the army, goes further by stating that not only was there never an order to fire on protesters but that Rachid Ammar never even sent this supposed telegram; Ayari claims that he himself invented this story so that the media would relay it to encourage people to protest.[25]

In any event, the army often provided cover and was considered an ally while security forces under the auspices of the interior ministry attacked protesters. Demonstrators cheered soldiers and armored vehicles on the streets. Videos and images showed soldiers saluting protesters and being thanked and kissed by them. Members of the armed forces likely supported, or at least sympathized with, the demands of the revolution.

The military's apolitical stance during the revolution was largely due to Ben Ali's having purposefully distanced himself in favor of the police and security forces. Resentment had built up among the forces after Ben Ali directed leadership purges in the 1990s, replacing both senior and junior military officers whom he accused of having Islamist leanings and allowing the police to attempt to exert authority over the armed forces. It is not entirely surprising, then, that when Ben Ali called in the army, soldiers deployed across the country fraternized with the protesters they were meant to intimidate.

The police, on the other hand, brutally suppressed protests in a number of locations, and dozens were killed, notably in Kasserine where snipers shot protesters from rooftops.[26] On January 8, some protesters were killed and others were injured when police took aim at a group that was setting a government building on fire in Thala.[27] But protests continued in Thala and Kasserine, as they did throughout the country.

The largest protests were held in Tunis on January 12, demanding the removal of Ben Ali. On the following day, January 13, Mouldi Jendoubi's story continues, he received a call from Abdessalem Jrad, asking that they meet at Jrad's home. Jrad, whose good relations with Ben Ali had always compromised his credibility within the union, reportedly told Jendoubi that he had just been to see the president at Ben Ali's request. Ben Ali demanded that Jrad lift the general strike that was scheduled to take place the next day in Tunis and the surrounding towns of Ben Arous, Manouba, and Ariana. Jrad, knowing that he would not be capable of succeeding even if he were willing, which he allegedly was not, told Ben Ali that he would try but that he was doubtful that anything could be done. Jrad reported to Jendoubi that he "had never seen Ben Ali as indignant." Jendoubi was allegedly advised by Jrad to stay away from his home that night, as things "were going to get ugly"—insinuating that his life was at risk.[28]

That same evening—January 13—Ben Ali, who had pleaded again with his people on January 10 on television, made a last-minute appeal to his people in a third television address. He admitted to the errors in his rule, condemned the use of live ammunition against protesters, and made a number of assurances that proved to be too little and too late. Among his promises were that he would lower food prices, loosen media monitoring and blocks on Internet sites, release political prisoners, and create a committee to investigate corruption. Ben Ali also vowed that he would not challenge the constitutional age limit of seventy-five for president, meaning that he would not seek reelection in 2014. In an act of desperation, Ben Ali broke with protocol and spoke to his people in Tunisian colloquial Arabic, or *Tounsi*.

The next day, January 14, 2011, Ben Ali abandoned his power, packed up what he could of stolen treasures, and boarded a plane with his family. He is said to have agreed to flee due to the influence of Ali Seriati, Ben Ali's security chief, who convinced him that he would be able to return at a later date.[29] General Rachid Ammar also told Ben Ali to leave but offered no illusions of a safe return.[30] The army secured the airport to ensure that Ben Ali could leave in one piece. In an overnight meeting held at the ministry of interior, a decision was made to bar the president from returning to Tunisia.[31]

In the wake of Ben Ali's flight, there was popular support for the army to take charge, at least temporarily, of Tunisia's affairs and achieve the influence that they had been denied for so long. But the leadership remained apolitical, preferring instead to "return to the barracks" and secure the country for elections.[32] After Ben Ali fled, Ammar told demonstrators that the army would protect the revolution, giving a clear message to security forces to stay out of politics.[33]

The international response was generally one of praise for the Tunisian people on their successful revolution. Some of the reactions were alarmingly disingenuous, however. During the revolution, France's Socialist Party condemned on December 30 the "brutal repression" of protests, but the French government of Nicolas Sarkozy remained silent. Just two days before Ben Ali fled, the French offered to send in French police to help the president restore peace. Sarkozy's minister of foreign affairs, Michèle Alliot-Marie, flew to Tunisia on the private jet of a Tunisian businessman close to the regime for a holiday as the protests were going on; she was subsequently forced to resign after an outcry over her actions.

The Arab public's response was one of jubilation, empathy, and hopefulness. Bouazizi's act of self-immolation had sent ripples of spontaneous energy and inspiration. Many Arab uprisings, subsequent to Tunisia's, began as demonstrations or marches in solidarity with the Jasmine Revolution, and then with the riots in Egypt. Social media and the Internet accelerated the spread of these sentiments. But it was forceful reactions by security forces that transformed many of these solidarity demonstrations into calls for regime change.

In Egypt, the military and police used brutal tactics to quell the demonstrations that had started on January 25 in Cairo's Tahrir Square. Within a little over two weeks, on February 11, 2011, the regime of President Hosni Mubarak fell. In Bahrain, an antigovernment "Day of Rage" on February 14 resulted in the regime's declaring martial law a month later. Security forces, backed by the Saudi and United Arab Emirates militaries, violently evacuated camps put up by the protesters, crushing the insurrection led by the subjugated majority Shi'ite population. In Yemen, supporters of President Ali Abdullah Saleh attacked peaceful marchers on January 29, and a state of emergency was declared on March 18, following persistent protests and the killing of fifty-two protesters at the hands of regime snipers at demonstrations at Sana'a University.[34] In Libya, what had started on

February 15 as a demonstration in Benghazi sparked a full-scale insurrection and international intervention meant to "protect" the Libyan people from the regime's brutality. On October 20, rebels killed President Muammar Gaddafi, who had been in hiding. In Syria, a vicious government crackdown on protests that started in March resulted in thousands of Syrians killed by June 2012 and spiraled into a civil war and a refugee crisis of gargantuan proportions.

This is what became known as the Arab Spring. The Arab Spring has also been called the "Arab Awakening," "Arab Winter," "Arab Uprising," and "Unfinished Revolutions." The revolts, whatever name is used to refer to them, went against a number of assumptions that had been held in Europe and the United States. The conventional view had been that Arab populations were passive and fatalistic and did not have a hunger for political reform—even culturally prone to authoritarian rule. The indigenous and spontaneous nature of the uprisings also disproved the assumption that meaningful political change required outside assistance and interference.

But was there really an Arab Spring, or is the term actually a misnomer? Is a "Tunisian Spring" a more apt descriptor, given where Arab Spring countries, with the exception of Tunisia, have ended up? Some have failed to bring about democracy, most crushingly in Egypt, which seemed to have been on a promising path. Other countries either brutally but effectively quieted dissent or became scenes of civil war, chaos, displacement, and utter disintegration.

The journalist and author Michael J. Totten wrote in 2012: "The political upheavals sweeping Tunisia, Egypt, Libya, and Syria are concurrent yet different phenomena, and it's premature to assume that any of them, let alone all of them, will bring their respective countries out of the long Arab winter of authoritarian rule. In the medium term, the number of genuinely liberal democracies to emerge in the Arab world is likely to be one or zero." Even then, Totten prophesized that of all the Arab Spring countries, Tunisia was the only one that "might be okay . . . It felt pre-democratic in ways that no other Arab country does, aside from Lebanon."[35]

Well educated and exposed to values of human rights and democracy, Tunisians proved predisposed to change and adept at bringing it about. The involvement of civil society, most notably UGTT, took the anger behind the early protests and channeled it into organized action, helping the protests spread throughout the country and across all strata of society, in a way that was sure to generate mass participation that could not be ignored. Social media and art forms were powerful tools that gave substantive, symbolic, and organizational force to the revolution.

The protests were relatively peaceful, and the revolution was surprisingly orderly. This was due in part to the organization brought to the revolution by civil society actors, but also because the army stayed out, intervening only to provide protection for protesters.

Looting was minimal; it mostly happened in the direct aftermath of Ben Ali's flight and was primarily directed at symbols of corruption associated with Ben Ali and his family. Houses belonging to members of the Trabelsi family and other relations of Ben Ali were looted and ransacked. In Sidi Bou Said, one café, belonging to a member of the Trabelsi clan, in the middle of two unharmed restaurants, "looked like it had been set upon by locusts."[36]

The protests were apolitical and areligious. They were led by youth who had no political aspirations and no Islamist affiliations, and who were not necessarily prepared, in any case, to take a leadership role and assume power following the fall of Ben Ali. Youth were driven by a quest for dignity, the denial of which had resonated as the underlying cause of the uprising, and by a desire for a redefinition of the relationship between state and citizens.

4

A Remarkable Transition

The period between Ben Ali's departure and the historic elections in 2014 was marked by a vigorous political coming-of-age. Turbulent divisions and coalitions, protests and protestations, triumphs and disappointments, and the consequential political awareness of civil society actors and ordinary citizens punctuated this critical phase of transition. Some of the greatest tensions were between the forces that sought a total break with the past and those that harked back to the old days.

During this transitional phase, Tunisians witnessed the handing over of power among four presidents and five prime ministers. Fouad Mebezaa—the second president, if one counts the one-day presidency of Mohamed Ghannouchi—oversaw elections for the Constituent Assembly that took place in October 2011 and had two prime ministers serving under him at different times: Mohamed Ghannouchi, followed by Beji Caid Essebsi.

With a long and clean record of public service and not believed to entertain future political ambitions, former president of the Chamber of Deputies Fouad Mebezaa was generally accepted as interim president. His caretaker prime minister, Mohamed Ghannouchi, however, had a tough go. The first government that Ghannouchi formed—positioned as one of "national unity"—was riddled with remnants of the old ruling party, the *Rassemblement constitutionnel démocratique* (RCD). He himself was, of course, a holdover from the Ben Ali era, but so were sixteen of the twenty-four provincial governors he appointed. RCD members controlled key ministries, including those of defense, finance, foreign affairs, and the interior.

Within a week, youth activists gathered in protest of the interim government, which they refused to recognize. The protests quickly turned into a movement and became a continuation of the revolution. Protesters did not have a cohesive strategy but were united by a shared sense of denunciation of the government and a strong resolve "to confront the ogre in his cave."[1] The rallies became known as the Kasbah protests, in reference to the place where they occurred: Place de la Kasbah, a central square in Tunis facing the office of the prime minister.

Inspired by the protests and eventually taking over the movement, a number of left-leaning opposition groups, including the Workers' Party and al-Watad, came together and formed the January 14 Front—providing leadership and demanding the removal of RCD members from the government.[2] Mohamed Ghannouchi reacted by dissolving the government, just ten days after it had been formed, and assembling a more inclusive cabinet. Ghannouchi also promised to hold elections within six months.

But it did not take long for protesters to gather at the Kasbah again, this time tens of thousands strong, for a second round of rallies. They called for the abolishment of RCD, the disassembling of the state security apparatus, and the establishment of a national constituent assembly, which would function like a parliament and be responsible for the formation of a new constitution. Protesters bemoaned the slow pace of change and called Ghannouchi's government an incarnation of Ben Ali's regime, one youth capturing the mood when he said, "we cut off the head of the beast, but the beast was still very much alive."[3]

The January 14 Front, which had morphed into the *Conseil national pour la protection de la révolution* and which Ettakatol and Ennahda also joined, provided political cover for the protests. The council was also supported by UGTT, which encouraged strikes as a means of applying pressure on the government and called on its members who had joined the new cabinet to resign. Three ministers who were representatives of UGTT had walked out of Ghannouchi's first cabinet, and a fourth refused to take his appointed position in the first place—all in protest over the inclusion of RCD members in the government.[4] The union used every opportunity it had—during and after the revolution—to bolster its credibility and to regain the trust that its central command had lost after years of collaborating with the Ben Ali regime.

In the second round of Kasbah protests, security forces confronted protesters, and Place de la Kasbah became a scene of burning tires, stone throwing, and gunfire. On February 27, Prime Minister Mohamed Ghannouchi resigned, and President Fouad Mebezaa appointed Beji Caid Essebsi as the new prime minister. As protesters left the scene, they removed garbage that had amassed and tried their best to return the area to its original condition—except for graffiti, which the youth now viewed as part of their national heritage.

The dynamics of the demonstrations underscored the existence of a generational divide. The youth had become increasingly disillusioned by the apparent inactivity of the government and demanded change. But they lacked the requisite political consciousness and the organizational skills that would enable them to take matters forward past the protests. Although they, in many respects, led the revolution, the youth were not organized nor united enough after the revolution to lead the political discourse or provide a viable alternative path for the transition.

The youth felt that the opposition parties hijacked the movement that they had started and appropriated the protests to advance their own agendas. Government attempts to engage the youth were limited. As an act of good faith, Slim Amamou, who had led anticensorship protests, was put in charge of the youth and sports portfolio, but he clashed with government officials, tweeting openly about it, and eventually quit.

Yet, according to Sami Ben Gharbia, cofounder—from exile—in 2004 of Nawaat, a collective blog that published TuniLeaks in 2010, even the most outspoken of the disappointed youth acknowledged that had the *Conseil national pour la protection de la révolution* not provided political leadership, all would have been lost. Ben Gharbia tells me that he sees the youth as having been "ideologically clean" and not "poisoned by all those ideologies that are part of the failure of the Arab world." But he recognizes that they also suffered because of their "political naïveté."[5]

Protesters had been united against Ben Ali and in their hope of revolution and zeal to bring about change, but they did not necessarily have a common vision of what they wanted next. In a sense, they were united in the negative space: they agreed on what they rejected but did not necessarily agree on what they wanted. There were splits among them in terms of priorities, drawn along geographic lines to some extent. Many who were living in the rural and poorer areas of Tunisia considered economic reform the biggest issue, while the urban elite youths were more focused on rights and individual liberties.

Ultimately, the youth of the Kasbah protests, with the *Conseil national pour la protection de la révolution* supplying political shelter and organization, succeeded in bringing down the Ghannouchi government, and they also sent a strong signal to the new prime minister that the revolution was still underway.

Prime Minister Beji Caid Essebsi had two things going for him in terms of his political biography: he had served under Bourguiba and had dissociated himself from Ben Ali. The choice of Essebsi, who had held the portfolios of the interior, defense, and foreign affairs at different times under Bourguiba, served as a poignant reminder that Bourguiba's legacy still held some sway in the minds of Tunisians. The fact that Essebsi had left politics in 1991 and remained at a distance from Ben Ali contributed to his credibility and acceptance.

Within weeks of Essebsi's appointment, the *tribunal de première instance de Tunis* dissolved RCD, liquefied its assets, and banned former RCD members who had recently held major positions within the party from running for elections or from being appointed to government positions. The government also dissolved the state security department, under which the secret police, the state's domestic spy agency, had operated.

Essebsi's government was primarily charged with seeing the country through to elections for the National Constituent Assembly, which it successfully did on October 23, 2011. Although the date for the elections was initially set for July 24, the authority that had been set up to organize and supervise the elections, *Instance supérieure indépendante pour les élections*, faced challenges in managing the necessary operations within the scheduled time frame.[6] The political environment, which reflected decades of political domination by RCD, was also challenging. The party had a reported 3.8 million members—nearly half of the adult population—in 2009, and it incorporated large segments of society into its networks, especially through local committees.[7] Membership in RCD did not, however, necessarily signify loyalty to the party; it was often the result of coercion or compliance as a pragmatic measure, including in terms of employment.

The revolution produced a confounding political scene. Only four months after the revolution, an estimated seventy new political parties had been formed, as well as hundreds of citizens' organizations.[8] A total of 112 parties were approved for the elections for the Constituent Assembly, and another 162 parties were denied.[9] The spectrum of ideologies represented by the emergent Tunisian political parties ran the gamut from Marxist to right-wing nationalist, Islamist, and pan-Arabist. Although many established opposition parties lacked electoral experience as well as popular appeal because of perceived inactivity or, worse, cooperation with the Ben Ali regime, some quickly acquired traction and secured themselves among the electorate in time for the first elections after the revolution.

There were profound cleavages across party platforms that reflected divisions within Tunisian society. These divisions, although somewhat distinct in character, overlapped significantly. Rifts were mainly defined along three contours: a religious versus secular dichotomy, conflicts in terms of an Arab or Tunisian identity, and tensions between modernity and conservatism. These sociopolitical schisms, which are part of an old Tunisian story, resonated in 2011 and throughout the transitional period, and they are likely to endure.

Harboring competing attitudes toward the place of religion in politics, hard-liners on both the secular and religious sides of the divide fought hard to carve out political spaces and exert their influences. Ennahda fashioned a place for itself within a landscape that had been dominated for decades by a sometimes violent repression of religious expressions that were not sanctioned by the state. The *Congrès pour la République* (CPR), which was founded in 2001 by human rights activist Moncef Marzouki but remained illegal until 2011, and Ettakatol had large secular followings—as did a number of other parties that followed the tradition set by Ben Ali and Bourguiba and capitalized on fears of looming threats of Islamism.

Foreshadowing what was to come was the scene at the Tunis-Carthage International Airport upon the return of Sheikh Rached Ghannouchi on January 30, 2011, after nearly twenty-two years in exile. Amid the jubilant crowds, estimated at 10,000 men and veiled women, there was a small group of protesters holding signs that read "No Islamism, no theocracy, no Shari'a and no stupidity!"[10]

A common thread between Ennahda and some of its secular opponents, however, was the promotion of a stronger Tunisian Arab and

Muslim identity. CPR and a number of Arab nationalist parties advocated for Tunisia to be affiliated primarily with the Arab and Muslim world, and for stronger relations with Gulf countries. Allegations, although not proven, of both CPR's and Ennahda's having received funding from Qatar were widely circulated. Fissures widened among political parties between those who aligned themselves as Arab, on one end, and protagonists of a non-Arab Tunisian identity—Mediterranean, North African, and African—on the other. Playing out on the scene was a familiar Tunisian scenario, dating back to the rivalry between Bourguiba and the Arab nationalist Salah Ben Youssef.

Ultimately, parties that fared best among Tunisians were those that had had no ties with Ben Ali and could actually claim a history of principled resistance to his authoritarian regime. Islamists marked the greatest break from the ancien régime and were able to quickly achieve credibility and draw massive sympathetic support. Ennahda—which was only legalized on March 1, 2011, thirty years after its founding as the *Mouvement de la tendance islamique*—had a long history, after all, of having its members tortured, killed, exiled, and imprisoned.

Ennahda exiles spent more than two decades in fifty different countries and were exposed to different systems of government, cultures, and ways of thinking—according to Ghannouchi.[11] Not all returned to Tunisia as benign as Ghannouchi suggests, however, and some found Ennahda too moderate for their taste, preferring instead to join extremist organizations. Similar to how Muslim Brotherhood leaders in Egypt forged their political agendas and became more radicalized while serving time in regime prisons, many Ennahda members cultivated extremist ideas while in exile in places like Yemen, Afghanistan, and Pakistan, or through relationships with various hard-liners, some in exile themselves, in the West.[12]

For his part, Ghannouchi, a theorist of Islam and democracy, wrote against the Saudi-nurtured Wahhabi form of extremism. He was influenced, along with other Ennahda exiles, by Europe's social movements. Throughout his time in exile, Ghannouchi consistently and publicly promised not to work to reverse family law, established through the 1956 *Code du statut personnel*.

Populist in its approach, Ennahda began to speak of mobilizing the common people even before the revolution succeeded in ousting Ben Ali. Ghannouchi understood the relationship between electoral support and the socioeconomic structure of Tunisia. The backing for the party after the revolution was strongest in poor urban areas on the coast and in younger districts where unemployment was high, particularly in the south of the country.[13] Ennahda's appeal reached well beyond its Islamist affiliation, and it was viewed as an honest party and an antidote to the corrupt practices of the former regime.

The Jasmine Revolution gave Ennahda just the opening that it had been waiting for. It rose to power quickly in 2011, setting itself apart from other Islamist groups as an advocate of democracy. When Ghannouchi returned, he immediately announced that Ennahda would participate in parliamentary elections, but neither he nor anyone from his party would run in the next presidential election. In his first interview after the revolution, Ghannouchi claimed: "We drank the cup of democracy in one gulp back in the 1980s while other Islamists have taken it sip by sip."[14] Ghannouchi emphatically claims that democracy is not incompatible with Islam.

The political genius of Ghannouchi exhibited itself in many scenes that have earned him a reputation as the best—according to some, the only— politician in Tunisia. When his *Majlis al-shura*, or Consultative Council, voted that he should push hard for inclusion in the new constitution of Shari'a—or Islamic law, the principles of which are drawn from the Qur'an and Hadith (recorded sayings of Prophet Muhammad)—he explained the futility of doing so: if the decision went to a referendum that resulted in a rejection of Shari'a, the door would be closed on the issue forever; and if it passed, Ennahda would make enemies of those who voted against the measure, deepening the polarization with secularists.[15] Ghannouchi convinced the council to revote to keep the door open, and 80 percent of members voted "no" in the second round.[16]

Ghannouchi's mastery of the political scene paid off in the October 23, 2011, parliamentary elections, which granted Ennahda 89 of the 217 seats of the Constituent Assembly. After multiple interim governments plagued with remnants of the old regime, it was no surprise that Tunisians opted for a sharp change.

Moncef Marzouki's CPR came in second in the elections, with 8.7 percent of the popular vote and twenty-nine seats in the Constituent Assembly. Al-Aridha (*Pétition populaire*), the only party formed after the revolution that did well in the elections, came in at third place with twenty-six seats, while Ettakatol was granted twenty seats. Eighteen of the 217 seats went to representatives of the 1 million Tunisians living abroad who had been organized into six constituencies for the purposes of elections.

In the spirit of cooperation, consensus building, and achieving balance, a coalition parliamentary bloc that henceforth became referred to as the Troika was formed among Ennahda, the secular revolutionary CPR, and the secular social Ettakatol. Although Ettakatol came behind al-Aridha in the elections, it was chosen over the conservative, populist, and socialist Islamist party in a promise to protect Tunisia's secularism. CPR's Moncef Marzouki was named president, and Ennahda secured its former secretary-general, Hamadi Jebali, the position of prime minister. Mustapha Ben Jaafar, leader of Ettakatol, became speaker of the Constituent Assembly.

The Troika was seen as an opportunity to craft a new vision for the relationship between religion and politics. Ennahda officials, including Ghannouchi, made concerted efforts to seem cooperative with secular parties and to appear supportive of democracy.

But despite its initial popularity and sympathy over the decades of torture, imprisonment, and exile at the hands of the ancien régime, once in power, Ennahda gradually fell out of favor and was accused of having used its government leadership position to try to Islamize Tunisia, introducing laws and amendments that were considered setbacks by secularists. There was pushback, both from the other members of the Troika and from citizens. In April 2012, as thousands celebrated the anniversary of the 1938 demonstrations against the French and marched along Avenue Habib Bourguiba, they protested the new government's handling of problems, including judicial reforms and socioeconomic programs. Violence erupted between protesters and the police.

Much of what Ennahda did or proposed seems innocuous, however, compared to its counterparts in other Muslim countries. Ennahda came into a different environment in Tunisia than the one the Muslim Brotherhood inherited in Egypt. Islamists in Egypt had already reversed much of the secular trend that characterized Gamal Abdel Nasser's Egypt; by the time Mubarak fell, the country was largely Islamized. Civil society was also largely Islamist, much of it controlled by the Muslim Brotherhood. Article Two of the Egyptian constitution, which enshrined the principles of Shari'a as the primary source of legislation, was just as sacred as the *Code du statut personnel* was in Tunisia. By the time Ben Ali left office, Tunisia had been largely secularized and transformed to such a degree that it stood in very sharp contrast to the rest of the Arab world.

The cleavages between secularists and Islamists came to a head during the process of writing the constitution by the National Constituent Assembly, which had adopted an interim constitution on December 10, 2011. The provisional constitution was drafted by the same commission charged with establishing electoral laws and procedures after the revolution and chaired by the secularist constitutionalist Yadh Ben Achour: *Haute Instance pour la réalisation des objectifs de la révolution, de la réforme politique et de la transition démocratique.*

The three most controversial areas that faced those tasked with writing the constitution concerned articles related to the incorporation of Shari'a, gender equality, and blasphemy.

Having retreated from its earlier position that would have allowed Shari'a to be adopted as law, Ennahda pushed hard to include language that would have prescribed Islam as the religion of the state, making way for Islamic Shari'a to regulate. But Ennahda had to eventually back down from its revised circuitous strategy after an estimated 25,000 protesters, joined by opposition parties, took to the streets on March 20, 2012.[17] In the end, Shari'a was kept out of the constitution altogether.

Ennahda also proposed an article that would have criminalized blasphemy and the defamation of religion, but this too was struck out. The article, introduced in June 2012, was proposed after Salafis stormed an art exhibition in La Marsa that purportedly insulted Islam. Later that year, Ennahda also tried to introduce a law against desecration, but that attempt failed, thanks to opposition by civil society actors, lawyers, and politicians.

In its insistence on the separation of mosque and state, the final draft of the constitution echoed the constitution that had been introduced during Ottoman times in 1861 and went further than the constitution that was drafted in 1959 following independence from the French. While the postindependence constitution had identified Islam as the religion of Tunisians, without prescribing it as state religion, the 2014 constitution firmly shut the door on Shari'a and ensured that Tunisia remained a civic state. The first article of both constitutions asserted that Tunisia is a free, independent, and sovereign state, and that its religion is Islam, its language Arabic, and its system republican. But the 2014 constitution added a second article, which cannot be amended: "Tunisia is a civil state based on citizenship, the will of the people, and the supremacy of law."

Yadh Ben Achour explained to me that the declaration of the state as civil in the second article prevented any potential interpretation of the inclusion of Islam in the first article as prescriptive or potentially leading to the implementation of Shari'a. He referred to the reference to Islam in the first article as a "sociological description" regarding the prevalent religion of the people, making a distinction between Islam being the religion of Tunisia as opposed to that of the state. For emphasis, Ben Achour further clarified that Article Two allowed Essebsi to run for president in 2014 on a platform of "a civil state for a Muslim people."[18]

One can only appreciate what an achievement the Tunisian constitution is in this regard when comparing it to constitutions in the rest of the Arab world.

Article Two of the Jordanian Constitution declares Islam the religion of the state. Matters of personal status fall within the jurisdiction of Shari'a courts in Jordan, including for non-Muslims, per Article 109 of the constitution. The scenario is not that different across the region, with the notable exception of Lebanon. In affirmation of religious pluralism, the Tunisian government contains an inclusive ministry of religious affairs, in contrast to a ministry of *waqfs*, or endowments by the state for Islamic purposes, as is typical elsewhere.

Perhaps the greatest "innovation" of the 2014 Tunisian constitution is its insistence on the freedom of conscience, protected by Article Six. But the inclusion of this article does not wholly represent a novelty for Tunisians; the same guarantees of freedom of belief, conscience, and religious practice were upheld by the 1959 postindependence constitution, albeit only in the constitution's French edition.

The freedom-of-conscience article squarely placed Tunisia well ahead of any other Arab country in terms of its respect for personal freedoms and human rights. It stipulates that the state undertake to disseminate the values of moderation and tolerance, and puts the state in the role of guarantor of the free exercise of religious practices and the neutrality of mosques and places of worship from partisanship. Freedom of religion in the Arab world, by contrast, essentially means the freedom to practice any monotheistic religion. An exception is Saudi Arabia, where the worship in public of any religion other than Islam is outlawed.

In a first for an Arab or Islamic country, Article Six outlaws accusations of apostasy—*takfir*—and the incitement of violence and hatred. The freedom-of-conscience article fundamentally guarantees the constitutional protection of agnosticism, atheism, and the full range of belief and nonbelief. Denouncing Islam for atheism or conversion to another monotheist religion is punishable across other Arab countries. These rights had been protected in Algeria by virtue of a clause included in the 1963 version of the constitution, but this changed in 1996 when the clause was removed.[19] In Saudi Arabia and Qatar, the penalty for apostasy, or *ridda*, is death, while in other countries, such as Jordan and Kuwait, the courts have the power to imprison apostates, annul their marriages, and strip them of child custody and inheritance rights.[20] So constitutionally enshrined is religion in Jordan that the constitution proclaims that the "family is the basis of society, the core of which shall be religion, morals and patriotism."

The new constitution, which was ratified by Tunisia's National Constituent Assembly in January 2014, was Tunisia's first popular constitution in that it was the outcome of public debate and much discussion that included large swaths of society. By contrast, the constitution of 1861 was the result of pressure by the French and the British, and the 1959 postindependence constitution, although indigenous, was mandated from above.

The 2014 constitution defined Tunisia unequivocally as a civil state, granting equal rights for men and women, freedom of speech and conscience, an independent judiciary, citizens' rights to health care, and progressive resource redistribution. According to Yadh Ben Achour, more than eighty fundamental laws will have to be legislated by the Constituent Assembly to implement the new constitution.

As a sign of the strong sentiments surrounding the corrupt practices that defined Ben Ali's reign and of the call for an abrogation thereof, anticorruption became enshrined in the 2014 constitution through Article 125 and the establishment of a good governance and anticorruption government agency. The agency is mandated with identifying and investigating corruption cases—in business and the public domain—and assigning them to the relevant institutional authorities.

The constitution went through four drafts, the last of which was submitted on June 1, 2013. A group of twenty-two lawyers, representing various points on the ideological and religious spectra, were brought in to advise and work with the six committees of the Constituent Assembly in drafting the constitution. Many had been members of the *Haute Instance pour la réalisation des objectifs de la révolution, de la réforme politique et de la transition démocratique*, which was dissolved following the formation of the Constituent Assembly. Yadh tells me that the most important role of these legal experts was in bringing the constitutional debate to the public. Through television and radio interviews and articles published in newspapers and online, they were able to put pressure on the Constituent Assembly to adopt certain measures and principles, such as freedom of conscience (Article Six) and the commitment to promote modernity, human rights culture, and foreign languages in Tunisia's education system (Article Thirty-Nine).[21]

During debates over the constitution, fears over Islamists' attempts at reversing advances made by women in the preceding decades came to life. A proposed article (Article Twenty-Eight), which referred to women as "men's complements," instantly became polemical, both within and outside the Constituent Assembly. The posting of the proposed language by an Ettakatol member of the assembly, Salma Mabrouk, sparked local and international controversy and generated more coverage in foreign French- and English-language news sources than practically any other single Tunisian event in 2012. Those arguing in defense of the article spoke about a mistranslation of the term used in the phrasing, which they insisted "has a deeper sense of enriching or integrating two parts to form a unified whole." Women staged a protest against Article Twenty-Eight on August 13, National Women's Day, which is also, advertently, the day that Tunisians celebrate the adoption of the 1956 *Code du statut personnel*. Thousands of women gathered, some in jeans and T-shirts alongside others who wore the hijab. The article was subsequently replaced with another, stating that "all male and female citizens are equal in rights and duties."[22]

Women's rights had actually come to the fore a year earlier during the 2011 elections, although the issue had not been a rallying point in the revolution. Hundreds of women demonstrated in Tunis on January 29 to reject a potential Islamic resurgence and to safeguard their hard-earned rights.

In the elections for the Constituent Assembly, the most obstinate and outspoken opposition to Ennahda came from middle-aged women from the middle and upper economic echelons of society. They accused Ennahda of wanting to return "Tunisia's *'femmes féministes'* to their kitchens." In the 2014 elections, Ennahda's competitor, Nidaa Tounes, tried to arouse fears among women voters, touting how it was women's role to preserve the democratic gains made during and after the revolution and painting itself as the successor of Bourguiba's secular and women-liberating regime, as opposed to the "obscurantist" and women-enslaving Ennahda.[23]

On the other end of the spectrum, *Nahdawiyat*, women members of Ennahda, spoke of how Ennahda and Islam were in favor of women's rights. Ennahda had actually succeeded in galvanizing female activists for the elections, and it ended up with forty-two of its own female members, out of a total of forty-nine elected women, in the Constituent Assembly. Ennahda was the only major party to capitalize on the gender parity law requiring parties to have alternating male and female candidates.[24]

It is also telling that, five years later, it was Ennahda that championed a 2016 bill in parliament to strengthen legislation on violence against women, introducing comprehensive definitions of gender-based violence, outlawing marital rape, and ending impunity for rapists who married their victims if they were under twenty years of age.

After the revolution and with the rise of Ennahda, expression of religious values by women became a contested issue. Women and men—on both sides of the divide—initiated protests over dress. It became more common for women to be seen wearing the hijab, especially on university campuses. This was opposed by some more Westernized women, while others—both religious and secular—argued that the freedom to express values was at the very heart of Tunisian Islam. The blogger Lina Ben Mhenni tells me that there was public pressure to wear the hijab under the Troika when Ennahda was in charge of government, especially in poorer neighborhoods, but this has since subsided.

During the October 2011 elections, militants from the political Islamist organization *Hizb al-tahrir* (Party of Liberation) demonstrated at the University of Sousse when young women were prevented from wearing the niqab and showing only their eyes. The demonstrations turned violent when protesters were met by counterdemonstrations led by women's groups who condemned what they saw as religious extremism. The decision to ban the niqab was upheld by Tunisia's education ministry, and in November 2015, the ministry suspended a primary school teacher and a supervisor for refusing to obey an order to stop wearing the niqab.

Confrontations between Islamists and secularists continued into the year 2013 and were ignited by increased activity of militant Islamist groups, debate over the constitution, and two high-profile political assassinations.

The murder in February of Chokri Belaid, the left-wing opposition leader and head of Watad, resulted in a general strike called for by UGTT. Work stopped across Tunisia, from the mines in the south of the country to the business districts of Tunis. Belaid had accused the Islamist-led government of encouraging political violence and subsequently had been stalked. Advanced state apparatus equipment seemed to have been used to track his movements and eavesdrop on his phone.[25] This caused suspicion that Ennahda was behind his murder and led to the resignation of Prime Minister Hamadi Jebali and his succession by Ennahda's Ali Laarayedh, marking the first step toward the dissolution of the Troika coalition.

Then, in July, Mohamed Brahmi, former leader and founder of the opposition *Mouvement du peuple*, was assassinated. Political parties in the opposition withdrew from the Constituent Assembly and refused to cooperate with the government, while a number of mass demonstrations took place.

Opposition drew inspiration from Egypt's Tamarod movement, which had just taken down President Mohamed Morsi. The *Front du salut national*, an alliance of smaller opposition groups, initiated a campaign titled *Irhal*, or Leave, to oust government officials appointed by Ennahda. Led by the *Front du salut national*, thousands of Tunisians demonstrated for more than a month, beginning in late July after the funeral of Mohamed Brahmi. Protesters, who gathered in front of the Bardo National Museum—adjacent to the National Constituent Assembly—demanded the disbanding of the Constituent Assembly and the resignation of the government.

The Ennahda government blamed Salafist extremists, including the Tunisian branch of *Ansar al-Shari'a* (Supporters of Shari'a) for the assassinations of Chokri Belaid and Mohamed Brahmi. It also put responsibility on Salafist militants for the killing of eight soldiers in the Chaambi Mountain region and for attacks against police in a number of towns—all in 2013—and declared *Ansar al-Shari'a* a terrorist organization. Ennahda accused Salafis of bearing a grudge against it because, in the words of Rached Ghannouchi, Ennahda presented "Islam in a way that differs from them" and preached the religion as one of "freedom and human rights."[26] Ghannouchi distanced himself from *Jabhat al-islah* (Reform Front), whose recognition as a Salafist political party he had pushed for in 2012.[27] Draw-ing similarities between the party and the militant groups *Hizb al-tahrir* and *Ansar al-Shari'a*, Ghannouchi claimed that, unlike Ennahda, they all "had failed to develop with modernity and our times."[28]

Once again, and as the situation was spiraling into crisis mode, civil society stepped in to save the day. UGTT was the only institution that had practice with political bargaining and could thus play a leadership role in resolving conflict among political adversaries and between the govern-ing and governed. It was also the only group that represented the working class and had geographic reach into the masses.

The union was experienced at adopting a two-pronged approach; dur-ing the authoritarian regimes of Bourguiba and Ben Ali, it often backed the ruling party's political line, for lack of choice or as a result of crony-ism, while at the same time bargaining hard with the private sector and state institutions to advance the rights of workers.[29] UGTT understood that given a specific organization of resource extraction and regional distri-bution, workers on the front lines could initiate crippling strikes to force political openings.

UGTT was singularly qualified to organize a round of talks among civil society organizations to deal with accusations against Ennahda and dis-cuss a path forward. Anchored by the union, the *Quartet du dialogue national* produced a timeline for the government's resignation and steps toward the selection of a more consensual government. Yadh Ben Achour and Pro-fessor Hafidha Chékir were brought in as legal advisers.

Ennahda accepted the Quartet's compromise and agreed to step down in December 2013—though not without pressure from unions, other politi-cal parties, and international institutions. The World Bank, the Interna-tional Monetary Fund (IMF), the African Development Bank, the United States, and Gulf countries forced Ennahda's hand by conditioning financial assistance for Tunisia on the party's acceptance of the Quartet's terms.[30] Ennahda's "willingness" to relinquish its power marked a first for an Islamist party.

The awarding of the Nobel Peace Prize to the Quartet in October 2015 was in recognition of the Quartet's "decisive contribution" to democ-racy when the country "was on the brink of civil war." Kaci Kullmann Five, chair of the Norwegian Nobel Committee, said that the Quartet's efforts in Tunisia were "directly comparable to the peace conferences mentioned by Alfred Nobel in his will."[31] That one of the awardees is a woman, UTICA's president Ouided Bouchamaoui, is a quintessentially Tunisian scenario.

The Nobel Prize also underscored the propensity of organizations such as UTICA and UGTT, which were often at odds with one another—one representing business interests and the other the rights of workers—to come together in times of crisis around broader national interests. But it was UGTT that was in a unique position to mastermind the negotiations process. Without UGTT, the Quartet would not have happened or succeeded in seeing a peaceful transition at a juncture that could easily have led to the disintegration of the process of democratic change.

The decisive role that UGTT was able to play in leading the Quartet negotiations with the government is a testament to its significant political, social, and economic clout—typical characteristics of strong labor unions that have had an important part in the development of democratic governments elsewhere. UGTT has historically served as the umbrella organization for social movements in Tunisia, a role that is likely to endure.

Let us not forget, however, that the union had to expend considerable effort in order to recover from decades of its subjugation to, and collaboration with, the Ben Ali regime, including as recently as the 2008 Gafsa corruption scandal. The weakening of its central authority resulted in fractures as smaller branches, harboring distrust of the hierarchical order and loyalty to their localities, acted independently.

But the union's active role in the revolution and its efforts to bolster its credibility were paying off. UGTT's reputation was also boosted as a result of an internal reform process that included democratic elections in December 2011 for a new thirteen-member executive board. These efforts helped it assume its leadership position within the Quartet, the success of which further strengthened its standing.

Other countries in the Arab world did not have similarly empowered and organized labor. In fact, the kinds of natural resources that countries like Saudi Arabia have been blessed with have meant the bypassing of the average worker and the concentration of political power at higher levels of management, encouraging a wealthy but unrepresentative state.[32]

In Egypt, where economic grievances and workers' demands played an equally important role in its revolution as they did in Tunisia, the unions worked against the protesters, siding with Mubarak and his regime in 2011.

Any planning and organization of protests that occurred during the revolution was led by Islamist organizations, not unions.

Leading up to the revolution, protests that were staged by workers between 2004 and 2010 occurred largely without the support of the leadership of the Egyptian Trade Union Federation (ETUF), the Egyptian equivalent—in name—to UGTT. In response to cumulative moves by Mubarak in 2004 to trim and privatize the public sector, labor unrest reached a level during that period that the country had not seen for decades. But ETUF, rendered politically impotent by the regime, supported only one strike during the entire reign of Mubarak.

Workers distrusted the federation, aware that its actions were often in the interest of the regime and at the expense of the worker. Faith in ETUF was so low among workers that the "Demands of the Workers in the Revolution" front demanded the dissolution of ETUF and described it as "one of the most important symbols of corruption under the defunct regime."[33]

Egyptian trade unions date back to 1919 and, as in the case of Tunisia, they played an important role in the independence movement. But Gamal Abdel Nasser brutally crushed unions; instead, he created a national labor federation in 1957 in the form of ETUF—originally named the Egyptian Workers Federation—as an instrument of the state. The creation of the federation, which focused almost exclusively on the public sector, marked the end of organized labor. Under Nasser, rank-and-file workers were given economic benefits, including job security, in exchange for their political quiescence; unions became tools for political control.

Whereas Tunisia boasts a strong labor movement and a small and relatively weak army, the opposite is true in Egypt, which shares a border with Israel and whose 1952 revolution was very much a military coup. Soon after the military ousted the Muslim Brotherhood and took control in July 2013, they quickly moved to reverse their marginalization under Morsi. The National Defense Council, which had become majority civilian under Morsi, reverted back to being majority military. Egyptians' distrust of Islamists led to the judiciary's dissolving the democratically elected parliament, following a precedent set by the Supreme Constitutional Court, first in 1987 and again in 1990. In Tunisia, no judicial body has the authority to nullify elections.

The presence of a strong army derailed Egypt's prospects for democracy, just as the strength of Tunisia's labor movement helped usher in its democracy. In sharp contrast to the situation in Egypt, UGTT mitigated political conflict and brought in other credible civil society actors to help move the process along. The accomplishments of the Quartet underscored a Tunisian scenario that offered more than just political parties and standard political processes.

The Quartet accomplished a smooth transition of power to Tunisia's fifth government since the revolution. Mehdi Jomaa, a former executive who had worked in France at the oil and gas company Total S.A., was picked to lead a technocratic caretaker government with no party affiliations. Jomaa's government was given a one-year mandate by President Marzouki to lead the country through parliamentary and presidential elections slated for late 2014. The consensual replacement of the democratically elected Islamist government with an appointed government of elites was inherently undemocratic, but it was seen as a way to provide stability and ward off violence.

A product of the private sector and having lived in France for the preceding twenty years, Jomaa assembled more than 300 curricula vitae and interviewed candidates, many living abroad, for his cabinet positions. He refused to appoint anyone he had previously known, and he forbade his cabinet members from resigning—in order to ensure continuity and effective progress.[34] Seven of his ministers returned from the diaspora, and three were women. The government reorganized the security apparatus for a more efficient response to terrorism, launched a national economic dialogue, and initiated several reforms in banking, taxation, and the national subsidies system.

Jomaa saw his role as prime minister as providing reassurances, at home and abroad, about security, stability, and the transparency of upcoming elections.[35] The technocratic government reacted forcefully in 2014 to violent radicalism—banning more than 150 Muslim civic organizations, closing a radio station, and arresting at least 2,000 young people on terrorism charges.[36] Numerous terrorist attacks meant to undermine the democratic process and spoil the upcoming elections were botched.[37] An estimated 80,000 security personnel and 22,000 election monitors, including 600 foreigners, were dispatched across the country at the time of elections.[38]

On October 26, 2014, Tunisia held its first legislative elections since the departure of Zine al-Abidine Ben Ali. More than a hundred political parties participated in the elections,[39] and voter turnout was 67.7 percent.[40]

Nidaa Tounes, the party assembled by Beji Caid Essebsi as a potpourri of secular oppositionists, achieved plurality in the parliamentary elections with 86 of the 217 parliamentarian seats; Ennahda won 69. In December, Tunisians participated in the country's first ever open and democratic presidential elections. Beji Caid Essebsi, former leader of Nidaa Tounes, became Tunisia's first democratically elected president. Aware of the danger of political divisions, Essebsi had renounced his political allegiance in order to run for the presidency as a candidate for all Tunisians.

5

The Morning After

Beji Caid Essebsi's ascension to the presidency marked the first voluntary transition of power in Tunisia between presidents and parties, excluding interim presidents. The year 2015 witnessed the emergence of a pattern of respect for democratic processes and a consolidation of the post-revolutionary transition toward democracy. But it also exposed strains within political parties, disappointments for Tunisian youth, menaces to freedoms, mounting economic challenges, and breaches of security that threatened to destabilize the country. The awarding of the Nobel Peace Prize to the *Quartet du dialogue national* was, however, a bright spot that shone lustrously on Tunisia and signaled a vote of confidence and a craving for hopefulness.

In my first meeting with President Beji Caid Essebsi, soon after he had assumed the presidency, he was keen to underscore that he saw himself as a "trustee" of Bourguibian principles and as a link between the generations formed by Bourguiba and Tunisia's present and future generations—a point punctuated by the larger-than-life picture of Bourguiba that is impossible to miss in the main reception hall of the presidential palace.[1] A polished diplomat and elder statesman, Essebsi is a product of the Bourguiba legacy. He uses this to his advantage and at times pays homage to the former president, as with his adoption of Bourguiba's iconic eyewear fashion.

Essebsi also bows to his more religious constituency with public displays of piety that have not gone unnoticed. State television, for example, filmed him praying at a mosque on the Prophet's birthday. On that visit to Tunis, the only time I came across a reference to a divine will was in the presence of Essebsi. At eighty-eight years of age, the president poignantly surrendered his chances of living out his term in office to the wishes of Allah.

On my second encounter with President Essebsi, in July 2015, a month after the Sousse terrorist attack, I found him to be understandably anxious about the security situation and the perceptions of Tunisia's stability in the rest of the world. A three-month state of emergency had been declared, but the president indicated—hopefully, but unconvincingly—that he thought it could be lifted in early August.[2] The state of emergency was ultimately revoked, only to be reinstated on the heels of the suicide bombing on board a bus that took the lives of twelve presidential guards. The country remained in a schizophrenic state of emergency and reassurance.

A little over six months into his presidency, Essebsi seemed to be consolidating power beyond what the constitution allowed him, raising concerns among Tunisians that the real power had returned to the presidential palace in Carthage. According to Yadh Ben Achour, Essebsi had become the de facto ruler of the country, with almost all powers resting with him as president—in violation of what is constitutionally a parliamentary regime. Ben Achour also saw this as a temporary and transitional situation in light of security concerns. He showed confidence that the Assembly of the Representatives of the People, which replaced the Constituent Assembly as of the October 2014 elections, and the will and capacity of Tunisians—as demonstrated at Kasbah and Bardo—would keep the president in check.[3]

Nidaa Tounes, Essebsi's former party, whose plurality in the last elections gave it the right to choose the prime minister, had picked Habib Essid, a former government official under Ben Ali. The choice of Essid, announced on January 5, 2015, was made after considerable consultation with the leadership of Ennahda, as confirmed to me by Sheikh Rached Ghannouchi.[4]

Ennahda saw in a coalition an opportunity to protect itself—locally, regionally, and internationally—following the fall of the Muslim Brotherhood in Egypt. From Rached Ghannouchi's perspective, Ennahda made sacrifices and was willing to accept representation by only one or two ministers in the government in order to avoid confrontation.[5] Ennahda might not have had much choice in the matter, however, given that it had lost the elections, had been driven out of office in 2013, and was weakened both in its own right and as a result of disastrous failures of political Islam elsewhere. Ennahda ended up with one ministerial position out of twenty-eight, and three of its members were among the fourteen secretaries of state in the new government. Seen by some as an "elite consensus," these power-sharing arrangements "regulated" competition among parties and helped ensure a continuation of a relatively smooth and peaceful transition.[6]

Secularists who claim that the process since the revolution has "democratized" Ennahda, some speaking of the "Tunisification" of the party, caution that Ennahda and Ghannouchi do not necessarily possess an ideological commitment to democracy but see democracy as the only rational choice in front of them—the only game in town, so to speak. There is deep distrust of the party and fear that should it return to power, Ennahda would not be so different from Egypt's Muslim Brotherhood or Turkey's Justice and Development Party, *Adalet ve kalkınma partisi* (AKP), and that it would strongly push its conservative agenda—a scenario that had materialized during its rule as part of the Troika in 2012 and 2013.

But Ghannouchi, consummate politician that he is, understood, especially after the failure of the Troika and of Egypt's Muslim Brothers, that he could not Islamize Tunisia. The move by Ennahda in May 2016 to drop its Islamist label and forbid its leadership from involvement in religious organizations, in essence "secularizing" itself in line with what it understood to be the prevailing mood, was an attempt to regain lost trust.

Corresponding strong leadership was lacking in the case of Ennahda's main competitor, Nidaa Tounes, which had been formed indubitably to counter Ennahda in the run-up to the 2014 elections. The party gained traction because it appealed to a wide swath of society through its leadership's inclusiveness of liberals and socialists, conservatives and moderates, as well as businesspeople and labor unionists. Its core support was concentrated among the upper- and middle-income classes in coastal regions and among those who favored stability, defended secularism, and, most importantly, did not wish for a return of Ennahda.

A patchwork of political alliances, Nidaa Tounes lacked a unifying vision and a socioeconomic agenda. Many of its private sector members had ties to the ancien régime, a point mostly ignored during the anti-Islamist election frenzy of 2014. These liabilities came back to haunt the party in the post-elections period as the public grew fearful that the party's rise to power meant a reinstatement of the old regime.

Such fears came to life in late 2015 with the emergence of two factions within Nidaa Tounes—one led by the president's son, Hafedh Caid Essebsi, and another by the party's secretary-general, Mohsen Marzouk, a human rights activist who had been imprisoned during Ben Ali's regime. In March 2016, Marzouk launched a new party, Machrouu Tounes, and based it on Bourguibian principles of maintaining a separation of religion and politics. Ironically, although Marzouk and his followers—determinedly secular— had objected to the formation of a coalition with Ennahda in the first place, their disavowal of Nidaa Tounes made Ennahda the majority party in parliament.

Secularists grew anxious that Ennahda would take advantage of a weakened Nidaa Tounes and its own potentially dominant presence in parliament to position itself for a return to power. But Rached Ghannouchi dismissed such reports, telling me that the party had "tasted the bitterness of power and is not eager to get back on top." By being an actor—but not the main actor—in the power structure, he explained, Ennahda was better able to effect change and introduce reforms without being "antagonistic." Ennahda sees itself as having paid a price for its dominance during the Troika phase, claiming to have withdrawn from government because staying in power would have "threatened the path to democracy." Underscoring the importance of stability in Tunisia's nascent democracy, Ghannouchi claimed that consensus building, not majority rule, was paramount.[7]

Political stability and compromise, however, translated into exclusion for the youth who felt that institutional actors had hijacked the revolution that they had led. "Half of Tunisia is marginalized," civil society actors have told me, citing this as a perceived failure of the political elite.[8]

Tunisian youth had proven to be adept at rising spontaneously and organically against absolute power—first in the case of Ben Ali, and then during the Kasbah protests when they realized that Ben Ali had been ousted but the regime had not changed. They had an expectation that their role would be recognized and that they, in partnership with established opposition parties, would help lead the country that they justly felt they had helped to set free. Instead, despite much progress toward democracy, this divide between the ruling elite and the revolutionary youth did not improve much. Trust in the political system was not helped by a growing sentiment that elite politicians appeal to youth voters during campaign seasons and, once elected, return to ignoring their needs, leading to frustration among young people and a perception of an aging political elite.

This tension was exacerbated by the sentiment that not much changed after the revolution. Political elites chose stability and compromise over deep reforms. They avoided addressing some of the central grievances of Tunisians and potentially divisive concerns—transitional justice and what type of economic reform. Building consensus was credited for Tunisia's relatively smooth and peaceful transition, but this was at the expense of limited improvement in the lives of ordinary citizens.

Historically at a disadvantage, the interior of the country continued to suffer from the presence of structural economic problems. The disillusionment of youth led to continued protests in cities like Kasserine, where the unemployment rate in 2015 was double the national average of 15 percent. In 2015 alone, 302 Tunisian youth are estimated to have committed suicide—105 of them through self-immolation.[9]

As I sat down with a group of young men sipping tea at a café in Kasserine's main square, I could not help but think that any one of them could be the next Mohamed Bouazizi or any number of youth who followed in his footsteps. I asked them about the appeal of Da'esh and other militant organizations at home and abroad. "We saw how well that has worked for those who joined, haven't we?" Youssef responded, adding, "these kids were idiots and now everyone knows that they were . . . no one in their right mind would fall into that sort of trap . . . at least, no one that I know." Others said that they knew people who had joined extremist groups but they did so only for financial reasons—religion was not a factor, they insisted.[10]

How do these young men spend their time? They go to sit-ins and they join demonstrations, but they do so in part to pass time and in large measure to protest that the government is not getting them the jobs that it owes them. They protest for jobs because every other trick they know—job applications, word of mouth, connections that they do not have—has failed them. Protesting has become their preferred job search process. "What is the point of looking for a job?" Mohamed retorted when

I inquired. "There are none to be had, and when there are, they are taken up by those with connections but with zero education," Moez chimed in, punctuating his bitterness by informing me that he has not one university degree, but three. Yes, there are jobs in Tunis and in the Sahel, but as one of them explained, "it would cost me more to rent a room and eat than I would make in wages." So they live with their parents and make do on the odd day-job here and there that they might be able to get their hands on.

Revolution? What revolution? "What good is democracy and how could you talk to us about freedoms when we have nothing to look forward to in life?" "Write about the corruption and do not hide anything" were their parting words to me.

Unemployment has risen since the revolution, as have food prices.[11] In 2015, roughly 10 percent of the 2.6 million Tunisians between the ages of eighteen and thirty were educated and unemployed, and another 1 million were "not in education, employment, or training."[12]

Four years after the revolution, the public was starting to lose its patience over the slow pace of treatment of the ills that had brought about the revolution in the first place. Although Tunisia's GDP stood at slightly over $48.3 billion in 2014, having grown at a somewhat higher rate than in previous years since the revolution, all other economic indicators were pointing in a negative direction. Debt as a percentage of GDP rose, as did the budget deficit—to almost twice its level before the revolution. Annual GDP growth, which had averaged 5 percent from 2003 to 2008, fell to 1.9 percent in 2011, bouncing back somewhat to a 2.3 percent level in 2014. Between 2011 and 2014, public debt as a percentage of GDP rose from 32 percent to 50 percent.[13]

Frustrations over the government's handling of economic problems eventually led to the voting out by parliament of Prime Minister Habib Essid in July 2016. The nomination by Essebsi of Youssef Chahed, a forty-one-year-old agricultural scientist and junior minister in Essid's government, was ratified by the Assembly of the Representatives of the People, despite disapproval by opposition parties. Critics claimed that Chahed lacked the requisite credentials and that he was chosen because of his familial relationship with Essebsi.

The public's patience has also been tested over the handling of corruption, which became "democratized" and widely practiced, at a smaller but broader scale, after the revolution.[14] Demands made by the youth during the Kasbah protests included the investigation and prosecution of past corruption crimes and the adoption of stopgap measures to restrain the practice. Protesters also called for perpetrators of human rights abuses and killings during the revolution to be brought to justice. This led to the formation of a number of commissions by then Prime Minister Mohamed Ghannouchi, many of which Ben Ali had actually first proposed in his last, desperate televised address on January 13, 2011. But these commissions produced mixed results.

The report of the fact-finding commission of abuse by the regime—*Commission nationale d'investigation sur les abus enregistrés au cours de la période allant du 17 décembre 2010 jusqu'à l'accomplissement de son objet*—included a 1,040-page list of all those killed or injured between December 17, 2010, and January 14, 2011, the period of the revolution. Pursuant to a trial of Ben Ali and many of his closest advisers and ministers, the former president and his wife were convicted in absentia on June 20, 2012, and sentenced to thirty-five years in prison for an array of crimes including drug trafficking, manslaughter, and conspiracy against the state.[15]

But another commission—*Commission nationale d'investigation sur les affaires de corruption et de malversation*—which listened to 10,000 complaints and brought 320 cases of corruption, resulted in only 120 cases being looked into by the courts.[16] A good show of fighting corruption and sanctioning culprits was put on, but in the end it was clear that a real effort had been withheld.

Efforts to bring justice to past incidents of corruption continued to suffer in terms of credibility and to be shrouded in controversy. In 2015, President Essebsi pushed for a contentious piece of legislation meant to achieve economic and financial reconciliation: *projet de loi de réconciliation nationale*. The proposed legislation would have provided general amnesty for public officials and businessmen accused of corruption who repaid stolen public funds. Purportedly, money from 120 corrupt businessmen would have been reclaimed and utilized for funding local development projects. Debate over the proposal raged so wild, as critics accused local elites of advancing transitional justice to serve their own interests and solidify their positions of power, that the proposed legislation was temporarily shelved.

The reconciliation proposal was a slap in the face of demands that anticorruption justice be served—firmly, fairly, and transparently. That it was finally dropped serves as another testament to the democratic nature of debate and the strength of resolve of revolutionary forces. But the mere fact that the legislation had been proposed ended up undermining the work of an important commission—*Instance vérité et dignité*—created in June 2014 by constitutional decree to investigate and prosecute political, social, and economic crimes committed since 1955. Sihem Bensedrine, a human rights activist who witnessed abuses under the Ben Ali regime firsthand, having been jailed in 2001 and then exiled to France in 2009, was brought in to lead the commission. Despite some significant early steps, the achievements of the commission were perceived to have been super-ficial. Complaining of a lack of funds and political support from govern-ment, Bensedrine ostensibly faced the same mind-set that characterized the regimes of Habib Bourguiba and Zine al-Abidine Ben Ali.[17]

Mohamed Salah Ben Aissa, former minister of justice, tells me that Bensedrine's truth and dignity commission accumulated more than 30,000 files on human rights abuses, but that holdouts from the ancien régime had planned to sink it from the outset. But in November 2016, testimony in some of the cases investigated by the commission—estimated at more than 10,000—began to be heard and broadcasted on radio and television.

Ben Aissa had come into government as an independent with deep convictions about institutional reform and transitional justice, but he quickly discovered that the environment was not conducive to his ideas. Ben Aissa ultimately quit the Essid government, feeling he had no option after being asked to sign onto a watered down and unconsti-tutional memorandum regarding independent judiciary powers. Things had already been piling up, and the memorandum episode served as the last straw.[18]

In his last few weeks as minister, Ben Aissa took a controversially bold position on the unconstitutionality of a law that criminalizes same-sex relations. Ben Aissa called for the repeal of Tunisian Penal Code Article 230, which punishes homosexual acts with a prison sentence of up to three years. President Beji Caid Essebsi publicly admonished Ben Aissa after he acknowledged that the code is contradictory to the constitutional right to private life and freedom of conscience, as enshrined in Article Six.

Civil society organizations, such as the LGBT (lesbian, gay, bisexual, and transgender) advocacy group Shams, have fought for repeal of Article 230, as has the organization Chouf, which has provided a feminist alternative to the repeal argument. Shams, one of the two legally recognized LGBT organizations in the Arab world, alongside Helem in Lebanon, had to reapply multiple times before it achieved its legal status in May 2015. With more than 81,000 followers on Facebook and a wide geographic reach, the group aims to provide a safe haven for members of its constituency who have been shunned by society and ostracized by their families. According to the vice president of Shams and one of its founders, Ahmed Ben Amor, the organization has already achieved quite a bit by bringing the issue of homosexuality to the fore, instigating debate among society and in the public sphere. Ahmed pointed to shifting public opinion, citing a poll that showed 67 percent of Tunisians in favor of punishment for homosexual acts—an improvement over the 89 percent reported in 2012.[19]

Shams has popularized the LGBT movement and helped advance it in Tunisia beyond its status in other Arab countries, even those with no penal code that criminalizes homosexuality—Jordan and Bahrain—but much social persecution. All other Arab countries either have penal codes that criminalize homosexuality or laws that may not explicitly mention same-sex relations but are used to target them. In Lebanon, where sexual intercourse that is considered contrary to the order of "nature" is illegal, Judge Rabih Maalouf issued a landmark ruling on January 26, 2017, refusing to prosecute a gay couple and declaring homosexuality a "personal choice." Iraq does not prosecute homosexuals, but they are violently targeted by nonstate actors such as Da'esh. Out of ten countries in the world where acts of homosexuality could lead to the death penalty, seven are Arab—Saudi Arabia, Qatar, Somalia, Mauritania, Sudan, United Arab Emirates, and Yemen—and all have a Muslim majority population.[20]

Openly gay Tunisians receive death threats on a daily basis, and there has been a severe backlash to the public debate on the issue. On the morning of July 9, 2016, Ahmed Ben Amor, fatigued by death threats and homophobic assaults, took a large quantity of medication in an attempt to end his life. He was taken to hospital in a coma, but came around, only to attempt suicide again unsuccessfully a week later. Ahmed bitterly tasted at a personal level the agony of being rejected by his own family when he came out to them at the age of sixteen. For three days, his father, an imam, and uncle beat him up so badly—as if to exorcise his demon—that Ahmed lost consciousness and was sent to hospital. He escaped from the hospital and has not seen his family since.

International human rights organizations—including Human Rights Watch, Amnesty International, and Frontline—have publicized cases of oppression and mistreatment of homosexuals and have condemned the government for not protecting gay rights, often putting pressure on the judiciary for the release from prison of sentenced individuals.

The story of Marwan, a pseudonym given to a twenty-two-year-old student sentenced to one year in prison on charges of gay sex, gained international attention and the indignation of human rights organizations in Tunisia and abroad. Facing the threat of a murder charge, Marwan denied any involvement in the crime but admitted to having had sex with the victim. He was then forced to undergo an invasive anal examination and was charged with sodomy. Human rights groups appealed for Marwan's release, and, according to Amnesty International, a petition to the Tunisian government obtained 80,000 signatures.[21]

Yadh Ben Achour tells me that on the heels of the Marwan controversy and our subsequent discussion on the matter, he tried to appeal to President Essebsi to call for the repeal of Article 230. According to Ben Achour, Essebsi was perplexed by the plea and at first failed to see merit in the argument. Initially opposed to the decriminalization of homosexuality, he seemed to come around, only to conclude that this would be too polarizing an issue and that the time was not ripe. Ben Achour emphasized that, constitutionally, the rights of sexual minorities and LGBT individuals are supposed to be protected. He conceded the contradiction and that the issue might come to a head when the new constitution gets translated into law.[22]

During one of my many interviews with Sheikh Rached Ghannouchi, shortly after the United States Supreme Court decision to allow gay marriage, I asked him what he thought of the decision and of the fight for the protection of same-sex relations in Tunisia. His immediate response regarding the Supreme Court decision was, in jest, that this was one instance where he was more closely aligned with the Republican Party. He then went on to explain that all religions agree in their recognition of marriage as only between a man and a woman and that, according to Islam and other religions, same-sex relations are "against nature." But he quickly went on to say that Ennahda respects people's private lives, that what happens behind closed doors is the private business of citizens, and that it is not up to him or Ennahda to interfere or judge.[23]

Surprising and refreshing, Ghannouchi's empathetic response was out of sync with attitudes I have encountered everywhere else in the Arab world—especially among the religious.

A younger Ennahda member, Zied Ladhari—at the time minister of vocational training and employment in Essid's government, later Ennahda's secretary-general and minister of industry and commerce in Chahed's cabinet—reinforced Ghannouchi's attitude, telling me he thought that private affairs, including homosexuality, should be protected.[24]

Tunisians, like other Arabs, have been exposed to Western references to homosexuality through television, the Internet, and the like, rendering the human condition a Western phenomenon and ignoring its abiding—and often celebrated—historic presence in Muslim society.

In a discussion I had with the imam of Kairouan, Sheikh Taieb Ghozzi, he insisted that homosexuality is an imported Western phenomenon—just like drugs and alcohol—that preys on "moral weakness and lack of faith." When I pushed Sheikh Ghozzi on the innate nature of homosexuality, he argued that it is well documented that homosexuality is a biological "disorder" that ought to be treated as a disease and that it would be acceptable for a person to go through a sex change operation so that any tension between masculinity and femininity might be resolved. Remarkably, though, it was the imam who brought up the subject of homosexuality in our conversation—a sign of public discourse that is rare elsewhere, if it exists at all—and he did not use the derogatory term that is commonplace in the Arab lexicon on the subject: shudhūdh, which literally translates as deviance. He used instead the appropriate reference to homosexuals: mathali al-jins.[25] Interestingly, the French version of Penal Code Article 230 criminalizes acts of sodomy while its superseding wording in Arabic uses an ambiguous term for offenders—al-luwat, in reference to Prophet Lot of Sodom and Gomorrah—which is commonly suggestive in an Arab context of both sodomy and homosexuality.

Tunisian homosexuals are rarely visible in public spaces, despite the presence of hammams, or public bathhouses, that cater to men looking for other men, or of men offering sexual services to Europeans on a vacation of sexual tourism.[26] In Egypt, where there are no gay bars or cafés per se, there was a somewhat tolerant attitude after the revolution. But this was short-lived: "gay-friendly" meeting places have been shutting their doors en masse because of repeated police raids. Even dating applications like

Grindr are not safe spaces; police have been creating fake profiles to crack down on homosexuals.[27]

Unlike in other Muslim and Arab countries, the subject of homosexuality is at least debated in the open in Tunisia. As negative as the discourse often (but not always) is, it is not taboo the way it is elsewhere. One member of the LGBT organization Shams sums it up: "The campaign, these attacks, don't get me wrong, they're really bad . . . but it's happening in the open now. People can't avoid us anymore. They're talking about it on the TV. Whether they like us or hate us doesn't matter. We exist."[28]

Still, for a secular country that is more pluralistic and liberal than any other in the region, when it comes to sexual freedom and protection of LGBT rights, Tunisia's record is inconsistent with its otherwise enlightened and progressive societal outlook.

Although Tunisia ranks better than any Arab country on freedom scores,[29] there are serious limitations to freedom of expression and the media. Journalists, bloggers, artists, and intellectuals are prosecuted for defamation, committing offenses against state agents, and harming public order. A committee to reform media and communications resigned less than a year after it had been commissioned by then prime minister Mohamed Ghannouchi. Kamel Labidi, its head, said he "does not see the point in continuing its work" given the lack of cooperation from the government.[30]

Civil society activists point to the need for reform within the interior ministry, in particular the Technical Agency for Telecommunications, which conducts expansive government surveillance. The focus on security and stability, following a time characterized by a lax security environment during and immediately after the revolution, raised concerns in terms of what it might mean for restrictions on freedom. Following the Bardo attack, lawyers, opposition leaders, and rights campaigners worried that "Tunisian security forces, traumatized by the attack on the capital, could once again embrace repression in their struggle to contain the jihadi threat."[31] Arbitrary arrests and police harassment increased, causing apprehension that the fight against terrorism and concerns about border infiltrations would bring back the deep state of the Ben Ali era and the later years of Bourguiba.[32]

Essebsi ran his presidential campaign on a promise to restore stability and crack down on extremism, something many Tunisians felt that Ennahda had failed to do. The president signed a new antiterrorism law in August 2015 after nearly unanimous approval in parliament on July 25. Following the passing of the bill, eight human rights organizations—including Amnesty International, Human Rights Watch, the Carter Center, and the International Federation of Human Rights—issued a joint statement explaining that the law "lacks the necessary safeguards against abuse" and "grants security forces broad and vague monitoring and surveillance powers."[33] The law extends pretrial detention time from six up to fifteen days for terrorism suspects. It allows for closed hearings and does not require the disclosure of a witness's identity to defendants.[34] Yadh Ben Achour believes that the law against terrorism is unconstitutional, especially with respect to the right to detain suspects fifteen days without due process.[35]

Parliament was debating the 2015 antiterrorism law when the Bardo attack took place next door. Concerns about terrorism had surfaced ahead of the Bardo attack, and there were fears about rising extremism, partially explained by the post-revolution free-for-all democracy and the effect of the porous borders with Libya.

Former minister of national defense in Mehdi Jomaa's government, Ghazi Jeribi, explained to me that border problems were often related to security staffing issues. Previous governments since the revolution had often placed heads of security in command of districts from which they came, thinking that this would bring in better security, but this was also sometimes done to indulge the requests by many to be stationed close to their homes. This ended up having the opposite effect to producing better security. Because of social, clan, and family ties, those in charge did not always report on suspected terrorists or terrorist activity. This was often the case with individuals involved in customs violations, smuggling, and trafficking, much of which took place at official border crossings where there was a lack of security.[36]

Another contributing factor to the challenging security situation is that a number of previously Salafist militants were given amnesty after the revolution and allowed to join post-revolutionary politics. Ennahda believed that Salafis could be contained through engagement in mainstream politics. Ghannouchi stated in an interview in 2012 that Salafis reminded him of his youth and "that Tunisians will make them change too just like they had changed Ennahda."[37] But this proved to have been wishful thinking, as violence by militant extremists intensified in the years following the revolution.

Militancy by the Tunisian branches of the largest Salafist group, *Ansar al-Shari'a*, was often directed at social and artistic expressions that they deemed blasphemous. Militants attacked the Afric'Art Cinema on June 26, 2011, when it showed the controversial Tunisian film *La rabbi, la sidi* (No God, No Master). They also reacted violently when the independent television channel Nessma aired the Iranian film *Persepolis*, which depicted God in human form. In September 2012, protests by Muslims erupted around the world when the American movie titled *Innocence of Muslims* was posted on YouTube. Many Muslims saw the film as anti-Islamic, denigrating of Prophet Muhammad, and an act of blasphemy. In Tunisia, militants belonging to other Islamist movements such as *Hizb al-tahrir* demonstrated in the streets and shouted for vengeance; several individuals were killed as demonstrators reached and attacked the American embassy and the neighboring American school. These acts prompted Ennahda to halt its attempts to engage Salafis in a dialogue and to encourage them to adopt the democratic process.

Ennahda recognized the need to fill the religious vacuum outside of politics, but it failed to do so itself. Although it branded itself as being more akin to Turkey's AKP than Egypt's Muslim Brotherhood, it did not take into account the plethora of religious organizations that had been around at least since the 1970s in Turkey, allowing AKP to be a chiefly political Islamist organization.

Whereas Bourguiba had closed down religious endowments, or *waqfs*—referred to as *habus* in the Maghreb—and he and Ben Ali imposed restrictions on religious bodies, Islamic foundations in Turkey (*vakıflar*) provided needed social services, especially in growing urban areas where state services were limited. Sūfi *tarikatlar*, or brotherhoods, and religious networks helped the poor and addressed religious, sociological, and economic struggles that were associated with rapid modernization. Turkey's AKP had been able, in essence, to partner with religious organizations and subcontract to them socioreligious programs, allowing it to focus on its political agenda. The buttressing of charitable organizations and of social welfare activities by AKP developed a wide network of support and was key to the party's success in national and municipal elections. Unlike AKP, Ennahda lacked a network of religious organizations that it could utilize to provide social and welfare services and, in turn, garner a stronger religious affiliation and the kind of loyalty that AKP could command.

With Ennahda dropping its Islamist label and declaring that it is getting out of the religious sphere, this has left the space even more susceptible to penetration by extremist ideology and Salafist currents. Ghannouchi believes that the state needs to step in and provide the necessary support and control. But he is also counting on some in Ennahda leadership positions to quit the party and help fill the vacuum, because as members they are forbidden by the party's new rules to preach in mosques or be engaged in religious organizations.[38] This could end up having the effect of Ennahda's subcontracting its religious function while appearing to be exclusively focused on the political sphere.

The majority of Tunisian militant Salafis belong to what may be called Soliman's generation, in reference to a town to the southeast of Tunis where clashes between members of an armed jihadist group and the police took place at the end of 2006 and the beginning of 2007.[39] Younger recruits, frustrated by the politically and religiously oppressive regime and lack of economic prospects, joined jihadis. Many had been radicalized through Salafist jihadist websites and chat rooms. Salafist jihadis were aided in their recruitment strategies by the idea that Salafist activism was "cool" and revolutionary—it provided a path to upsetting generational hierarchies and acquiring social status when the traditional economic route held little promise.[40]

Ben Ali's tight control over the religious domain, including religious education and mosques, made the population more vulnerable to radicalism. The dearth of religious organizations under Ben Ali meant that the religious space was open for radical and Salafist groups to fill. Those seeking a greater identification with Islam were forced to turn to radical interpretations of the Qur'an and to an extreme ideological rhetoric dominating Internet and satellite spaces. The diminished role of Zaitouna soon after independence also meant that there has been for decades a scarcity of Islamic scholarship coming out of Tunisia—leaving the door wide open for alternative, radical influences. By not engaging in institutionalized religious thought and offering moderate alternatives, the state ceded space to radicalism.

Forced secularization and the suppression of religion under Ben Ali had the effect of creating a "black market" for ideas. Ben Ali went farther than Bourguiba ever did and used Draconian measures to mandate secularism. He did not possess Bourguiba's charisma, diplomacy, and nationalist credentials, which allowed his predecessor to use moral persuasion as a tool to secularize. Ironically, Ben Ali was more of a believer than Bourguiba was, and some members of his immediate family were quite religious. Ben Ali did not necessarily think in terms of secularism and religion; his "forced secularization" came under the banner of his authoritarianism and oppression of all forms of opposition, including Islamists.

After the revolution, Salafist jihadist preachers took advantage of the power vacuum and eruption of freedom in the post–Ben Ali era. They preached in the suburbs of Tunis and rural areas such as Sidi Bouzid, Jendouba, Kairouan, and Kasserine. Official imams were marginalized both because of their association with the ancien régime and because they could not compete with or hold their own next to Salafist preachers. These preachers claimed superior knowledge of Islam and usurped the state-trained imams, propagating that they were "imams lite."[41]

Imam of Kairouan Sheikh Taieb Ghozzi explains that the way Salafist preachers and their recruits have gone "backwards" in adopting principles of jihad and takfir is very un-Tunisian. He blames foreign influences that infiltrated Tunisia during and after the revolution and gave Tunisians the illusion that they offered "salvation." Sheikh Ghozzi tells me that in the Tunisian Maliki tradition of Islam, he and others had "opened the door" and invited dialogue and debate with these groups but that they were rebuffed.

Contrary to common belief, Salafism does not always equate with jihad-ism. The name originates from the Arabic word for ancestor, salaf. Salafism has its roots in the Salafiyya doctrine that grew out of the Islamic modernist reform movement of the late nineteenth and early twentieth centuries, as chapter 9 will discuss. Salafiyya called for the reassertion of Islam's rational aspects and for freedom from the rigidities that had inhibited the religion's development. It attracted followers from across the Arab world and beyond with its calls for the restoration of traditional Islamic values as a way to strengthen the Muslim community, or umma. Its ambition was the purification of Islam and the moral, cultural, and political reform of the conditions of Muslims. The movement was essentially intellectual and modernist in its origins, calling for the adoption of Western innovations as a way to counter the economic and political hegemony of the West.[42]

As a movement, on the whole, Salafism did not condone violence. Militancy within Salafism is a modern phenomenon. As Salafism evolved, it has morphed into three distinct, although at times overlapping, groupings: purist, political, and militant.[43]

The Salafism that rests on ideas from the early development of the movement—the purist, or scientific, kind—called for the spreading of the ideology solely through preaching and education. Ben Ali had tolerated the proliferation of this scriptural ideology (*al-Salafiyya al-'ilmiyya*) so long as the movement did not adopt political ambitions.[44]

Political Salafism calls for the institutionalization of Islam, including Shari'a, through political action. This branch of Salafism rests on the idea that political reform is a critical requirement, necessary for the revitalization of Muslim societies.[45]

Salafist jihadism, which is a "minority within a minority" in Tunisia, advocates violent opposition to current regimes as a means of establishing an Islamic state and instituting Shari'a.[46] *Ansar al-Shari'a*, which does not believe in democratic principles, belongs to this group and has acted as a spoiler of the democratization process.

Terrorist acts, whether carried out by *Ansar al-Shari'a* Salafist militants, al-Qaeda in the Islamic Maghreb, or lone radicals who might have pledged allegiance to, or been trained by, the likes of Da'esh, ultimately share an objective: to destabilize and bring havoc to Tunisia's budding secular democracy. Salafis who had been exiled or jailed were bitter and eager to put their ideas into practice and to react against the republic. The prospect of a thriving democracy and the freedom and modernity that it entails is in and of itself a threat to what radical groups, which have defined themselves around a narrow interpretation of Islam as the "savior," espouse as a utopian Islamist alternative. As much as they see the West as their nemesis, a far more dangerous adversary is the positive adaptation of Western values and influences by fellow Muslims.

By specifically targeting Westerners in Tunisia, extremists have attempted multiple gains, directly and indirectly. They have hit the economy where it hurts most, shrinking the tourism industry, which accounted for roughly 15 percent of GDP and 14 percent of employment in 2014.[47] Extremists have endeavored to shake the foundation for a successful democratic transition and to foment a sense of insecurity among Tunisians and competition between freedom and security—attaining martyrdom and killing a few "infidels" in the process.

Tighter border control and successful attempts by the government to preempt terrorist attacks have introduced a greater sense of security among Tunisians and a gradual bouncing back of tourism activity. Civic society and community actors have also played an important role in curbing the spread of extremist ideology. Imam Ghozzi believes that the state has assumed greater control over mosques where *takfiris*—those who incite accusations of apostasy—had found their pulpit and that many adolescents who had been lost to extremist rhetoric are being won back to a more rational and sensible discourse. The imam believes in a secular state and that a balance between the study of Shari'a and "Western thought" is what will continue to keep Tunisia strong in the face of invading extremist ideologies.

In an effort to combat susceptibility to extremist teachings, and cognizant that many would-be militants were being recruited in prison, the blogger and activist Lina Ben Mhenni started a social media campaign to collect books for prison libraries that she discovered were filled with books that taught extremist ideologies. Lina was able to collect more than 10,000 books in less than two months and has been working with the interior ministry on the vetting and distribution of books. Ben Mhenni believes that the issues of jihadism and Salafism in Tunisia are often exaggerated in the media, which tend more often than not to focus on what is wrong rather than what is right.[48]

There will continue to be spoilers, and the prospect of terrorism and increased radicalization will continue to loom over the country, as it has all over the region and beyond. Polarization between religionists and secularists will also continue to define the Tunisian landscape. For the first time since independence, the role that Islam plays in politics and in Tunisian society has been up to Tunisians. Under Bourguiba and Ben Ali, religion was part of the official discourse, but in reality there was no application of Islam, and religion had been removed from the public sphere. To hardline Islamists, the absence of any mention of Shari'a and Islam from official discourse in the new democracy represents an additional loss in the sphere of the rhetorical.

From both an historic and a regional perspective, however, Tunisia's smooth and peaceful transition to democracy is remarkable. What the country has achieved in a very short period of time is extraordinary—in four short years, Tunisians took a revolutionary dream and made it a reality.

Tunisians insist that the future of democracy cannot be threatened. Yadh Ben Achour remains ultimately optimistic. He references security threats and a concentration of power in the presidency as contributing to "a complicated and unstable situation," but stresses that Tunisians can say that they have succeeded in getting a real democracy.[49]

Ghannouchi, for his part, speaks of the focus in the next period on fighting injustice everywhere and on economic growth through infrastructural improvements, tourism, and trade.[50] He is confident that "the police state, the single party state, is not about to return. The days of president for life are over."[51]

The vulnerabilities are real—whether on the security, economic, or political front—but so is the sense of optimism and pride among Tunisians. The country may still have a long way to go before it can claim consolidation of the gains made since the 2011 revolution, but few question that the country is on the right path and that it continues to shine as the only real success story of democracy in the Arab world.

One civil society activist summed up the Tunisian spirit perfectly to me when he quoted the English biologist and early adopter of Darwinism, Thomas Henry Huxley: "It is far better for a man to go wrong in freedom than to go right in chains."[52]

PART II

Roots of Tunisian Identity

6

Carthage

egend has it that a woman founded Tunisia.

Across the Mediterranean, on the Great Sea's eastern shore, King Belus II ruled over the Phoenicians of Tyre in modern-day Lebanon. By the king's side were his son Pygmalion and daughter Elissa, to both of whom he bequeathed his throne.

When Elissa, also known as Elissar, mourned the death of her husband, a high priest who had acquired much wealth and authority, little did she know that it was none other than her own brother Pygmalion who had done the deed. Elissa only unraveled the mystery around her husband's death in a dream.

Knowing that her brother had an insatiable appetite for gold and intrigue, Elissa tricked Pygmalion into believing that she was going to travel in pursuit of riches that she would send back to him. With gold and friends in tow, she set sail, never to return home.

According to myth and poetic tradition, Elissa—or Dido, as the ancient Roman poet Virgil called her—landed in the early ninth century BCE on the African coast of what we now know as Tunisia. From Virgil's *Aeneid*,[1] we learn:

The rising city, which from far you see
Is Carthage, and a Tyrian colony
Phoenician Dido rules the growing state

Who fled from Tyre, to shun her brother's hate
Great were her wrongs, her story full of fate

Upon her arrival at the African coast, Hiarbas—the local Berber chieftain—greeted Elissa with a magnificent gift: she could have as much land as could be covered by a single ox hide. Elissa cut the hide into very thin strips and laid them end to end until they encompassed all of the hill of Byrsa.

As they dug to lay the foundation for their new city, Tyrian settlers unearthed the head of an ox; considering this a bad omen, they moved farther away. Instead, it was the head of a dead horse that foretold where Elissa's new city would rise. A Phoenician symbol of courage and conquest, the horse became the emblem of Carthage—from the Phoenician *Qart-Hadasht*, meaning "New City"—which was built in 814 BCE, making it older than Rome.

Elissa died a tragic death. One myth has her dying a martyr, while Virgil tells us that she died of a broken heart. In either story, she builds a funeral pyre and, in front of her people, throws herself into the fire.

From one account, we learn that Elissa surrendered her life to the gods after Hiarbas threatened her with war or marriage. But according to Virgil, Dido was already in love—with a Trojan prince. Fleeing the fallen city of Troy, Aeneas had come upon Dido's shores. When Aeneas chose Rome over her, Elissa wanted to live no more—her dying curse on the Trojans providing a mythical backdrop for one hundred years of war between Rome and Carthage.

Elissa became a national symbol, an identity that connects Tunisia to Europe and anchors it in the Mediterranean. Tunisian women have been referred to as the "Daughters of Dido." References to Elissa in contemporary Tunisia include a regular section titled *"Les indiscrétions d'Elyssa"* in *La Presse*, a leading French newspaper. The ten-dinar currency note featured Elissa until about 2010.[2]

Long before Elissa is said to have landed in Carthage, Phoenician merchants had established trading routes along the central and western Mediterranean. They built ports along the North African coast, in western Spain, and across the islands dotting the Mediterranean.

Ancestors of the modern-day Lebanese, the Phoenicians were direct descendants of the Canaanites. When Phoenicians arrived on the North

African coast at what was to become Carthage, the indigenous people they found living there were Berbers, the first people in recorded history known to have inhabited what is today Tunisia.

Throughout ancient history, the indigenous populations in North Africa were lumped together and given different monolithic names, although they were heterogeneous and did not belong to the same tribes or communities. The Greek historian Herodotus and the Roman historian Sallust called them Moors; they have also been referred to as Libyans and Numidians.

Berbers were also known as *Imazighen* (singular *Amazigh*), meaning "proud men of the west." The origin of the term Berber is somewhat controversial because of its relation to the term Barbarian. The term is likely from the Latin word *barbarus* or the Greek plural of the noun, *barbaroi*, used to describe foreigners and non-Latin and non-Greek speakers, respectively.[3] When Islam spread to North Africa in the seventh century CE, Arabs referred to the indigenous peoples that they found as *barbar*, which came to denote barbarian in the Arabic lexicon.

For the Phoenicians, whose civilization was famed for its maritime abilities, Carthage provided the ideal setting for the building of a commercial empire. Two major trade routes ran through Carthage. One was between Cadiz in southern Spain—whence the supply chain sourced precious metals—and Tyre, where these metals were manufactured into luxury goods and then traded back. The other trade route was between North Africa and the northern Mediterranean—specifically Sicily, Italy, and Greece.

Carthaginian ships reached as far as Brittany in northwest France and Cameroon in West Africa. Its exceptionally innovative mercantile and naval fleets dominated the Mediterranean for centuries. Carthage's dependence on maritime trade made it infamous for attacking, without mercy, aggressors who threatened its shipping routes.

Carthaginian wealth became legendary. Carthage became a major hub for manufacturing and an exporter of terra-cotta figurines and masks, jewelry and delicately carved ivories, blown ostrich eggs, and all sorts of foods and wines.[4] Affluent Carthaginians bought land in the countryside and took pride in their gardening and breeding of animals. As Carthage's economy grew, so did its size, reach, and importance.

The population of Carthage reached 30,000 within a century of its founding, and it grew to one of the largest cities on the Mediterranean

Sea. By the third century BCE, the city's population is estimated to have reached as high as 250,000.[5]

In 264 BCE, Carthage's territory hugged the northern coast of Africa, reaching far into modern Libya and Morocco, the southern coast of Spain, and the islands of Corsica, Sardinia, and most of Sicily. Though it later lost the islands, its territories continued to expand into the interior of northern Africa and eventually covered half of the Iberian Peninsula. Carthage became the most prominent Phoenician colony in the central and western Mediterranean, with its economy, military, and population far exceeding those of its closest counterpart. Only Rome and Syracuse in Sicily matched its domination of the Great Sea.

Carthage's prominence was largely due to the leadership and influence of the Magonids, a wealthy political clan that dominated Carthaginian politics from 550 to 390 or 380 BCE. In the fifth century BCE, the Magonids introduced a series of political reforms, including the formation of an elite constitutional body: the Tribunal of One Hundred and Four. While the constitution called for an oligarchic Council of Elders, it also introduced a democratic People's Assembly, which allowed for the participation of all citizens.

The Carthaginian political system won the praise of Aristotle, who credited it for the absence of tyranny and rebellions. Aristotle also considered the constitution of Carthage to be "one of the best balanced in the Mediterranean world," an honor he otherwise bestowed only on Sparta, Crete, and his own Athens.[6]

"Democracy is not a new phenomenon in Tunisia," Tunisians like to remind a listener. Tunisia's—already pioneering—1861 constitution was not its first, they also like to boast.

On the international front, Carthage's strongest ally was the Roman Empire, but it then became its greatest foe and, ultimately, its annihilator. Carthage and Rome shared trading and security interests, regulated through a number of treaties. Carthage was the dominant power at first, and new treaties had to be formed as Rome's power and sphere of influence grew.

The peaceful coexistence between the two powers came to an end when Roman colonists in Sicily called upon both Rome and Carthage for help in settling a dispute between the city-state of Messana, which they were both protecting, and the more powerful Syracuse. Rome, which had never fought a war outside of Italy, and Carthage each saw the efforts of the other as a pretext to extend their power over Sicily.

War broke out between the two empires in 264 BCE when a lack of political will on either side failed to prevent it. After its surprising success at sea, Rome extended the battlefield to the Carthaginian islands of Sardinia and Corsica. Seeking a broader victory over the Carthaginians at their home base, the Roman commander Regulus sailed his fleet to North Africa and marched by land to Carthage, destroying the Carthaginian army along the way and taking Tunis before peace negotiations finally began. Carthage refused to surrender and instead built a new army of cavalry and elephants that it put under the stewardship of General Hamilcar Barca. But it was too late: by 241 BCE, Rome had gained control of sea routes, and Carthage had no option but to capitulate and pay huge war reparations.

The conflict between Rome and Carthage over the strategic islands of Corsica and Sicily became referred to as the First Punic War, the first in a series of three wars between the two empires that spanned more than a century—from 264 to 146 BCE. Punic, from the Latin word *punicus* for Carthaginian, is how these wars are described, for it was the victorious Romans who wrote the surviving history of the conflict.

Carthage's defeat significantly weakened its Mediterranean trade and devastated its economy so that it could not pay back the money owed to its mercenaries. When an inexperienced military commander attempted to convince the mercenary soldiers to forgo the debt owed to them by the government, a revolt erupted and turned into a full-blown war that lasted for more than three years.

Hamilcar Barca's generalship proved decisive in the final victory of the Mercenary War. With his newfound glory, and Carthage in dire financial need, the general took off to Spain in a bid to take over the Iberian Peninsula and the silver mines of Tartessus. Following Hamilcar's death in battle, his son Hannibal led his legendary army to the gates of Rome, which had seen Carthage's encroachment on Spain as a threat and declared war. Hannibal made multiple displays of military genius as he traveled overland across Spain and Gaul and through the rough terrain of the snow-covered Alps, drawing comparisons to Hercules. But he was able to get only within 250 miles of Rome. Neither Spain nor Carthage sent him reinforcements in time to complete his heroic expedition.[7]

Just as they did to emerge victorious in the First Punic War, the Romans took the war to Africa. The two great rivals, Hannibal and the Roman general Scipio, met for a final battle at Zama in central modern-day Tunisia in 202 BCE. Hannibal met his first real defeat in the field, and the Second Punic War (218–201 BCE) ended.

It took Carthage fifty years to rebuild its wealth, primarily through trade and agriculture. When the Roman senator Cato the Elder visited Carthage in 153 BCE, he was amazed by its agricultural wealth. He returned to the senate in Rome—with Carthaginian figs in hand—and famously declared, "*Carthago delenda est* (Carthage must be destroyed)!"[8]

In no time, Rome had just the pretext to do exactly what Cato had resolutely professed. When Carthage declared war on the advancing Numidian king Masinissa, the king called on Rome for help. Rome intervened, and this led to the Third Punic War (149–146 BCE). A Roman siege of Carthage lasted for two years and ended with the final destruction of the city in 146 BCE. General Scipio Aemilianus, the adopted grandson of Scipio Africanus, sacked and burned down the city, and for six days and nights he sent in killing squads to eliminate any Carthaginians who survived the flames. Only about one-fifth of Carthage's nearly 250,000 residents remained at the final surrender, and they were enslaved.[9] Very little survived of Carthage's libraries and archives; much of it was destroyed with the fall of the city. The destruction was so horrible that Scipio himself is said to have shed tears and lamented the fate of Carthage, meditating alone afterwards and reflecting on the fall of cities, empires, and peoples, and perhaps the inevitable fall of his own nation one day.[10]

Thus began six centuries of Roman hegemony over the western Mediterranean.

"Great Carthage waged three wars. It was still powerful after the first, still inhabitable after the second. It was no longer to be found after the third," declared, two millennia later, the German playwright and poet Bertolt Brecht.[11]

But Carthage had its revenge. When North Africa produced its first Roman emperor, Septimius Severus (r. 193–211 CE)—three and a half centuries after the fall of Carthage—he spoke with a strong Phoenician accent.[12] It was centuries before people abandoned the Carthaginian culture and language, which were deeply rooted in North Africa.

The Romans founded a colony at the site of Carthage in 122 BCE, but the city was not fully rebuilt until Augustus decided in 29 BCE to anchor it as the center for Roman North Africa. The borders of the new province, Africa Proconsularis, extended south to the Sahara, incorporating the kingdom of Numidia along the western border of Carthage and, further west, Mauretania—spanning modern-day western and central Algeria and Morocco.

The province of Africa became one of the most prosperous and urbanized regions of the Roman Empire. The economy fully switched from a reliance on trade to agriculture—granting Carthage the title "Granary of Rome." Annual grain production is estimated to have been more than a million tons, one-quarter of which was exported. By the first century CE, the province produced two-thirds of the grain consumed by the city of Rome. In the second century CE, the cultivation of olives spread such that Carthage produced more olive oil than Italy.[13] By then, Carthage had become the third most important city in the Roman Empire, after Rome and Alexandria.

The Romans embarked on ambitious public works and infrastructural projects. The Antonine Baths in Carthage, commissioned by Emperor Hadrian in 116 CE and completed during the reign of Emperor Antonius Pius in 162 CE, spanned nine acres to the sea and were the fourth—or third by some accounts—largest public baths in the Roman Empire and the largest outside of Rome. Construction of the best of Roman infrastructure included a wide network of roads that stretched 12,500 miles—mostly built for military purposes.[14] Aqueducts, dams, bridges, and irrigation systems abounded. The Roman aqueduct and water temple in Djebel Zaghouan, still visible near the town of Zaghouan, took eleven years to build and delivered 8.5 million gallons of water each day to Carthage.[15]

The amphitheater in El Djem, built around 238 CE, is one of the most "accomplished examples of Roman architecture of an amphitheater, almost equal to that of the Coliseum of Rome." One of the largest coliseums in the world, and the largest still standing in North Africa, it could hold up to 35,000 spectators.[16] Theaters, baths, temples, and statues, as well as public feasts and celebrations, rivaled those in Rome and the rest of the empire.

African Roman art spread throughout the Mediterranean. Buildings and floors were covered with mosaics. Ceramic production flourished. North Africa first imported Roman pottery, or *terra sigillata*, but soon African *sigillata* became the favored ware in the region and was exported across the Mediterranean and to a good part of the Atlantic coast. With the dawning of Christianization, art celebrated biblical themes, framed in a new religious and political context.[17]

Bilateral influences between Carthage and Rome extended into the political spheres. Many natives and whole communities were given Roman citizenship before it was granted to the entire empire in 212 CE.[18] Some wealthier, generally land-owning, Africans entered Roman imperial politics. Fifteen percent of Rome's senators and one emperor came from the Roman province of Africa.[19]

Carthage also produced a number of important Christian personalities during the Roman era—including saints, bishops, and theologians. The first wave of Christianity gained its followers among the poor and the enslaved and then spread to the elite circles. Historians are unable to trace the exact beginning of the Christianization of Africa. However, the persecution and oppression Christians suffered in Roman Africa in the early days is well documented.

The Passion of Saints Perpetua and Felicity, one of the oldest surviving Christian texts, recounts the imprisonment, trial, and condemnation to death of Perpetua, an African noblewoman, and Felicity, a pregnant slave who gave birth in prison, for their wanting to convert to Christianity. The story was read every year, for centuries, in Carthage's churches in memory of the Carthaginian martyrs.

Among Carthaginian converts who contributed to theological thought and to church leadership was Father Tertullian (c. 160–240 CE). A prolific author, a notable early Christian apologist, and a polemicist against heresy, Tertullian has been called "the founder of Western theology."

By the middle of the third century CE, Carthage also had its own Christian bishop: Saint Cyprian (200–258 CE). Born to a high social class, Cyprian was a well-known rhetorician and lawyer before he converted to Christianity and quickly rose through the ranks. He led the North African church during the Decian persecution, when thousands of Christians renounced their faith under an edict from Emperor Decius that commanded everyone residing in his empire to perform sacrifices for the Roman gods. When the persecution ended, Bishop Cyprian readmitted into the Church those who had apostatized, and he established the Church's authority to forgive deadly sins, including that of apostasy.

But the greatest and fastest reformation occurred decades later at the hands of Saint Augustine of Hippo, who made reconversion his life objective and advocacy of the Roman Catholic Church his principal cause. A sinner turned saint, Augustine was born in the northeastern highlands

Numidian village of Thagaste, 150 miles from Carthage, at the border between modern-day Tunisia and Algeria. Saint Augustine later moved to Carthage to finish his formal education and became one of the most significant Christian scholars; his prolific writings, including *Confessions* and *City of God*, shaped Christian thought in the Middle Ages.

But as with all civilizations, the Roman saw its eventual and inevitable decline. Six centuries after Scipio humiliatingly defeated Hannibal and Cato declared that Carthage must be destroyed, Rome's hold on Carthage came to an end.

The East Germanic tribe known as the Vandals brought about the end of Roman hegemony in the province of Africa. The Vandal occupation lasted just about a century. It ended early in the reign of Emperor Justinian, the first great ruler of the Byzantine Eastern Roman Empire. Justinian's armies set out to conquer parts of the former—western—Roman Empire to round out the empire's holdings on the Mediterranean Sea. As a first step, Justinian sent an expedition in 533 CE to expel the Vandals from North Africa.

The Vandal kingdom was destroyed in two spectacular battles that occurred within a few months of one another, leading to their ultimate surrender in 534 CE. Unlike previous and future occupiers, the Vandals did not leave a lasting mark on Tunisia, "surviving only here and there in the gene pool in the shape of an unexpected fair headed child in the countryside"—the legacy of opportunistic marriages between Vandal women and Byzantines to keep their former husbands' lands.[20]

Byzantine rule lasted for 165 years in Carthage, until 698 CE and the culmination of the Arab conquest. The empire's territory stretched over modern-day Tunisia, Algeria, Libya, and Morocco.

Richard Edis, British Ambassador to Tunis in the late 1990s, argues that historians have largely recounted the Carthaginian, Roman, and Arab heritage of Tunisia at the expense of the Byzantine era, which is not deemed to be an essential element of Tunisian national identity. This neglect seems unwarranted, for Byzantine Tunisia, at its height, was "more stable and prosperous than most parts of the then known world," and it made important contributions to religious intellectual thought.[21]

Just as in Italy and Constantinople, Justinian mounted an ambitious building campaign in North Africa. Contemporaneous scholars Evagrius and Procopius claim that Justinian led the restoration of 150 towns and the construction of thirty-five castles, a governor's palace, two public baths, two forums, five churches, and a monastery in North Africa.[22] Byzantine influences in Tunisia are evident in the style of churches: the use of cupolas, ornamental capitals of columns, and mosaics. The Domus Caritatis basilica at Carthage is an example of Byzantine grand church designs.

Under Byzantine rule, the church in Carthage continued to adhere to the orthodox Catholic doctrine led by the pope in Rome, but there was great religious debate in the early days, specifically over the divinity or humanity of Christ. An old religious controversy came to a head as a result of an influx of Egyptian priests and monks who practiced Monotheletism. The Catholic Church considered Monotheletism, a doctrine positing the dogma that Jesus had a dual nature but only one will, heretical. A Greek monk, Maximus the Confessor, and his followers in North Africa led a religious opposition to the doctrine and its adherents and appealed for support from the pope in Rome. But with the ascension of a new emperor, Constans II, state doctrine turned in favor of Monotheletism, and in 653 CE both Maximus and Pope Martin were arrested and tried for heresy. Constantinople's rule over the province of Africa was interrupted when the exarch of Carthage, Gregory the Patrician, declared secession in 646 CE and named himself emperor.

By this time, Arabs had taken over Byzantine territories in Syria, Palestine, Egypt, and Tripolitania in modern-day Libya and were encroaching on the modern borders of Tunisia. It took fifty years more for the Muslim invaders to capture *Ifriqiya*, the name given by the Arabs to the Roman province of Africa, than it did to seize Syria or Mesopotamia. The Caliph Omar Ibn al-Khattab (583–644 CE) had warned that *Ifriqiya* was "a dangerous land which leads you astray and dupes you and which no one will attack as long as I live."[23]

Unlike Phoenician, Roman, Vandal, and Byzantine settlers, who had invaded from the sea, the Muslim Arabs came by land. The entry point for the Muslim Arabs was through Sufetula—Sbeitla in modern-day Tunisia— the new capital of Byzantine Tunisia after the split from Constantinople. A decisive battle was waged between the Arabs and the armies of Gregory the Patrician. The Arab forces won, capturing and looting Sufetula and parts of Byzacena in 648 CE, but they soon withdrew—for a large sum of gold raised by the local elite. With Gregory's death in battle, the province returned to its imperial allegiance. The Battle of Sufetula is considered especially important not only in that it marked the beginning of the end of Byzantine rule in the region, but because it eventually led to Arab conquest and the spread of Islam over North Africa and into Spain.

A series of raids and retreats occurred between 665 and 669 CE, ending with the capture of Capsa—modern-day Gafsa. The first permanent presence was established by 'Uqba Ibn Nafi' al-Fihri in 670 CE in Kairouan. 'Uqba had accompanied his uncle 'Amr Ibn al-'As as he led the Islamic invasion of North Africa and the expansion of the Umayyad dynasty in the region. Kairouan, positioned on a steppe on the outer edge of the Sahara, became the first Arab administrative center in the Maghreb and the oldest Muslim city in Africa, from which Islam spread to sub-Saharan regions.

The Byzantine naval fleet was eventually defeated, and the Byzantine imperial force was driven out of Carthage in 695 CE. The city of Carthage was finally secured in 698 CE after a number of counterattacks were crushed. But the Umayyad army decided that the site of Carthage was too vulnerable to naval attacks and so turned its attention to Tunis, which had been settled by native Berbers. As daunting as it was, defeating the Byzantines proved less challenging for the Muslim Arabs than subduing the local Berber populations. Natives had reclaimed Kairouan in 683 CE and continued to make things difficult for the invading Arabs. So obstinate was Berber resistance in *Ifriqiya* that the Muslim armies had to desperately call upon the chief commander of the entire Umayyad army, Hassan Ibn al-Nu'man, who reconquered Kairouan in 691 CE.

But it would take almost another decade for Ibn al-Nu'man's army to squash the Berbers' tenacious defiance. The legendary *Amazigh* warrior, princess Kahina, staged what was to be the last major defense against the Arabs in the Maghreb around 698 CE. Kahina proved to be an elusive target. The Muslim armies had to chase her to the Aurès Mountains in modern-day Algeria, where she ultimately met her death.

Amazigh elites adopted Arabic and Islam and soon saw themselves as allies in the effort to spread the religion. Some *Amazigh* tribes had assisted 'Uqba Ibn Nafi' al-Fihri and his Muslim armies against the Byzantines. Berbers aided Tariq Ibn Ziyad (670–720 CE), who was rumored to have been born to Princess Kahina, in crossing over from the Maghreb into Spain at Gibraltar—derivatively named after him (Jebel Tariq, or Mountain of Tariq)—and establishing the capital of an autonomous and lasting Umayyad caliphate, al-Andalus, or Andalucía, at Cordoba in 711 CE.

Tunisia was subsequently ruled at different times by a number of Muslim Berber dynasties and Arab caliphates—both Shi'a and Sunni. It is important to note, however, that although Muslims ruled Tunisia almost uninterruptedly until the French declared Tunisia a protectorate in 1881, continuous Arab rule extended only until early in the tenth century and returned only intermittently afterwards. Various Muslim Berber dynasties reigned, longest among them being the Hafsid dynasty (1229–1574), which had Tunis as its capital and whose rule ended with annexation to the Ottoman Empire.

Tunisia has been non-Arab and non-Muslim longer than it has been either. The late Tunisian diplomat and former minister of culture Habib Boularès argued that, by referring to the "Arab Conquest" of North Africa as if it marked the beginning of Tunisia's historical significance, Arab historians have neglected the 1,750 years of history before the Muslim Arabs arrived.[24]

Tunisian civilizations—Carthaginian, Roman, Byzantine, Arab, and Berber—contributed as much to Mediterranean culture and history as they absorbed from it. The proud cognizance of this by Tunisians, particularly in Tunis and along the Sahel, is critical to the way they see themselves: as *Mutawassittiyeen*, or Mediterranean. This has kept them integrated into, and not isolated from, the West, which they do not perceive as imposing as Arab Muslim populations generally do.

Bourguiba insisted on this age-old "Mediterranean" character of Tunisia, which served him well on a number of fronts. It justified his Eurocentric policies, and it won him the support of the French against his domestic adversaries, most notably Salah Ben Youssef. Positioning Tunisia toward the Mediterranean and Europe helped distinguish the country from the rest of the Arab world, and it provided an alternative to the Arab and Islamist orientations of Bourguiba's political enemies.

Zine al-Abidine Ben Ali also was mindful of the multifaceted nature of Tunisian identity. In a foreign policy speech in early 2003—ahead of a meeting of Mediterranean nations—he stressed Tunisia's bond to the sea, speaking of a Euro-Mediterranean space as one of "security, peace and prosperity, and a bridge that links the different cultures and civilizations of the peoples of the region." While he proclaimed a desire to strengthen relations with "brotherly Islamic states," he stressed the importance of regional economic and diplomatic integration through Tunisia's participation in the Maghreb Union and the African Union.[25]

Abdelbaki Hermassi, who served as minister of culture under Ben Ali for almost a decade, defines Tunisian civilization not as Arab or Islamic, but as an amalgamation of "African, European and Eastern civilizations," which "passed through and met in this land [Tunisia] where the wealth of elements making up our heritage, are juxtaposed, superimposed, and intertwined and the sum total of all three elements constitute our Tunisian civilization." Hermassi, who is known to have been quite pro-Western in his attitudes, describes Tunisia's reference groups as "the French and the Italians, not the Algerians and Libyans."[26]

Neither Libya nor Algeria had a history as an organized state before the arrival of European colonial mapmakers. Unlike Tunisia, these countries had been obscure "geographical expressions."[27] Libya, within its modern borders, lacked a common heritage and consisted for most of its history of different states inhabited by various indigenous Berber tribes. Algeria had no historical territorial legitimacy; its modern borders did not begin to be defined until the nineteenth century. Its people's collective identity emerged late in the nineteenth century out of anticolonial necessity. Its ancient cities, like Thagaste—the birthplace of Saint Augustine—were oriented toward Carthage.

Robert Kaplan explains that "the economic and political fault lines that separated Carthage and Numidia are the ones that separate Tunisia and Algeria—and the Romans drew them." Upon defeating Hannibal at Zama in 202 BCE, the Roman general Scipio dug a demarcation ditch, the Fossa Regia (Royal Trench), also known as the Fosse Scipio. The trench, parts of which are still visible, ran from Tabarka in the northwest, southward, and then eastward to Sfax, forming the boundary between the province of Africa and the kingdom of Numidia—roughly the same as the boundary between modern-day Tunisia and Algeria.[28]

Unlike neighboring Algeria and Libya, and farther afield in the rest of the Arab world, Tunisia's boundaries have changed little for more than two millennia, and it has been a cradle of significant civilizations and settlements since ancient times.

Tunisians are very aware of their rich heritage and of the multiple facets of their identity that make them distinctively Tunisian. They learn their history in school. Architectural, archeological, and artistic reminders surround them. And unlike in other Arab countries, that history is celebrated rather than relegated to a sidebar in the journal of an Islam-dominated narrative.

It is telling that Tunisia's former minister of education, Neji Jalloul, starts every conversation I have had with him with a reminder of the Roman saints and martyrs who were Tunisian and of the great and rich history of Carthage, which he believes is not taught sufficiently well to Tunisian pupils.[29] Emna Mizouni, founder of Carthagina, an association for the raising of awareness of Tunisia's history and heritage, tells me of the special significance after the Jasmine Revolution of Tunisians' consciousness of their varied and Mediterranean history as they chart their futures.[30]

In a 1972 speech, Habib Bourguiba famously said, "Carthaginians, Romans, Arabs, Turks, Spaniards, have successively occupied this country, and they have left a trace of their spirit."[31] Bourguiba used this rich diversity of the Tunisian cultural fabric as a point of amalgamation with Berber populations, evoking in another speech that "the interaction between the native Berbers and the Phoenician settlers created the Punic culture, a specifically Tunisian variant of the Phoenician civilization."[32]

Bourguiba relied on a stronger identification with Tunisia's ancestral roots in fighting what he considered "foreign" concepts brought by the Arab invaders. In discouraging all forms of traditional dress, including the hijab, which he viewed as impractical and demeaning to women, Bourguiba cast his justification within the contexts of both Islam and an originally Tunisian identity. He argued that Islamic standards of modesty did not require the wearing of a hijab. But he also maintained that unveiling is not a European or colonial imposition but a truly Tunisian practice.

During the debate over the hijab in 1958, the official newspaper *L'Action* published an article titled *"Pin-up d'hier et d'aujourd'hui"* that showed a mosaic in the Bardo Museum of the Roman goddess Venus brushing her long, lush hair, naked except for robes covering her legs and back, next to a photo of a modern Tunisian woman in the latest swimsuit fashion. The "anonymous" author of the article wrote of Tunisian ancestral Phoenician grandmothers as having "had a strong taste for lipstick, painted eyelashes, and indecent draperies. They had an arsenal of beauty creams and ointments that would embarrass Miss Elizabeth Arden herself, by their complexity and efficacy."[33] Juxtaposing Roman and Phoenician imagery, the implicit connotation is that there was a distinct Tunisian identity that rested somewhere between West and East, but was not a cloning of either. Bourguiba's anti-veiling policy rested on an argument that it was "un-Phoenician" for a Tunisian woman to wear the hijab and to succumb to a relatively recently imported custom, almost suggesting that Elissa, the mythological founder of Carthage, would disapprove.

7

Tunisian Islam

By the dawn of the eighth century, Tunisia was firmly in the hands of the Arab Muslims who had arrived from the Arabian Peninsula, the birthplace of Islam and the only part of the so-called "Arab world" where the ethnonym Arab correctly applies. With the Arab conquests and the Islamization and Arabization of the peoples of Mesopotamia, the Levant, Egypt, and the Maghreb, "Arab" began to identify the now Arabic-speaking peoples of those regions, who had their own ancestral civilizations, cultures, languages, and genealogies. Common threads of language and religion began to overshadow otherwise very divergent peoples and regions, lumping them over time into a homogeneous identity: Arab.

Islam, which sees itself as the successor to Judaism and Christianity, spread with ferocity during the seventh century, particularly following the death of Prophet Muhammad in 632. Political intrigue, struggles for power, assassinations, civil wars, violent conquests, and mass conversions characterized an era of rapid empire expansion.

The foray into the Maghreb took some six decades to complete. It culminated with the coalescence, in 705, of the area roughly encompassing Tunisia and parts of modern-day Libya and eastern Algeria into an African Muslim province, *Wilayat Ifriqiya*. With Kairouan as its capital, the province was ruled from Damascus by Umayyad caliphs.

The Umayyads (661–750) came into power after they had emerged victorious in the first Muslim civil war, or *fitnah*, which was fought over caliphate succession. The war was triggered by the murder of Uthman Ibn 'Affan, third of the four *Khulafa' Rashidun* (Rightly Guided Caliphs). Uthman's kinsman Mu'awiyah Ibn Abi Sufyan defeated Ali Ibn Abi Talib, Muhammad's cousin and son-in-law and fourth caliph, and established himself as the first Umayyad caliph, with Damascus as his capital. Supporters and descendants of Ali, who had been assassinated, became known as Shi'ites (from *Shi'at Ali*, or Party of Ali), giving rise first to the political, then religious, faction of Islam known as Shi'a.

After the eventual bloody demise of the Umayyad caliphate, the Abbasid dynasty (750–1258) moved the seat of power of Islam to Baghdad, which they built in 762. The Abbasid caliphate was more interested in expanding Islamic rule eastward into the mainland of Asia than it was in the Mediterranean, which had been largely secured during the Umayyad dynasty. The former *Wilayat Ifriqiya* became an Arab kingdom ruled by the Arab Muslim Aghlabids, or Banu al-Aghlab. The Aghlabids ruled from 800 to 909 and were nominally subject to the Abbasid caliphs of Baghdad. The Aghlabid ruler was recognized as the emir of a hereditary power, and not a mere *wali*, or governor, giving rise to what was to become the first self-governing dynasty in the Abbasid caliphate and a precedent for the autonomy that was to characterize much of Tunisia's history in the second millennium.

The rest of North Africa was split into various other Muslim kingdoms, including one in modern-day Morocco that was ruled by a Berber dynasty. *Amazigh* communities in Morocco accepted Islam but rejected Arab rule, preferring to establish their own Muslim dynasties instead. Neither the Abbasids nor their predecessors, the Umayyads, were able to impose Arab rule over most of the areas west of *Ifriqiya*.

The widespread conversion to Islam in *Ifriqiya* marked an eventual change in the relationship between Berbers and the Arab invaders and the beginning of an era marked by assimilation of traditions, customs, and language—though the Arabic language spread much more slowly than the Islamic faith.[1]

This assimilation was aided by a shared lifestyle between Arabs and Berbers: both were nomadic herders who preferred the interior to the coast. The egalitarian spirit and emphasis on communal existence in Islam appealed to the tribal Berber communities, who were able to synthesize their tribal beliefs with Islamic ideals. Berbers appropriated principles and practices of Islam but held onto some of their traditional rituals and beliefs, such as in spirits and saints.[2]

Islam was "tolerant" toward other monotheistic religions as it spread in North Africa. *Ahl al-kitab*—or "People of the Book," as followers of the three Abrahamic religions are called in Islam—were allowed to continue to practice their faiths, but they had to pay *jizya*, a form of tax. However, the local Berber populations of *Ifriqiya* were mostly nonmonotheistic and did not belong to *ahl al-kitab*. The grim options available to them, if they chose not to adopt Islam as their religion, were enslavement or submission to the sword.

Jews and Christians were permitted to restore their old temples and churches, but were forbidden to construct new ones.[3] Followers of both faiths continued to practice long after the Arab conquest, and there continue to be small minorities of each living in Tunisia. It was not until the end of the twelfth century that Christians were given the choice of conversion or exile, with most ending up proselytized.

Ifriqiya prospered under Aghlabid rule. Aghlabid emirs leveraged *Ifriqiya*'s geostrategic position and built a fleet that reigned supreme in the central Mediterranean, undertaking the conquest of Malta and Sicily, which remained under Muslim rule for more than two centuries. Aghlabid emirs also invested heavily in public works, including the conservation and distribution of water. They built aqueducts, bridges, water storage basins, and a complex sewage system, originally attributed to the Carthaginians and Romans until disproven by the French historian Marcel Solignac in the 1950s.

But perhaps most important, a marvelous Kairouanese civilization evolved under Aghlabid rule. Kairouan quickly became the capital of great Islamic thought, culture, and scholarship, and established a moral code that held through generations in the Islamic world. Kairouan became known for its rich market for books, in both Arabic and Hebrew, and as a flourishing hub for the study of medicine, astronomy, engineering, and translation.

Kairouan was defined by its great mosque, the Mosque of 'Uqba, which was commissioned in 670 by the founder of the town, 'Uqba Ibn Nafi' al-Fihri. The first mosque to be built in the Maghreb, it underwent major expansions under Aghlabid rule in the ninth century and became known as the Great Mosque of Kairouan. The grandeur of the mosque rivaled any wonder found in the East. Architecturally appealing and seamlessly integrative of different influences, there is a Sūfism-like spirituality and calmness to it—felt most notably in its large and welcoming courtyard. The mosque gained Kairouan a reputation as a holy city and a destination for pilgrims and devout Muslims.

The mosque also quickly became a great place of scholarship, attracting students from all areas and across faiths. The historian Luis del Mármol Carvajal compared its significance to Islam with what the *université de Paris*, founded three hundred years later, meant for Christianity.[4] A mosque was considered the center of a Muslim community, not just a place of worship or religious instruction but also a place for political discussion, debate, and education. Wherever Islam spread, mosques were built, and they led the education—both religious and nonreligious—of the local populace. By 900, nearly every mosque in the Muslim world included at least an elementary school—for both boys and girls age five and above. The Qur'an was at the core of early instruction. Elementary education began with writing the ninety-nine names of God and memorizing verses from the holy book. Later on, reading and writing were taught by means of a thorough study of the Qur'an. Arithmetic was also typically taught, and at larger and more advanced mosques, instruction was available in history, law, science, poetry, and algebra.

Performing the role of a school and a university, the Great Mosque of Kairouan taught the Qur'an and Islamic jurisprudence alongside mathematics, grammar, medicine, and astronomy. The mosque's library collection includes one of the earliest examples of Arabic writing and some of the oldest Islamic legal manuscripts, dating back to the ninth century.[5]

Under the leadership of Kairouanese scholars, Tunisia achieved one of the best medical traditions outside of the East at the time. Ishaq Ibn Imran (d. 908), a Muslim physician born in modern-day Iraq, established a medical school in Kairouan, where one of his students would become one of the most influential medical experts of his time: Ishaq al-Israeli (c. 832–932), also known as Isaac Israeli Ibn Salomon—a Jewish man born in modern-day Egypt. Al-Israeli was also a philosopher, and he wrote a number of books on logic and metaphysics. His students included the renowned Tunisian physician Ibn al-Jazzar (898–980), who was born in Kairouan.

Ibn al-Jazzar published works on diet and pathology, melancholy and forgetfulness, and sexual intercourse. His most famous body of work was a comprehensive general medical handbook titled *Zad al-musafir wa qut al-hadir* (Provisions for the Traveler and Nourishment of the Sedentary), which consisted of seven volumes dealing with a wide range of medical topics and included descriptions of various diseases. Considered one of the most influential texts in the development of European medicine, it was translated into Greek, Latin, and Hebrew. Ibn al-Jazzar also wrote a treatise on women's health and debated the role of the male physician in female examinations—challenging the prevailing common wisdom of the time that a physician should only examine or treat a female under circumstances that were beyond the knowledge or capability of a midwife. When Ibn al-Jazzar died at more than eighty years of age, he left behind more than 1,000 kilograms of books, mostly on medicine.[6]

The translated works of Ibn al-Jazzar were taught at the *Schola Medica Salernitana* in Italy, the world's first medical school and the forebearer of the modern university. The school's reputation peaked during the eleventh and twelfth centuries because of the works of one of its most important scholars, the Tunisian Christian Constantinus Africanus, also known as *Magister Orientis et Occidentis* (Master of the East and of the West). Born in Carthage, Constantinus traveled and studied throughout the Arab world, including Alexandria and Baghdad. Constantinus translated Arabic and Greek texts into Latin, and the school taught Roman, Greek, Jewish, and Arab science. The school, which had great influence on Europe's cultural renaissance in the twelfth century, played a significant role in spreading knowledge of the Arabs and the Greeks through the Western world.[7]

Kairouan was also a center of Islamic *fiqh*, the study and interpretation of Shari'a. As Islam spread through the Levant, Mesopotamia, and North Africa, it became necessary to examine how the religion could be adapted to new societies and cultures in these regions. This opened the door for scholars to apply *ijtihad*, or independent reasoning, and debate over the precepts of Shari'a and the foundation of the four Sunni schools of jurisprudence, or *madhabs*: Maliki, Shafi'i, Hanafi, and Hanbali—each named for its respective imam and founder.

For a while, the local populace of *Ifriqiya* wavered between the Hanafi *madhab*, introduced by the Abbasids, and the Maliki school. Over time, however, the Aghlabid rulers became overtly pro-Maliki, favoring the more marginal school at the time—as did religious scholars. The jurists, *fuqaha'*, of Kairouan likely found that they had more discretion in defining the legal culture of the Maghreb by being early adopters of the Maliki school of thought.

Imam Malik Ibn Anas (c. 708–795), founder of the Maliki *madhab*, believed that the mores observed by the first three Islamic generations of Medina should form the basis for an Islamic way of life. These adherents of Sunnah emphasized practical interpretations of the Qur'an and Hadith and appreciated the sociopolitical context of religion, in contrast to the strict religious dogma of more conservative *madhabs*. The approach taken by Malikis to the interpretation of Islam was marked by great flexibility and an emphasis on the importance of various cultural practices in shaping religion.[8] This adaptiveness helped define a Tunisian Islam that would characterize modern Tunisia and would shed light on why the country has been able to follow a markedly different trajectory than other Arab Muslim countries.

That much of Maliki scholarship was forged by *ulama*, or scholars of Islam, at the Great Mosque of Kairouan was a crucial factor in this development. The mosque was essential in supporting and promoting the Maliki *madhab*. Imam Malik considered Kairouan to be one of the three primary centers of Muslim learning and sciences, along with Kuffa in Mesopotamia and Medina in the Arabian Peninsula.[9]

Kairouanese scholars shaped the debate that took place in Kairouan and elsewhere, and they wrote what are considered to be the most influential works on Malikism. The Andalusian Yahia Ibn Salam al-Basri (c. 745–815) wrote and taught his *tafsir* (interpretation of religious text) at Kairouan; his writings triggered the beginning of Islamic scholarship in Andalucía.[10] The Kairounese Abdelsalam Ibn Said (d. 855)—better known as Sahnun— wrote what is considered to be the defining treatise on Maliki thought: *al-Mudawwana al-kubra* (The Great Code). The book was a major factor in the spread of the Maliki *madhab* across North Africa and Andalucía; it was considered the "Vulgate of North African Malikism" and an essential step in the unification of Maliki ideology in the Maghreb.[11]

Another of Kairouan's famous Maliki scholars, Ibn Abi Zayd al-Qayrawani (d. 996), wrote *al-Risalah*, or the Epistle, one of the most important expositions of Maliki law. Al-Qayrawani was a proponent of Ash'arism, a theological school of thought founded by the Mesopotamian Shafi'i scholar Abu al-Hassan Ali Ibn Ismail al-Ash'ari (873–935). Predicated on the supremacy of rationality and logic over dogma, and ascribing a larger degree of responsibility and free will to the individual, Ash'arism became the dominant Sunni school of thought in the Maghreb.[12]

Kairouan also became famous for producing a legal code that was centuries ahead of its time in terms of granting women rights in matters of marriage and divorce—rights that are still absent in almost all Arab and Muslim-majority countries. Though rooted in the lessons of the Qur'an, the code was influenced by social custom and demand, underscoring that Shari'a is a human product, far from being absolute or static. Especially in the Maghreb, customary law played a critical role in modeling accepted legal and judicial practice.

Polygamy had been common in pre-Islamic societies and was, as it continues to be, conditionally permitted in Islam: a man can marry up to four women, provided that he can treat them equally. But marriage contracts in the city of Kairouan were an exception and included clauses whereby a husband pledged fidelity to his wife. If the husband breached these clauses, such as by taking a second wife or bedding a concubine, the wife had full right to divorce and would be supported by the Islamic judiciary. So widespread was this "voluntary" practice that the expression a "Kairouanese wedding" came to imply a monogamous marriage.[13] Two stories, both set in the eighth century, are said to have been the genesis of the famous Contracts of Kairouan. According to one, the future second Abbasid caliph Abu Ja'far al-Mansur had evaded pursuit by the Umayyads by taking refuge in Kairouan. There, he married Arwa, the daughter of a nobleman, who stipulated in their marriage contract that he could not take another wife or a concubine. In another account, the governor of *Ifriqiya*, Yazid Ibn Hatim al-Muhallabi (r. 770–787), married a noblewoman from the Hejaz in the Arabian Peninsula who had settled in Kairouan. Their marriage contract included a similar clause to Arwa's, stipulating monogamy. After many years of marriage, Yazid took a concubine, and his wife took him to court demanding a divorce. The judge, "well known for his righteousness," ruled in the wife's favor, and the governor was forced to choose between his wife and the concubine.[14]

During the century-long rule of the Aghlabids, Malikism took deep root in Kairouan and throughout *Ifriqiya*, and a base of Islamic scholarship was established. This would shape the future relationship between Tunisians and Islam. What started under the Aghlabids withstood the strains brought by other dynasties that came to dominate the land.

In the early tenth century, Shi'a rule was established over much of *Ifriqiya*. Husayn Ibn Zakariyya, also known as Abu Abdullah al-Shi'i, led a successful rebellion against the Aghlabids, entering Kairouan in 909. When Ubayd Allah al-Mahdi, leader of the Isma'ili fringe and esoteric branch of Shi'a Islam, got wind of this, he marched west from the Levant, where he had declared himself the *Mahdi*, or messianic deliverer.[15] Al-Mahdi proclaimed himself caliph in Kairouan and executed Abu Abdullah al-Shi'i. Thus began Fatimid rule, named after Fatima, daughter of the Prophet, from whom Ubayd Allah al-Mahdi claimed decent.

The Fatimids first established their capital at the Tunisian coastal town of Mahdia, named after al-Mahdi. In 969, under the caliph al-Mu'izz li-Din Allah (c. 930–975), who was of Tunisian stock and born in Mahdia, the Fatimids captured Egypt, and in 973 they established *al-Qahira*, the Arabic name for Cairo, as the new capital of the Fatimid caliphate. In Cairo, al-Mu'izz commissioned the founding in 970 of the world famous al-Azhar Mosque, which would later become a leading Sunni theological center. From Cairo, the Fatimids, who reigned until 1171, expanded their possessions northeast to Syria and southeast to Mecca and Medina.

The Zirids, or Banu Ziri, a Berber tribe, pledged allegiance to the Fatimids and became rulers over *Ifriqiya* during their reign. Maliki scholars remained true to their Sunni school, however, and opposed the Fatimids. Riots by Malikis broke out in 1016–1017, killing an estimated 20,000 Shi'ites. The Zirids finally made their break from the Fatimids and from Shi'ism in 1044 and retreated from their capital in Kairouan to the former Fatimid capital and stronghold of Mahdia on the coast.[16]

In the middle of the twelfth century, *Ifriqiya* was taken over by the revolutionary Almohad movement, led by the Berber Muhammad Ibn Tumart, who had fought and defeated the reigning Almoravid dynasty in modern-day Morocco. Political and spiritual unity was established under the Almohads. For the first and last time in its history, the entire Maghreb was unified under one central indigenous authority.

In a move that ended up contributing to their own undoing, however, the Almohads appointed members of the Masmudah Berber tribe Banu Hafs as governors of Tunisia in the late twelfth century. As soon as the enterprising Banu Hafs found an opening, which they did around 1229, they broke away from diminishing Almohad rule and established their own Hafsid dynasty. Wars and rebellions had started breaking out throughout the Maghreb, and it was not long before the convulsive process brought to an end the Almohad dynasty. The Hafsid dynasty was to govern until the middle of the sixteenth century, when Tunisia fell into Turkish hands.

The Hafsids established their capital in Tunis, where the Kasbah became the seat of power, as it continues to be. Cities became centers of learning, and rulers financed beautiful mosques and prestigious schools. Religious thought and education flourished, and the Maliki *madhab* witnessed a renaissance. But religious scholars were barred from interfering in state affairs, as there was separation between mosque and state under the Hafsids; the state relinquished control over Islam, and religious life developed freely.

Concurrent with Almohad rule, and Hafsid after it, was the development of Sūfism, which had started making its way into Tunisia and influencing the development of its Islam. Sūfism, commonly referred to as the mysticism of Islam, sees itself as the elaborate extension of the spiritual implications of the religion and as "the completion of Islam, its living embodiment, in contrast to legal formalization and theological scholasticism"; Sūfism is to the spirituality of Islam what Shari'a is to the legal aspects of the religion.[17] The practice of Sūfism blends the performance of conventional religious duties, such as the five daily prayers, with additional spiritual rituals, such as *dhikr*, or the chanting of God's attributes, and the veneration of saints. Among the most popularized Sūfi orders, or *turuq*, are the Mevlevi order, based on the teaching of Jalal al-Din al-Rumi (c. 1207–1273), and the Naqshbandiya, named after Baha-ud-Din Naqshband Bukhari (d. 1384) from Bukhara in Uzbekistan.

It is difficult to trace the exact origin of the term Sūfism, rendering its genesis as enigmatic as the orders themselves. According to some explanations, the term stems from the Arabic word for wool, *sūf*, suggesting that early Sūfi movement followers were influenced by the habits of monks in Eastern Christianity who usually wore wool as "a sign of world renunciation,"[18] or in reference to Moses's wool clothing when he supposedly spoke to God. It has also been said that the term Sūfism is a reference to poor and humble immigrants at the time of the Prophet. In contrast to the politicized and corrupt tendency to attribute religiosity to elites and nobles, the Sūfi lifestyle embodied simplicity, and poverty was seen as an essential element of Sūfism.[19]

Sūfi masters came into conflict with Almohad rulers, not surprising given that Sūfism considers the principles of sovereignty and legitimacy to be attributes that belong to God only. Under Sūfi principles, roles were reversed in the relationship between political rulers and Sūfi leaders: the representative of the temporal power must bow before the vehicle of God, not the other way around. Instead of gifts bestowed by the caliph or sultan becoming the object of indebtedness, as was commonly the case, it was the ruler who became beholden to the Sūfi saint for being the recipient of the saint's spiritual testament and of *walaya*, or proximity with God. The Sūfi masters' influence on the common people and the potential threat they represented to established power led them to be viewed as dangerous and deviant by the political elites.[20]

Centuries later, Sūfi masters led the resistance to colonial influence and expansion. This made it necessary, at least for European orientalists, to label the movement as fanatic and foreign to Islam.[21] The European interpretation of Islamic Sūfism through the prism of Christianity, and their biased colonial experiences, resulted in a cultural condemnation that is quite clear when examining writings on Sūfism in the French language.[22]

Despite attempts by some modernists and reformist Islamic thinkers to disassociate Sūfism from Islam, Sūfism's ethical and theological contributions to Islam cannot be easily dismissed. Sūfism is considered to have been highly influential on Islamic society, shaping its culture as well as its character. This is especially true in Tunisia, where every town and village had a Sūfi clerk and almost every Tunisian belonged to one of the main Sūfi orders, at least until the nineteenth century. Sūfi Islam is the "popular Islam of Tunisia," as opposed to the scholarly Islam of the religious elite, passed down through generations of families that held influential positions at Zaitouna Mosque in Tunis, which was built in 734 and later assumed the role of Tunisia's center for modern intellectual thought.[23]

Considered the patron saint of Tunis, Sidi Mahrez Ibn Khalaf (951–1022) was a Maliki scholar who became a political and religious leader known for having defended the city of Tunis during political upheavals in the final days of the Fatimid dynasty. He was also famed as the guardian of the Jewish community. At a time when only Muslims lived within the walled city of Tunis, Ibn Khalaf called for Jews and Muslims to live side by side, leading to the creation of the first Jewish neighborhood in Tunis—known to this day as the Hara quarter.

Other prominent Tunisian Sūfi figures included Sidi Abu Said al-Baji (1156–1231), who established a sanctuary that became the town of Sidi Bou Said. Abu al-Hassan al-Shadhili (1196–1258), a Moroccan who moved to Tunis and became a mentor to several notable Tunisian Sūfi figures, established the Shadhili order. His protégés included Aicha Manoubia (1180–1257), considered an early Islamic feminist and one of the few females to have been granted the title of saint.

Ibn Khaldūn, the fourteenth-century "son of Tunisia"[24] who would become a vital point of reference in Tunisia's modern reform movement, approved of early Sūfism. He respected the sobriety, *sahw*, of the early Sūfis but condemned their ecstatic successors, often rumored to engage in the consumption of drugs in their rituals. He blamed Sūfism for what he saw as its adverse effects on social cohesion and political stability. Ibn Khaldūn's negative view of later Sūfism was likely related to the common perception at the time of a connection between the growing influence of Sūfism and the political and economic decline of the Maghreb and Andalucía. Given the elitism of his heritage, Ibn Khaldūn is likely to have been prejudiced against the social order imposed by Sūfism rather than opposed to the nature of its beliefs.[25]

Ibn Khaldūn, whose ancestors came from Andalucía in 1248, reached high administrative and political posts under different dynasties. He lived during a rather tumultuous period in the Maghreb, witnessing the end of Almohad rule and diminishing Muslim control in Spain during the Reconquista. During his political career, Ibn Khaldūn encountered both Pedro the Cruel of Castile in Seville and the Mongol conqueror Tamerlane near Damascus, both of whom sought his council but were refused.[26] He had a certain capacity for making adversaries, changing employment frequently and often complaining about "enemies and intriguers" who turned his employers against him.[27]

Centuries before Adam Smith introduced modern economics and the early theories of political economy and David Ricardo brought us the concepts of comparative advantage and value theory, Ibn Khaldūn had studied and written about the theory of productivity, human labor, and the social organization of production.[28] But the widespread dissemination of his writings outside the Arabic-speaking region did not take place until late in the nineteenth century.

Considered to be one of the greatest polymaths of all time, early in his career Ibn Khaldūn began to question the perils of urban luxury and the distance between rulers and their people. A political and philosophical realist, he is most remembered for his seminal work *Muqaddimah* (Introduction), which discussed the philosophy of history and addressed Islamic theology, political theory, and science. Ibn Khaldūn was fascinated by the notion of the state, which for him was synonymous with the dynasty that led it—there being no distinction in Arabic between the two, with the word *dawlah* being used for both. Believing that political and power dynamics emerged from tribal communities and remained at play in larger states or empires, he wrote on the relationship between a civilization's development and its environment. On religion and politics, Ibn Khaldūn wrote in the *Muqaddimah*: "The truth one must know is that no religious or political propaganda can be successful, unless power and group feeling ['*assabiya*] exist to support the religious and political aspirations and defend them against those who reject them."[29]

The *Muqaddimah* dedicated an entire chapter to the human ability to think, which according to Ibn Khaldūn sets humans apart from other living beings. He offered his interpretation of the meaning of the Qur'anic verse "He gave you hearing and eyes and hearts" (The Qur'an, *al-Nahl* (The Bees) 16:78), inferring *fu'ad* (heart) as the ability to think—as opposed to emotions or the organ itself.[30]

Ibn Khaldūn's theories on education were both profound and advanced in their development. He argued that it was harmful to be too strict, objected to severe punishment for students, and stressed the importance of a close relationship between student and teacher. He believed that subjects should be taught gradually, one at a time, in the correct—not broken—sequence, and according to students' level of comprehension. Ibn Khaldūn found handbooks that condensed material and provided abridgments to be harmful to a student's learning. Arguing for the importance of a student's comprehending the larger topic at hand, he took a position against presentation of a plethora of scholarly works with complex technical terminology and methodological differences. Ibn Khaldūn encouraged practical learning through travel and meeting with scholars.

Defying common, then and now, norms of inculcation, especially when it came to the teaching of religion and the Qur'an, Ibn Khaldūn was an opponent of the method of rote memorization. Despite his general disparagement of Sūfism, Ibn Khaldūn concurred with the Andalusian scholar of Islam and Sūfi mystic Ibn al-'Arabi (1165–1240) that a student's instruction should begin with the Arabic language and poetry, followed by arithmetic, rather than the practice of teaching the Qur'an first, which was common at the time.

Ibn Khaldūn's theses advocating critical and analytical thinking is clearly discernible in Tunisia's, and particularly Bourguiba's, approach to teaching and learning. They stand in remarkably sharp contrast to the pedagogical emphasis on rote memorization that has dominated Arab classrooms for decades, instilling the prohibition against debate or dispute with authority figures—both political and religious—and against interpretations that do not toe the "party line."

Acknowledged as the father of sociology and the science of human civilization (*'ilm al-'umran*), Ibn Khaldūn is viewed as continuing the "Aristotelian-Averroist" current of Islamic thought and as a precursor to modernist secular Islam.[31] Although some sixteenth- and seventeenth-century Ottoman scholars and statesmen became interested in his work, it was not until the *Muqaddimah* was translated into French in the 1860s that Ibn Khaldūn gained international recognition.

Ibn Khaldūn has been claimed by countries across the Maghreb and the Middle East, and even north to Spain, as part of their Islamic intellectual heritage. Perhaps more than any other people, Tunisians rightly lay proud claim to Ibn Khaldūn. It is no wonder that when Habib Bourguiba needed validation for his regime and his policies of reform in 1978, he erected the statue of Ibn Khaldūn that still stands on Avenue Habib Bourguiba, facing one of the modern "father of Tunisia" himself.

Liberal secular ideals have been born out of the traditions of Ibn Khaldūn and earlier Maliki scholars. These principles have carved out spaces for Islam to play an important role in the private lives of Tunisians, while not regulating their political and public spheres. Habib Bourguiba understood this very well.

The Iranian scholar Javad Haghnavaz contends that Islam was never opposed to learning and integrating ideas from other civilizations as long as the principles of the religion were upheld.[32] Tunisian Islam was no exception. In his book *Histoire de la Tunisie*, Habib Boularès argues that throughout Tunisia's history, Tunisians were inclined to adopt unorthodox interpretations of religions.[33] Tunisian Islam evolved over a period of eight centuries, weaving together teachings that were homegrown in intellectual centers such as Kairouan and Tunis with scholarly, theological, and spiritual developments that were being shaped in places as far as Persia or as near as Andalucía. Deep scholarship, an insistence on adaptation to local traditions and values, and interspersion with different civilizations produced a living version of Islam that was robust and far from dogmatic. Tunisian Islam contributed to the fertility of a unique Tunisian identity and to the tapestry of Tunisia's rich civilization.

Tunisian Islam was helped in that it did not suffer the fate of other corners of the Muslim world that had been cradles of a great Muslim civilization. Invasions by the Mongols that brought an end to the Abbasid dynasty in 1258 destroyed entire cities that were centers of intellectual activity, where science and education had flourished. Their defeat in 1260 at the hands of the Mamluk Sultanate that ruled over Egypt prevented the Mongols from venturing farther west, averting similar destruction in the Maghreb.

At the time of the Mongolian invasions of the Levant and Mesopotamia, while Islamic scholarship was at its height in Kairouan and Tunis, a long period of stagnation began in the eastern frontiers of the Arab world, and seeds of fanaticism were planted by the likes of the prominent Hanbali jurist and scholar Taqi al-Din Ahmad Ibn Taymiyya (1263–1328). Attempts at an Islamic revival that held much promise in the nineteenth century were ultimately aborted, ceding space for extremist ideologies that took hold during the twentieth century.

What evolved in the first half of the past millennium in Tunisia was preserved, helping make possible the modern reform movement that started in the middle of the nineteenth century and continued well into the twentieth, as the next two chapters will elucidate.

8

Influencing Rivalries

Two momentous world events that took place in the fifteenth century had huge consequences for Tunisia, determining its fate for much of the remainder of the second millennium.

In 1453, the Ottoman Turks drove the Romans out of Byzantine Constantinople, establishing it as the capital of an Ottoman Empire under Sultan Mehmet II and setting into motion one of the largest imperial projects in human history. What began as a *ghazi* (raider) state around 1300 in Asia Minor under Osman I ended up expanding into an empire through conquest and the spoils of war, uniting tribes across Anatolia in a holy war against Christian Byzantium. By 1520, the Ottomans had gained control of territory that stretched from the gates of Venice in the west to Mesopotamia, the Levant, and the Arabian Peninsula in the southeast, also dominating Egypt and capturing regions to the west of Tunisia.

The second major development was the conclusion of Spain's centuries-long Reconquista and the end of Andalusian Muslim rule in 1492 with the capture of the Iberian Peninsula by Isabella I, queen of Castile, and her husband Ferdinand II, king of Aragon. Explorations, settlements, and empire building quickly ensued as Spaniards ventured into the Americas and traveled as far east as the Philippines. Spain also had its heart set on conquests across the Mediterranean, setting up presidios in port cities along the African coast.

The Jews and Muslims of Andalucía faced forced conversion to Christianity or expulsion. Aided by geographic proximity and the appeal of Kairouan, Tunisia had already benefited greatly from links to Andalucía and the emigration of Muslim and Jewish intellectuals. The defeat of the Muslim king of Granada saw a surge of such emigrants who sought refuge from the Spanish.

The valuable coastal strip of North Africa, which Europeans referred to as the Barbary Coast (after the Berbers), attracted the attention of what had now become the two most powerful and competing Mediterranean states: Habsburg Spain in the west, and Ottoman Turkey in the east. The Spanish-Ottoman rivalry along the North African coast lasted for much of the sixteenth century. The Ottomans eventually won, using quite unorthodox means: they allowed the infamous Turkish pirates, or corsairs, to establish themselves along the coast, seizing territories, to which the Ottomans then gave formal status as protectorates of the Ottoman Empire. Thus, the coast of Algiers was captured in 1512, and two other protectorates were firmly based east of Tunisia by 1551. Tunisia was briefly taken in 1534 by the corsair Khayr al-Din Barbarossa, then recovered for Spain in 1535, before finally being brought under Ottoman control in 1574.

Tunisia's borders, having contracted somewhat under the Ottoman Empire, roughly matched its modern ones, except for some parts of the south. Tunisia, like other Ottoman jurisdictions, became a semiautonomous province administered by a bey, or governor. Central authority rested with the sultan in Constantinople, assisted by his grand vizier.

Tunisia was one of the last acquisitions of the Ottoman Empire. The slow decline of the empire had commenced by the time of its capture. While subjugation of the Arab world had doubled the revenues of the Ottoman treasury, there were no longer any new conquests that could generate fresh sources of income. The Ottoman military, famed for its extraordinary conquests and efficiency, began to weaken, and its inactivity led to military defeats and rising costs of battle. Corruption, nepotism, and economic troubles led to social unrest in various parts of the empire.

A reform era beginning in the seventeenth century attempted to tackle the malaise but failed to address the roots of the problems. The empire continued to decline, and it lost much of its European territory. Local provincial rulers amassed greater powers and exercised more authority as centralized governance deteriorated. This was especially true in the more distant provinces of the Ottoman Empire. In North Africa, local military corps ruled, paying mere tribute to the Ottoman sultan. By the nineteenth century, the Ottoman Empire had almost no control over its territories in North Africa.

But autonomous rule had commenced in Tunisia much earlier. Military revolts toward the end of the sixteenth century and local control over decision making resulted in the Ottomans' recognizing Tunisia's de facto independence in 1606. Following rule by the Muradids, the first line of hereditary beys to govern Tunisia from 1613 until 1705, al-Husayn Ibn Ali, founder of the Husaynid dynasty, passed a law of succession in 1710, ensuring that his descendants would reign over Tunisia for generations. Indeed, the Husaynids ruled continuously until 1957, when Tunisia's postindependence constituent assembly ended beylical rule, which had already become only a symbolic position during the French protectorate.

Territorial conflicts between the weakening Ottoman Empire and the rising European powers continued during much of the life of the Ottoman Empire, and they intensified in the nineteenth century. Tensions escalated over control of North African territory when the Turks seemed to be encroaching militarily on Tunisia in 1840, prompting France to send its own fleet. France's advocacy of Tunisian autonomy within the Ottoman Empire was intended to keep the Turks away from neighboring Algeria and to prepare for its own eventual annexation of Tunisia. The Husaynid Ahmad Bey, who ruled from 1837 until 1855, understood this. The bey solicited the support of a third strong foreign power, Britain, to keep his neighbors at bay, and a military confrontation was avoided.

Economic interests were at the heart of the allure of Tunisia to the Europeans, who saw the province as an entry point to greater economic integration with the Ottoman Empire. After the 1818 Congress in Aix-la-Chapelle to address common problems following the Napoleonic Wars (1799–1815), European powers, interested in ensuring safe passage for ships that carried their products to international markets, forced North African governments to put an end to piracy. Until the early nineteenth century, booty, ransom, and slaves—extracted by Barbary pirates from weaker Mediterranean and Atlantic powers—were a major source of revenue for beys in Tripoli, Tunisia, Algeria, and Morocco. With the termination of the practice of piracy, European products and ideas started flowing into Tunisia at an unprecedented rate.

As part of Ahmad Bey's strategy to protect Tunisia from European and Ottoman intrusion, he set out to launch a program of military modernization. Ahmad Bey's father, Husayn Bey (r. 1824–1835), had established a modern *nizami* army based on a European-influenced Ottoman model, training for which was provided by a French military mission, a sign of rising nineteenth-century French influence. Husayn Bey considered the Ottoman army, with its "flamboyant cavalry and the use of swords, spears and other 'white arms,'" to be severely outdated and invested in a strong infantry equipped with modern weapons, most notably the musket. But by the time Ahmad Bey came to rule, the army's European equipment too had become obsolete, and officers were mostly illiterate and had not been trained in military science. The army consisted mainly of elite formations of Turks, mercenary Berbers, and some Ottoman slaves, or *mamluks*. Ahmad Bey expanded the *nizami* army, up to 16,000 men at its peak, and made a number of improvements to it. He changed the practice of conscription, allowing peasants into the army. Native Tunisians, distrustful of Turks who traditionally filled the ranks of the military, resisted at first, with many buying their way out of conscription or exempting altogether.[1]

A stronger, modernized Tunisian military meant that Tunisia was better equipped to resist European encroachment. But France supported improvements and updates to the army, including its weaponry, as a means of ensuring Tunisia's autonomous status, at least from the Ottoman Empire. France was in effect ensuring Tunisia's independence and clearing the way for its own eventual annexation, putting itself in the peculiar position of helping modernize the very army that could one day turn against it.

Ahmad Bey's modernization project included the establishment of foundries, textile mills, and small factories to support the budding army and to enhance the economic autonomy of Tunisia. He also founded Bardo Military Academy in 1840 to train an officer corps in the new equipment and latest military strategies and tactics, based on the model of the *Eski saray* (Old Palace) military school in Istanbul. The academy was small, so the army could not be staffed exclusively from the ranks of its graduates, but it still had strong influence on the military through the new ideas and training that its alumni brought to the overall force.

Subjects taught at Bardo consisted of military art and history, artillery, topography, French and Italian languages, and Arabic language and literature. In contrast to the teaching at Zaitouna Mosque, which specialized in religious sciences and related topics, Bardo introduced its students to the civilization of the northern Mediterranean region. The school employed modern European pedagogic principles that fostered active and participatory learning, and a Socratic approach to debate and inquiry. Professors at Bardo came from a diversity of backgrounds and nationalities, including Italian, British, French, and Tunisian. European teachers mostly taught the modern curriculum, while more traditional subjects were taught by the likes of Zaitounian Sheikh Mahmud Qabadu (1812–1871). Qabadu, who would influence Tunisia's modern reform movement, taught Arabic language and literature and, with some of his most brilliant students, translated European works and military treatises into Arabic.[2]

Marking a new era of secular education, Bardo was the first school in Tunisia not to be run by religious authorities. The academy predated al-Madrasah al-wataniyyah (The National School)—established in Beirut in 1863 and recognized as the "first independent and religiously unaffiliated school in the Arab world"[3]—by more than two decades. Its students were the first to study modern mathematics, sciences, and engineering, setting them apart as an influential elite whose impact was felt long after Ahmad's military aspirations had faded. The academy led to the formation of a core of Tunisian reformists who would later seek to modernize their country in the spirit of the Enlightenment.

Most of the initial graduates were the sons of mamluks. Bardo also allowed entry to the baldiyya, or merchant class, of Tunis. This, along with the entry of the peasantry into the armed forces, presented a wholly novel proposition that locals would have a say in the future affairs of their country.

But the army modernization project in which Bardo played a crucial role created a substantial financial burden, which weakened Ahmad Bey's resolve. The bey had increased taxes and tariffs on agricultural exports to help pay for his military program, but these measures proved insufficient. Then in 1852, Ahmad Bey suffered his first stroke, and one of his ministers fled to Paris with most of the treasury, crippling the state's finances. This could not have happened at a worse economic time for Tunisia, as the country was reeling from the devastating effects of several years of bad agricultural crops.[4] The nineteenth century witnessed repeated epidemics and crop failures; one-quarter of the Tunisian population had died in 1818 as a result of the plague.[5]

Toward the end of Ahmad Bey's rule, he could no longer afford to maintain his military program, and he disbanded most of his army. But when the Ottoman Empire called on its vassals to send troops to help fight in the Crimean War (1853–1856), in which it was aligned with France and Britain against Russia, Ahmad Bey obliged by sending 10,000 men to the frontline. Despite shortages of funds and men, this was an opportunity to exert Tunisia's autonomy and play a military role in international affairs that the bey felt he could not pass up.[6]

The military exercise turned out to be an unprecedented and unmitigated disaster. Typhoid and cholera took their toll on the allied troops; there were reports that the Tunisians were too weak even to fight and were just left to die from disease. This was a major blow to the bey, who had staked his reputation and personal wealth, having sold his own jewelry, on the expedition. The military program came to an end after the war, and Ahmad Bey's successors allowed the army to disintegrate to such a condition that when Tunisia fell to the French in 1881, it did so without much of a fight.[7] Thus, the lasting legacy of a small Tunisian army, which would help save the day and preserve a democratic transition a century and a half later, was established.

Ahmad Bey's reforms, starting with his army modernization program, took place at a time that the Ottoman Empire was introducing its own reforms from Istanbul. Sultan Mahmud II (r. 1808–1839), the first in a line of nineteenth-century rulers who attempted to reform the waning Ottoman Empire, had introduced some internal reorganization. He disbanded the defunct Janissary corps of loyal guards and soldiers of the sultan—composed primarily of slaves from newly conquered territories—and abolished remaining military fiefs and *waqfs*. Schools were created to train civil servants, doctors, and military officers; an official newspaper was launched; and students were sent to Europe. Primary education was made compulsory, but this was hardly enforced across the empire. Mahmud II also introduced European dress, which was adopted for official purposes. These piecemeal reforms were somewhat superficial, however, and did not address the central ethical and legal problems of the time, including the status of Christian subjects and other minorities within the empire.

Mahmud's sons, Abdulmecid I (r. 1839–1861) and Abdulaziz (r. 1861–1876), extended the reform movement that their father had initiated but with an emphasis on deeper and more substantial social reforms in the empire.

Their reforms became collectively known as *Tanzimat*, and they were heavily influenced by European ideas and pressures from European powers. Internal demands, mostly from the non-Muslim population, also played a role in bringing about the reforms, and *Tanzimat* statesmen soon came to embrace the program as their own, believing it to be necessary in order to resuscitate the deteriorating Ottoman Empire.

Heralding the *Tanzimat* era was the promulgation of the *Gulhane hatti sherif* (Noble Edict of the Rose Chamber) in 1839. The edict kept the status of Islamic law, but made subjects of all religions equally members of the political community. Central and local governments were reorganized, and tax collection was regulated. Military conscription was introduced. Civil, military, and commercial courts were set up, and new penal and commercial codes inspired by the French precedent were drafted. The Imperial Edict, or *Hatti humayun*, introduced in 1856, identified the "happiness" of his subjects as the aim of the sultan. It banned discrimination on the basis of religion, race, or language in matters of taxation, conscription into the army, or entry into government schools or positions.

Tunisia did not immediately implement the *Tanzimat*, but external forces—similar to those experienced by the Ottoman rulers—and internal developments led to the enactment by the Tunisian bey of similar reforms. Although Ahmad Bey's military modernization program was short-lived, the social reforms he introduced were historic and lasting. Tunisia became the most liberal and rights-friendly polity in the Muslim and Arab world over the course of the nineteenth century.

The first significant social reform was the abolishment of slavery. Ahmad Bey banned the trade and the ownership of slaves in a series of three decrees between 1841 and 1846. Tunisia became the first state in the Muslim world to do so, predating by 116 years the abolishment of slavery in Saudi Arabia and Yemen, both of which officially ended slavery in 1962. Mauritania, another Arab country, abolished slavery only in 1981 and criminalized it as late as 2007.

Tunisia had imported black slaves, mostly from Central Africa, and exported the vast majority of them—numbering in the hundreds per annum—to Muslim countries in the Ottoman Empire. By the time of Ahmad Bey's rule, unprecedented traffic in black slaves across the Mediterranean from Tunisian ports triggered pressures for abolitionism from Britain, which had outlawed the Atlantic slave trade in 1807.[8]

On April 30, 1841, Thomas Reade, the British consul in Tunisia, met with Ahmad Bey and implored him to put "some sort of check" on the slave trade. To Reade's surprise, not only was Ahmad Bey receptive to his arguments, but he sent a telegram shortly after Reade left Bardo Palace promising to deliver a "death blow to slavery in this Regency." The bey boasted that he had already freed all the slaves in his possession and had issued orders to ban the export of slaves from Tunisia.[9]

The bey followed up in August with a decree to shut down the slave market and to prohibit the export of slaves from Tunisia. The bey's decree was enthusiastically met with letters of encouragement from the British and Foreign Anti-Slavery Society and from the Institut d'Afrique in Paris, created in 1842 with the mission of "regenerating" Africans after the abolishment of slavery.[10] A year later, Ahmad Bey issued a second decree, proclaiming that anyone born in Tunisia would be free. This time, it was French pressure that precipitated the act. The decree occurred after a family of black slaves—afraid that they were going to be sold separately—sought refuge in the Chapel of Saint Louis in Carthage. The French consul intervened, giving the family asylum in the French consulate and calling upon the bey to free them, which he did.

An anonymous pamphlet from Malta that spread among the ruling elite prompted the third and final decree. The pamphlet was brought to Tunisia in 1845 during a dispute over the execution of a Maltese colon, or European settler. Resting its argument on the Qur'an and Hadith, the pamphlet called for the abolition of slavery. These developments solidified the bey's resolve, and in 1846 Ahmad Bey issued his third decree on the subject of slavery, ordering the immediate release of all black slaves.

The abolition decree had profound repercussions outside the city of Tunis, and particularly in the oases of the south where slave labor in agriculture was common. The exploitation and trade of slaves was a lucrative business for many Tunisians, and its final abolition contributed to an insurgence that shook the country that year. A pragmatic yet resolute politician, Ahmad Bey responded by introducing a measured program of phased abolition in an attempt to alleviate the financial losses experienced by large slave owners.

Ahmad Bey also needed the sanction of his ulama, and once again he put his diplomatic skills to good use. In a most cleverly crafted letter addressed to his Majlis al-Shari'a, or High Religious Council, he explained the reasoning behind his abolition decrees. Ahmad Bey based the crux of his argument on religious grounds: although Islam permitted slavery under certain conditions and obligations of ownership, the ill, and often illegal and unethical, treatment of slaves by their owners put at risk the masters' access to heaven in the afterlife. The bey argued from within Islam, citing the Qur'an and Hadith, and emphasizing freedom as one of the leading principles of the egalitarian religion. The word *maslaha*, public interest of the greater good, was used twice in the bey's letter, and he referred to the Malta pamphlet and to positive European reactions to his first decree. He also explained that he wanted to prevent slaves from seeking refuge in other territories whose populations were not Muslim. The bey's masterful blending of religious, political, and social arguments left the *ulama* with no choice but to concede.[11]

The argument put forth by Ahmad Bey to his *ulama* concerning slavery was not very different from one used by Habib Bourguiba regarding the abolishment of polygamy a century later. The conditions of fair and equal treatment of wives that are set forth in Islam are just as impossible to fulfill or enforce. In Bourguiba's abolishment of polygamy, which he described as anachronistic, he invoked the emancipation of slaves as an example of how social circumstances had necessitated the abandonment of a religiously sanctioned practice. Both Ahmad Bey, in arguing against slavery, and Bourguiba, in his justification of the abolishment of polygamy, relied on justice being a basic tenet of Islam.

The bey's minister and mayor of Tunis, General Husayn Pasha (1802–1887), was a main protagonist in the emancipation tale. Deeply driven by ethical considerations, Husayn Pasha played a key role in advancing the abolition of slavery outside of Tunisia and in helping put Tunisia on the world stage in this respect.

When the United States consul, Amos Perry, wrote to Ahmad Bey in 1863—two years before slavery was abolished in the United States—asking for advice on the benefits of the emancipation of slaves, Husayn Pasha replied on the bey's behalf. In the letter to Amos Perry, Husayn Pasha put forth a political-economic argument that had not been brought forward by the bey: "Countries where full liberty exists and no enslavement is permitted are more prosperous than other countries."[12] The argument was reinforced by his proposition that there were three different types of workers: a very hard worker who works for himself, a paid worker who is not as hard working as the first, and an unpaid worker—slave—who does not work hard or perform at all.[13]

Shedding light on how far advanced Tunisia was with respect to the issue of slavery—followed by France, which abolished slavery in its colonies in 1848—and on Husayn Pasha's own attitude toward the matter is the story of an encounter at the Paris Opera in the spring of 1856. Husayn Pasha was in the company of a black man when an American accosted him, hurling insults at the black man and at Husayn Pasha for his "outrageous" act. Husayn Pasha retorted: "Take it easy my friend, we are in Paris and not in Richmond!"[14]

The pivotal role of abolitionism in placing Ahmad Bey and Tunisia at the forefront of the world stage cannot be overstated. Ahmad Bey won the praise of many around the world and emerged as an "enthusiast and energetic reformer," according to his French military adviser, Phillippe Daumas.[15]

In a multivolume chronicle of Tunisian history of the times, *Ithaf ahl al-zaman bi akhbar muluk Tunis wa 'Ahd al-aman* (Presenting Contemporaries with the History of Rulers of Tunis and the Fundamental Pact), Ahmad Ibn Abi Diyaf (1804–1874), the bey's secretary, spoke of Ahmad Bey as possessing a natural inclination toward a civilization that held freedom as its true core and foundation.

Ahmad Bey's lifestyle set an example that was followed by the urban elite. His court was open to the ideas of the times and included members of the ruling class, *ulama*, and *mamluks*. The *ulama* served as his interlocutors with the High Religious Council, presenting the ideas of modern times and embedding them in an Islamic context.[16] *Mamluks* were well treated in the court of Ahmad Bey, and many reached some of the highest and most influential posts in government and in the military. Purchased at a young age in Ottoman slave markets, *mamluks* received an excellent education, including in Islam and often with the children of the royal family, and their studies culminated in their conversion to Islam. The status of *mamluks* was tied directly to the bey, so they were incredibly loyal and often married the sisters or daughters of beys. Both *ulama* and *mamluks* traveled abroad and were in close contact with foreign consuls, who informed them about the state of affairs in Europe.

Among the most consequential *mamluks* who were members of Ahmad Bey's inner circle were Mustapha Khaznadar (1817–1878) and Khayr al-Din al-Tunisi (circa 1822–1890). Khaznadar served as treasurer and later as prime minister under Ahmad Bey and his successors, becoming arguably the most influential government personality in Tunisia for more than forty years. Khayr al-Din al-Tunisi began his career as a colonel, rising to the position of minister of the navy and later prime minister. An Islamic modernist, Khayr al-Din al-Tunisi introduced economic and administrative reforms to address the country's financial crisis at the time and authored a seminal work on reform and modernization.

Reformists who were cultivated during Ahmad Bey's rule sustained his path after his death. His cousin and successor, Muhammad Bey (r. 1855–1859), did not share Ahmad's appetite for reform initially but ended up succumbing to pressures from foreign powers and the influences of Tunisian reformers. It was during the time of Muhammad Bey, also known as Muhammad II, that the most important social reform since the abolishment of slavery in 1846 took place: 'Ahd al-aman (Security Covenant, or Fundamental Pact), granting civil and religious equality to all subjects—Muslim and non-Muslim, Tunisian and foreign.

Following the example of the Ottoman Tanzimat, 'Ahd al-aman was written in 1857 by Ahmad Ibn Abi Diyaf under orders from Muhammad Bey. It promised reforms in the criminal and commercial codes, the dismantling of state monopolies, and the establishment of a special mixed court for Europeans. A multiplicity of texts was written to support and provide explanations for 'Ahd al-aman. Its issuance was followed by the publication of a textual analysis in 1857 as well as a decree related to the organization of a "Great Ministry," the precursor to a full-fledged government. This was followed by another decree, issued on February 25, 1861, regarding the rights of the sovereign and his subjects, which served as a forerunner to the constitution that would shortly be introduced. The publication of supporting documents as antecedents or successors to a reform, as well as the overall slowness of the process, suggests that the drafters were interested in citizens' understanding and acceptance of the reforms and their implications. It also suggests some resistance to a departure from the old practices of a government based on principles of absolutism.[17]

Until the introduction of 'Ahd al-aman, Islamic law had applied across the land, causing serious conflicts of jurisdiction between the bey and European consuls when Christians took refuge in consulates. The effects of discrimination in matters of criminal justice, property ownership, and employment were felt by *colons*, whose numbers were increasing with rising economic migration from Mediterranean islands.

European Christians living in Tunis had grown from less than 1 percent of the city's 85,000 inhabitants at the dawn of the century to an estimated 12,000 by 1856.[18] Tunisian Jews significantly outnumbered European Christians, and they fell into two categories. The larger community, which numbered around 18,000, lived in self-contained, poorer communities in both rural and urban areas. This community traced its origins to a wave of immigrants from Palestine in the first and second centuries CE. A second, smaller Jewish community, numbering between 1,000 and 2,000, were descendants of refugees from Spain in the sixteenth and seventeenth centuries or Italian economic immigrants who came to Tunisia subsequently.[19] We also know from Jewish oral tradition from the Tunisian island of Djerba that Jews started arriving in Tunisia as exiled Israelites after the Babylonians destroyed the Jerusalem Temple in 568 BCE. Jews also migrated from all areas of the Mediterranean to North Africa—some as traders, others on slave ships.[20]

It was the case of a Tunisian Jew, Batto Sfez, who was executed according to Shari'a on charges of blasphemy, that prompted the introduction of *'Ahd al-aman*. Sfez was implicated in an accident that killed a Muslim child and was subsequently arrested for allegedly making derogatory remarks about Islam in the altercation that followed.

Uncharacteristically liberal for the time with regard to its treatment of minorities, *'Ahd al-aman* was nonetheless a top-down reform, and it was considerably encouraged by outside forces. European powers were interested in increasing their local influence by compelling the introduction of reforms and the granting of equal rights to Jewish and Christian minorities. European encouragement was also motivated by economic interests—namely, opening up the Ottoman market to Western influence. Britain and France vied for dominance, both pushing for favorable economic conditions for their own constituents. The rivalry was often played out between the two countries' respective consuls, the British Richard Wood, who served from 1855 until 1875, and the French Léon Roches, who was stationed in Tunis between 1855 and 1863 and whose skills in the Arabic language earned him the nickname Sheikh Omar.

Britain initially prevailed, primarily because of a cozy relationship between Wood and Mustafa Khaznadar. An example of the preferential treatment that the British received and of the corruption involved is the Anglo-Tunisian Bank, set up in 1857 to promote British investment in Tunisia. Subsequent to his facilitation of its establishment, Khaznadar was made an officer of the bank—despite his position in government. Following objections from the French, the Tunisian government later broke its links with the bank, which led to the introduction of Tunisia into the international monetary system.

Khaznadar also pushed for the Anglo-Tunisian Convention of 1863, which granted British subjects living in Tunisia the same status as Tunisians in matters of commerce, justice, and the law. Khaznadar awarded many lucrative concessions to the British, hoping to steer support away from his rival Khayr al-Din al-Tunisi. But the bey eventually dismissed Khaznadar in 1873, under pressure from the Italians and the French, and replaced him with none other than Khayr al-Din.

The French proposed a financial partnership in 1858, but Muhammad Bey summarily rebuffed their advances. Five years later, however, failed government initiatives—some pushed by Roches himself—left the Tunisian government in desperate need of an international loan. The terms of the loan that was then negotiated with a Parisian bank ended up driving the country toward financial ruin.[21]

Tunisia also owed its trade imbalance to the Europeans. The country was dependent on foreign—mostly European—imports, which had doubled between 1816 and 1829, while exports had increased by only 45 percent.[22] The bey's concessions—or rather, capitulations—to European powers had given rise to the importation of European cotton, leather, and silk, causing Tunisian industry to suffer and triggering the gradual disappearance of the Tunisian artisan trade.[23] Although Tunisians found foreign markets for their agricultural products, such as wheat and olive oil, this resulted in the inflation of prices for basic foodstuffs in local markets, prompting demonstrations that took place in the souk of Tunis in 1861. The abolition of slavery two decades earlier had disrupted the caravan trade with West Africa, and this weighed considerably on the treasury, for which such trade had been an important source of revenue.

By the time of Muhammad Bey's death in 1859 and the ascension to the throne of his brother, Muhammad III al-Sadik (1813–1882), known to the French as Sadok Bey, the state was in economic disarray. Excessive borrowing, royal extravagance, badly planned projects, and bureaucratic corruption had contributed to a worsening financial situation that led to gigantic debts to foreign creditors and a devaluation of the currency.

Sadok Bey completed the reforms started by his predecessors and accepted them willingly, thinking that they would give Tunisia greater autonomy vis-à-vis the Ottoman Empire. He also introduced, early on, a number of reforms on the educational and press fronts. These included the publication of *al-Ra'ed al-tunisi* (The Tunisian Pioneer), the first Tunisian newspaper, in 1860, as well as the creation of the first official printing works.

But perhaps no nineteenth-century Tunisian innovation was as significant as Sadok Bey's issuance of a constitution. The adoption of the constitution, the first in an Arab or Muslim country, took place at the Bardo Palace on April 26, 1861. *Qanun al-dawla al-tunisiya* (Law of the Tunisian State) was read aloud at its proclamation by Khayr al-Din al-Tunisi.[24]

The constitution established a political power that was separate from religion and, by so doing, set an important precedent for all Tunisian constitutions since then. Islam was barely mentioned in the text, except to emphasize that constitutional tenets were not in violation of those of the religion. The constitution did not even explicitly state that the ruler had to be Muslim.[25]

The constitution's thirteen sections established various institutions, including a Great Council, a constitutional court, and a court of appeal. With Khayr al-Din as its president, the Great Council was tasked with ensuring the application of *'Ahd al-aman*, the constitution, and the newly created institutions.[26] The council was made up primarily of foreigners, but one-third of its sixty members were government officials appointed by the bey, Ahmad Ibn Abi Diyaf among them. The bey's ministers were made to be constitutionally responsible to the Great Council.[27]

The *ulama* did not support the constitution and were wary of European influence in general—perhaps for good reason, given the limits such influence placed on Tunisia's financial and political autonomy. The *ulama* agreed with the principle of affording non-Muslim subjects their security but opposed the notion of equality in tax and legal matters between Muslim and non-Muslim subjects, as *'Ahd al-aman* dictated. Some went so far as to advise the bey to avoid interacting with Europe altogether. For the most part, though, they did not oppose Europeans' instigating and carrying out projects that were infrastructural, like the building of a major aqueduct, or technical, such as setting up a telegraph system.[28]

The rejection by the *ulama* of the 1861 constitution was manifest inasmuch as they refused to partake in drafting it or to sit in the newly created courts. There were some exceptions, and a few *ulama* played influential roles in the reformism project. Some eventually agreed to participate in institutions created by the constitution, including the Great Council, the penal court, and the court of appeals. That Ahmad Ibn Abi Diyaf, who wrote *'Ahd al-aman* but was reluctant to apply its principles, went on to write the constitution in 1861 and was an ardent partisan of Khayr al-Din's reforms underscores the notion that modernist political reformism could not be dissociated from Islamic reformism. They interacted with one another—albeit often ambivalently.

The political reform period ended abruptly when an insurgency erupted in 1864 in the aftermath of the government's doubling the *majba*, or personal tax, to pay off its debts. Inflated prices in local markets because of increased exports, mostly bound for Europe, added fuel to the fire. The revolt was led by Ali Ben Ghedhahem, a tribal leader from the interior province of Kasserine, and quickly spread to all regions of Tunisia. It was brutally suppressed by Sadok Bey; however, he did subsequently annul all increases in taxation. In some respects, the revolt—one and a half centuries ahead of the Gafsa riots of 2008 and the uprisings in December 2010 and January 2011—underscores that the problems associated with the marginalization of the poorer interior and south of the country are an old story for Tunisia.

The French under Napoleon III blamed the new constitution for the insurgency and tried to pressure the bey into revoking it. They also tried to get the bey to fire some of his ministers and members of his close circle, including Mustafa Khaznadar, Khayr al-Din al-Tunisi, and Ahmad Ibn Abi Diyaf. Although Sadok Bey had shown Napoleon III a draft of the constitution before announcing it and had obtained his approval, France was now anxious lest the insurgency be used as an excuse by rival foreign powers, chiefly Britain, to intervene, thus threatening its own dominance.[29]

France, arguably, also did not want Tunisia to be reformed from within, thinking it easier for French diplomacy to deal with only one interlocutor: a bey with absolute power. The commitments of the *'Ahd al-aman* as they related to the rights of foreigners were now sufficient for France. And so on May 1, 1864, Sadok Bey notified the institutions that he had created through the constitution that he was suspending their activities.[30]

Although the suspension of the courts, the tribunals, and the Great Council was a major step back to the status quo ante, the constitution did make a durable impact on reformist thinking in Tunisia.

Khayr al-Din al-Tunisi had foreseen the events that were about to unfold when he resigned from the ministry of the navy and from presiding over the Great Council in 1862, keeping his distance from the constitution's repeal.[31] Khayr al-Din's resignation also followed a dispute with Khaznadar over further borrowing from abroad. He spent the next seven years living in Europe, leading several diplomatic missions of the bey between 1863 and 1867. These were otherwise years of relative inactivity that allowed him the space to think in depth about necessary reforms in Tunisia and across the Muslim world.

Khayr al-Din was accustomed to moving across different lands. He was born in the Caucasus and, like many of his countrymen, taken as a *mamluk* to Istanbul in his youth to seek a military or political career. He was then brought into the service of Ahmad Bey in Tunis and given a modern and religious education. Khayr al-Din learned French and Arabic, and he quickly rose through the ranks.

While in self-imposed exile, Khayr al-Din published in 1867 a seminal work that would forever establish his legacy as a great reformer. In *Aqwam al-masalik fi ma'rifat ahwal al-mamalik* (The Surest Path to Knowledge Regarding the Condition of Countries), he argued for stability in political institutions and for the rule of law as requisites for the power and prosperity of nations. *Aqwam al-masalik* was preceded by the publication of an introductory essay on necessary reforms in Muslim states. The essay and *Aqwam al-masalik* were based on a series of studies of countries that Khayr al-Din had visited—both Muslim and European.

Khayr al-Din contended that a ruler's power had to be checked either by revealed or natural law or in consultation with the *ulama* and notables—so-called "men of affairs."[32] He also called for an advisory system against the excesses of a regime based on absolute power. Khayr al-Din supported the notion of a constitutional monarchy. Although he did not discuss universal suffrage, Khayr al-Din argued for equality before the law, the regulation of public finances, and peaceful coexistence among different sectors of society.

Khayr al-Din proclaimed that Islam did not contradict the values of freedom, justice, and the primacy of law and that Shari'a was not opposed to Tunisian reforms or Ottoman *Tanzimat*. *Aqwam al-masalik* appealed to men of religion and tried to convince them that not everything Western was corrupt and that Muslims had much to learn from the Europeans regarding modern subjects that would lead to the betterment of their lives and to proper governance. Khayr al-Din used the argument that scientific knowledge had been initiated by the Muslims centuries before and that it was now time for Muslims to benefit from the advancements made to what were originally their contributions to civilization.[33] Khayr al-Din understood the importance of consulting with the *ulama* in order to gain their support for his reform program and that excluding them over the constitution had been a mistake.[34]

At the end of his foreign sojourns, when Khayr al-Din returned to Tunis in 1869, he rejoined the government as head of the International Finance Commission (IFC). Established in 1869, the IFC included France, England, and Italy; it was designed to regulate public finances and, above all, to reimburse the Tunisian debt amounting to 160 million gold francs. Because of the steady decline of Tunisia's financial situation, the IFC became a sort of supranational government for foreign powers to protect their own interests.[35]

Then in 1870, Khayr al-Din was appointed executive minister, and in 1873, he became prime minister. With Khayr al-Din by his side, Sadok Bey introduced new government policies based on *Aqwam al-masalik* that he pursued over the ensuing four years. Khayr al-Din also worked to alleviate the tax burden on farmers in the different regions and to encourage the agricultural sector. But his administrative and economic reforms in this respect were limited, as was their impact.

Hard as he tried to introduce a constitutional monarchy system of government, Khayr al-Din did not succeed—largely because of opposition by the bey and his close circle. He was widely criticized for failing to bring back constitutional laws, but in his view, Tunisia was not ready for them. In a memorandum addressed to his critics, Khayr al-Din stated that constitutional laws could only have meaning if the ruler were willing to respect them and if the people truly understood them—rendering the constitution otherwise a "word without meaning."[36]

What Khayr al-Din was unable to achieve on the constitutional front, however, he made up for on the educational dimension. Under him, the state increasingly took control of educational institutions and proceeded to "modernize" their teachings on the example of Europe, whose material success, he believed, rested on education. Khayr al-Din saw reforming the education system in Tunisia as crucial to the country's economic recovery and as a counterweight to foreign interference. In his *Aqwam al-masalik*, Khayr al-Din posited education and knowledge as the main bases for the advancement of civilization. In his introductory essay to *Aqwam al-masalik*, he argued for broadening the scope of science and knowledge, as well as establishing good governance and effective administration, toward a gradual improvement in each field.

At first, Khayr al-Din set out to reform teaching at Zaitouna Mosque. The reform that he attempted in 1874 maintained religious education but added a multiplicity of other subjects, including literature, history, logic, arithmetic, geometry, and astronomy. He further organized the education system at Zaitouna into three cycles: primary, secondary, and higher education. These measures were aimed at reforming, not revolutionizing, Zaitouna, and were meant to diversify and better structure its education. Khayr al-Din was frustrated, however, by the limits of his attempts at modernizing an institution that was governed by the *ulama* and was set in its ways.

His inability to reform Zaitouna led Khayr al-Din to create a new secular institution in Tunis: Sadiqi College, named after Sadok Bey and created by decree on January 13, 1875. The curriculum preserved an Arab Islamic culture and helped establish a gateway system between Sadiqi and Zaitouna for students anxious to continue their education at the mosque. Sadiqi was organized into three sections: legal studies, religious education, and rational sciences, or *al-'ulum al-'aqliyya*. This last field represented a major innovation in that it introduced foreign languages and exact sciences into the curriculum. In doing so, the curriculum responded to two yearnings of nineteenth-century Tunisian reformists: opening the country to the rest of the world—especially Europe—and equipping students with new knowledge that was necessary for the country's development. Instruction was in French, Italian, and Arabic, and subjects such as mathematics, arithmetic, geometry, and technology—deemed essential to good administration—were taught.[37]

Students at Sadiqi were recruited on the basis of merit, as opposed to otherwise prevailing traditions of enrollment through cooptation and nepotism. Sadiqi attracted students from all backgrounds and was noted for its religious diversity; Tunisian Jews constituted as much as a third of the student body in the 1950s.[38] All students received a free education, room and board, and school supplies, and enjoyed privileges that were simply unavailable to counterparts at other Tunisian educational institutions. This egalitarianism extended geographically in that students were intensively recruited from every region of the country. A sense of national belonging was cultivated through relations that were forged among students who were otherwise socioeconomically and provincially diverse.

The college quickly became the most prestigious learning institution in the country, and over time it educated generations of Tunisia's modernist elite. Sadiqi, along with Bardo Military Academy before it, produced Western-influenced, secular-minded, nationalist ideologies that competed with the narrower Islamic teachings of Zaitouna. The founding of Bardo had set a precedent of ensuring the emergence of a new elite with fresh values who were to confront the traditional governing elite. Both Bardo and Sadiqi prompted the process of change and the restructuring of the state apparatus, giving rise to an indigenous elite who would challenge the status quo.

In the first three decades after independence from the French in 1956, 124 out of 137 government ministers were Sadiqi graduates, and it is estimated that roughly two-thirds of the Tunisian political elite between 1955 and 1969 had been educated at the college.[39] This is not surprising given that Habib Bourguiba, who had studied at Sadiqi himself, was attracted to the secularism and positivism that permeated the college's teachings and found among its graduates suitable recruits for his nationalist agenda.

Sadiqi became Khayr al-Din's enduring legacy. With his removal from power in 1877, the last hope for further reform that would strengthen Tunisia in fending off European powers faded. Enemies, both domestic and foreign, conspired against Khayr al-Din and convinced Sadok Bey to remove him, prompting him to retire to Istanbul, where he would serve as grand vizier under Sultan Abdulhamid II (r. 1876–1909) from 1878 to 1879.

Foreign intrigue in Tunisia throughout the 1870s made European encroachment virtually preordained. Sadok Bey had become increasingly unpopular with his people following his ruthless suppression of the 1864 insurgency, and he was seen as acquiescing to European powers.

Sadok Bey's long and difficult reign ended with the French invasion—ostensibly to protect Tunisia from an Algerian tribal assault. The signing of the Treaty of Bardo in 1881 established Tunisia as a French protectorate, stripping the bey of most of his powers and subordinating him to a French resident-general. Sadok Bey died less than a year after signing the treaty, and Ali III Bey (1817–1902) succeeded his older brother.

Under the Bardo Treaty, all official acts required approval by the French hierarchy, and although traditional administrations remained under the control of Tunisians, Tunisian government ministers had French directors as counterparts and new administrations were assigned to the French. The French redrew boundaries of administrative districts to form divisions based on geography rather than tribal populations, thus curbing the influence of tribal leaders, who were now supervised by French *contrôleurs civils*. This would have a decisive effect in helping Bourguiba—before and after independence—build a strong national identity that was not compromised by tribal affiliations.

At an 1883 convention at La Marsa, France guaranteed the repayment of Tunisian debt, which by then amounted to eleven times the government's annual income, and dissolved the International Finance Commission, which it saw as a symbol of British influence.[40]

By that time, reformism had introduced progressive innovations— abolition, *'Ahd al-aman*, and the 1861 constitution—and put in place secular-leaning educational institutions that would play an influential role in spawning further reform and producing political, intellectual, and social leaders. The era marked the beginning of a reform movement in Tunisia that would go on for much longer and would have a critical part in shaping the country's modern development and its nationalist path. The fundamental, pioneering reforms of the middle nineteenth century proved transformative and sturdy enough to set the stage for modern Tunisia as the special case that it is today.

Although exogenously influenced, nineteenth-century reforms would not have been possible had it not been for the committed and visionary leadership of Husaynid beys and the intellectual courage of important collaborators, most notably Khayr al-Din al-Tunisi and Ahmad Ibn Abi Diyaf. Al-Tunisi and Ibn Abi Diyaf were among Tunisia's first secularist thinkers, having sought to identify Shari'a as an entity separate from religion and reconcilable with Western law and politics.

The advent of reformism in Tunisia was nonetheless intrinsically linked to Western domination and European powers' imperialistic interests—their struggles for control and their cultural and ideological influences in the region. Reformism was not, however, always aligned with Western liberal thought: there was no mention of democratic practices either in the Fundamental Pact or in the 1861 constitution. Europeans pushed for reform as long as it suited their needs and protected their interests but did not threaten their hegemonic designs.

But in the end, it was this reformism that principally explains Tunisia's trajectory and prospects relative to the rest of the Arab world. In her article *Le réformisme, grand récit politique de la Tunisie contemporaine*, political analyst Béatrice Hibou describes the phraseology of reformism as "opening up to the West without renouncing the Islamic religion or culture; it is based on the primacy of the law and the constitution; it gives priority to order and stability, and to moderation and the fair middle; it is the expression of a rational political practice; it embodies modernity and integrity."[41] The reformism that started in Tunisia in the middle of the nineteenth century continued cumulatively into the twentieth century and provided the foundation for Habib Bourguiba's building of a modern nation.

9

The Age of Modern Reform

rabs lament the passing of the golden age of Islam, when it spread all the way to China in the east and modern-day Morocco to the west; established glorious dynasties in Damascus, Baghdad, and Andalucía; and produced great scholarship and lasting contributions to the arts, letters, and sciences—some of it, it must be noted, at the hands of Muslim non-Arabs, including Persians and others from farther east, and non-Muslims. They mourn the decay of Islamic civilization that culminated in destruction at the hands of Mongol invaders in the thirteenth century. They live in the dreamy past of such glories that are the subjects of Arab folklore, rhetoric, and school curricula. They have blamed the Turks, and then the West and Israel, for their failures to reinvent themselves and to awaken from their cavernous stagnation.

There were, however, episodic attempts at an Arab renaissance of intellectual thought, the most significant of which began in the nineteenth century and continued into the first decades of the twentieth. *Al-Nahda*, as the movement that emerged in Cairo and Beirut came to be known, was an extraordinary intellectual development defined by Islamic modernism and aimed at reviving Islamic thought through the reinterpretation of sacred texts. Notable scholars rebelled against Islamic orthodoxy in search of an ideological response to growing Western influences. But this revival was ultimately short-lived—hijacked, interrupted, and stampeded by forces from within and without that saw to it that there would be a closing of the minds and an unthinking surrender to dogma, religious and otherwise.

Al-Nahda paralleled the reform movement that started in Tunisia around the middle of the nineteenth century. Its scholars interacted with their Tunisian contemporaries, both movements benefiting from each other. But while Nahda intellectuals concerned themselves primarily with Islamic reform, the efforts of Tunisians were far more expansive and delved into social, constitutional, and secular education domains.

Tunisia's also was not a renaissance per se, as there was no sleep to wake up from. Tunisia did not suffer the destruction of its civilization that much of the rest of the Arab Muslim world experienced at the hands of the Mongols, and it remained autonomous under Ottoman rule. Tunisia's geographic distance and enlightened trajectory in the realm of Islam helped protect it from later Islamist currents that took hold further east, Wahhabism and the Muslim Brotherhood chief among them.

Al-Nahda failed to produce similar outcomes at home or have as lasting an impact as Tunisia's modern reform. Militarism, failed political ideologies, and the rise of Islamism got in the way, with some Nahda intellectuals actually changing course and helping breathe life into extremist ideologies.

Tunisia's modern reform movement continued well into the twentieth century; it evolved and grew, leading to a nationalist movement that succeeded and in an education system that has helped define the country's uniqueness. It was during the late nineteenth century that the seeds of Bourguiba's reforms, and of Tunisia's trajectory that facilitated its transition to democracy, were securely planted.

By the time Tunisia came under French rule in 1881, Western powers were taking over everywhere in the Arab world, in some places allowing for a semblance of a symbolic and ineffectual Ottoman presence—as in the case of Tunisia, where the Husaynid bey was left with no authority to speak of. By the dawn of the twentieth century, the British had exerted their control over Egypt, Sudan, and the southern coast of the Arabian Peninsula. Egypt's bankruptcy, the result of enormous debt caused by the modernization projects of Isma'il Pasha (r. 1863–1879)—most notably the Suez Canal—and high interest rates imposed by European banks, led to British conquest in 1882. Elsewhere in North Africa, the Italians invaded Libya in 1911, and the French—already entrenched in Algeria—conquered

Morocco in 1912, but allowed for the carving out of a coastal protectorate for Spain. No realm seemed safe from European intervention, and every political issue required taking into account European interests.

An Ottoman Empire whose influence in its provinces was waning, and European powers whose hegemony in these same territories was growing, provided a pretext and a context for a number of like-minded Muslim scholars who questioned classical concepts of jurisprudence and searched for new methods of Islamic theology and Qur'anic exegesis. They challenged the dominant reliance on the four principal sources that informed matters of Islamic jurisprudence, societal norms, and governance: the text of the Qur'an, Hadith, *ijma'* (consensus of theologians), and *qiyas* (juristic reasoning).

Scholars argued for the adaptation of Shari'a to the times, and they called for the reopening of the gates of *ijtihad*, the principle of independent reasoning that reformists relied upon and which, it was thought, had been shut since the tenth century. The primary question posed by reforming intellectuals concerned the validity of knowledge derived from sources outside of Islam, such as modern science, philosophy, and methods of government. They thought hard about the direction that reform ought to take and sought to identify and articulate factors that defined a successful society. Heavily influenced by Western thought and what the West defined as "modern" and "civilized," they questioned whether Shari'a was compatible with Western practices that they argued were important for Muslims to adopt in order to evolve as a society. These reformers did not seek to replace Arab or Islamic thought. They instead labored to produce new Islamic interpretations that were not dissociated from past thinking. They placed greater emphasis on modern Western technical innovation than on European thought per se.

Almost all of the modernist reform movements focused on education—some calling for a reconciliation of antagonistic interpretations of Islam with the Western world, while others advocated a puritanical approach that was less than enthusiastic about embracing modern ideas that had originated in the West. Some were predominantly political in their orientations, but most were primarily intellectual movements with some overtones of political thought permeating them.

Among the very first modern Islamic thinkers who stressed the value of Western sciences was the Egyptian Rifa'a Badawi Rafi' al-Tahtawi

(1801–1873). Al-Tahtawi led the way in calling for a reform of Islam and Muslim society and in developing nationalist ideals among Egyptians. He argued that Islamic laws did not differ from the natural laws adopted by European countries and that Shari'a could be adapted through the practice of *ijtihad*.

Like many of his contemporaries and successors, al-Tahtawi was trained according to prevalent traditional schooling methods, having studied and then become an imam at al-Azhar in Cairo. But al-Tahtawi left al-Azhar to pursue his studies in Paris, where he learned French, ancient history, and classical Greek philosophy. He became versed in the ideas of the French Enlightenment, studying the works of Voltaire, Condillac, Rousseau, and Montesquieu. Al-Tahtawi later wrote a narrative of his time in Paris—*Takhlis al-ibriz ila talkhis Bariz*—in which he noted the Europeans' education systems, intellectual curiosity, social morality, and work ethic.

Al-Tahtawi's mix of a traditional religious education and a modern European one influenced his advocacy of a balanced approach in education that combined both pedagogies. He did not rebel against either, but rather fused the impacts of each into the views and philosophies that he would develop. Drawing the sharpest distinction between French and Egyptian society on the basis of their systems of education, he argued that Western education was more advanced because of its emphasis on the sciences.[1]

Al-Tahtawi was quite selective, however, about which aspects of French culture he thought should be admired. He considered it bizarre that European women were able to compete with men and described them as lacking in morality: "They are like men in all that they do. You may even find among them young women who have an affair with a stranger without being married."[2] Al-Tahtawi deemed it a good thing that he did not encounter in France love relations between men, telling in that the practice was common enough at home for him to have made note of its absence in Europe. In *Takhlis al-ibriz ila talkhis Bariz*, al-Tahtawi commends the French language for its "refusal" of the declaration of male-male love, arguing that the French would find "abhorrent speech" in this regard in Arabic books.[3]

Influenced by Montesquieu's *amour de la patrie*, al-Tahtawi spread his conception of *hub al-watan*, or love of the motherland, similar to Ibn Khaldūn's idea of *'assabiya*—the solidarity that binds together members of the same community. Al-Tahtawi believed in the Egyptian—as opposed to Muslim—*umma*, or community, as deserving of its own historic consideration. He did not dwell on the past accomplishments of an Islamic civilization, but praised the golden age of ancient Egypt and believed that education ought to instill nationalistic values.[4] Al-Tahtawi's statements on the Egyptian *watan*, or motherland, are considered to be the first expression of nationalism in the Arab world. Unlike Khayr al-Din al-Tunisi, who also insisted on learning from the Europeans but addressed the entire Muslim *umma* in his rhetoric, patriotism for al-Tahtawi was an Egyptian notion that was inclusive of Jews and Christians, setting the tone for some later Egyptian thinkers.

Divergent attitudes toward nationalism underscored distinctions in terms of how modernist reformers at the time defined the scope of their communities—a precursor for what was to later emerge as national versus pan-Islamic or pan-Arab identities.

A contemporary of Khayr al-Din and al-Tahtawi, Butrus al-Bustani (1819–1883) was born to an aristocratic Christian Maronite family from Mount Lebanon, but he later converted to Protestantism. Al-Bustani shared with al-Tahtawi a nationalistic orientation and wrote about territorial patriotism. He appealed to his Arab Muslim compatriots on the basis of their shared monotheism and similarities between Christianity and Islam, and advocated for a separation between a secular state and the religious sphere. A consequential scholar in the Arabic language, al-Bustani advocated modern European-style education and strived to use the Arabic language to convey complex modern concepts, calling for the acceptance or rejection of European ideas based on their individual merit.[5] Butrus al-Bustani believed that education was key to the development of secular nationalism. The pioneering school that he established in 1863, *al-Madrasah al-wataniyyah*, accepted boys of all faith backgrounds and socioeconomic strata.[6]

The Maronite community to which al-Bustani's family belonged benefited from strong ties with the West, especially with Paris and Rome. Its members were well educated, establishing schools and producing an active clergy. Maronites, Roman Catholics who had retreated to Mount Lebanon following persecution in the seventh century, exercised autonomous control under the Ottomans over Mount Lebanon, starting in 1861. Somewhat insulated—but at once fraternal with the West and nestled in an Arab milieu—Maronites, as well as their Eastern Orthodox brethren who comprise a sizable minority in modern-day Lebanon, contributed to Arab intellectual advancement during *al-Nahda*, some postulating that the future of the community lay within an Arab identity.

But it was naturally Muslim scholars who led the Islamic modernism movement, which took off amid growing feelings among Muslims of a great European imposition that threatened their *umma*.

The most enduring and far-reaching impact was of those, like al-Tahtawi, who labored both to revive the religion and to reconcile it with positive modern influences. Jamal al-Din al-Afghani (1839–1897) played a pioneering role in this domain. He argued that Muslim society was in need of a reformation—just as Christianity had undergone its own. Al-Afghani believed that salvation of the *umma* lay in its adoption of Islam as a civilization rather than just a religion. He spoke of the principles of Islam as essentially the same as those of modern rationalism or natural law, comprising a perfect religion the interpretations and adoption of which into a civilization were in need of amelioration. Like al-Tahtawi, al-Afghani placed heavy emphasis on the use of *ijtihad* to bring Islam and Muslim society into the modern world.[7]

Al-Afghani called on Muslims to unite in the face of a Western threat that was more advanced—scientifically and intellectually—by adopting the very best of what the West had to offer. Al-Afghani postulated not only that Islam and science were compatible but that Islam was indeed the "friendliest" religion toward science—a fact that Muslims had forgotten, unable to recognize their own historic contributions to European science.[8] His origins disputed—many believing that he was born a Persian Shi'ite, despite his claim to having been born in Afghanistan—al-Afghani lived in Cairo, Constantinople, Paris, Iran, and India, where he learned European sciences and mathematics. Like Khayr al-Din al-Tunisi, al-Afghani was more politically inclined than his peers and wary of absolute rulers. He believed that power should be constitutionally checked—an attitude that caused him to often face exile.

On his return to Cairo in 1871 from one of his expatriations, Jamal al-Din al-Afghani made the acquaintance of a young man, Muhammad Abduh, who would become one of his most devoted students. Abduh and al-Afghani worked together on an influential and modernist periodical, *al-'Urwa al-wuthqa* (The Indivisible Link), which provided analyses of European intervention. The two collaborators became known for their development of a purist doctrine that called for the reaffirmation of Islam's rational tenets, which grew to be a sub-trend within *al-Nahda* known as *Salafiyya*.

Like al-Tahtawi and al-Afghani, Abduh encouraged the practice of *ijti-had*. He asserted rational aspects of Islam and called for liberation from what he considered to be structural rigidities that restricted Islam's evolution. In presenting a new, pluralistic view of studying Shari'a, Abduh blended elements from the four Sunni jurisprudence schools and picked what he deemed most suitable for the times, enacting the practice of *talfiq*, or piecing together. His open-minded and flexible approach that combined the best interpretations of sacred text, irrespective of their authors, was a truly extraordinary and innovative feat. But he was widely criticized for this, many believing that his indulgences were perilous. Wary of those who were suspicious of his theories and teachings, Abduh often met with his students at his home, away from the watchful eyes of his detractors. Exiled to Beirut for his involvement in the Egyptian nationalist movement, it was there that Abduh delivered lectures on theology that would later comprise his most famous book, *Risalat al-tawhid* (Treatise on Unification).

Abduh was concerned with how to deal with modern problems that had not existed at the time of the Prophet, and—like al-Afghani—he made the controversial claim that Islamic principles could be easily reconciled with modern ideas. He argued, for example, that *shura* is basically a form of European parliament, and he tried to convince secularists and Europeans of the compatibility of Islam with modern life, reason, and science. Abduh, who was profoundly Egyptian, believed that the best form of government was an Islamic state in which non-Muslims would be equal to their Muslim counterparts, and he quarreled publicly with the Syrian Christian journalist and novelist Farah Antun (1874–1922) over the latter's advocacy for a secular state.

Muhammad Abduh argued vociferously for modernizing education through the learning of modern European sciences. He believed that only through education could the Islamic world be restored from its decay and that even if external intervention or autocratic rule was needed to carry out an education reform, Egypt could not aspire to be a modern nation or to have a modern form of government until such reform took place.[9]

Considered the father of Islamic modernism, Abduh extended his reach far beyond Egypt and well into Tunisia, influencing its modern intellectual and education movements far more than any other non-Tunisian before or after him. Young and educated Tunisians both contributed to and benefited from the teachings of Muhammad Abduh, who twice visited Tunisia—in 1884 and again in 1903. Abduh was invited on both occasions by reformist Zaitouna *ulama*, his ideas having reached them through his journal, *al-'Urwa al-wuthqa*.[10]

On his first visit to Tunis, Abduh attended classes at Zaitouna and met with famous *ulama* who contributed to the foundation of his modernist doctrine. The Zaitouna liberal reformist Sheikh Muhammad al-Sanusi (1851–1900)—an academic, writer, judge, and poet—had been influenced by Egyptian thinkers and had spent time in Cairo in 1882 and 1883 before returning to Tunis and founding the first *Salafiyya* group in Tunisia.[11] Al-Sanusi, who hosted Abduh on his first visit, had been a close collaborator with Khayr al-Din and was also a follower of the celebrated poet and Bardo instructor of Arabic Sheikh Mahmud Qabadu.[12]

During his visit in 1884, Abduh recognized the entrenchment of the French in Tunisia and advised that Tunisians work within the protectorate system for reforms that reflected Muslim values of equity and justice, as he had done with the British in Egypt.[13] Abduh did not share al-Afghani's antagonism toward authority; he worked within the system to successfully advance his ideas. His advice in this regard would prove invaluable to Tunisian reform efforts.

Abduh's ideas found a home among a group of young Tunisian reforming elites who were members of al-Sanusi's *Salafiyya* group.[14] These intellectual, reformist elites were a product of the Tunisian educational innovations of the nineteenth century, many of them having studied at Sadiqi, Bardo, and Zaitouna, with some having traveled to pursue further education in Europe, primarily in France.

The Tunisian intellectual class assiduously read Egyptian journals, including the newspaper *al-Manar*, which was founded in 1897 by Abduh's disciple, Muhammad Rashid Rida.[15] The Egyptian journals *al-Hilal* and *al-Dhiya*, which provided access to the social sciences and literature, penetrated the elite circles in Tunisia, while *al-Muqtataf*, published in Lebanon, inspired Tunisian writers and journalists in the field of scientific research.[16]

Inspired by counterparts in Egypt and Lebanon, Tunisian reformers began to opine in their own newspapers. In 1888, Muhammad al-Sanusi and colleagues founded the weekly newspaper *al-Hadira*, the first private Arabic newspaper in Tunisia, which devoted a considerable portion of its coverage to education. *Al-Hadira* targeted the *baldiyya* and the *ulama*, calling for modernity and social reform that upheld Muslim values and culture. Elites used *al-Hadira* as a platform for presenting their opinions on the country's social, intellectual, and moral life. Even though it was supported by some protectorate officials, including the resident-general René Millet—whose encouragement of indigenous reform eventually led to his removal from office in 1900—the paper came under pressure from the French colonial administration to change its editorial line and focus on positive aspects of the protectorate.[17]

Young Tunisian reformers came to be known as *Jeunes Tunisiens* by the French settler lobby *Prépondérants*, as a term of derision, equating them with the nationalist Young Turks or the Young Ottomans before them.[18] The *Jeunes Tunisiens* initially cooperated with liberal French officials and supported the French presence, believing that it would facilitate Tunisia's entrance into the modern world and enhance Tunisia's economic productivity. But incipient demands for economic and political rights eventually set in, and they turned against the French and formed a political party in 1907.

The *Jeunes Tunisiens* led education reform and were responsible for the early stages of a cultural revitalization movement in Tunisia. Insisting on French education, the *Jeunes Tunisiens* argued on economic grounds that a modern French curriculum was better suited for teaching the sciences of the time. They believed that their calls for the adaptation of Western sciences and the use of European languages did not conflict with their commensurate emphasis on the Arabic language as instrumental to accessing the Qur'an. They themselves had a mastery of French methods and thought and understood that through education, Tunisians could achieve greater autonomy in the protectorate.[19]

Reformers were assisted at times by French officials who believed that Western education could sway the populace in favor of the protectorate. But there was also a discouraging attitude by some French toward Tunisian education, as captured in a statement by a high official in the early days of the protectorate: "Let us not seek to make pseudo-Europeans of them. . . . Let us recall that fifty years of living with us have glided over the Algerians without modifying them."[20] This sort of derogation captured the generally low esteem in which the French regarded their colonized subjects. Ironically, it was Tunisians' emphatic attention to educating themselves that ultimately brought them their liberation from the chains of French rule. Education was their most potent weapon, and they wielded it with great effect to achieve their independence and, decades later, their democracy.

French educational reforms were ultimately driven by necessity. An explosive growth in the number of Europeans, mostly Italian, living in Tunisia required the establishment of schools for the children of *colons*. The *colon* population grew from 12,000 in 1881 to 77,000 in 1895 and to 129,000—or 6.4 percent of the total population—by 1905.[21]

By this time, the French administration's adoption of education as a priority and a responsibility was taking center stage. This resulted from the gradual evolution among the French of the notion of a modern state and the acknowledgment that the populace should get something in return for government taxes, which had until then been seen as merely for the benefit of the state.[22]

Schools and universities became the battleground for reform, with the fiercest confrontations taking place at Zaitouna between conservative and reforming scholars. This polarization manifested itself during Muhammad Abduh's second visit to Tunis, when many among the *ulama* opposed his ideas vehemently while reformists hailed him as the "grand master of Islamic reformism."[23]

Elementary, or primary, education under the local Husaynid dynasty of the Ottoman Empire was exclusively religious and in dire need of reform, as was the case in much of the Arab world at the time. At the start of the protectorate in 1881, there were more than 1,000 Qur'anic madrassas—also known as *kuttab* schools—and many of them were affiliated with Zaitouna. The primary occupation of masters at these schools was to produce students who had memorized the Qur'an, with only a handful going on to study at Zaitouna.[24] This constituted the only form of school education available, except for schools for European children run by Christian religious orders and Jewish institutions that were similar to *kuttab* schools.

Neither Muslim nor Jewish girls went to school until Louise Millet, wife of the resident-general René Millet, pushed for the establishment of a private elementary school for Muslim girls—*École rue du Pacha*, as it was later named. Eight years later, in 1908, the French directorate of public instruction established the first official public school for girls.[25]

The colonial administration was reluctant, for the most part, to interfere in reforms of *kuttab* schools or at Zaitouna. Louis Machuel, who was director of public instruction from 1883 until 1908, understood the sensitivity and avoided direct intervention, choosing instead to oversee religious education from afar and to introduce alternative secular reforms that would stimulate assimilation. He established Franco-Arab elementary schools that were open to Tunisian, French, and other European boys and offered a tailored French curriculum that included the teaching of Arabic as a subject. Franco-Arab schools were welcomed by some Tunisians as an entry point to the more privileged European communities. Among government officials, some enrolled their children to gain favor with the French, while others were pressured to do so.[26] Most Tunisians opposed the schools on religious grounds. When Machuel proposed a plan whereby *kuttab* schools could benefit from the Franco-Arab school system for two hours a day, his idea was vigorously opposed.[27]

The *Jeunes Tunisiens* wanted Tunisians to rid themselves of fatalism and "all prejudices that shackle their evolution, destroy their faculties, and hold them outside the movement that carries humanity toward progress," in the words of Muhammad Lasram (1858–1925) at the 1906 colonial congress.[28] They disparaged the state of degradation of *kuttab* schools across Tunisia. They objected to the *kuttabs'* outdated methods of teaching, including memorization of the Qur'an by heart, and protested against the widespread practice of aggressive sanctions and corporal punishment. They called for the realignment of *kuttab* schools according to rational, rather than religious only, principles so that pupils could develop critical thinking and reasoning skills. Some argued for their attachment to Franco-Arab schools in order for pupils to receive a bilingual education that would prepare them for a modern world.[29]

Thanks to the efforts of the *Jeunes Tunisiens*, the first reformed *kuttab* schools aimed at Muslim students who rejected the Franco-Arab model were established in 1907. The reformed private primary schools applied French pedagogic methods and incorporated modern subjects into the curriculum, while maintaining an emphasis on Arabic and religion.[30] Newly introduced subjects included literature, grammar, arithmetic, geometry, geography, and history. Not everyone was convinced, however, and some *Jeunes Tunisiens*, like Ali Bash Hamba (1876–1918), argued that these reformed schools kept Tunisian pupils in an inferior position because of the incompatibility of Arabic with new scientific ideas and the poor quality of textbooks imported from Cairo.[31] This line of thinking would inform Bourguiba's education policies following independence and would form the basis for Tunisia's bilingual education system ever since.

Resistance also came from the French authorities, but from a diametrically opposite position: they were not in favor of Tunisians' gaining access to the French education system and French culture, except when it served their needs to produce "assimilated" elites to fill positions in the colonial administration. The French thus objected to not being able to control these schools. But in the end, French authorities—succumbing to pressure by colons, who objected to the mixing of Tunisian and European pupils—considered the reformed kuttab schools to be a lesser evil and eventually favored them for Tunisians over their own Franco-Arab schools.[32]

Reformed schools gradually replaced the old kuttab schools, and by the end of the protectorate, roughly one out of four students in the public school system were enrolled in them.[33] Tunisian urbanites continued to study at Franco-Arab schools, while reformed kuttab schools were favored everywhere else.

But once students completed their primary school education, they had few options in the way of further schooling. The only nonreligious postprimary school, Sadiqi, had a limited student body of around 150.[34]

Sadiqi presented a conundrum for the French. On the one hand, it was a largely secular institution of high quality that was producing a new generation of Tunisian elites that could work within the colonial administration as auxiliaries to implement French policies. The French patronizingly referred to these elites as évolués, considering them "civilized" and "advanced in their evolution." On the other hand, Sadiqi College was also creating new generations of freethinking liberal men who could in time turn against the colonial power and fight for independence, which is exactly what ended up happening.

The French ultimately brought the reform of Sadiqi under their control, aligning it with a French education model and setting up a national competitive examination to recruit students. Sadiqi was reorganized in 1911 as a diploma-granting institution and in 1930 completely integrated the French lycée—high school—system, becoming a secondary school with both middle and high school components. Sadiqi College was now more than a breeding ground for public servants; it had turned into an authentic educational institution that prepared graduates for all types of professional lives.

Other options were also starting to become available for Tunisians. *lycée Carnot* attracted middle school graduates from Sadiqi. Founded in 1875 and renamed in 1894, *lycée Carnot* had been set up to serve a predominantly European student body but later accepted some of the best Muslim and Jewish students from Franco-Arab schools. Before Sadiqi added a *lycée* component to its offerings, students who wished to gain access to higher education in France had to first obtain their *baccalauréat* at *lycée Carnot*.

Even with the reform of Sadiqi and the creation of new schools like *lycée Carnot* and *collège Alaoui*, which started off as a school for training teachers for the new Franco-Arab schools, the supply of graduates continued to be outstripped by the needs of the French authorities for intermediate agents in the civil service. René Millet thus proposed to the *Jeunes Tunisiens* the establishment of an educational institution that would be dedicated exclusively to the teaching of Western sciences, using modern pedagogical methods. The *Jeunes Tunisiens* welcomed the idea and in 1896 established, as an association, *al-Jam'iyya al-khaldūniyya*—named after Ibn Khaldūn.

Students at Zaitouna were now able to take modern classes through the association that they would not have been able to access otherwise. *Al-khaldūniyya* introduced modern subjects that included natural sciences, physics, topography, economics, and French.

The *Jeunes Tunisiens* wanted to further invoke the modernist project and to democratize education by offering a parallel means that was accessible to all. Led by Ali Bash Hamba, they founded the *Association des anciens élèves du collège Sadiqi* (Sadiqi College Alumni Association) as an informal education group in 1905. The alumni association was formed in the same spirit as *al-khaldūniyya*. Its goal was to prioritize the dissemination of ideas of progress and the advancement of citizens' quality of life over traditional ideas of piety, religious community, and happiness in the "hereafter." The mandate of the association was to organize cross-generational encounters among Sadiqi alumni and to offer evening classes on topics that were not discussed at traditional institutions, including European ideas, Islamic modernism, and Arab politics.[35]

The *Association des anciens élèves du collège Sadiqi* aimed to be inclusive and to reach into Zaitouna, so the founders invited Zaitouna *ulama* to participate in its development. Under Khairallah Ibn Mustafa (1867–1965), who had led the *kuttab* schools' reform of 1907, Tunisian imams gave lectures in Arabic centered on progressive aspects of Islam, occasionally infusing notions of Arab unity and Arabism and underscoring an ideal that progress could be achieved through the Arabic language. The venerated Sheikh Tahar Ben Achour (1879–1973) gave the first such evening talk, collectively known as *musamarat*, in May 1906. Others from Zaitouna participated, including the Maliki scholar Ahmad al-Nayfar (1864–1926) and Muhammad al-Khidr Hussein (1876–1958), who later became the grand imam of al-Azhar.[36]

Zaitouna continued to produce an elite class of Islamic scholars whose function in society was limited to the religious sphere: carrying out the legal and ritual duties of an Islamic society and training the next generations to do the same. But by offering a parallel track that taught modern subjects and challenged Zaitouna's traditional teachings of Islam, the two associations—*al-Jam'iyya al-khaldūniyya* and the *Association des anciens élèves du collège Sadiqi*—and Sadiqi College triggered the beginning of a phase of profoundly consequential reform at Zaitouna. This reform was far more complex and controversial than any of the educational reforms that had preceded it, including that of *kuttab* schools.

Very few Zaitounians had been won over to the reformist movement that was sweeping Tunisia during the first couple of decades of the protectorate. The mosque presented a unique and daunting set of challenges: not only had it been around for fourteen centuries and become set in its ways, but it also occupied the religious, and thus most sensitive, domain. Formidable forces were caught in the war that ultimately brought about reform at Zaitouna: The *Jeunes Tunisiens*, French colonialists, Zaitouna students, and—most decisively—Zaitouna *ulama*, both traditionalist and reformist.

Reform-minded *ulama* included Tahar Ben Achour, Salim Buhagib (1827–1924), and Muhammad al-Sanusi. Perhaps most notable among these, Tahar Ben Achour descended from—and extended—a long line of intellectuals, Islamic scholars, and lawyers. Ben Achour completed his basic studies at the mosque before serving as a lecturer at Sadiqi and then becoming a professor at Zaitouna at twenty-four years of age. He believed that the state was responsible for the education of its citizens and that this responsibility extended to providing universal education. Ben Achour believed that Tunisia's Islam could be reformed from within and that the Qur'an should not be seen as a holistic source but studied linguistically to derive meaning from it. He wrote about the compatibility of Islam with natural law and the importance of Islamic values at the societal and individual level for a modern state.[37]

Opposing Ben Achour and other reformers were conservatives who wanted to preserve the old educational structures and protect them against foreign influences. Some of these traditionalists were not necessarily inclined toward religious dogmatism as much as they were, at least in part, protecting their societal status in the face of threatening change. Powerful *ulama* typically descended from extended families of religious scholars who had high-ranking careers and formed the core of aristocratic society.[38] They represented the strongest and most influential sector of society and assumed powerful positions in the judiciary, education, and *waqfs*—as muftis, *qadis* (judges), teachers, muezzins, and religious instructors.

The powerful position of the *ulama* of Zaitouna was further solidified by the fact that Islamic education had been the only type of education previously available to Tunisians. For a while, everything—thought, literature, and even craftsmanship—revolved around Zaitouna Mosque. Sheikh Rached Ghannouchi contends that to some extent, "all of Tunisia was produced at Zaitouna."[39] The *ulama*, therefore, must have seen any discussion of reform at Zaitouna, which was their own turf and last bastion of authority, as a serious threat. The resistance, at least by some, was not necessarily in opposition to reformism per se as much as it was imbedded in their not wanting to relinquish their power and privilege.

But this was not the case for all reactionary *ulama*. The objections of some *ulama* were dogmatic and related to their broader philosophical perspectives on education and Islam. Many believed that knowledge was self-contained and could be deduced from reason alone; it could not be gained through exogenous experience. Education that evolved outside a closed, religiously based system of knowledge was dismissed a priori. Traditionalists valued deference to what had come before them and to social and religious hierarchy. They were content with education's consisting of the memorization of a static whole, an "indisputable" set of information.[40] Thus, religious education was not subject to change and had to remain a closed system, protected from outside influences and new interpretations.

The colonial administration, which understood the importance of Zaitouna, supported its reform only halfheartedly, keeping a distance from this sensitive domain. In 1898, the administration set up a Zaitouna reform commission consisting of reformist *ulama,* led by Salim Buhagib, and members of the French bureaucracy. The reform commission culminated in Zaitouna's being removed from the directorship of public instruction and attached instead to the prime ministry, giving it greater autonomy.[41] The French thus ensured that Zaitouna was kept at arm's length and that they averted being drawn into the religious sphere.

Seeing attempts at reform as benign and cosmetic, students at Zaitouna sustained their demands for real change over the next decade. Encouraged by protests in 1909 at Cairo's al-Azhar—demanding curricular reforms—students insisted that subjects such as history and geography be integrated into the curriculum, that they be granted the right to take exams after three years instead of seven, and that they be exempted from paying taxes and serving in the army. Zaitouna students felt inferior to their counterparts at Sadiqi College, who were gaining knowledge in modern subjects, including the sciences. They deplored the obtuse conservatism of the majority of Zaitouna professors and the absence of a number of subjects such as philosophy, sacred exegesis, and metaphysics.[42]

But it was not until 1929 and students' persistent calls for reform that a second Zaitouna reform commission was formed. The debates this time were not confined to the walls of the mosque but were carried out in newspapers and public discussions. Battles were waged between the minority reformers who sought a radical reorganization aimed at considerably broadening the field of knowledge and traditionalists who wanted to preserve the status quo. The reform commission culminated in an education decree in 1933 that allowed the mosque to grant three diplomas, one for each cycle of education: *ahliya* for primary, *tahsil* for secondary, and *alimiyya* for the postsecondary cycle.[43] It also resulted in the appointment of Sheikh Tahar Ben Achour as rector of Zaitouna in 1932, a position he left after a year.[44]

Meaningful reform finally came to the mosque only in 1944, when Ben Achour returned as rector. Against a backlash by conservatives, the teaching of the English and French languages became mandatory at Zaitouna, modern subjects were introduced, and the quantity of religious material taught was decreased.[45] Ben Achour also saw to it that the Zaitounian spirit was widely spread, setting up twenty-five annexes across Tunisia and in Algeria and expanding the student population from 3,000 to 20,000 during his tenure.[46]

While Tahar Ben Achour was implementing his reforms at Zaitouna, his son, Sheikh Fadhel Ben Achour (1909–1970), was strengthening the emphasis on Arabic at *al-khaldūniyya*, where he was president. Fadhel Ben Achour had studied the Qur'an at home and started learning French at the age of ten. He was admitted directly into the second year at Zaitouna and later taught at Zaitouna and Sadiqi. Fadhel believed that the educational institutions set up by the French in Tunisia were too Western in their orientations and did not sufficiently take into account an Arab and Islamic context, so he pushed for the creation of the Institute for Islamic Research and the Arab Institute for Law, both founded in 1946.

At *al-khaldūniyya*, Fadhel Ben Achour introduced the first Arab *baccalauréat* degree to reinforce modern teachings in Tunisian educational institutions and to enable students to continue their studies at Arab universities in the Middle East. He forged ties with universities in Cairo and worked with Egypt's minister of education at the time, Taha Hussein (1889–1973).[47]

Taha Hussein, the leading twentieth-century figure of Arab modernism, wrote novels and plays in Arabic that earned him thirteen nominations for the Nobel Prize in Literature between 1949 and 1964. He had a yearning for freedom of scholarship that got him expelled from the conservative al-Azhar, whose outdated teachings he had rebelled against. In his 1936 book on educational policy, *Mustaqbal al-thaqafa fi Misr* (The Future of Culture in Egypt), Hussein contended that there was no divide between Europe and Egypt, an argument that rested upon the notion of a Mediterranean culture. With Taha Hussein, Fadhel Ben Achour created equivalencies between Tunisian and Egyptian diplomas, facilitating the path for Tunisians to pursue their higher studies in Cairo.

Fadhel Ben Achour also paved the way for, and supported, Bourguiba's progressive reforms postindependence. Sheikh Fadhel's advocacy for women's rights and his staunch backing of Bourguiba's *Code du statut personnel* were especially meaningful given his theological base and public persona. There were others who defended women's rights and paved the way for Bourguiba's reforms. Reformers faced just as much, if not more, backlash on this topic from traditionalist *ulama*, and their ideas ultimately did not take root until after independence.

Sheikh Muhammad al-Sanusi led the way by publishing a book in 1897 titled *Tafattuq al-akmam* (The Ripping of the Calices) in which he provided an analysis of the condition of women in the Muslim world and of women's rights within an Islamic context. The book was followed two years later by another influential work authored in Cairo by one of Muhammad Abduh's most consequential disciples, Qasim Amin. Amin's book, *Tahrir al-mar'a* (The Liberation of Woman), argued for the emancipation of women on the premise that equality between the sexes was grounded in Islam and evident in Shari'a, but that distortions of it were the result of traditions brought into the religion by converts. Qasim Amin also held the belief that interpretations of the Qur'an and Hadith were not sacred—that they orig-inated in human thought that could change over time and according to social context.

Despite his advocacy for the emancipation of women, Amin did not call for equality of rights between women and men, positioning women instead along traditional gender roles as wives and mothers. His was a "modernization" of patriarchy by aligning it with Western notions.[48] He did not believe that the education of women should necessarily be equal to men's, arguing that it ought to consist of basic schooling. But Amin went even further than al-Tahtawi, who was an early advocate for universal pri-mary education for boys and girls. While al-Tahtawi was driven by a belief that women's education would lead to more harmonious marriages and better rearing of children, Amin argued for women to be educated so that they could earn their own living and not have to be financially dependent. But Amin agreed with al-Tahtawi that women should not be able to partici-pate in government or have a political voice.[49]

Other prominent Tunisian figures who advocated for equality included the Zaitouna sheikh Abdelaziz Thaalbi (1876–1944), a disciple of Salim Buhagib, who argued in his 1905 book *L'esprit libéral du Coran* that Islamic principles favored gender equality and called for equal access to educa-tion for women as well as abolition of the Islamic veil.[50] Thaalbi provoked the wrath of older *ulama* and was tried in 1901, an event that precipitated further support for his opinions and for the reformist movement. Thaalbi, who would later become a leader of the Tunisian nationalist movement but who remained foremost a religious preacher and social reformist, called for the evolution of religion and for its in-depth understanding.

But no one advocated as strongly for women's rights or was as respon-sible for Tunisia's progressive legal status of women as the Islamic scholar and reformer Tahar Haddad (1899–1935). Hailed as one of Tunisia's most important social thinkers, Haddad has been widely credited for the tolerant, liberal, and progressive nature of Islam in modern-day Tunisia. Haddad opened the path for Bourguiba's *Code du statut personnel* by shaping the dialogue about women's rights in Tunisian society; his positions on women's rights became the basis for Bourguiba's code.

Born in southern Tunisia to a poultry dealer and growing up most likely in a religious and socially conservative milieu, Haddad studied at a *kuttab* school before attending Zaitouna, where his thoughts started taking shape. At Zaitouna, where he also taught, Haddad studied Muhammad Abduh and was influenced by Muhammad al-Sanusi and Abdelaziz Thaalbi.

Haddad understood Islam as a religion capable of adapting to societal developments and believed that Shari'a should be dynamic and not limited to rigorist and unchanging interpretations. Like other reformers of the time, Tahar Haddad believed that the reason Muslim society lagged behind Europe lay with Muslims' misunderstanding of the tenets of Islam.[51] Arguing from within an Arab and Islamic context rather than looking at Western practices, Haddad put forth the idea that fundamental human and civil rights, including those of women, could not be separated from Islam.[52] He argued that Islam, at its inception, had already established equality between men and women. The reason behind the degraded status of women in society, therefore, was not religion but a misunderstanding of religious texts and a misguided application of religious edicts. Haddad's elucidations were similar to Qasim Amin's in that both scholars attributed women's inferior position in society to tradition and not to Shari'a or Islam itself.

In Tahar Haddad's treatise *Imra'atuna fi al-Shari'a wa al-mujtama'* (The Status of Women in Islamic Law and Society), published in 1930, he argued for a paradigm shift in how women were viewed in Muslim society. Haddad assigned the same rights to women as those of men, such as the right to testify in court and to sign contracts.[53] In the sphere of marital relationships, Haddad advocated for mutual consent before marriage, and he called for an end to polygamy, unilateral divorce, and automatic child custody for the father.[54]

Haddad argued for women's education, framing the empowerment of women as part of the broader anticolonialism movement. But like some of his Egyptian predecessors, Haddad cited a woman's role in the family as the basis for her education and did not envision a professional future for women.[55] Haddad's argument was nonetheless progressive in a context where few discussed whether women should even be literate.

In arguing that women should have equal access to education, Haddad posited that Islam did not call for the segregation of sexes in school. In his treatise, Haddad devoted two chapters to the subject of the veil, arguing that it prevented couples from knowing each other before getting married and that it led to the isolation of women and the prevention of equal access to education, going so far as to compare the veil to "the muzzle that is imposed on dogs."[56] Haddad echoed Qasim Amin, who had postulated that wearing a niqab could incite sexual desire rather than promote chastity and that men enforced women's seclusion out of lack of respect and appreciation for a woman's attributes beyond her physical body.[57]

Tellingly, in terms of his attempts not to provoke but rather to encourage Zaitouna *ulama* to implement Shari'a reforms, Haddad interviewed several of them about his arguments concerning women's rights for the purposes of his book. Although some, as expected, were not supportive, notable exceptions included Tahar Ben Achour, who referred to men's and women's "shared rights" in marriage, and another Zaitounian who contended that the Qur'an did not order women to cover their faces in public.[58]

The publication of Haddad's book sent shock waves across Tunisia, and he was violently criticized for a number of his beliefs, most especially for denouncing polygamy and condoning abortion when the mother's life was at risk. Conservatives at Zaitouna ran a personal defamation campaign against him. Among *ulama* who published rebuttals of Haddad's treatise was Mohamed Salah Ben Mrad, a major Zaitouna figure, who issued one of the most scathing and effectual attacks on his work in a pamphlet, only for it to be later discovered that he had not even read the book.[59] Zaitouna scholars eventually revoked Haddad's distinction as a notary, practically annulling his degree and expelling him from the religious establishment. Although he had enrolled in a newly established two-year study program in law, Haddad was prevented from taking his final examination and denied his law degree.[60]

It was later discovered that Haddad had praised the institution that shunned him as a center of Islamic education. In a book published posthumously in 1981, titled *al-Ta'lim al-islami wa harakat al-islah fi Jami' al-Zaitouna* (Islamic Education and the Reform Movement at Zaitouna Mosque), he wrote: "This institution today is the only institution that allows us to protect our essence from perishing by reviving our language and our authentic literature, and by studying the sciences of life in our own tongue." But he also acknowledged Zaitouna's limitations and called for reform and for broadening the scope of teaching. Haddad wanted Zaitouna to be revitalized, both as a center of Islamic thought and a modern institution teaching secular subjects, and he suggested that students needed to lead the process of change in defiance of what he described as unyielding teachers.[61]

Accused of atheism and heresy, Haddad became subjected to physical assaults on the streets of Tunis, prompting him to seek a permit to carry a gun.[62] With smear campaigns against him in the press and many of his political allies turning their backs on him, Haddad spent the rest of his young life depressed and in poor health, having retreated from society. He died at the age of thirty-six from heart disease and tuberculosis, but his legacy, which became influential only after Tunisia gained its independence, would prove to be unquestionably enduring.

Tunisian modernists like Tahar Haddad had a permeating impact on education, women's rights, and the relationship between religion and society, and they helped define Tunisia's position in the modern world and its attitudes toward the West. Arguing from within Islam and reforming, as opposed to circumventing, religious institutions, like *kuttab* schools and Zaitouna, established both a harmonious relationship between religion and modernity and precedents for working within the system to ensure a balanced approach.

Reformers were deeply influenced by Cairene *Nahda* intellectuals, but Tunisia's reform movement was more expansive, and it evolved into the political sphere and a nationalist movement. The works of major Egyptian scholars were primarily motivated by a quest for the awakening of the Muslim *umma* and the adaptation of religion to the times through the application of the practice of *ijithad*.

Some *Nahda* reformers reversed themselves and moved toward the rigorous and narrow views of influential reactionaries. The onetime disciple and follower of Muhammad Abduh, Muhammad Rashid Rida, turned from a unifier of Sunnis and Shi'ites to an adopter of the exclusionary and extremist teachings of Muhammad Ibn Abdelwahhab (1703–1792), founder of the Wahhabi dogma. Rida perceived the extrapolation of Abduh's ideas to secular forms as subjugation of Islam to the West. He was inspired by the work of Taqi al-Din Ahmad Ibn Taymiyya, who planted seeds of extremist ideologies in the thirteenth and fourteenth centuries that would materialize centuries after his death. Ibn Taymiyya believed that *ulama* ought to reopen the doors of *ijtihad*, but that in doing so they should revert to the original seventh-century sources rather than rely on the interpretations of scholars. Ibn Taymiyya warned of the dangers of *'assabiyya*, the solidarity of a clan irrespective of the religions of its members that Ibn Khaldūn would advocate a century later. Ibn Taymiyya's orthodox views would inform the doctrine of Wahhabism that took shape in the middle of the eighteenth century and that of the Muslim Brotherhood in the early twentieth century.

Rising Islamism and the power of reactionary currents interrupted the work of *Nahda* scholars and severely limited their ability to effect change. The most significant project to modernize Islam was sadly terminated, giving way to a regression, the effects of which will continue to be felt for generations to come. Conditions for Tunisian influential thinkers, on the other hand, enabled them to persevere in their reforms and to continue on a generally cumulative and uninterrupted trajectory. Over the course of the twentieth century, Tunisia's path of reform would morph into a nationalist movement and produce an enlightened postindependence society.

10

1956

Tunisia's independence movement and nation-building project were formed, over decades, by intellectual forces and the
fight for workers' rights. It was a gradual, indigenous, mostly
cohesive, and peaceful endeavor—setting a tone and an example for the
country's revolution against tyrannical rule and its democratic transition
henceforth.

The *Jeunes Tunisiens* and other contemporaneous reformers who gave
birth to the intellectual reform movement of the late nineteenth and early
twentieth centuries were ultimately the champions of the anticolonial
movement that would lead to Tunisia's liberation. In the decades leading
to independence, intellectual currents adopted socioeconomic grievances
and the rights of women, workers, and the colonized more broadly—
breathing life into both a vibrant civil society and a sophisticated political
movement.

Anticolonial sentiments were spreading widely throughout the larger
region as world events—punctuated by two world wars—shattered the
myth of the invincible colonial power and exposed its vulnerability.
France's attention turned toward its troubles in Europe and on protecting
its sovereignty—providing space for indigenous political activity in Tunisia and elsewhere in the Maghreb to grow.

The battle for independence forged improbable alliances and brought together disparate constituents: Zaitounians and secularists, workers and elites, rural agrarians and urban industrialists, and women and men of all backgrounds and dispositions. Newspapers and journals were at the center of nationalist debate. Political parties had their own papers, often reincarnated under different names as the French colonial power labored to suppress dissent and oppress expressions of solidarity against its hegemony. Tunisian leaders lobbied for their demands on the world stage; they shared ideas and—at times—found commonalities of purpose with other Arab national movements taking place concurrently.

The most hotly contested issues at the turn of the century, pitting Tunisians against the authorities and the *colons* that they supported, were over land ownership and taxes.

The French had employed a strategy of attracting French citizens to Tunisia through promises of land grants that would create a material attachment to Tunisia among *colons*. Small parcels were transferred from Tunisians, often displacing peasants, at such a rate that by 1892, French citizens owned 400,000 hectares of land. In just over a decade, the French population, a mere few hundred out of the mostly Italian *colon* population in 1881, had grown by more than 10,000, much faster than the non-French.[1]

Further confounding the land transfer issue was that significant portions of Tunisian agricultural lands were held as religious *habus*. In their quest to entice French citizens, protectorate officials forced the local *habus* council in 1896 to give several thousand acres of its land each year to the newly established French-led Directorate of Agriculture to sell to settlers.[2]

The French did not stop at the acquisition and transfer of land away from Tunisians. To help finance infrastructure projects—including the building of roads, which were used mostly by the *colons*—the French increased the *majba* tax on Tunisian citizens in 1903.[3] Tunisians did not take this news quietly, and just as the doubling of *majba* at the hands of the Husaynid Sadok Bey had led to riots in 1864, the countryside erupted in protest. Matters came to a head in 1906 when an uprising at Thala-Kasserine against land seizures and the onerous tax burden resulted in a massacre, leaving twelve dead and seven injured at the hands of the French. A number of prominent Sadiqi graduates were involved in rousing the masses, including Bashir Sfar (1865–1917), who had delivered an impassioned speech just a month earlier against the new French resident-general, Stephen Pichon.[4]

Sfar had originally favored the French presence but became disenchanted following two decades of colonization, and he often spoke publicly against the French administration, demanding reforms on behalf of the Tunisian people.[5] His consequent isolation by the French led to other activists, most notably Ali Bash Hamba, rising to leadership positions within the *Jeunes Tunisiens* movement.[6]

The issues of taxation and landownership continued to divide Tunisians and the settler populations—with the protectorate government at times acquiescing in attempts to prevent another violent altercation.

The *Jeunes Tunisiens* embraced these economic grievances as part of their political platform. In 1907, they founded the *Parti évolutionniste*. Ali Bash Hamba used his newspaper *Le Tunisien*, the successor to *al-Hadira*, to promote the party's various programs. The first indigenous newspaper to be published in Tunisia in French, *Le Tunisien* quickly became the venue that propagated ideas of the nationalist movement. An Arabic version of the paper, *al-Tounsi*, was created two years later in 1909, with the Zaitouna modernist scholar Abdelaziz Thaalbi as its editor-in-chief.

With *Le Tunisien* and *al-Tounsi* as its mouthpieces, the party that the *Jeunes Tunisiens* founded took a stance against the systematic eviction of Tunisian farmers from their lands for the benefit of newly arrived settlers. It also took on new economic and political agendas, demanding equality between colonizer and colonized, and comparable treatment between European and Tunisian workers. The *Parti évolutionniste* called for the admission of Tunisians into public positions and for the widening of access to primary education and vocational agrarian instruction.

European settlers regularly mocked the *Jeunes Tunisiens*' demands in their own newspapers. In an article dated June 16, 1907, the French *colon* Victor de Carnières demeaned calls by the *Jeunes Tunisiens* for equal rights, asserting that the "[Tunisian] race has been rendered inferior by its depressing religion and a long hereditary tradition of laziness and fatalism."[7]

Tensions between *colons* and indigenous leaders became more charged as the nationalist movement developed further. Popular protests over land issues grew in frequency and in size in the years following the 1906 Thala-Kasserine riots.

Protests turned violent when the Tunis Municipal Council ordered a survey of the Jellaz Cemetery and the land surrounding it in 1911.

Tunisians were concerned that the burial grounds would be defiled and that this might lead to the registration of more land that would cease to be part of their national heritage. The French reacted pugnaciously, condemning thirty-five protesters and sentencing seven to death—two were guillotined. Colonial authorities declared the country under siege, imposing a state of emergency that was not lifted until 1921.[8] The event became an important marker and part of the collective memory of the Tunisian struggle for independence.

Every incident became a trigger that exposed profound distrust and unleashed deep resentments. When an Italian tram driver ran over a young Tunisian in February 1912, Tunisians boycotted the tram company, and Tunisian tram workers demanded equal pay and better working conditions.

The *Parti évolutionniste* projected its concerns on the international stage, voicing them at the 1908 *Congrès de l'Afrique du Nord* in Paris. But these attempts were not successful in garnering support for the aims of the *Jeunes Tunisiens*. In fact, airing their grievances outside Tunisia had the effect of backfiring against them at home, where they were looked upon ever more suspiciously by the French administration and *colons*, who suspected them of organizing the Jellaz Cemetery riot and the tram boycott as part of a greater political plot.[9]

The French suspended *Le Tunisien* and banished Ali Bash Hamba, Abdelaziz Thaalbi, and a number of their collaborators. Thaalbi and others were able to return to Tunisia after a few months, but Ali Bash Hamba chose to stay in exile in Istanbul until his death in 1918.[10]

With a state of emergency gripping the country and the leadership of the *Jeunes Tunisiens* beleaguered, there was not much opportunity for new leadership to emerge. It took two more decades for the momentum initiated by the *Jeunes Tunisiens* to successfully resume.

Attempts, futile as they may have been, at reaching independence were not in short supply in the intervening period, with some former *Jeunes Tunisiens* persisting in their efforts. Chief among them was Abdelaziz Thaalbi, who joined other compatriots in 1919 to form *al-Hizb al-horr al-destouri al-tounsi* (The Constitutional Liberal Tunisian Party), or Destour for short. These nationalists hoped that their solidarity with the French during the First World War would pay off—80,000 Tunisian troops had fought, and 12,000 had lost their lives.[11] Joining the war effort had been driven by strategic objectives and the hope that this would help Tunisia's case for independence. Economic motives played a role as well, as soldiers were financially compensated.

The *Jeunes Tunisiens* found reason for optimism in Woodrow Wilson's Fourteen Points and wrote the U.S. president a letter petitioning for Tunisia's right to self-determination.[12] They also sent a delegation composed of Destour members to participate in the Versailles Peace Conference of 1919 to advocate for greater autonomy for Tunisia. But none of these efforts paid off. Tunisia did not factor into the bigger agenda concerning Europe and the Middle East.

Tunisians attempted again to get a sympathetic ear in France. Destour leaders headed a second delegation to Paris in June 1920, but demands were once again unheeded. In the same year, Thaalbi wrote—in Paris—the first nationalist book to come out of the Maghreb, *La Tunisie martyre*. Published anonymously at the time but later largely attributed to Thaalbi, the book is considered to have been the unofficial program of Destour.

Their petitions rebuffed by the French, and having learned from the mistakes of the *Jeunes Tunisiens*, Destourians at first adopted an uncompromising position toward the colonial power. Destour became a movement away from the forthright adoption of "modernization *à la française*."[13] The founders of the party demanded restoration of the 1861 constitution— a point emphatically made by their use of the shortened party name, Destour, meaning "constitution" in Arabic.

Destour's political program consisted of nine points, including the setting up of municipal councils and of a mixed legislative assembly to which Frenchmen and Tunisians would be elected. The program also addressed Tunisians' rights to land ownership, freedom of assembly and of the press, and equal pay for equal work. Not surprisingly, given the evolution of the intellectual and educational reform movements over the preceding few decades, compulsory primary education—following the model of France— was one of the key components of Destour's program.[14]

France was quick to undermine Destour's demands for reform, fearing encouragement following the granting of partial independence to Egypt by the British authorities in February 1922. The French cunningly attempted to drive a wedge between the leadership of Destour and the nominal ruler, Nasser Bey, who had thrown his support behind the nationalist party.

After having been set up by the French in a distorted newspaper interview that made it seem as if he had dismissed the need for a constitution,

Nasser Bey put forward several conditions for agreeing not to abdicate: that the French flag be replaced by the Tunisian one; that a government and a council of ministers, presided over by the bey, be set up; and that land occupied by settlers be restituted. The bey also demanded that the 1921 naturalization decree that gave French nationality to children born to non-French parents in Tunisia be annulled; becoming a French citizen was perceived as an act of betrayal that was irreconcilable with a Muslim identity. But France ignored Nasser Bey's protestations, as well as a previous Hague International Court ruling that had declared the 1921 decree unlawful. France reacted instead by issuing a new decree in December 1923, allowing Muslims to be naturalized as French citizens.[15]

The bey's conditions, most of which were unmet, did result in one small victory in that France set up in 1922 a council to rule on budgetary and taxation matters. This *Grand Conseil* had fifty French members and twenty-six Tunisians, at least one of whom had to be Jewish.[16]

A pattern was thus established: the more France exerted its sovereignty over Tunisia, the more Tunisians—with the succor of the bey—opposed the protectorate.

Workers' grievances continued to be in the fore. The injustices bestowed upon Tunisian laborers in the form of underpayment and ill treatment worsened as the protectorate endured and as the exploitation by the French of Tunisia's natural resources increased. This, in turn, gave rise to an organized labor movement that would have nationalist aspirations and would come to be at the forefront of every major political development in the country's future.

During the protectorate, Tunisian workers were typically employed by a European business—or at least supervised by a foreigner—and they earned roughly a third of what their European counterparts did. The differential wage structure, known as *tiers colonial*, was used, along with the land grants, to lure French citizens to immigrate to the colonies.[17]

Miners comprised the largest segment of the industrial workforce, as the most prized Tunisian natural resources were phosphates and metals—iron, zinc, and lead. Mining activities did not bring benefits to Tunisians, however, beyond the low wages that miners received. In typical colonial fashion, resources were syphoned for the benefit of the colonizer. A case in point was the company whose workers' riots more than a century later would mark the beginning of the Jasmine Revolution: *Compagnie des phosphates et des chemins de fer de Gafsa.* In 1899, the company completed a pipeline connecting the interior town of Gafsa to the coastal city of Sfax, and from there phosphate was shipped out without contributing to any economic development in Tunisia.[18]

Ironically, the first Tunisian labor union was formed by non-Tunisians to exploit Tunisian workers. In order to preserve their privileged status, French and Italian workers—primarily in transport, construction, and postal and other public services—set up in 1919 a branch of France's *Confédération générale du travail.* The union was comprised of French socialist and communist party members who envisioned a future socialist Tunisia led by a new and advanced French working class. In another ironic twist, the union's refusal to support a 1924 dockworkers' strike by Tunisians— demanding equal wages to those in Marseille—led Tunisians to form the first independent labor union of their own: the *Confédération générale tunisienne du travail* (CGTT).[19]

The communist-leaning union was formed by Muhammad Ali al-Hammi (c. 1890–1928) and Tahar Haddad, both of whom had recognized the French labor movement in Tunisia as racist and exploitative.[20] Although they had received different types of education—traditional in the case of Haddad and Western in al-Hammi's—they reached the same conclusion in terms of the necessity to build a strong labor movement.

Haddad, a nationalist, was a Destour activist during the time that he taught at Zaitouna. In his book *al-Din wa al-jinsiyya wa mas'alat al-yawm* (Religion, Nationality, and Today's Problems), Haddad celebrated Tunisia's unique personality and decried France's efforts at naturalization of Tunisian Muslims. He argued that there was an indivisible link between religion and nationality and that integration of one community with another put at risk elements of culture and identity, particularly when the assimilator represented a community that was hostile toward the assimilated. As a member of the propaganda committee of Destour, Haddad's political activities took him across Tunisia and put him in intimate contact with workers and their grievances.[21]

Al-Hammi had interrupted his studies to fight against the Italians in Tripoli and lend his support to regional resistance movements. When he later studied in Berlin, al-Hammi became involved in the political and social activism of European unionists, communists, liberals, and workers. He became convinced that "the power and the progress of the West resided in the multidimensional and global dynamic of these societies, particularly with regard to the organization of work and the economic and political systems." Al-Hammi returned to Tunis in 1923, and the following year he founded cooperatives for Tunisian workers, led strikes, and formed regional unions across Tunisia.[22]

Destour leaders at first supported the founding of CGTT, but later distanced themselves from the union out of fear that its activism would compromise the party's agenda.[23] A 1925 national strike called for by al-Hammi—and supported by nationalists, communists, and socialists—underscored the threat that al-Hammi posed to the French. The French subsequently dissolved the union and exiled al-Hammi, who died in a road accident in Saudi Arabia in 1928.[24]

Tahar Haddad, frustrated with Destour's withholding of support, had already quit the union before it was dissolved.[25] In 1927, he published a book titled al-'Ummal al-tounisuyyun wa dhuhur al-haraka al-naqabiyya (Tunisian Workers and the Birth of the Unionist Movement), in which he discussed the travails of the working class and presented a biography of CGTT cofounder al-Hammi. Haddad wanted to highlight underlying structural problems, including the growing taste for European goods in Tunisia at the expense of local craftsmen, as well as the failure of Destour to ally with CGTT and its meager interest in the working class in general.

The Destour party grew factious as Tahar Haddad and others grew impatient with its pervasive conservative postures and its nonconfrontational approach. Destour leaders were, in the end, unwilling to challenge the French colonial power directly. The party was largely ineffectual from its inception, and under its leadership, the nationalist movement went through a period of inactivity in the 1920s.[26] The circumstances under which Destour came into being almost ensured its conventional makeup and stance. Its cadre consisted mainly of traditional urbanites from the capital of Tunis—technocrats, religious leaders, and notables. They were inward looking and did not represent anything beyond a separatist movement that was not concerned with workers' rights.[27]

But it was during this time that a new generation of leadership was starting to emerge. The introduction of competitive national exams for student recruitment, scholarships, and government posts meant that young men from all over Tunisia had an opportunity to join a new elite. Many continued their studies in France and returned to Tunisia prepared to push against the French more severely than those they were starting to replace. This new Tunisian cadre benefited from the educational opportunities provided by their colonizers. But unlike their counterparts in other colonized lands, Tunisians were able to extend the impact of Western education on their society without becoming any less Tunisian.

Trumpeting their Western education as an essential credential for their leadership, the new class of elites were not unlike the *Jeunes Tunisiens*, who had earlier proclaimed, "Our new mentality is the product of the French mind. We have taken over its vast domain and made it our own."[28]

Habib Bourguiba was among this emerging group of new elites. Bourguiba attended Sadiqi College and *lycée Carnot* before going to Paris to study law and political science at the Sorbonne. In Paris, Bourguiba took his political inspiration from Rousseau, Lamartine, and Hugo. Upon his return in 1927, Bourguiba became an activist, often writing on the discontent of Tunisians under the French.

Bourguiba voiced his opinions in Destour's *La Voix du Tunisien*, but later founded—with Mahmoud Matri (1897–1972) and Tahar Sfar (1903–1942)—a new paper, *L'Action tunisienne*, which published competing views with those of the conservative Destour.

Bourguiba and his like-minded Destourians were looking for an opportunity to resurrect the nationalist movement and to rally the masses, having observed the relative success of the labor movement. The French unwittingly gave Bourguiba just the opening he needed in the early 1930s. While much of the Tunisian population felt the pinch of an economic crisis that was gripping the country, the colonial power made a few grave mistakes that touched on national and religious sentiments and played right into the hands of Bourguiba and his compatriots.

The first such mistake, which proved to be one of the decisive factors in the revival of the nationalist movement, occurred in 1930, when the government gave permission to the Catholic Church to hold its International Eucharist Congress in Carthage. The streets were filled with Catholics dressed as crusaders, handing out pamphlets encouraging the Muslim populace to convert. As if this had not delivered enough insult, the French also organized lavish and extravagant public celebrations of the subjugation of Algerians on the centennial anniversary of the capture of Algiers.[29]

But the issue that ultimately fanned the flames of the nationalist movement was the revival of the naturalization controversy of the early 1920s.

Between 1932 and 1934, tens of thousands of Tunisians demonstrated against the burial of French-naturalized Tunisians in Muslim cemeteries—an avowed act of apostasy. That many of those who got naturalized were public servants within the French administration further fueled perceptions of them as collaborators. Muslim cemeteries became the symbol of Tunisian sovereignty.

Bourguiba and some of his fellow Destourians seized the opportunity and called on Tunisians in 1933 to blockade burials of naturalized individuals in Muslim cemeteries. They capitalized on, and further spread, unfounded rumors that the French had exerted their authority over the religious sphere and ordered the issuing of a *fatwa*—a ruling by a recognized religious authority—in favor of granting burial rights for naturalized persons. The nationalist movement used the burial issue to underscore French interference in Tunisian affairs in general. Ultimately, Tunisian Muslims settled the question once and for all themselves. The *Ligue des Français musulmans* published a letter in 1936 acknowledging that being French was incompatible with being Muslim and calling on the French president to allow them, as well as their children, to be denaturalized.

In the aftermath of the naturalization crisis and the swelling of public resistance, the French tightened their grip, shutting down nationalist newspapers and suspending the Destour party. But the older and more conservative Destour leaders, who had not sanctioned the antiburial campaign in the first place, acceded to French conditions of moderation, and the party was allowed to resume its activities.[30] Bourguiba was arrested by the French authorities for his role in the antiburial campaign. But before he was held in exile in southern Tunisia, he convened a congress at Ksar Hellal in March 1934 at which a new party was formed from the ranks of younger, more frustrated factions of Destour that had spearheaded the resurrection of the naturalization campaign.

In establishing the new splinter party, Neo-Destour, Bourguiba was once again joined by his cofounders of *L'Action tunisienne*: Tahar Sfar and Mahmoud Matri. Bourguiba was named secretary-general of Neo-Destour, while Matri was named the party's first president. Bahri Guiga (1904–1995), who had studied with Bourguiba at *lycée Carnot* and then earned degrees in law and public finance in Paris, became treasurer.[31] Had Tahar Haddad not died in 1935, perhaps he would have joined the foundational ranks of Neo-Destour as well.

Another of Bourguiba's friends, Mohamed Chenik (1889–1976), provided the financial support that was critical to the new party's launch and its eventual ascendancy over Destour. A wealthy business owner, Chenik cooperated with the French—a common practice among large landowners and rural merchants—and served twice as prime minister under the protectorate. Much of the early party funding came from large landowners in the semiarid region of the Sahel that had for the most part been spared incursion by European settlers. This early relationship evolved so that the postindependence state became tied to the rural bourgeoisie.[32]

From the outset, Neo-Destour represented a departure from what Destour had become in that it took a bolder and more radical anticolonial stance and relied extensively on propaganda efforts to rally the masses behind it.[33] Bourguiba had learned from his efforts during the naturalization crisis the importance of setting up cells in rural areas, especially in regions hit by economic depression. Party branches were established throughout the countryside to recruit and politically educate a new "liberation army" of peasants.[34]

The party also adopted views that were akin to those of the *Jeunes Tunisiens* in their pro-Western outlook, as many of its members had been formed by the same education that the party's founders had received. In several respects, Bourguiba was a product of the colonial power, having studied in its schools and evolved a Western mind-set. He fought against French oppression while adopting many of their principles, which he would implement once he was in charge.

Bourguiba and other Neo-Destourians saw Islam as central to achieving a national identity, and they used religion as a means to rally the masses to the nationalist cause and to instill a spirit of resistance—invoking the notion of martyrdom and its heavenly rewards in the fight against the colonizer.[35] But Neo-Destour was also inclusive and careful not to allow schisms among Tunisians to surface, mindful of its substantial Jewish minority.

Unlike the old Destour party, which had vigorously denounced Zionism, Neo-Destour applied a more nuanced approach to the issue and was careful to differentiate between Judaism and Zionism. The party suppressed Zionist media activities while insisting that there was a place for the religion, but not the political movement, in Tunisia.[36]

Jews, most of whom had become naturalized French citizens, were resented for the preferred status they enjoyed under the French. Violent clashes between Tunisian Jews and Muslims had erupted in the Sahel and Tunis area during the summer of 1932. Tensions arose as a result of economic grievances, but also because of sympathy with Zionism on the part of some members of the Tunisian Jewish population.[37] Contrasting attitudes on the issue naturally emanated from the leadership of the new and old versions of the Destour party. Neo-Destour's Salah Ben Youssef chanted, during a demonstration in 1934, "the Jews are our brothers."[38] On the other end of the spectrum, the old Destour's leader Abdelaziz Thaalbi had close links with the uncompromising Palestinian nationalist leader and mufti of Jerusalem, Hajj Amin al-Husseini, and helped spread anti-Jewish propaganda.[39]

Women were also center stage, as Tunisian feminism started taking shape in the 1920s. There were demonstrations by women for their rights, and female figures who fought for their liberation and against the hijab were emerging onto the scene. Manoubia Ouertani—the first Tunisian woman to take off her hijab in public at her own lecture on feminism in 1924—was one such personality whom others modeled themselves after, including Habiba Menchari in 1928.[40] These women followed the example of Huda al-Sha'rawi, the mother of the Egyptian feminist movement, who in 1923 dramatically cast off her hijab at a train station in Cairo as a show of resistance against the oppression of women.

Bourguiba, who would later scorn women for wearing the hijab, took a stance against unveiling in 1929 and joined other national leaders in criticizing Habiba Menchari's and Manoubia Ouertani's public removal of their headscarves. In a derisive article in 1929 that appeared in the newspaper *L'Etendard tunisien*, Bourguiba questioned the wisdom of unveiling given the prevailing circumstances.[41] Politically, Bourguiba thought that Islamic traditions such as wearing the hijab served as an important differentiating symbol from the French. Habib Bourguiba played Islam to his advantage leading up to independence, changing his tunes quite dramatically once he became president of a free Tunisia. For him, everything was political, and the end of liberation justified any means that he found useful.

It was not until 1936 that the first women's organization in Tunisia was founded: *Union musulmane des femmes de Tunisie* (UMFT). The organization's founder, Bchira Ben Mrad (1913–1993), was the daughter of the Zaitouna sheikh Mohamed Salah Ben Mrad who had fiercely and publicly opposed Haddad's treatise on women in 1930. In many respects, the organization was set up expressly to counter the ideas of Tahar Haddad.[42] The organization, which stood for the advancement of women's education and their social inclusion—in the spirit of Islam—did not advocate for equality of the sexes or seem to have the aim of improving women's living conditions in Tunisia.[43] UMFT was close to Neo-Destour, with which it shared an anticolonial doctrine; Bourguiba's niece Chedlia Bouzgarou (1917–2005) and his future wife, Wassila Ben Ammar (1912–1999), enrolled in UMFT.[44]

Other women's organizations also came to the fore during that period. Prominent among them was *al-Qiyada al-nissa'iya* (Women Leadership), which adopted, along with a number of nationalist groups, an increasingly popular medium of protest: the arts. *Al-Qiyada al-nissa'iya* helped women found their own theater groups and, unlike UMFT, advocated for equality, but with little influence.[45]

The arts scene in Tunisia had blossomed along with the nationalist movement as Tunisians sought ways to preserve their culture and identity. They set up the Rashidiyya Institute in 1934 to preserve indigenous music and as an antidote to the French music conservatory, the *Conservatoire français de musique*, now the *Conservatoire national de musique de Tunis*.[46]

A group of artists and intellectuals gathered at night in cafés in the Bab Souika neighborhood in the Medina of Tunis. They exchanged ideas and conveyed their political views and anticolonial sentiments through various artistic expressions—poetry, fiction, painting, sculpture, and film. The group, which became known as *Taht al-sur* (Under the Wall), wanted to create a literary cultural milieu that built national character, denounced colonialism, and promoted social and economic justice. Tunisia's most celebrated poet, Abu al-Qasim al-Shabbi, was a member of *Taht al-sur*.[47] His poem "The Will to Live," which became a mantra for the Jasmine Revolution, exemplified the objectives of this group. For al-Shabbi, submission and indifference were synonymous with death, and he condemned the passivity of Tunisians in the face of colonial oppression. "The Will to Live," which continues to be taught in Tunisian textbooks, was al-Shabbi's parting gift to his people; he died just a year after it was written, at the age of twenty-five.

Al-Shabbi's denunciation of submission and fatalism was echoed in 1940 in the play *al-Sudd* (The Dam), authored by Mahmoud Messaadi, who would later serve for ten years as Bourguiba's minister of education. A symbolic drama, *al-Sudd* depicted two conflicting ideologies: one a deep faith in God and a fateful surrender to a life of inexorable hardships, the other free will and control over one's destiny.[48] The play served both as a challenge to the fatalism of religion and as an allegory of Tunisian resistance against the French and of human resilience.[49] Like "The Will to Live," *al-Sudd* became part of the Tunisian school curriculum.

Messaadi was Tunisia's most renowned author of the twentieth century, and he was highly praised by other Arab writers. Best known for his articulate and precise use of language, Messaadi's work is thought provoking and experimental, exposing tensions between tradition and modernity.[50] A product of both traditional and modern Tunisian education—having studied at Sadiqi, Zaitouna, and *al-khaldūniyya*—Messaadi was also trained by the French at the Sorbonne. Traversing both worlds, Messaadi taught Arabic literature at several French universities before returning to Tunis and becoming an important figure in the nationalist movement. Messaadi's direct impact on the education and culture of Tunisians was of such great consequence that it is fair to say that no other influence, besides Bourguiba's, was as significant as his in helping Tunisia avert the path taken by other Arab countries following independence.

Both al-Shabbi and Messaadi called on their people to hold onto hope and to seize opportunity for advancement of their nationalist aspirations and struggle for freedom. Neo-Destour leaders did just that when, in 1936, the *Front populaire* rose to power in France, giving new hope that cooperation might now be possible.

Indeed, the antifascist, socialist Léon Blum (1872–1950), who presided as prime minister over an alliance of leftist political parties, supported greater autonomy for Tunisia. Freedom of the press and of assembly were restored, and *L'Action tunisienne*, which had been shut down when Bourguiba was exiled, resumed publication—in time to widely publicize the decision of the *Ligue des Français musulmans* to denounce naturalization. Bourguiba and other militants were freed by the new resident-general Armand Guillon in April 1936 and were given a warm welcome and hailed as heroes. Bourguiba's exile had made him a martyr in the eyes of the nation and further catapulted him onto the scene.[51]

Bourguiba immediately took it upon himself to negotiate with the *Front populaire* for a power-sharing agreement in line with the 1881 Bardo Treaty so that Tunisia would progressively transition to greater autonomy. But Abdelaziz Thaalbi opposed Bourguiba's efforts and argued publicly against cooperation with the French. The rise of the *Front populaire* coincided with the Arab rebellion in Palestine in response to increasing Jewish emigration. Destour was openly skeptical about the *Front populaire*, accusing Prime Minister Léon Blum in its newspaper, *La Charte tunisienne*, of being sympathetic toward the Jewish cause in Palestine.[52] Bourguiba's attempts ultimately failed, and France proclaimed its presence in Tunisia as definitive.

Careful to neither alienate the French nor concede to Destour's hard-line strategy—and wanting to keep Neo-Destour at the center of the nationalist struggle—Bourguiba continued to adopt a conciliatory approach in the form of Franco-Tunisian cooperation, while stating that his end goal was now independence. He enunciated his strategy in *L'Action tunisienne*, asserting that independence without French cooperation would not be possible, and that "Tunisian independence must be accompanied by a treaty guaranteeing French supremacy vis-à-vis other foreign powers, in political as well as economic matters."[53]

Bourguiba's strategy rested on achieving short-term gains while patiently and methodically working toward realistic and clear long-term goals. Bourguiba understood that glorifying the past, projecting victimhood, and resorting to blame tactics would weaken his position and be counterproductive. He also believed there was no benefit in denying that Tunisian society had not yet matured. His strategy of political flexibility and of working to win over, rather than defeat, his opponents served Bourguiba well, both in the struggle for independence and in running Tunisia's affairs postindependence. Bourguibism was not simply "good political common sense" but rather "uncommon good sense presented with deceptive simplicity and clarity."[54] It was predicated on a set of principles that Bourguiba applied with cunning tenacity.

But cooperating with the French did not mean that attaining independence through militancy, if need be, was ruled out. So when tensions over naturalization were revived in 1937 and 1938 over the gradual reintroduction by local French authorities of the burial of French Muslims in Muslim cemeteries, Bourguiba reverted to rebellion and spearheaded civil disobedience through noncompliance with conscription and taxation. Coinciding with the fall of the *Front populaire* in Paris, demonstrators—incited by Bourguiba—took to the streets on April 9, 1938, and were brutally repressed by the French. The official account reported twenty-two deaths, but nationalists challenged that account and contended that the real number of deaths was close to 220.[55] Bourguiba and several of his compatriots were subsequently jailed in France, and both the old Destour and Neo-Destour parties were dissolved.

It was around this time that Bourguiba, who enjoyed being in the leading role and was not very successful in working with others, began to isolate colleagues. Stifling the political maturity of the nationalist movement, he started falling out with many of his close associates, including Mahmoud Matri and Tahar Sfar.

With the outbreak of the Second World War, Bourguiba, in jail, at first called on Tunisians to support the French and take an unconditional pro–Allied Forces stance. Utilizing a characteristically Bourguibian two-pronged approach in dealing with the French, he concurrently exploited France's weakness by adopting a rejectionist attitude to certain things like taxation. Tunisians were at first apprehensive about supporting the French as the outbreak of war seemed imminent, especially given the events of April 9, 1938. In galvanizing support for the Allies, Bourguiba exploited anti-Italian sentiments, which were fueled by a large wave of Italian migration to the country and Mussolini's public expressions of his desire to incorporate Tunisia into his "African empire."[56]

With the Nazi invasion and occupation of France in 1940 and the installation of the Vichy regime, France suffered a huge credibility blow that made it difficult for younger Neo-Destourians to lend their support. There were also repeated calls by Hajj Amin al-Husseini of Jerusalem to Muslim populations across the region to support the Axis. Tunisians gave a warm welcome to the Germans when they entered Tunis in November 1942, thinking this meant that French colonization was over, and at a meeting at Alhambra Cinema on February 21, 1943, Neo-Destour youth proclaimed their support for the Axis powers.[57]

Seeing Bourguiba as a potential political asset, the Germans released him in 1942 and allowed him to return to Tunisia, which he did in April 1943. Bourguiba, for his part, tried to make the most of the political opportunity this presented to him and started negotiating with the Germans and Italians to form an alliance. In return for support of the Axis powers, the Germans would liberate his country.

The nominal Husaynid ruler Moncef Bey (r. 1942–1943) took advantage of the brief German occupation, which lasted until May 1943, to implement reforms without asking the permission of French officials. He restructed the *habus* administration and annulled the *tiers colonial*, including for Tunisian public servants, who could now earn the same wages as their foreign counterparts.[58]

German occupation dealt Tunisian Jews, who had lost faith in the French as their protectors, a deadly blow. The Jewish population, which numbered around 100,000 at the time, was adversely affected by the reach into Tunisia of discriminatory laws issued by Vichy France. The French authorities seized goods from Tunisian Jews and took over Jewish matters. Jews were identified by mandatory yellow badges, and as many as 5,000 Tunisian Jews were forced to work in labor camps, often building weaponry and other goods for the war effort.[59] Acts of violence against the Jewish population included massacres that took place in Dagache in 1940 and in Gabès in 1941.[60]

But Germans also faced obstacles in implementing measures that would have threatened the legal status of naturalized Jews and their economic position. Some Jewish Tunisians had influential status, and the Jewish population received support from powerful non-Jewish segments of Tunisian society. To assure them of their protection under him, Moncef Bey convened a delegation of Jews from different Tunisian communities and stressed their equality with all other Tunisians in the face of prejudicial directives from Vichy France.[61]

Protection was also provided by Tunisian Muslim citizens. Khaled Abdelwahhab, a young man from a powerful and wealthy family, hid—at great risk—a number of Tunisian Jewish families at his farm in the countryside until the German occupation ended. He also saved a young Jewish woman from being raped by German officers.[62] Abdelwahhab is the only Arab to have ever been nominated for the Righteous Among Nations honor, reserved for non-Jews who helped save Jews during the Holocaust.

Once the Nazi occupation of Tunisia ended, the newly gained freedoms that nationalists had achieved were lost. Political parties were once again banned, and a state of emergency was reinstated. The French removed Moncef Bey from office and replaced him with Lamine Bey (r. 1943–1957). But with the colonial power vulnerable, independence resolve was strengthened, and Tunisian nationalists grew more militant and uncompromising in their attitude toward French rule. Independence now seemed inevitable, given that France—wrecked by years of war—had to focus on reconstruction and on domestic and economic priorities.

The war had fragmented the political scene in Tunisia, but Bourguiba still emerged as the unrivaled leader of the nationalist movement and France's preferred negotiator. Bourguiba's strategy was to turn Neo-Destour into the only nationalist party in Tunisia, acting as an umbrella body for all mass organizations. Neo-Destour needed to collaborate with other nationalist entities intent on independence, so it joined forces with the loyalists and with Destour, communist parties, and *ulama*. Bourguiba also formed an alliance with labor organizations, which were uniting. The national movement for independence would assume a labor union political framework.

On January 20, 1946, a meeting of several labor unions took place at *al-khaldūniyya*, the outcome of which was the founding of the *Union générale tunisienne du travail* (UGTT). From the outset, UGTT distanced itself from the communist proletarian international movement that supported class warfare and the Soviet Union. The departure from socialist or communist dogma, unusual at the time, underscored a Western-leaning worldview, which was in line with the ideology of Neo-Destour. [63]

Sheikh Fadhel Ben Achour, president of *al-khaldūniyya* at the time, chaired the constituent session of the union and was appointed honorary president of UGTT. The sheikh launched a campaign to build support for UGTT by insisting on the need for Tunisians to unite based on their common Arab and Muslim identity. His participation, an affirmation that UGTT was not communist nor against Islam, was critical to convincing the religious establishment to adopt the union as part of the nationalist movement.[64] UGTT leaders acknowledge that the support of a revered religious leader like Sheikh Fadhel Ben Achour demonstrates that this movement came out of the "womb" of all Tunisians.[65] They see the formation of UGTT and Ben Achour's sponsorship of the union as an effort to save the cultural identity of Tunisia and not as motivated only by political or labor considerations.

Farhat Hached (1914–1952) served as UGTT's first secretary-general. Personally and politically close to Bourguiba and the Francophile faction of Neo-Destour, Hached dedicated his life to the union movement in Tunisia. He served until 1944 as undersecretary of the Tunisian branch of the *Confédération générale du travail*. Hached later founded several unions himself, including one of the three main syndicates that came together at the founding of UGTT—*Union des syndicats autonomes des travailleurs du*

Nord—which he set up in 1945. Leadership within UGTT also hailed from the southern axis of Gafsa-Sfax-Kerkennah, providing a broad regional base for the nationalist movement.

Workplace contentions became inseparable from the nationalist struggle, and workers proved to be a critical political asset for Neo-Destour, as workers generally lived in densely populated urban areas and could be more easily mobilized than rural peasants for political action. Schoolteachers, postal workers, health care professionals, and telecommunications workers became the most militant members of the nationalist movement.[66]

Farhat Hached became the de facto new leader of the national struggle for independence after Bourguiba, who had come under constant surveillance by the French, left for Cairo in 1945, remaining there in voluntary exile until 1949. Hached's famous line *"uhibuka ya sha'ab"* ("I love you, people") captured the depth of his passion for the cause.

While Hached attended to nationalism at home, Bourguiba became the spokesperson for Tunisia's independence abroad. He traveled in the Middle East and to the United Nations in New York to plead the case of the nationalist movement. He met with other Arab nationalists, including representatives of the newly founded League of Arab States. In Cairo, Neo-Destour contributed to the establishment in 1947 of the *Bureau du Maghreb arabe*, which brought together nationalists from Morocco, Algeria, and Tunisia.

Habib Bourguiba and Farhat Hached together promulgated their joint cause in the United States when the union leader was invited to a conference of the American Federation of Labor in San Francisco in 1951. Bourguiba and Hached, who was celebrated in the West for the model—and, importantly, noncommunist—labor movement that was UGTT, leveraged the conference as a platform to familiarize the American public with the Tunisian nationalist cause.

The two organizations—Neo-Destour and UGTT—had become so intricately interconnected that by 1952, 80 percent of union members were also members of the party.[67] Neo-Destour had the greater number of members, but UGTT had more activists among its ranks. Politically aligned, the union and the party remained structurally independent.[68] Bourguiba, who wanted to keep the entities separate, was nonetheless wary of the union's independence, so he had two new organizations established under the directive of Neo-Destour: *Union tunisienne des artisans et commerçants* (UTICA) and *Union générale des étudiants tunisiens.*[69]

Women's organizations rallied behind the unionist-nationalist cause. Many formed communist organizations, such as the *Union des femmes de Tunisie* in 1944 and, for younger women, the *Union des jeunes filles de Tunisie* in 1945. Both unions consisted only of French, Italian, and Jewish Tunisian members at their inception. Muslim Arab women were slow to enter the scene and adopt the cause. But starting in 1946, the unions widened their membership base by attracting female Destour members as well as apolitical Tunisian women. More Muslim women joined, and by 1951, Nabiha Ben Miled (1919–2009), a Tunisian Muslim woman, became the president of the *Union des femmes de Tunisie.*

Both the *Union des femmes de Tunisie* and the *Union des jeunes filles de Tunisie* offered literacy courses—in French and Arabic—and encouraged women's economic participation in the labor market and their financial emancipation. Unlike religiously leaning women's organizations, communist organizations stressed the idea of a woman's right to work to gain her freedom.[70]

Neo-Destour's support for women's organizations was circumspect. As liberation loomed closer, however, Neo-Destour, which was careful to elucidate that the national question came first, established an official feminist entity within the party in 1950.[71] Neo-Destour understood that in the context of the nationalist struggle, women were seen as the repository of Tunisian identity, national values, and traditions that needed to be preserved.[72]

Partially as a result of women's integration into Neo-Destour, the *Union des femmes de Tunisie* and the *Union des jeunes filles de Tunisie* began to lose their momentum by the mid-1950s.[73] With independence, institutional feminism took over, and the fight for women's rights became embodied in the state-led *Code du statut personnel* and the creation of the *Union nationale de la femme tunisienne* in 1956.

Bourguiba returned from Cairo in 1949, still an adamant believer in the necessity of French-Tunisian cooperation. He presented his independence agenda to the French in 1950. Bourguiba wanted Tunisia to be a sovereign state, run by an all-Tunisian government, and he demanded that the French gendarmerie and French posts—such as the resident-general and technical inspectors—be abolished. The program also called for the creation of a national assembly, elected by universal suffrage, whose first task would consist of drafting a democratic constitution, and the creation of elected municipalities, including representation of French interests in cities with a strong French presence. In his quintessentially two-pronged manner, Bourguiba appealed to a Tunisian symbiotic relationship with France: "We consider that our country's military is too weak and our strategy too strong to do without the support of a great power [France], as long as [France] acknowledges the legitimacy of our demands. . . . We are always ready to cooperate [with France] on an equal footing from people to people."[74]

Neo-Destour had put forth the *Manifeste du front tunisien* back in 1945, demanding self-governance in the context of a constitutional monarchy, but France had failed to respond to the document adequately. The timing of Bourguiba's 1950 petition, however, was right. France was preoccupied with struggling to retain control over its Indo-Chinese territories, where it was enduring heavy military losses and humiliations. With the scars of the Second World War still fresh, France was already considering decolonization in sub-Saharan Africa and abandoning its protectorates in Tunisia and Morocco, but wanted to remain in Algeria.

France conceded to the principle of Tunisian independence and appointed a new resident-general, Louis Perillier, in June 1950, tasking him with initiating the transition. A new government of negotiation was formed, and it included both French and Tunisian members. Neo-Destourians held important portfolios, including Mohamed Chenik as prime minister, but as a sign of French unwillingness to relinquish any meaningful semblance of power, the resident-general had veto power over decisions.[75]

Bourguiba and the Neo-Destour leadership came under heavy criticism from pan-Arab and pan-Islamic proponents, including the Arab League, for cooperating with the French. The old Destour party thus dissociated itself from Neo-Destour and in February 1951 launched a newspaper, *Indépendance*, that took a strong position against the government of negotiation and Neo-Destour's cooperation strategy, presenting it as a betrayal of the Tunisian people.[76] The position taken by the old Destourians and their pan-Arab supporters would serve as a defining feature of Arab politics for generations to come: rejection of opportunities for cooperation and compromise, invariably leading to a worsening of the status quo.

Pressured by the *colons*, and lacking a strong and unified counterweight, the French authorities were disinclined to implement legislative reforms they had introduced in 1951. They dismissed Louis Perillier, the symbol of Franco-Tunisian cooperation, and replaced him with the far less cooperative and more brutal Jean de Hauteclocque. Tunisian nationalists, led by Mohamed Chenik, sent a petition to the United Nations Security Council in January 1952 to pressure the French into accepting their demands, but the Security Council decided that the Tunisian question would not be on its agenda. When demonstrations erupted throughout the country, Jean de Hauteclocque ordered security forces to intervene and placed Bourguiba under house arrest.

With Bourguiba under some semblance of control and knowing that they could always get him to compromise, the French turned their attention to Farhat Hached, whom they perceived as the main threat to their interests. In a telegram sent to the French president on May 16, 1952, Jean de Hauteclocque asserted, "Farhat Hached is as dangerous as was Bourguiba," adding, "only the annihilation of Farhat Hached will enable us to restore order."[77] On directives from the French that were carried out by a terrorist *colon* ring, *La Main rouge* (The Red Hand), Farhat Hached was assassinated on December 5, 1952.[78] Hached has survived in Tunisians' collective memory as a champion of the nationalist movement and a symbol behind the organization that would play a crucial role in Tunisia's affairs—leading up to independence and well beyond.

Negotiations and the path to independence were only resumed when the radical-socialist, Jewish-born Pierre Mendès-France was elected French president. In a July 31, 1954, speech that became known as the "*discours de Carthage*," Mendès-France announced France's intention to grant Tunisia full internal autonomy while protecting the rights of Frenchmen in Tunisia as well as those of their children. During his short tenure as president (1954–1955), Mendès-France terminated France's involvement in Indochina and paved the way for Tunisia's autonomy.

Franco-Tunisian negotiations started in Tunis on September 4, 1954, and produced six conventions that were signed in Paris in June 1955. The agreements were then ratified in August by the French parliament—marking the end of French interference in Tunisia's internal affairs. The 1955 conventions fell short of full independence for Tunisia in that they granted the country only internal autonomy and established a transitional period of two years during which France was responsible for maintaining public order. The French government, headed by Prime Minister

Edgar Faure, viewed internal autonomy as the end point, but Bourguiba accepted the 1955 conventions firmly believing them to be an intermediary step toward full independence.

Bourguiba made himself central to the negotiations with the French in 1954, but the nationalist movement had become divided. Salah Ben Youssef, who was secretary-general while Bourguiba was president of Neo-Destour, was opposed to any alliance with the French, and he outright rejected Bourguiba's conciliatory approach. Bourguiba fought hard for a strong—if redefined—relationship with France, but his former friend and Neo-Destour cofounder favored pan-Islamic forces and believed that a revitalization of the party's alliance with Zaitouna was critical to its development. Bourguiba, already pushing for a separation between religion and politics, insisted on distancing the party from Zaitouna as independence came within reach.

The animosity between the two grew as their worldviews became increasingly divergent. Their competition had also become a "clash of constituencies."[79] Bourguiba had the support of the lower middle class of merchants and landowners from the Sahel as well as the UGTT, while Ben Youssef was buoyed by religious authorities and conservative, religious elements of society that were skeptical of any compromise with the French.[80] Bourguiba's tight grip on the party, his alliance with the French, and the support of the powerful UGTT ultimately rendered Ben Youssef's attempts to counterweigh him futile.

Ben Youssef then turned to arms and appealed to a group of unemployed workers with links to UGTT known as the *fellaghas*, a name literally meaning bandits that was given to guerilla nationalist groups in French North Africa.[81] The *fellaghas* attacked French farms and police stations, especially in southern and western Tunisia, throughout 1954. The nationalist movement considered the possibility of turning the *fellaghas* into Tunisia's "liberation" and national army. Officially, Neo-Destour repeatedly condemned the *fellaghas*' "terrorist actions," but unofficially, some Neo-Destour leaders at first encouraged and even helped organize their attacks as a way to pressure the French into giving Tunisia greater autonomy. Pressure from France and from within Neo-Destour eventually led Bourguiba to work out an amnesty agreement for the *fellaghas*, who turned in their weapons.[82]

Bourguiba marginalized Ben Youssef within the party, eventually expelling him in October 1955. He also minimized his influence by, for instance, limiting the number of Ben Youssef supporters—referred to as Youssefists—who could attend the party's congress in Sfax in 1955.[83]

Bourguiba's distaste for Arab nationalism and for a role for religion in politics, set against Ben Youssef's vision for an independent Tunisia that was integrated into an Arab and Islamic world and aligned with Gamal Abdel Nasser's pan-Arabism, ultimately won the day. Salah Ben Youssef left Tunisia in 1955 and spent the remainder of his life in exile. He was assassinated in Frankfurt in 1961.

Had Ben Youssef won the fight with Bourguiba, things could have turned out differently for Tunisia. It is quite plausible that Tunisia would have turned east in its orientation and adopted a stronger Arab and Muslim identity. Nasserist political ideologies would have probably taken root, and Tunisia would have become entangled in the costly confrontation and acrimony that have defined the Realpolitik of the Arab world. All that had been accomplished in terms of reform, however, would likely have helped create some balance. It is perhaps even fair to say that Tunisia's enlightened trajectory up to that point abetted Bourguiba's victory over Ben Youssef and contributed to his support.

Bourguiba had promised to maintain a preferential link with France postindependence, and the French, wary of a Youssefist alternative, hastened the independence process.[84] French Prime Minister Guy Mollet acknowledged Tunisia's right to be independent before the National Assembly on January 31, 1956. Tunisia was helped by a declaration on November 6, 1955, that marked the end of the French protectorate in Morocco and anticipated full-fledged Moroccan independence, which was granted a year later.

Tunisia became an independent republic on March 20, 1956.

The nationalist movement, and Bourguiba's role in it, continued to define Tunisian identity long after 1956. The struggle for independence dominated the public narrative, including in school curricula and state-sponsored arts, for decades.

Unlike independence movements elsewhere in North Africa, Tunisia's was mostly indigenous and largely nonviolent. Libya's "liberation," by contrast, required the heavy involvement of the United Nations and

European states. The three main regions of Libya—Tripolitania, Fazzan, and Cyrenaica—only united in 1929 as a single colony under the Italians. There was no united, indigenous independence movement. Libya became independent by default after Italy's defeat in the Second World War, and its new king Idris al-Sanusi (1890–1983), a product of British patronage, had little support outside of his native Cyrenaica.[85]

Algeria was regarded as part of France rather than just a colony, and more than 1 million French men and women had settled there. At the time of Tunisia's independence, a bloody and costly war was raging, having started in Sétif, a small town in eastern Algeria, on May 8, 1945, where 10,000 Muslims had gathered on the morning after the exuberant celebrations of Victory in Europe. Demonstrations began peacefully with Muslims calling for equality and the end of colonialism, but then turned violent when a young man holding up the Algerian flag was accosted by a French police officer. Scuffles and gunshots followed; the twenty-six-year-old man "staggered out of the parade, dripping with blood, clutching the Algerian flag, and fell to the floor, shot dead." Fighting lasted five days, during which time more than 100 Europeans were killed in Sétif and neighboring towns, and countless women were raped. Bodies were grotesquely mutilated, and atrocities were committed on both sides—"it was as if the rage of over a hundred years was now being unleashed in this paroxysm of violence." The immediate reaction was the killing of an officially reported 6,000 Muslims in a few weeks, though what Algerians took as fact was the number 45,000 that was reported by Radio Cairo.[86] By the time a cease-fire was declared and Algeria gained its independence in 1962, two decades of carnage had claimed an estimated 1 million Algerian lives. On the European side, an estimated 18,000 French soldiers and 10,000 French settlers had been killed.[87] A mass exodus of approximately 1.35 million *pieds-noirs* (*colons*) back to Europe ensued, representing one of the largest mass migrations in history.[88]

When Morocco achieved independence in 1956, it did so both from the Spaniards, who ruled over the north and southwest provinces, and the French, who had held the rest of the country as a protectorate. Rebellions, violence, and the return of the exiled sultan, Muhammad V, who then became king in 1957, marked the final days of colonization. Tangier—a playground for Westerners and, later, Gulf Arabs—was made into an international zone under French, Spanish, and British control.

British intrigue and conquests by the al-Saud clan culminated in the creation of the Kingdom of Saudi Arabia in 1932. An alliance, the genesis of which dated back to the middle of the eighteenth century, between al-Saud and followers of Muhammad Ibn Abdelwahhab, underscored the construct of the new state. The forefather of the Saudi clan, Ibn Saud, had teamed up with Ibn Abdelwahhab in 1744, each having found something of great value that the other could offer. In Ibn Abdelwahhab's radical teachings and concept of jihad, Ibn Saud found an opportunity to seize power, an excuse for the use of force against "infidels," and a pretext to conquer more lands and expand the tribe's hegemony. Ibn Abdelwahhab, for his part, sought in the alliance an opportunity to shape what was to become known as the Wahhabi doctrine and to put into practice Ibn Taymiyya's vision of an Islamic society—intolerant and harsh, especially towards Shi'ites. The tribe of al-Saud controlled political, military, and financial matters, while Ibn Abdelwahhab and his descendants took over the religious and judicial spheres. That was the case in the second half of the eighteenth century, and such continued to be the scenario in the modern Saudi state of the twentieth century.

As Saudi Arabia started to claim a leadership role for the rest of the Islamic world, particularly after oil was discovered in the 1930s, the financial support of Wahhabism became a priority for the state. Wahhabism would change in the twentieth century from a revolutionary jihad waging ideology to a conservative institution with a royal Saudi family as its patron, spreading its extremist tentacles around the world and into the twenty-first century.

Wahhabism helped shape the ideology of the Muslim Brotherhood, founded in Cairo in 1929 by Hassan al-Banna (1906–1949) as the Society of the Muslim Brothers. The society adopted a political program that called for the eradication of all Western influences, particularly in the sphere of education, and the purification of Islamic society as the only means toward its salvation. The emblematic book of al-Banna's protégé Sayyid Qutb (1906–1966), *Ma'alim fi al-tariq* (Milestones), has served as a manifesto for Islamist fundamentalism.

Egypt had achieved nominal independence in 1922, but continued to be under the control of Britain, which installed a puppet monarchy and later dragged the country into the Second World War, turning it into an army base for British troops. The largest political party, Wafd, had lost credibility for its cooperation with the British during the war. Egyptians joined extreme, fascist-inspired nationalist groups such as Young Egypt, later renamed the Islamic Socialist Party. The Society of the Muslim Brothers conducted violent attacks and political assassinations. The Free Officers Coup toppled King Farouk (1920–1965) in 1952, and a military dictatorship took hold for the next sixty years.

The signing of a treaty between British diplomat Sir Mark Sykes (1879–1919) and former French consul in Lebanon François Georges-Picot (1870–1951) in 1916 had artificially divided up the Arab territories of the former Ottoman provinces of Syria and Mesopotamia into spheres of influence. The Conference of San Remo in 1920 granted new states independence, subject to British and French mandatory powers until "political maturity" was attained. New countries emerged where there had been none.

Three countries were created out of the Ottoman province of Syria: Lebanon, Syria, and Palestine. The state of Lebanon was born in 1926, but it did not gain independence and hold elections until 1943, when the last reigning French high commissioner left. Syria was declared a state in 1920 and became independent in 1946. The British established their mandate over Palestine in 1920, with the aim of realizing the promise they had made in the 1917 Balfour Declaration for the creation of a national home for the Jewish people.

Iraq was carved out of Mesopotamia, and the British installed the Hashemite Faisal (1885–1933) as king in 1921, granting the new state independence in 1932. Trans-Jordan was created in 1921, and the British named Faisal's brother Abdullah (1882–1951) emir of the new state. Jordan became an independent kingdom in 1946.

The smaller—compared to Saudi Arabia—nations of the Gulf came into being in the following decades as they gained independence from the British. Kuwait was the first to become independent in 1961, followed by Oman in 1970, and Bahrain, Qatar, and the newly formed United Arab Emirates in 1971.

With the departure of colonial powers from the region at large, instead of nations becoming states, we had states that were—for the most part—in search of nations. Many such states had been carved out—without much consideration for the histories, peoples, and geographies of the land. Former colonizers and "protectors" left a legacy of monarchical regimes and family dynasties to rule—with the exceptions of Algeria, Tunisia, Syria, and Lebanon.

New Arab leaders, few of whom had participated in national struggles for independence, relied on the populism of anticolonial sentiments and Islamic values to legitimize their authority. Some found in a military dictatorship and totalitarian model the path to constructing a national narrative, suppressing, for the time being, sectarian and tribal divides. Intent on nurturing an exclusionary and intolerant attitude, they provided their populaces with a poor education, thwarting citizens' abilities to think for themselves. When free Arab armies lost the war with Israel in 1948 and the Arab world became ensconced in a decades-long Arab-Israeli conflict, anti-Western rhetoric joined the ranks of religion and national fervor in ensuring that Arab citizens could only know absolute truth.

PART III

L'École, la Femme, et la "Laïcité"

11

The Father of Tunisia

Having finally achieved independence from the French, Bourguiba turned his immediate attention toward ensuring his grip on power and paving the way for his nation-building project. He wasted no time. Among his first tasks was to force a weakened and aging Lamine Bey to sign off on a decree that would create a constituent assembly. This would in turn clear the way for Neo-Destour to build governing bodies and get a constitution-writing process under way.

Elections were held on March 25, 1956, only five days after the independence protocol was signed. The *Front national destourien*—composed of Neo-Destour, *Union générale tunisienne du travail* (UGTT), *Union générale des agriculteurs tunisiens*, and employers—won 80 percent of the popular vote for the Constituent Assembly, and Bourguiba was appointed president of the new entity.[1] The Constituent Assembly would have the power to completely shape the future of the young country.

In April, the bey named Bourguiba prime minister and charged him with forming a government, an act that would forever ensure that it was the last one of any consequence by a bey.

Bourguiba would settle for nothing less than absolute power. Sixteen of the seventeen ministers that comprised his government were Neo-Destourians.[2] The diversity of the *Front national destourien* helped ensure that he got the support he needed to control the Constituent Assembly, but once in power, he showed no interest in a pluralistic approach to governance.

Thus the daunting task of building a nation started in earnest. Compared to many Arab countries that had little in the way of a national history, Tunisia had much to fall back on: experience with procedural democracy through its political parties and labor unions; the legacy of a constitution that it had once adopted; the institutionalism of a functioning state with local civil administrators; and an educated political leadership that grew out of an intellectual reform movement. Tunisia had already had many of the characteristics of a budding nation-state as far back as the middle of the nineteenth century and the reign of Ahmad Bey.

The first session of the Constituent Assembly took place on April 8, 1956. Five specialized commissions were formed to deliberate the conditions within which executive and legislative powers would be exercised. Much as in the case of the drafting of the 2014 constitution, divisions on the place of religion in Tunisian society and the role and rights of women surfaced immediately. In another parallel, the more liberal voices ultimately got their way.

The first question before the assembly concerned the form of government Tunisia should have. The assembly debated a constitutional monarchy model, but concluded that Tunisia would be a republic. A decree placing the beylical family under the purview of the state was passed, and the bey was stripped of the power to choose the prime minister.

The constitution of 1861 served as a model of sorts for the new constitution. Neither used Shari'a as the source of its laws, and both created civil, commercial, and criminal courts and legal codes that buttressed them. The new constitution additionally insisted on an independent judiciary and a supreme court that could try government officials.[3] In this, as in so much else, Tunisia was way ahead of other Arab countries and, in some respects, ahead of its time.

Western constitutions, particularly the American, were a source of inspiration in that the new constitution defined Tunisia as a democracy and upheld the separation of powers among the executive, judiciary, and legislature. The constitution established a parliamentary body in the form of a national assembly, which would replace the Constituent Assembly and would be elected every five years by popular vote. The assembly would have legislative powers and fiscal responsibilities, but constitutional articles stipulated circumstances under which the president was afforded legislative authority. Executive power would be exercised through the president, who would be popularly elected for a five-year term and have a three-term limit—provisions that both Bourguiba and Ben Ali would amend in due course in order to extend their hold on power.

Separation of state and religion was not as clearly delineated, however. Reservations about proclaiming Islam the religion of the state, in part for fear of alienating non-Muslim communities, and suggestions that the state should be civil were met with strong opposition from conservative members of the Constituent Assembly.[4] Ultimately, and as echoed in the 2014 constitution, Islam was identified descriptively as the religion of Tunisians but not prescribed as the state religion, thus arguably closing the door on the possibility of introducing Shari'a. The 2014 constitution went further in explicitly defining Tunisia as a civil state.

There were other innovations for which the 2014 constitution is celebrated but which were actually established by the postindependence constitution. The idea of freedom of conscience being constitutionally protected goes back to Bourguiba's constitution. But while the 1959 constitution included explicit language about freedom of conscience in its French edition, its Arabic version only spoke of freedom of religion. The 2014 postindependence constitution, in both languages, ensured that freedom of conscience was protected. In this respect, Tunisia became the only Arab country in which nonbelievers are protected by the law and cannot be prosecuted for apostasy. Tunisia remains the only such country in the entire Arab world.

Opinions were divided on whether voting rights should be granted to all Tunisian citizens, including women. Progressive thinkers, such as cofounder of *L'Action tunisienne* and Neo-Destour's first president, Mahmoud Matri, contended that women should have the right to vote as they were as well educated as men. Traditionalists—primarily men who hailed from the interior of the country—objected.[5]

But Habib Bourguiba had already granted women the right to vote in the 1957 municipal elections, thus setting a precedent. Universal suffrage became cemented with the passing of the constitution, which included an article that stated: "All citizens have equal rights and duties and are equal before the law."[6]

The assembly adopted the first constitution of an independent Tunisia on June 1, 1959.

Tunisia held two elections on November 8, 1959: presidential and parliamentary. Ninety-one percent of eligible Tunisians voted. Bourguiba won the presidency, for which he, unsurprisingly, had run unopposed. The *Front national destourien*, led by Neo-Destour, won all ninety seats in the new parliament.[7] A woman won one seat, and another seat went to a Jew.[8]

The transformation of Tunisia into an independent republic was sealed. But there were enduring remnants of the colonial era.

France would remain Tunisia's largest trading partner, as was the case with postindependence Morocco and later Algeria. But the lingering colonial presence in Tunisia, which France continued to treat as its domain, was problematic. The sustained existence of the French military, particularly in Bizerte, and Tunisia's support of Algerian rebels became the thorniest issues between the two countries.

Algerian nationalists in 1954 created the *Front de libération nationale* (FLN). With the support of the civilian population, a guerilla war ensued—exhausting the French army and causing ruinous damage to *colons'* farms and installations. Tunisia, newly independent itself and with immense public backing for the revolution in Algeria, gave its support to FLN.

Bourguiba walked a tightrope. He called for peaceful steps toward Algeria's independence, but permitted FLN guerillas to establish camps inside Tunisia, where they would regroup when their battalions had been weakened. This led to the targeting of Algerians by the French within Tunisia. Bourguiba's sanctioning of Algerian camps inside his borders created a precarious scenario, given the presence of the French military. Tunisia was acting as a launching pad for both sides of the war, and it was thus natural that the violence sometimes spilled over.

French military presence had been a condition set forth in the independence agreement. France considered it strategically important for it to station its troops in Tunisia, given its war effort in neighboring Algeria. French president Charles de Gaulle agreed in 1958 to withdraw French forces, but insisted on retaining an air base in Bizerte, France's largest foreign Mediterranean base. De Gaulle wanted to secure the Algerian border and to keep an eye on French oil interests to the south in the loosely defined Sahara region.

Conflict over the presence of French troops in Bizerte escalated to a crisis point in 1961 and eventually led to French evacuation, but only after causing heavy Tunisian casualties—mostly civilian.

On July 4, 1961, on the pretext that the French had illegally expanded the Bizerte air base—apparently by two meters—Bourguiba directed Tunisian volunteers to infiltrate the base and blockade it.[9] The scene became violent when the army opened fire on any French military personnel who tried to move out of the base. De Gaulle, who was losing the war in Algeria and could not afford to appear weak, sent several thousand paratroopers and four warships to the scene.

Tunisian youth organizations, students, women's unions, labor unions, and even the Children of Bourguiba—an organization for orphans—joined a carefully orchestrated "spontaneous demonstration" toward the Bizerte base. The cynical French troops, hardened by the violence in Algeria, fired on the marching civilians indiscriminately. Fighting went on for three full days. By the time it was over, between 1,300 and 2,000 Tunisians had lost their lives. France evacuated the forces it had sent to Bizerte, but restored the status quo ex ante on September 29, 1961.

Remarkably, Bourguiba was compelled in his acquiescence by his desire to ensure that instruction by French teachers in Tunisian schools, on which he relied heavily, would not be jeopardized, especially with the beginning of the academic year. French instructors, for their part, made demands for their security and safety before resuming work.[10] Bourguiba's education agenda trumped all else.

Tensions with the French eased after their eventual withdrawal from Algeria in 1962 and their subsequent evacuation from Bizerte in October 1963, and relations ever since have tended to be better than between France and her other former colonies. Tunisia remained a desirable and safe destination for French travelers, and driven by economic opportunity, many Tunisians migrated to France.

While working to define Tunisia's new relationship with its former colonizer, Bourguiba was outwardly projecting an identity that he was building at home. Bourguiba's astuteness, charisma, and diplomatic skills allowed him to catapult Tunisia onto the world stage, making it a player that often punched above its weight in regional and world affairs.

But he maintained a noninterventionist stance, and his ambitions for Tunisia did not include territorial or hegemonic aims. In a famous speech at the Palmarium Theater in Tunis, in response to an overture by Libya's Muammar Gaddafi for a union between the two countries, he said in 1972: "Every country is free to have its own system. If it wants to change it, it should be the one to change it and fix it for the better. We shouldn't interfere in what is not ours, and encourage revolutions and send arms."[11]

Bourguiba was unabashedly pro-Western, taking bold positions against the Soviet Union in the Cold War while some Arab leaders aligned themselves with the Soviets—distrustful as they were of the United States and its support for Israel. He publicly snubbed pan-Arab movements, and he initially declined to have Tunisia join the League of Arab States. Bourguiba's relationship with the league was always tenuous, boycotting it as he did in 1968 in protest over what he saw as acquiescence by Arabs to the Soviets.

Less than a week after independence, Bourguiba published an article in the *New York Times* in which he pledged Tunisia's unequivocal support of the West and made a case for the country to join the North Atlantic Treaty Organization. In Western foreign policy journals, he published pro-Western articles, such as one in 1957 titled "Nationalism: Antidote to Communism," and another in 1958 titled "We Choose the West."[12]

The first major power to do so, the United States recognized Tunisia's independence in 1957 and supplied it with financial aid that grew in the 1960s to account for one-sixth of the country's economic growth.[13] American assistance helped compensate for France's withdrawal of its subsidies between 1957 and 1963 in retaliation for Tunisian support of Algeria's *Front de libération nationale*.[14]

Relationships between Bourguiba and his American counterparts became close, and there were state visits by him to the United States and by American officials to Tunisia.

When President Dwight Eisenhower visited Tunisia on December 17, 1959, he asked Bourguiba how the United States could be most helpful. Bourguiba responded with a request not for arms but for food, education, and shelter for his people. Bourguiba asked for an additional 80,000 to 90,000 tons of wheat on top of the 40,000 tons Tunisia had already received, for access to schoolteachers and opportunities to train technicians and engineers, and for help in financing public housing.[15]

Habib Bourguiba's first state visit to the United States took place on May 3–5, 1961, and included a stop in New York, where he was met by cheering crowds. President Kennedy drew parallels between Bourguiba and George Washington in his praise for the Tunisian leader's attainment of independence for his country.[16]

Motivated by an opportunity to increase its influence in the country at France's expense, the United States acted in line with the Truman Doctrine of 1947, which established that it would assist—politically, militarily, and economically—democracies that were under threat from Soviet encroachment. Cooperation between the two nations included opening Tunisian ports to the U.S. Sixth Fleet. Scenes of U.S. Navy helicopters rescuing Tunisian civilians who were injured and trapped after a large dam had broken in the Majerda Valley in 1973 bore testament to the special relationship between the Western superpower and the small North African country.[17]

The United States brandished Tunisia as a model of democracy, especially for other African states, whose leaders soon looked toward Bourguiba's example when planning their own postindependence programs.[18] In a *Harper's Magazine* article published in 1957, Bourguiba was described as "far more friendly, rational, and long-sighted than the hysterical [Gamal Abdel] Nasser types further East—and his country offers a test case of immense importance to America."[19]

Bourguiba's alignment with the West was in line with his ideological independence from popular ideologies that were taking hold elsewhere in the Arab world—Ba'athism and Nasserite pan-Arabism most prominent among them.

Ba'athist ideology had its roots among Arab students, such as the Damascene, Christian-born Michel Aflaq (1910–1989), who had studied in Paris. Drawn to the anti-Western and anti-imperialist stances of communist and socialist movements that were on the rise, Aflaq and his compatriots sought a regenerative process to reform Arab society in the face of imperialism. They were fellow students of Tunisian would-be Neo-Destourians, many of whom had also studied at the Sorbonne and other elite institutions in Paris in the 1920s and 1930s, but who, unlike their peers from further east, returned home to contribute to a determinedly Tunisian anticolonial movement—drawing inspiration from the West.

With pan-Arab aspirations, the Arab Socialist Ba'ath Party, founded in 1947, accepted members irrespective of their religion, sect, or nationality— to the extent that meaningful state nationalism existed at the time. The movement had Marxist underpinnings and attracted communists, but it lacked a clear and consistent manifesto. It was secularist, but it had Islamic undertones: Ba'athism rested on an appreciation of exclusionary blood ties that were linked to the lineage of Islam.

A successful coup led by the military branch of the party in 1963, without the civilian leadership's knowledge, activated an enduring and authoritarian Ba'athist rule in Syria. The Iraqi regional branch of Ba'ath came into power through a military coup in 1968 and was sustained by Saddam Hussein until the 2003 U.S. invasion.

As Ba'athism was taking hold in Syria and Iraq, a comparatively less ideological but more ambitious, hegemonic, and dogmatic Arab nationalist movement grew out of Cairo in the 1950s. The leader of the movement, Gamal Abdel Nasser, who, like Bourguiba, was an all-star nationalist leader who came to power after independence, led the Free Officers group that overthrew King Farouk in 1952 before becoming prime minister of Egypt in 1954 and president in 1956.

Charming and charismatic, Nasser played on the romanticism of the notion of a pan-Arabism that would give a consciousness to Arabs—transcending tribal, ethnic, and territorial divides. Nasser adopted an Arab and Islamic identity and wanted to move Egypt to the center of a great Arab nation and away from an ancient Egyptian or Pharaonic ancestral distinctiveness.

The great Arab nation that Nasser was attempting to create was a revival of an idea that had been put to rest decades earlier. Pan-Arabism, whether in the form of Ba'athist ideology or Nasserite rhetoric, had its roots in the time of the decline of the Ottoman Empire, and it peaked prior to and during the First World War. Hussein Ibn Ali, the Hashemite emir of Mecca who led the Great Arab Revolt against the Turks in 1916 and whose sons would later rule Iraq and Jordan, called for the establishment of an Arab nation and saw himself as "King of the Arabs."

Nasser broadcasted his captivating speeches, ripe with fantastical hyperbole, on his radio station *Sawt al-Arab* (Voice of the Arabs). *Sawt al-Arab* reached living rooms across the entire Arab world, capturing the imagination of Arab publics. Egyptian teachers did their bidding on behalf of Gamal Abdel Nasser as well. In ample supply and sought after throughout an Arab world that had shortages, they became emissaries of Nasserism, with classrooms as their stages.[20]

Nasser's appeal was so compelling, and viable alternatives were so lacking, that Michel Aflaq and Syria's Ba'ath government at the time sought a union with Egypt in 1958. The United Arab Republic, which hoped to bring other Arab countries into its fold, lasted for only three years, however.

Syrians quickly became suspicious of Egypt, perceiving it as imperialist in its designs and exploitative of their resources in its actions. Nasser's despotic policies and Cairo's domination over the union prompted Syria to secede in 1961. Distrust and accusations grew on both sides, a scenario that would quintessentially characterize intraregional politics more broadly for much of the Middle East's postcolonial history.

Bourguiba had distaste for the notion of an Arab union, and he did not believe that it could be attained. Having brought independence to his country, Bourguiba emerged more confident and successful than his Arab counterparts. He was not emotionally stuck, as others were, in the nostalgia of the long-past golden era of Arab Muslim greatness or the fantastical aspirations of an Arab *umma*.

"People can only unite when their minds change and when they understand the meaning of nationhood, which we created," he declared in his famous 1972 Palmarium speech. Bourguiba spoke of his connectedness to his people and of his determination to change their mind-set, reminding them of the uniqueness of their national identity, rich heritage, and unity over the ages. In the same speech, he said: "Why Tunisia and not the Arab world? Because: for thousands of years, since the time of Carthage, Tunisia has had its own personality. We lived together, generation after generation. The Arab world was never as united as we are."[21]

Tunisia's unique history and identity served as a point of differentiation from the Arab world. Bourguiba much preferred a Mediterranean identity and Eurocentric policies for his nation, not unlike how the founder of modern Turkey, Kemal Ataturk, steered his young nation at the time of its founding in 1923. Bourguiba completely subscribed to the Western paradigm and pushed for Western modernization, not surprising given his education and that he was very much a product of French colonialism. He was fixated on demonstrating that Tunisia could realistically aspire to a European benchmark.

Bourguiba altogether distrusted the Egyptian leader and considered his pan-Arab ideology a threat to Tunisia's security. Tensions had developed ever since Egypt provided refuge to the exiled Salah Ben Youssef in the mid-1950s, and they grew in intensity over the question of Palestine. Except for a temporary lull in friction between 1961 and 1963, when Nasser expressed solidarity with Tunisia against the French over the Bizerte crisis, the relationship between the two leaders was openly and vehemently contentious.

Acrimony between the two countries escalated in 1966 when Bourguiba tried, unsuccessfully, to intervene to prevent the execution of the Muslim Brotherhood leader Sayyid Qutb and a number of his collaborators. Bourguiba was unsympathetic toward the Muslim Brotherhood, but he felt more threatened by the populist appeal of Nasser's pan-Arabism.[22] Bourguiba's attempted intervention was ironic in two respects: Bourguiba himself would suppress Islamists in his own country later on, and Sayyid Qutb went against everything that Bourguiba stood for, having famously declared that the affairs of human beings should unequivocally be governed by the system that God had "decreed." Diplomatic relations were ultimately severed in October 1966 when Radio Cairo accused Tunisians of collaborating with imperialist powers.[23]

The rivalry between Nasser and Bourguiba often played out on the stage of the League of Arab States. Arab countries that also felt threatened by Gamal Abdel Nasser and his pan-Arabist dogma—including Iraq, Lebanon, Saudi Arabia, and other Gulf countries—saw Tunisia as a natural ally. But Bourguiba's stance on Palestine and his compromising attitude toward Israel made it difficult for him to sustain alliances within the Arab League.

In the years leading to independence, Bourguiba had leveraged the Palestinian cause to win popularity and had written in 1946 in support of it to the Anglo-American Commission charged with investigating the question of Palestine.[24] He had branded Israel's existence as a form of colonialism and had likened its policies to those of apartheid in South Africa.[25] Bourguiba did not, however, promote hatred toward Israel, and he drew distinctions between Jewishness and Zionism.

True to his pragmatic and diplomatic ways, Bourguiba later called for a resolution with Israel—as early as in 1952. He was more open to reconciliation than any other Arab nation, and he offered to mediate the conflict in the Arab League. Just as he had done in dealing with the French regarding his country, Bourguiba called for a gradual and flexible approach of working in stages toward a resolution.

In a highly controversial speech delivered on March 3, 1965, in Jericho, Bourguiba pleaded with Palestinians to accept an Israeli state as a starting point. He advised that *siyaset al-marahel*, the "policy of stages" that he had practiced successfully in Tunisia, be employed. "In Palestine," he said, "the Arabs pushed away the compromise solutions. They refused the division and the clauses of the White Paper. They regretted it then. If we had in Tunisia refused in 1954 the internal autonomy as a compromise solution, the country would have remained until this day under the French domination."[26]

Bourguiba persisted in his advocacy for a phased solution to the Palestinian problem. He called on Arabs to accept the 1947 United Nations Partition Plan for Palestine into an Arab and a Jewish state. His argument appealed to self-interest: he argued that should Arabs accept Israel's existence, they would then gain the support of the international community on moral grounds and would create room for making further demands. He pleaded with Arabs to be less emotional and more pragmatic on the issue of Palestine, and to dispose of empty rhetoric. "Enthusiasm and passionate demonstrations of patriotism are not enough to achieve victory," he declared.[27] In a speech in Lebanon, which he visited after Jericho, Bourguiba openly challenged Abdel Nasser's ideology, urging Arab leaders to be transparent with their people and not to propagate a culture of faulting the West for all of the region's ills. "Look forward to building your nation and stop blaming the past," Bourguiba instructed.[28]

Strong condemnation of these views forced Bourguiba at times to adopt an apologetic attitude. In an April 1965 note to Gamal Abdel Nasser, Bourguiba wrote that he shared Nasser's wish for Palestine to be free but that he was interested in helping break the political stalemate and in making way for future concessions from Israel. Nasser continued to denounce Bourguiba and his ideas, portraying them as betrayal of the Arabs and of the pan-Arabism cause. Bourguiba's condemnation by the Arab League— endorsed by all members except Lebanon, Morocco, Kuwait, and Saudi Arabia—almost led to the expulsion of Tunisia from the league. Just as the old Destour had accused him of betrayal when he negotiated with the French for Tunisia's independence, and just as he was proven right in that instance, Bourguiba knew better than his Arab peers.

While the Jericho speech alienated Bourguiba from an Arab critical mass, it resulted in the opening of a number of back-channel communications with Israel. Israel's foreign ministry made efforts to demonstrate support for Bourguiba, arranging for his candidacy for the 1966 Nobel Peace Prize, which he did not win. Bourguiba's reach within Israel included the reinforcement by Israel's intelligence apparatus, Mossad, of his security detail on a November 1965 visit to Liberia .[29]

Bourguiba's neutrality was stoic. When the Arab-Israeli Six-Day War broke out in 1967, Arab states and the Tunisian population put pressure on Bourguiba to sever his ties with the United States and Britain, but he refused. Tunisia, along with Morocco, also maintained relations with West Germany when the rest of the Arab world cut off ties with the Western power over its supply of arms to Israel in the mid-1960s.

Although some at home viewed Bourguiba as brave, others criticized his foreign policy and found him to be too daring and even reckless. Tunisians did not necessarily share Bourguiba's compromising stance toward Israel, nor his pro-Western bias. Anti-Zionist demonstrations erupted across the country during the 1967 Six-Day War. Bourguiba denounced assaults on Jewish citizens and properties, which included looting Jewish-owned shops and setting fire to the Great Synagogue in Tunis.[30] Sustained emigration of Tunisian Jews followed the war—diminishing by half the Jewish population that had existed at the time of independence.[31]

Bourguiba's foreign policy stance became conciliatory toward the Arab world in the 1970s. He supported the Arabs in the 1973 Arab-Israeli War and contributed a small number of forces to the effort. But his support was more for show than anything else: he had his troops parade for days on end across the country before being shipped to the battlefront, in an attempt to avoid physically joining the war effort.

Then, in 1978, Tunisia was drawn closer to the Arab world when the headquarters of the Arab League moved from Cairo to Tunis after Anwar Sadat (1918–1981, r. 1970–1981) signed the Camp David Accords with Israel.

But when Israel invaded Lebanon in 1982, Bourguiba was reluctant to allow the Palestine Liberation Organization (PLO) to move its headquarters to Tunisia—an eventual move that was orchestrated by the United States. Bourguiba wanted to dissociate his country from the conflict and feared that the move would hurt Tunisia's thriving tourism industry. He was mindful of how the PLO had virtually governed large areas of Lebanon and, before that, Jordan.

Ironically, relations with the United States reached a low point in 1985 over the very presence of the PLO in Tunisia. Bourguiba considered cutting off relations with the United States when President Reagan publicly sanctioned an Israeli Air Force bombardment of PLO headquarters on the outskirts of Tunis. Nearly one hundred people were killed or injured, a large number of them Tunisians.[32] But Bourguiba was later pacified when the U.S. government retracted its support for the attack.

Bourguiba's unconventional foreign affairs positions were driven partly by his conviction and partly by his strategic and political astuteness. He wanted to spare Tunisia from entanglement in the conflict and from having the question of Palestine dominate political and domestic affairs, as became the case in much of the Arab world. He was also cognizant of how critical it was for him to appease the West, and the United States in particular, vis-à-vis Israel. Bourguiba longed for Tunisia to receive the international attention it had enjoyed before its independence.[33] Bourguiba wanted to match Nasser's presence on the international arena, and he was therefore driven to assume controversial and dramatic stances.

By the 1970s, Bourguiba was beginning to be viewed as impulsive. His health was starting to deteriorate following his first heart attack, in 1967. Tunisians worried when he signed a union agreement with Libya's Gaddafi at a meeting in 1974 on the Tunisian island of Djerba. The rash decision to enter into the agreement caught everyone by surprise, coming just over a year after Bourguiba declared: "Muammar Gaddafi told me he was ready to give me the power to rule both countries . . . but Libya needs to unite its own people first. Tripoli is in one end of the country, Fezzan is in another—and the desert between them . . . Libyans are not even living in the Middle Ages—they are living in the time of the Prophet Adam!"[34]

The Tunisian-Libyan marriage lasted a mere twenty-four hours until Prime Minister Hedi Nouira, who had been traveling at the time of the announcement, blocked it. Gaddafi was slow to forgive Bourguiba, and relations between the two countries declined precipitously after Tunisia pulled out of the union plan. Libya launched an insurrection campaign inside Tunisia, and Tunisian officials accused Gaddafi of attempts to depose the regime. In 1980, insurgents, trained and supported by Libya and Algeria, led an attack on Gafsa.

Despite these hostilities, Bourguiba was about to make the same mistake a decade after the "Djerba incident," as the signing of the union charter with Gaddafi on hotel stationery came to be known. It was through the intervention of the American and French embassies that a repeat union was avoided; the U.S. ambassador at the time referenced the averted decision as reflecting "a low point in [Bourguiba's] psychological state."[35] In retaliation, Gaddafi expelled 32,000 Tunisian workers in 1985, bringing

the two countries to the brink of a border war, which Algerian intervention avoided.[36] In all likelihood, Tunisia would have been defeated had war
broken out, given the size and state of its army.

Nonbelligerent and noncombatant, Tunisia did not need a large army,
and Bourguiba never invested in building one—developing it only enough
to effectively carry out its basic security goals and meet pressing issues.
Bourguiba drew his foreign policy strength from his diplomatic skills, not
from a large army, on which countries like Egypt spent heavily. By the end
of the 1950s, Bourguiba spent 10 percent of the national budget on the military, compared to 18 percent on education, with spending on the latter
eventually reaching almost 35 percent of the government budget.[37] Unwittingly, Bourguiba protected postrevolutionary Tunisia from the imperious
and undemocratic reach of a strong army.

Tunisia had maintained a small military since the late 1850s when
Ahmad Bey recoiled from his expensive army modernization programs.
That legacy survived and was reinforced by the French, who did not allow
armed forces to develop beyond a certain point under the protectorate.
Bourguiba extended French colonial policy and deliberately kept the military weak and apolitical, with little or no chance of exerting the kind of
influence armies had in other parts of the Arab world.

Deep personal distrust of the army was another motivation. Shortly after
the disastrous Bizerte gamble, a plot to overthrow Bourguiba was hatched,
and it was uncovered afterward that elements within the military—militant
Youssefists and communists—were responsible. The ten individuals implicated in the assassination attempt were summarily executed, following a
rushed tribunal and a live media broadcast of the sentencing. Bourguiba's
suspicion of the army marked the beginning of his obsession with boosting
internal security forces under the auspices of the interior ministry, mold-
ing Tunisia into a police state.

But after the 1980 Libyan-led attack on Gafsa, Bourguiba launched a
military modernization plan. Toward the end of his presidency, Bourguiba
invested heavily in developing his armed forces, increasing spending on it
from $18.8 million in 1981 to $125 million in 1982. Spending was projected
to reach nearly $1 billion by 1986 had the expenditure not strained the
economy and threatened the regime's stability.[38]

On the home front, although Tunisia's independence had been achieved
through a nationalist struggle in which the whole country came together,

nation building still required the creation of a cohesive Tunisian identity and the fusing of different orientations and class divisions.

Tensions often occurred along geographic and topographic lines: between the Sahel and the interior, urban centers and the countryside, and the north and the south of the country. They were also naturally evident in disparities between those who were members of the political elite and those who were not; the latter tended to be not as well, if not poorly, educated. The persistent rivalry between followers of Bourguiba and those aligned with Salah Ben Youssef, or Youssefists, also continued to divide the country.

Tribalism, to the extent it existed, was another factor that needed to be considered in building a uniform postcolonial Tunisian identity. Divisions across tribal lines posed a threat to the unification of the nation—in terms of both politics and identity. The threat was tempered, however, as tribal affiliations were far less prevalent in Tunisia than some countries in North Africa and the Middle East.

Tribes across the Maghreb had been free to run their own affairs, independent of any central authority. In Libya, tribes had little interaction with the central government under Ottoman and then colonial rule. But in Tunisia, the bey kept tribes in check by imposing administrative controls and through the army. Central control of tribal affairs increased under the French protectorate government, which exerted its authority over tribes in the interior of the country and imposed a territorial-based reorganization. France carved out thirty-six administrative units known as *qiyadas*, or governorates, so that tribes were now identified through their territorial, and not tribal, affiliations.[39]

Neo-Destour played the tribal issue to its benefit on two competing fronts. On the one hand, the party took advantage of the discontent and set up relationships of patronage with tribes, providing them with services and aid in exchange for their support against the French.[40] But Neo-Destour also furthered the policy started by the French. By setting up party bureaus throughout the country along geographic contours that sometimes cut across tribal lines, Neo-Destour ignored loyalties and rivalries defined by kinship and replaced existing structures with those of the party.[41]

In postindependence Tunisia, Bourguiba sought a transition from tribal and religious cohesions to state solidarity. He saw the prevalent tribal tradition of marrying within one's own family or clan as serving a "greedy objective of preserving the patrimony of the kin group from strangers." He pontificated on the potential health hazards associated with the practice and the danger it posed in terms of producing "children who are deformed and retarded."[42]

Bourguiba often referred to tribal structures as "archaic," and he implemented a series of reforms aimed at limiting tribal power. A 1958 law abolished collective ownership of tribal lands, which were to be redistributed to individuals. Other reforms, such as the setting up of a unified judicial system and the imposition in 1959 of patronymic family names for all Tunisians—clearly directed against tribal members who had been named according to their paternal lineage—helped in the further disintegration of a tribal structure.[43] In this, as in other instances, Bourguiba may have looked to Kemal Ataturk for inspiration. Turkey had adopted a similar law in 1934, requiring all Turkish citizens to adopt a Turkish family name and banning all honorific titles inherited from the Ottoman Empire, including tribal titles.

Tribal members began to self-identify as Tunisian first—not as members of a given kin group—and to develop loyalty toward the nation. There were exceptions, especially in the underdeveloped south, which was much less influenced by the central government and therefore much less integrated into the national fabric.[44]

In comparison, state building in Morocco was predicated on limited interference in local tribal affairs by the monarchy, which needed the support of rural elites. Tribes became the repositories of independent Morocco's traditional and Islamic identity. Through land redistribution schemes and power sharing agreements, tribes became the backbone of the monarchy and political system in Morocco—a scenario that is not very different from ones that emerged in countries further east, such as Jordan.

Bourguiba understood that the path to building a modern nation-state and to sculpting a Tunisian character necessitated the eradication of tribal structures. This proved to be one of the most significant differentiating factors in his nation-building exercise, compared to other countries in the region.

Tunisia's comparatively homogeneous—ethnically and religiously—populace and its small territory assisted Bourguiba in his goal of achieving national integration. Bourguiba promoted the notion of Tunisia as "one family, united like the foundations of a structure without defects."[45] In a

1961 speech, Bourguiba compared the nation and its citizens to a "human being whose organs are interdependent."[46] Bourguiba was cognizant of the need to erase internal divisions and to transcend them with the unifying idea of a nation. But he also erased from memory others who fought and died for independence, focusing the narrative of the birth of the nation on himself.

In the arts, which government patronized and used as a mouthpiece for its national agenda, Bourguiba ensured that he was at the center of the nationalist rhetoric. The figure of Bourguiba was prominent in the works of the contemporary visual art movement *École de Tunis*, founded in 1947 by the *pied-noir* painter Pierre Boucherle (1894–1988) and home to Tunisian, French, and Italian painters. The *École de Tunis* marked a clear departure from the colonial period by attempting to create an authentic *tunisianité*, mixing descriptions of the origins of Tunisia with modern motifs.[47]

In 1962, a leading figure of the *École de Tunis*, Zoubeir Turki (1924–2009)—a graduate of Zaitouna, the *École des beaux-arts* in Tunis, and the Stockholm-based Academy of Art—painted a mural titled *La Procession des Mourabtines* in the lobby of the now demolished Hotel Ribat in Bourguiba's hometown of Monastir. In this painting, Turki portrayed a scene from Tunisia's early Islamic history: a religious procession of volunteer warriors departing from Monastir's eighth-century *ribat*, or Islamic fort, with Bourguiba in the lead. Bourguiba's depiction as a twentieth-century figure in the middle of an eighth-century historical scene brought to life at once his self-propagated image of a modernizing force and *al-mujahid al-akbar*, or the greatest warrior.[48]

In part to encourage cultural works in Arabic, Neo-Destour campaigned to designate Abu al-Qasim al-Shabbi as the national poet of Tunisia, two decades after his passing. The party inserted the first four lines of "The Will to Live" into the national anthem, which was later suspended by President Bourguiba in favor of a new anthem that glorified him—only to be later reinstated by Ben Ali.

In addition to the role of the arts, Bourguiba, like many a postcolonial nation builder, believed that education could help cultivate an authentic national identity. Bourguiba also saw education as a means to fight what he termed *les structures mentales* of Tunisians who were opposed or indifferent to his programs of modernization. He believed that schools would develop respect for the party, build support for his programs, and help overcome what he saw as a lack of national unity.[49] This was going to be accomplished through primary education, which would perform a social function, so he set out to implement a universal national education system.

Bourguiba wanted to produce a specific version of a Tunisian narrative, aimed at projecting a glorious past and rooted in the history of the nationalist movement. He thought that this would counter internal divisions and have a homogenizing effect, reminding the population of how the entire nation had come together around a common goal.

Within a few years of independence, the "Bourguibization" of national history became evident in textbooks. The objective was to create a "national mythology as a basis for collective memory" around Bourguiba the leader.[50] There was a personification process at work whereby, in the modern history of Tunisia after the 1934 Ksar Hellal congress at which Neo-Destour was founded, Bourguiba's personal history and the history of the country merged into a single narrative. Textbooks presented Tunisia's history in two clearly demarcated parts: a pre-1934 history, and a post-1934 national history.[51]

Works of literature challenged Bourguiba's monopolization of the independence narrative while still reinforcing the centrality of the nationalist movement in the Tunisian identity. Bashir Khurayyif's (1917–1983) *Digla fi 'arajiniha* (Dates in Their Branches), published in 1969 and set in southern Tunisia in the 1920s, described the Tunisian labor movement and the struggles of mineworkers as precursors to the independence movement. Mohamed Laroussi al-Matwi (1920–2005) produced two fictional works, *Halima* in 1964 and *al-Tut al-murr* (The Bitter Berries) in 1967, both of which depicted the suffering of southern Tunisians and the beginnings of the independence movement. These and other important works of literature published in the decades following independence provided an alternative narrative, underscoring the part played by everyday Tunisians in the decolonization project.[52]

Set against works critical of Bourguiba were many that gave his narrative a strong voice, such as Omar Khlifi's 1966 feature film—arguably Tunisia's first—*al-Fajr* (The Dawn), which documented the story of the nationalist struggle against the French and ended with the heroic return of Bourguiba from exile. Some of Khlifi's later works—*Le rebelle* in 1968, *Les fellaghas* in 1970, and *Hurlements* in 1972—reproduced the official history of the nation with Neo-Destour and Bourguiba at the center.

In his own mind, Bourguiba was responsible for the nationalist movement and Tunisia's independence, and he could not envision that the
country could be ruled by anyone but him. Bourguiba's biggest mistake
was that he did not know when to withdraw from the political arena. When
his three consecutive terms as president were over in 1975, Bourguiba
declared himself president for life, ending any illusion of even a pseu-
dodemocratic form of government. He did not believe that Tunisians could
demonstrate sound judgment—it had not occurred to him that, with time,
they would start to question his own judgment—or that they were ripe for
a full-fledged democracy. "How can we trust the decision-making capacity
of the multitude?" he quibbled in a 1970 speech.[53] Bourguiba was singularly responsible for Tunisia's successes and failures—he alone ran what
he termed a "controlled democracy."[54] Bourguiba thought that he was the
nation and that the nation was he. He perceived himself as being above the
law—indeed, he thought of himself as the law. When asked about Tunisia's
political system, he famously answered: "The system? What system? I am
the system!"[55]

Bourguiba saw himself as the nation's savior and educator, projecting
a persona of a moral being who was rational and capable of self-sacrifice
and, therefore, had the aptitude to lead the nation.[56] He spoke of being
inspired to dedicate his life to Tunisia as a young student in Paris by the
inscription on the statue at Place de la Sorbonne of the French philosopher
Auguste Comte that read "Vivre pour autrui" ("Live for others").[57] He also
spoke of how his time in France had helped him understand the French so
that he could later know how to negotiate with them and achieve his aims.
Boasting of how his experience in France had been crucial to Tunisia's
independence, Bourguiba said: "I invented my own way, after learning and
travelling and living in France for three years. I learned their weaknesses
and their strengths."[58]

Wanting to appear available and approachable to his people, Bourguiba took regular trips across Tunisia and addressed local populations.
He frequently used colloquial Tunisian Arabic, Tounsi, intertwined with
formal Arabic in his speeches in order to get closer to his citizens and earn
their favor. Tunisians were drawn to his charismatic personality and to
the eloquence of his tongue. He said that he went to his people so that he
could "speak directly to them in their language, in order to educate them,
to organize them, to make them the architects of their own destiny."[59]

But that architecture was not intended to include democratic governance, at least not while he was still around.

Bourguiba's authoritarianism was built around a cult of personality that he erected for himself. His figure pervaded the public sphere—on radio and television and in print—and his portrait hung everywhere. His vanity and attention to detail regarding his image naturally extended to his wardrobe. He was always immaculately dressed—showing a preference for dark, striped suits—with his iconic round bifocals framing his vibrant blue eyes. He was a show-off who took pride in his physical fitness; in fact, the nightly national news program's opening shot sometimes featured Bourguiba taking his daily swim in the Mediterranean. He saw himself as an authority on all things, even giving Tunisian housewives cooking tips during speeches broadcast on radio and television. Drawing a comparison with another self-absorbed nation builder, the journalist Andrew Borowiec captured it best when he commented: "While Ataturk loved his feet and frequently padded around barefoot while receiving his foreign guests, Bourguiba loved all of himself."[60]

Bourguiba provided intimate details of his life, often causing embarrassment among Tunisians with some of the particulars that he shared. Most of what is known about his personal life came from him, much of it focused on his early childhood and the time prior to independence, thus reliably providing his stories with a happy ending. Bourguiba spoke of how he was sent to Tunis from Monastir when he was five years old to study at primary school. He often related the sadness he felt at being separated from his mother at such a young age. Bourguiba highlighted his education when he spoke of his life—his time at Sadiqi College, lycée Carnot, and the Sorbonne, and the time in between that he spent in El Kef recovering from pneumonia in the care of his older brother, whom he described as cruel. Regarding his first wife Mathilde, fourteen years his senior and mother to his son Habib Jr., Bourguiba spoke of how he chose to bring her back to Tunisia with him from Paris, despite his friends' discouragement.[61]

The more his authoritarianism set in and the more advanced his irrationality and erraticism grew, the more bizarre some of Bourguiba's self-narratives became. In a society that did not openly discuss personal issues, Bourguiba shocked his audience when he revealed in a television interview that he had only one testicle, most likely bragging that while other leaders needed two, he built a nation with only one—making him twice as great.[62]

Bourguiba's actions became increasingly spasmodic as he searched for ways to secure his power base following the abandonment of a failed socialist experiment that lasted for much of the 1960s. With his health declining, Bourguiba's capacity to lead started to be questioned, particularly after his 1974 announcement of a union with Libya. In the eyes of many, the Djerba incident became a defining moment as the beginning of the end for Bourguiba.

It was at around that time that his second wife, Wassila Ben Ammar, likened Bourguiba to "a candelabrum of one hundred candles of which seventy are extinguished" and a Swiss psychologist warned the president's advisers that occurrences like Djerba were likely to come up again.[63] In his later years as president, his contemporaries speak of a president who was ruined by medication and who spent many months abroad getting treatment. They debate the point in time at which his illness started to show itself, but they remark that through it all, he had moments when he exhibited remarkable coherence and eloquence.[64]

The worse Bourguiba's condition got, the greater that palace intrigue lurked. Corruption, manipulation, and arrests were rampant. Freedoms that had been afforded the press, unions, and the judiciary following independence were curtailed. Mechanisms of normalization gave way to methods of exclusion and the muzzling of any dissent by those deemed dangerous to the regime. Bourguiba never had much tolerance for political opposition or for threats to his rule; the reliance on the French army to suppress Youssefist resistance and the subsequent assassination of Salah Ben Youssef served as telling examples and dark points in the first years of independence.

Throughout his presidency, Bourguiba made sure he surrounded himself with trusted associates, recruiting disproportionately from the Sahel and his hometown of Monastir for his party and his bureaucracy. Bourguiba chose his own ministers and made sure to place people from his party in positions of power. The vast executive authority granted to the presidency by the constitution gave him much latitude to center the political system around himself.

Bourguiba established himself as "the maker and breaker of political careers," installing and removing politicians as he pleased.[65] The government and Neo-Destour formed a symbiotic relationship and had intersecting functions and staff, with Bourguiba at the helm of both.[66] He allowed political parties, but did not legalize any besides his own until 1981; he formulated policies unilaterally and considered any form of discord as sedition.

Ideologies that threatened the nationalist narrative or did not toe the party line were not tolerated. The government under Bourguiba cracked down on students returning from Cairo, Damascus, and Baghdad with Arab nationalist ideals—making arrests en masse as early as 1963. Detainees were tortured in an attempt to extract intelligence that would help the regime thwart the dissemination of pan-Arabist ideology.[67]

Abuses under Bourguiba also included prolonged detentions incommunicado, surveillance and phone tapping, and police violence. His creation of the Arab world's first independent human rights organization in response to President Carter's human rights campaign was seen as a charade.[68] Bourguiba never contested the principle and validity of human rights—as long as they did not interfere with the regime's agenda.

Communists were especially targeted. The *Parti communiste tunisien*, which had favored cooperation with the French and had not involved itself in the nationalist struggle, was sidelined once Tunisia gained independence. Bourguiba suspended the party and its publications in 1963. Party leaders were taken into custody on allegations that they had collaborated with Youssefists in a conspiracy to overthrow Neo-Destour and Bourguiba—despite these same leaders' denunciation of the Youssefists in *Le Monde* in January 1963.[69]

Suppression of the communist party was motivated by its having gained popularity among Tunisian students and workers and the threat it represented to Bourguiba's monopoly on political power. In the early 1960s, a number of left-leaning students and intellectuals organized themselves into the *Groupe d'études et d'action socialiste tunisien*—commonly known as *Perspectives*. They criticized Bourguiba for his pro-Western leanings and for having implemented state capitalism, despite socialist policies. Bourguiba, whose strategies were always nuanced, maintained a dialogue with leftist groups, attempting persuasion as a tool to influence their direction. But when demonstrations broke out in 1967 and 1968—in tandem with similar protests that were taking place worldwide—Bourguiba clamped down violently on *Perspectives* and other student leftist organizations and young professionals. The crackdown included kidnappings, imprisonment, and torture, all aimed at thwarting further protest movements.

Leftist leanings also underpinned UGTT, but Bourguiba could not suppress or dismiss the union the way he did the *Parti communiste tunisien* or *Perspectives*. It was imperative for Bourguiba that UGTT be part of the nation-building project, especially given that many unionists were also public servants.

Bourguiba approached UGTT and any inclusion thereof very cautiously. He ensured his party's dominance in UGTT affairs, placing Neo-Destour members in key positions within the union and playing musical chairs with the leadership—removing UGTT officers when they pushed too far and reinstating them when he felt that they had redeemed themselves.

But Bourguiba also gave UGTT some latitude in running its elections and autonomy in choosing its leadership when he did not feel threatened. As one of the few institutions that were democratically transparent, it was important for Bourguiba that the union serve as an outlet for debate, disagreement, and dissent. This was a delicate balancing act that Ben Ali would also later strive to achieve. Begrudgingly, both Bourguiba and Ben Ali allowed the sustenance of labor activism and a vibrant civic society.

A prime example of how UGTT leadership was in favor one moment and out the next is Habib Achour. At the time secretary-general of UGTT and a member of the political bureau of the ruling *Parti socialiste destourien*, Achour was first arrested in 1964 when a crisis over an IMF-induced devaluation of the Tunisian dinar and a consequential decrease in nominal wages led to protests. Reinstated as secretary-general in 1970, Achour was arrested once again in 1978 for organizing the "Black Thursday" strikes. Achour's third imprisonment occurred in 1985 when UGTT rejected a program imposed on the Tunisian government by the World Bank and the IMF.

But perhaps no one enjoyed as much power and wrath bestowed upon him by Bourguiba as Ahmed Ben Salah.

Ninety years old and frail, but with a sharp wit and pleasant demeanor, Ahmed Ben Salah seemed to rejoice in recounting to me his acrimonious history with Bourguiba. At his modest and mostly unkempt villa on Avenue de France in the Radès neighborhood of Tunis, the living room's furnishings and surroundings provided the perfect historical setting for the subject of the conversation. Tellingly, most prominent among the framed photographs adorning the walls was one of Farhat Hached, whom Ahmed Ben Salah was quick to characterize as the best thing that had happened to modern Tunisia.

Ahmed Ben Salah was in Paris studying when Farhat Hached founded UGTT in 1946. Born into a modest family in Moknine in the Sahel region, Ben Salah graduated from Sadiqi College before heading to Paris to pursue his studies in French and Arabic literature. Already a member of Neo-Destour, Ben Salah joined UGTT upon his return from Paris in 1948. He set up the UGTT branch in Sousse and was then sent to Brussels as the UGTT representative at the International Confederation of Free Trade Unions.

Following the assassination of Farhat Hached in 1952, Ben Salah was elected secretary-general of UGTT in 1954. During his tenure, he pushed forward a socialist economic program that he had created based on his study of economics in Brussels. Ben Salah saw himself as heir to Farhat Hached and as responsible for ensuring an egalitarian Tunisian society. "What is the use of independence," he proposed rhetorically, "if we do not take care of our people?"[70]

Lacking an economic program of its own, Neo-Destour hesitantly adopted Ben Salah's socialist program at its 1955 Sfax congress. According to Ben Salah, when Bourguiba first saw the plan, he waved it at him and yelled: "I cannot do this! This is a communist program!" Ben Salah protested Bourguiba's allegation of communist tendencies on his part. He claims to have tried—in vain—to get the Egyptian labor movement to move away from communism and to join the International Confederation of Free Trade Unions. Ben Salah described to me his first trip to Egypt as a "sad" occasion, for he came into contact with a union leadership that seemed to be overly hierarchical, "backwards," and structured like an "army"—in contrast to the "grassroots Tunisian movement that had been founded by Farhat Hached."

Eventually, Bourguiba's growing impatience with Ben Salah pushing his socialist economic program led him to sponsor the founding of the *Union tunisienne du travail* by Habib Achour in September 1956.[71] Bourguiba took it a step further in December 1956, when he removed Ahmed Ben Salah as secretary-general of UGTT. Ben Salah tells me that he learned of his dismissal on the radio while on a visit to Rabat. Bourguiba then replaced Ben Salah with Ahmed Tlili (1916–1967), a member of the Neo-Destour political bureau.

With Ben Salah out of the way, Bourguiba mediated a reunification congress on September 22, 1957, bringing together UGTT and the Habib Achour splinter union. Bourguiba laid down the condition that UGTT would stop trying to impose its socialist agenda on government policies.[72] But Bourguiba still lacked any economic program, and there were not many people he could trust and turn to, or that he had not eliminated.

In typical Bourguibian fashion, and after a multiyear hiatus, Ben Salah was back in favor almost as abruptly as he had fallen out of it. But he climbed so high a ladder in the next decade that when he ultimately fell, as he was bound to do, he came down crashing.

In 1960, Ben Salah was put in charge of public health and social affairs for the state, and the following year, he was appointed minister of planning and finance. The portfolios he accumulated in the 1960s reached a total of five ministries, making him in effect "first man" of Tunisia.[73]

In charge of the economy, Ben Salah immediately went to work on the implementation of a ten-year socialist plan that defined 1960s Tunisia. The plan introduced a collectivist policy of nationalizing lands, some previously owned by French *colons*, and converting them into cooperatives for peasants. The program intended to enhance the status of small peasants by giving them access to land and teaching them modern farming methods. By 1968, 27 percent of the rural population, or 750,000 farmers, were working in cooperatives.[74]

But in economic terms, productivity rates remained poor. Between 1960 and 1967, the annual national growth rate was 3.3 percent—compared to a projected 6 percent rate.[75] Several bad harvests adversely affected agricultural production. Bureaucratic controls by urban elites who were insensitive to the needs of the peasantry were also blamed.[76] Despite concerns that Ben Salah's program was threatening to the bourgeoisie, it was ordinary peasants who were most deeply affected by it.

When small landowners rioted in the Sahel in January 1969 and the experiment was declared an utter failure and abandoned, Ben Salah was made to take the fall. He was sacked in September 1969. Accused of financial mismanagement and treason, he was tried and sentenced to ten years of hard labor. Ahmed Ben Salah broke out of prison in 1973 and fled to Switzerland. He would only tell me that his brother Mohamed had arranged for his escape.

Despite his proclaimed failure, Ben Salah is credited with contributing to building a solid physical infrastructure, including bridges and roads, along with forests and artificial lakes, during his tenure. As the Tunisian historian and Ben Salah's contemporary Abdeljelil Temimi insists, "Ben

Salah never recognized his mistakes." He preferred instead to contemplate that the country was just not ready for the progressive socialist thinking that he had introduced.[77]

The failed socialist experiment of the 1960s made a bad economic situation even worse. Hopes that had been built around successful agricultural growth in the 1950s were dashed, and the 1960s ended with the economy in critical condition—a situation made worse by declining grain production. Land collectivization was accompanied by a policy of rapid nationalization of a number of industries, causing disturbances in the industrial sector as well. The departure after independence of French technicians and engineers caused a loss of knowledge and capability, thus weakening the manufacturing sector.

This occurred against a backdrop of national fiscal malaise, which had caused the currency devaluation of 1964. With the dawn of independence, foreign direct investment in Tunisia had already decreased by more than 10 percent between 1953 and 1957.[78] The flight of French citizens meant the retreat of their capital, and investors were discouraged by the low purchasing power of the local population. Aid from the United States that commenced in the late 1950s did not sufficiently offset the suspension of French financial assistance because of Tunisian support of Algerian guerilla rebels.[79]

In the 1970s, government policy became generally biased toward the rural bourgeoisie, large landowners who had been excluded from access to nationalized land in the 1960s, granting them large portions of land and agricultural credit facilities. But more often than not, loans made by the state were not repaid.[80]

Following the failure of socialism, the government adopted a policy of infitah, or economic liberalization. Low wages were maintained in an attempt to attract foreign investment, but this proved insufficient. Economic liberalization led to trade imbalances as cheap French goods flooded the Tunisian market—even the traditional Tunisian hat, sheshiya, was cheaper when sourced from France.[81] Tunisia's mining sector was also in decline, facing tough competition from Morocco. The government encouraged tourism and developed the industry on the model of Franco's Spain—cheap, mass market for continental Europeans seeking the sun. But tourism could not be immediately relied upon as a mainstay of the economy, as it took a while for hotels to be properly managed and serviced.[82]

Although Tunisia's GDP grew by 9 percent annually between 1970 and 1976, the rate of economic growth dropped by 50 percent in 1977, and unemployment rates doubled.[83] By the late 1970s, 30 percent of the Tunisian population was considered poor, according to the World Bank.[84]

Bourguiba's failures on the economic front stood in sharp contrast with the successes he scored in the social sphere. In the years after independence, Bourguiba put Tunisia on a modernization path based on social liberalization and mainly secular inspiration. He was intent on remodeling his country and "civilizing" its people, as he would often say, in order for Tunisia to become an advanced nation. Bourguiba understood education and the law far better than he did economic matters.

"It is necessary for [the people] . . . to aspire to dress better, to eat better, to support their family appropriately, to instruct their children, to care for themselves—in a nutshell, to live honorably like advanced nations," Bourguiba pronounced in a June 24, 1961, speech.[85] His orations often spoke of quickening Tunisia's evolution and of inducing his people to take important initial steps toward progress.

Bourguiba supposed that he needed to lead a psychological revolution in order to change what he saw as prevalent "backward" mind-sets. His contemptuous hauteur was so unfettered that he described some men he had encountered as bearing a resemblance to animals—making his mission to "civilize" all the more necessary.[86] The revolution that Bourguiba set out to effect entailed instilling in Tunisians values essential to developing the country: rationality, citizenry, responsibility, and morality. To do so, he thought it imperative that he put religion under state control and strip religious authorities of their monopoly over moral guidance.

The civilization mission that Bourguiba envisioned for his people extended to improving the state of public health and providing access to health services for the entire population. Bourguiba saw to it that public health care services and facilities were widely expanded. The state improved access to clean water and tackled endemic health issues such as tuberculosis, trachoma, and malaria. Community clinics were set up across the country to help mitigate overcrowding in hospitals.[87]

Prioritizing public health conditions and medical care paid off. Between the late 1940s and 2004, life expectancy increased from 37 to 73 years.[88]

Bourguiba beat his own country's life expectancy by a good one-third, living to be ninety-seven years old; his life spanned virtually the entire twentieth century. By the time he was forced out in a doctor's coup in 1987, at eighty-four years of age, Bourguiba had ruled for three decades and had been the principal nationalist leader for more than two decades before independence.

A cunning statesman and adept politician, at once charismatic and narcissistic, Bourguiba was a thinker and a brilliant visionary who was ahead of his time. But he also exploited his power, and his methods often included abuse of human rights, torture, execution, and breaches of the judiciary. He was arrogant and ruthless and—by any definition—an authoritarian and a dictator. But Bourguiba also protected certain human rights by legislating deep reforms in the spheres of education, healthcare, and women's rights. In the end, he is mostly remembered for his better qualities and for the positive path on which he set Tunisia.

Perhaps Bourguiba's most enduring legacy is his emancipation of women. The *Code du statut personnel* reshaped religion's relationship with society, and it continues to grant women in Tunisia more rights than anywhere else in the Arab world. Women became the pillars of the culture of expression and debate that started within the nuclear family unit and that defined Tunisian society and set it apart from the rest of the Arab world.

The second most important mark that Bourguiba made was in the sphere of education. Tunisians educated under Bourguiba were better prepared for the modern world than their counterparts elsewhere in the Arab region. The breadth and depth of Tunisian education—mainly secular and deeply rooted in the humanities and liberal arts but also strong in the sciences—enabled a genuine transition to democracy that the country has uniquely witnessed in the Arab world. Bourguiba accomplished his enlightenment mission: Tunisia emerged under him as a country of cultivated, cultured, and well-educated citizens who were more liberal minded than their counterparts in the Arab region.

In both of these endeavors, Bourguiba ameliorated the role of religion in Tunisian society, curbing an otherwise overbearing religious presence that was starting to creep into Arab society at large. He helped save the country from a downward spiral for which the rest of the Arab world has been paying a very heavy price.

Bourguiba institutionalized and put into law the liberal reforms—whether with respect to women, education, or religion—that intellectual forces, within and without the religious establishment, had advocated for almost a century and that rested on a much longer history of moderation and modernity. Bourguiba translated thought into reality and into facts on the ground.

In half a century of indirect and direct rule, the "Father of Tunisia" set the country on a track that would be very difficult to reverse. Bourguiba was aided by a long history, a fortuitous geography, and a resilient identity that predated him. Elsewhere, religion was quickly becoming the emblem of national identity when neither territorial nor ideological notions of nationalism succeeded in gaining any durable traction.

On Avenue Habib Bourguiba, Tunis's main thoroughfare and the site of the protests that brought down Zine al-Abidine Ben Ali, stand two statues of two great Tunisian men facing one another. One is of Ibn Khaldūn, and the other is of Habib Bourguiba—riding triumphantly on a horse and looking away from the old city of Tunis toward the modern Bourguiba Avenue. Bourguiba's statue was brought back to its natural home in 2016 after an absence since 1987, when a bitterly jealous Ben Ali had moved it to La Goulette.

The original placement of the two statues facing one another was deliberate. Ibn Khaldūn's statue was erected in 1978 as validation of Bourguiba's policies of reform and to send a strong message that Ibn Khaldūn, a figure from the past, was decidedly focused on Tunisia's future. The juxtaposition of the two figures was intended to signify the legacy of Ibn Khaldūn as a romanticized symbol of the Tunisia that Habib Bourguiba was building.[89]

12

Putting Religion in Its Place

S eeing religion as a double-edged sword, Bourguiba master-
fully turned the conundrum that it presented to him to his
advantage. On the one hand, he recognized that religion was
entrenched in Tunisian society and that Islam could be a legitimizing factor for the independence movement and a mobilizing factor for the people. On the other hand, he marginalized religion when he thought it could
retard the pace of modernizing change that formed the core of his vision
for the young state he was building.

Bourguiba was thus careful to strike the right balance and to allow room
for religion while working on promoting a modern and reformed application thereof. He was circumspect not to remove religion from people's daily
lives or to eradicate religiosity. He instead wanted to promote a reformist
version of religion in which Islam would liberate individuals from what he
considered to be backward customs and mind-sets. He sought the practical
side of the religion, wanting to make sure that Islam would not hinder the
country's development but rather would enable it. He argued that unless
the true purpose of religion was understood, faulty reasoning—not religion itself—would be responsible for the country's decline.

Bourguiba's psychological revolution and *nūr al-'ilm* (light of knowledge) project entailed a moral revival of an Arab Muslim society that was
to be predicated on rationality and technological progress in an attempt to

keep up with the West. "Our concern," Bourguiba declared in 1959, "is to return to the religion its dynamic quality."[1]

To achieve his aim, Bourguiba set out to adopt a pedagogic approach, elucidating for Tunisians modern interpretations of the religion. Despite his lack of a religious education and his presumed agnosticism, Bourguiba, audacious as he was, portrayed himself as an Islamic reformist and a *mujtahid*—an authority capable of independently interpreting, through reason, Islamic tenets from the Qur'an and Hadith.

Founded on the principles of *ijtihad* that were promoted by nineteenth-century reformers of the *Nahda* movement, Bourguiba's ideas were infused with elements of reason, rationalism, and pragmatism. Bourguiba's use of *ijtihad* echoed the arguments of Rifa'a Badawi Rafi' al-Tahtawi, Jamal al-Din al-Afghani, and Muhammad Abduh for the adaptation of Shari'a to the times in order to bring Islam and Muslim society into the modern world.

Although he may not have publicly given them credit, Bourguiba also undoubtedly relied on his Tunisian predecessors who had, to some extent, prepared the population for the reforms he was about to introduce. The labors of Tunisian reformers who had argued for the emancipation of women from within Islam—most notably Tahar Haddad, but also Muhammad al-Sanusi and Abdelaziz Thaalbi—were invaluable to him in his modernization project.

Islamic justification for the emancipation of women had already been attempted by the time Bourguiba was in a position to introduce his reforms. The *Code du statut personnel*, the main pillar of Bourguiba's modernization project, echoed Tahar Haddad's 1930 treatise *Imra'atuna fi al-Shari'a wa al-mujtama'*. Bourguiba in effect extended earlier debates, and he now had the power to legislate changes in which he firmly believed but which he had cast aside for political reasons during the colonial era.

Neo-Destour had not wanted debates stirred up for fear of creating divisions at a time when national unity and holding onto local values in the face of French colonization were necessary; they saw promoting women's rights as a task for after independence. This was evident in Bourguiba's own denunciation of the unveiling of women in 1929. Debate in Tunisian society on the emancipation of women was entirely silenced following Haddad's discrediting and banishment as a heretic.

As independence loomed closer, however, Bourguiba and Neo-Destour started making their positions publicly known through the party's publications, which discussed women's rights, employment, and education in far more liberal terms than those of the competing, more conservative factions of Ben Youssef and the old Destour party.[2] The formation of a feminist entity within Neo-Destour in 1950 underscored the party's formal adoption of the cause of women's rights.

Bourguiba understood that the first step toward modernization had to be the granting of women their rights. This was an end in and of itself, but also a prerequisite to further reforms that he would introduce. Liberated women would form a backbone of support as he pushed to restructure religion's relationship with society.

Women were also vital to Bourguiba's plans for economic development. Their education, which necessitated their emancipation, was crucial for the country's growth—economically and socially. Economic needs dictated that administrative jobs that had been left vacant by the departing French be filled by Tunisian men *and* women.

Cognizant of the necessity for his reforms to be buoyed by credible experts on Islam, Bourguiba labored to garner the support of contemporary Islamic scholars and judges. When he was ready to introduce the *Code du statut personnel*, he ensured that they were present in the process. The sanction of Tahar Ben Achour, the revered sheikh of Zaitouna, was crucial to Bourguiba at this juncture, and he made sure that Ben Achour gave the code Islamic credence. "I worked with [Tahar Ben Achour] on the code, and it does not contradict the teachings of Islam," Bourguiba proclaimed.[3]

It was equally important that Bourguiba get on his side the Maliki Sheikh of Islam at the time, Mohamed Abdelaziz Dja'it (1886–1970). In his attempts to give the code Islamic credence, Bourguiba claimed that it was similar to Sheikh Dja'it's 1949 *Majalla*, which was a compilation of answers to questions regarding family laws and women's rights.[4] Bourguiba also sought Dja'it's approval of the text of the code, but, alleging that its language was changed after he had initially approved it, Sheikh Dja'it issued a *fatwa* in September 1956 against the code, characterizing it as contrary to Qur'anic principles and religious tradition.[5] Dja'it ultimately came around, however, and was appointed to the newly formed position of Mufti of the Republic, a role in which he served from 1957 until 1960.

Bourguiba cast the code within Islamic justification, arguing that he had used *ijtihad* and his own critical thinking skills to arrive at the proper reinterpretation of Islam. He framed the code as a necessary step toward freeing Shari'a from archaic misinterpretations and reinstating the genuine essence of Islam. Bourguiba contended that the change "represented in our minds a choice in favor of progress," calling for "the end of a barbaric age and the beginning of an era of social equilibrium and civilization."[6]

Bourguiba spoke not only of equal rights, but also of equal respect for women. "The Tunisian people," he said, "whether woman or man or child, have to have dignity. Women should have the same dignity and respect and appreciation as men. I think religions—all religions—were made for the betterment of human kind, especially Islam, which is suitable for every day and age. It cannot contradict or prevent development."[7]

The code was not so much about liberating women from men as it was about freeing them from themselves and from the shackles to which they had grown accustomed. Bourguiba explained: "In the task of changing people's mentality, we have difficulty not only with the men but also with the women themselves, who cling to this state of servility, decadence, and bondage just as if they considered it their normal state in this base world."[8] Bourguiba was inspired in this by the views of Qasim Amin and Muhammad Abduh, sharing their beliefs that this was not the Prophet's intention.

It was, in fact, men who liberated Tunisian women. No feminist grassroots movement had demanded the changes brought about by the code. Women who were active in the national struggle had not yet begun to speak on women's issues. Women's organizations collaborated with Neo-Destour during the fight for independence, but their advocacy for rights was focused mostly on economic participation and financial emancipation. Ultimately, it was men who came up with the code, and they imposed it from the top. The "women's revolution" was neither a revolution nor led by women; it was a carefully planned and executed decision of Habib Bourguiba.

The code acted as a state power-consolidating move at the expense of more conservative and tribal social structures. It had been customary, for instance, for individuals, especially females, to marry at a very young age. But the *Code du statut personnel* mandated a minimum age for marriage of fifteen for females and eighteen for males. When this proved insufficient, the code was amended in 1964 to raise the minimum legal age for marriage to seventeen for a woman and twenty for a man.[9] A subsequent amendment, this time in 2007, established the minimum age as eighteen for both sexes.[10]

Progress has been slower, or entirely absent, in other parts of the Arab world. In Egypt, the minimum age for marriage is sixteen.[11] The legal age for marriage in Jordan was raised from fifteen to eighteen only in 2002. There continues to be no minimum age for marriage in places like Saudi Arabia and Yemen.[12]

Acting as a further deterrent to early marriage, the code discouraged arranged marriages, advocating instead that decisions regarding marriage be left to those entering into it. The code stipulated that both parties must be present at a marriage, thus ensuring that a wife's consent is explicitly given. It became compulsory that a marriage be registered with the state so that the woman's legal age and agreement to the marriage could be validated.[13] The removal of a father's or guardian's power to give a woman away in marriage, with or without her consent, represented a revolutionary departure from accepted norms. It continues to be the case in a number of Arab countries that a woman needs her male guardian's permission to get married.

But where the *Code du statut personnel* was perhaps most revolutionary was in its abolishment of the age-old practice of polygamy, which is still legal throughout the rest of the Arab world. Bourguiba's code even introduced punishment for an offending male: a year's imprisonment and a fine equaling approximately $500—a year's income for the average Tunisian at the time.[14]

A century after the Husaynid Ahmad Bey outlawed slavery, Bourguiba used the same religious argument against polygamy: although sanctioned by Islam, the condition set forth of fair treatment of all wives was impossible to fulfill. Bourguiba went so far as to suggest that in the spirit of equity, should polygamy be allowed, a woman ought to be permitted to become polyandrous in the event her husband turned out to be sterile.[15]

Bourguiba's code also formalized the matter of divorce, requiring that it be carried out in court. The new laws stipulated that either husband or wife could apply for a divorce, and that both had to mutually consent to it.

Even though the Prophet denounced divorce, and all four schools of jurisprudence agreed that divorce is only permitted when it is "essential" and there is no chance of reconciliation, divorce could not be easier in Islam if a husband desires it. *Talaq*, or divorce, occurs when a husband simply pronounces that the marriage is dissolved, followed by a three-month period, *iddah*. This waiting period, during which the wife is not allowed contact with any male except unmarriageable kin, or *mahram*, allows for reconsideration and confirmation that the wife is not pregnant. In general, the default legal position on a woman's right to initiate divorce is that she has none; women are granted the right to divorce only in very specific and restricted circumstances.

The advancement of women's family rights included the granting of child custody to a mother in the case of divorce or death of the father, with her relatives favored in the event of her death. Although the father maintained the right to request custody of his children once they reached a certain age—seven for a male and nine for a female—an amendment in 1993 granted courts the power to determine custody based on what they deemed the best interest of the child.

But a patriarchal hierarchy continued to dominate in certain respects. If a woman remarries, for example, she loses custody of her children. Also, as is the case elsewhere in the Arab world, even when custody is in the hands of the mother, the father, or an agnate in the case of the father's death or inability, remains the legal guardian. In a major breakthrough in November 2015, however, a law was passed allowing Tunisian women to travel with their minor children without the father's permission.[16]

Bucking another male chauvinistic trend that continues to be the norm in Arab countries, the code extended Tunisian nationality to all children born in the country to a Tunisian mother and a foreign father, reversing a previous decree from 1914 that made Tunisian nationality nearly an exclusive right of the father. A 2010 amendment to the nationality law gave Tunisian women married to noncitizens the right to pass on their nationality to their child even if the child was born abroad.[17]

In Jordan, by contrast, nationality is still primarily the exclusive right of fathers. Women with Palestinian husbands who are not Jordanian citizens, for example, cannot pass their nationality to their children. Campaigns to amend the law in favor of equal citizenship rights have been met with strong opposition.

Interfaith marriages are also the exclusive domain of men, according to Islamic norms that permit only men to take non-Muslims as spouses. In another major breakthrough that granted equal rights to women and defied revered Islamic tradition, the *Code du statut personnel* allowed a Muslim woman to marry a non-Muslim man. A memorandum that went into circulation in 1973 banned judges and civil officials from performing wedding ceremonies between a Muslim woman and a non-Muslim man, but the law preserved a loophole: if an interfaith couple got married outside the country, their marriage would become legal in Tunisia.[18]

In yet another significant departure from Islamic teachings, Tunisia allowed adoption by virtue of a 1958 amendment to the code. As long as a prospective adoptive parent had the physical, mental, and financial capacity to adopt, she or he could do so. Going a step further, a condition set forth in the code that an adoptive parent had to be married was subsequently relaxed in a 1959 amendment so that a widowed or divorced person could be exempted from the requirement.[19] Bourguiba set an example when he and his second wife, Wassila Ben Ammar, adopted a young girl, Hejar.

Elsewhere in the Arab world, compliance with Shari'a allows for the system of *kafala*, or guardianship, whereby a family can raise a child that is genetically not its own, but cannot pass on either the family name or inheritance rights. The only exceptions, besides Tunisia, are Somalia—to the extent that it can be considered an Arab country—and Lebanon, where adoption is legal but only for Christian citizens.

The one area in which Bourguiba acquiesced to *ulama* and failed to grant women equal rights was in the domain of inheritance, where he allowed for Shari'a to dictate the principal tenets of the code. The code was faithful to the Maliki *madhab* and to practices elsewhere in that regard. It granted predetermined shares to a deceased's kin, giving preference to patrilineal relatives according to a two-to-one ratio between males and females. Tunisia did, however, grant a woman's testimony in court the same weight as a man's, making it, along with Oman, the only Arab country in which a woman's testimony is not valued at half of a man's.

Bourguiba's attempts to change inheritance in favor of equality were resisted, then and later, by *ulama* on the premise that the text of the Qur'an was incontrovertibly clear on the subject. According to Yadh Ben Achour, when Bourguiba tried to introduce the notion of equality in inheritance between the sexes in 1973, the respected sheikh Mohamed Salah Ennaifer (1902–1993) drew a red line, reminding Bourguiba that it had already been a major concession for him and other *ulama* to go along with the code.[20] Attempts at extending equality to inheritance have continued—including during the summer of 2016, when a proposed change in the law was discussed in parliament—but all such efforts have failed.

Still, the code granted Tunisian women fairer treatment in matters of inheritance than their counterparts elsewhere in the Arab world. A 1959 amendment undermined agnate privileges by granting a larger share of inheritance to a female spouse and advancing some female relatives over agnates; daughters and granddaughters were favored over uncles and brothers of the deceased, for example. By favoring descendants of both sexes over collateral relatives, and a spouse over other descendants, the code in that regard was revolutionary. The lot of women when it came to inheritance was further enhanced by the eradication of religious endowments. Males had often donated property to *habus*, a permitted practice, as a means of excluding female heirs. With religious endowments closed down, that loophole was securely shut.[21]

As progressive as the code was, it nonetheless maintained a conservative tone. While it called on both spouses to treat each other with kindness and respect, the husband was positioned as the head of the household.

In these respects, and in congruence with Tahar Haddad's stances, Bourguiba's emancipation of women was still confined within traditional gender norms. Women remained subordinate to men, and a woman's primary duties were to her husband and family. The code also failed to address the status of single mothers and did not recognize children born out of wedlock.

Bourguiba knew well that his code was nonetheless ahead of its time, and he presented it to Tunisians as an aspirational scenario, conceding that the law "may precede the ability of citizens to apply it." Bourguiba called upon public institutions to educate the populace and elucidate the application of new laws through conferences and workshops.[22]

Compliance with the new code did not occur right away, especially in the more conservative countryside. Some judges resigned over its issuance, and the press offered criticisms. The staunchest opposition came from conservative and religious elites, both at home and abroad, who argued that the code violated Islamic norms. Some considered the code an outright act of aggression against Arabic culture and Islam. Although polygamy was not widely practiced, its prohibition concerned Islamic scholars, who saw that as working against the doctrines of the Qur'an. From Egypt, Salah Ben Youssef called on the Tunisian population to rise up against the reforms and Bourguiba, whom he described as "the one who prohibited what God had authorized and authorized what God had prohibited."[23]

But the code *was* Islamic—in a Tunisian sense. The *Code du statut personnel* adopted moderate Islamic values that defined Tunisian Islam, and it relied on arguments put forth and defended from within Islam by Tahar Haddad more than two decades before.

The code was ultimately, if not immediately, sanctioned by major religious figures. The modernization that had taken place at Zaitouna in the 1940s and early 1950s under Sheikh Tahar Ben Achour had a tempering effect on initial resistance to the code. Acceptance was a milestone achievement, as the code was, after all, inspired by secular values and did not leave open a door for consulting Shari'a in matters for which answers could not be found within the code—except in the case of inheritance.

Amendments made to the code in 1959 reflected improvements and lessons learned during the first period of its implementation. These were followed by later enhancements and popularization of modern customs, as when Bourguiba and Wassila Ben Ammar got married in 1962 and introduced the practice of giving a symbolic dinar rather than the mandatory *mahr*, or dowry, in celebration of the marriage.[24]

When Ben Ali took over in 1987, he set up a commission to comprehensively review the code. The outcome of the review was a set of amendments introduced in 1993. In addition to updating laws surrounding child custody, amendments dealt with the marriage of minors, domestic violence, and the mutual obligations of husband and wife.

While Tunisia's *Code du statut personnel* purged conservative social structures of kinship and tribalism, Morocco's postcolonial personal status code, *Mudawwanat al-ahwal al-shakhsiyya*, reinforced them—not surprisingly, as King Mohammed V (1909–1961, r. 1956–1961) had come into power through a number of tribal alliances. The *Mudawwana*, which was drafted in 1957 and 1958, essentially codified existing Maliki family laws and institutionalized patrilineal ties. It did not require a woman's explicit consent to marriage, and her presence was not required for the marriage contract, which was signed by her guardian. Marriage thus remained a matter between male representatives of the two families. The right of a guardian to marry off a woman against her will—in cases of "bad conduct," such as loss of virginity—was removed, however, and the age of marriage was set at eighteen for both men and women in 2004.[25]

It took Algeria more than two decades after it achieved independence in 1962 to introduce a family status code, which it did in 1984. Codification was attempted numerous times in the intervening period, but factional disputes and resistance stampeded the efforts.[26] Prior to the code's adoption, anticolonial and rising Islamist sentiments saw the introduction of a number of laws reversing gains made by women under the French. In 1973, all remnants of French rule were comprehensively reversed when power was given to judges to decide on family matters according to Shari'a.[27]

The code that was ultimately imposed in 1984 further retarded the status of women, for it was meant to appease antigovernment Islamist movements that were on the rise. The approval of a woman's guardian for marriage was codified, as were polygamy and repudiation, which at least now had to be registered with a judge.[28] As would become common elsewhere, a husband became legally obligated merely to make his wife or wives aware of his decision to marry another woman.[29]

Personal status codes in the rest of the Arab world echoed those introduced in Algeria and Morocco and were closely based on Shari'a. Egypt did not even establish a personal status code; the task of legal interpretation was completely left to religious clerics, who retained their monopoly over religious affairs.

Iraq served as an exception for a while, introducing in 1959 a family status code that outlawed polygamy, revised inheritance laws, and set the minimum age of marriage at eighteen.[30] But the Iran-Iraq War, which lasted through the 1980s and resulted in grave loss of life among men, served as a pretext for allowing men to take on widows as additional wives.[31]

With eighteen recognized sects, Lebanon in 1936 established a decentralized system of fifteen separate personal status laws. Rules are enforced and interpreted by independent religious courts, with little government interference, save for the review and ratification of submitted laws and trial proceedings to ensure constitutionality. When Christian and Jewish confessionals complied but Sunnis reneged, a decree was issued that exempted Muslim courts from oversight by the state.[32]

The granting of Tunisian women their equal rights in family matters, enshrined in the Code du statut personnel, signified a major milestone for Bourguiba, who would go on to introduce other measures that would further improve the condition of women, including in matters of reproductive health. Bourguiba was also motivated by economic considerations; in the 1960s, the fertility rate was seven children per Tunisian woman.[33] Birth control to curb population growth became a priority for the state.

Family planning measures, including awareness building and instructional courses, were introduced, and women were encouraged to use contraceptives, the distribution of which was facilitated by the state.[34] The *Union nationale de la femme tunisienne*, which by 1960 had 14,000 members in more than 115 branches, played a key role in raising awareness in the field.[35] The *Association tunisienne pour le planning familial*, established in 1968, and the *Office national de la famille et de la population*, set up in 1973 and funded by the government and the World Bank, contributed to the efforts and oversaw family planning centers throughout the country.[36]

Religious leaders, research institutions, and the media also lent their support. Unlike in other Muslim countries, where family planning is considered sacrilegious and birth control is a taboo subject, some Tunisian *ulama* supported the new policies on the grounds that they did not conflict with the teachings of Islam.

Opposition came instead from the left. According to Selma Hajri, who runs the women's health organization named for Tawhida Ben Cheikh (1909–2010)—one of the first female physicians in the Arab world—liberals objected to the infringement on freedom caused by family planning policies. Of particular concern was the practice of forced tubal ligations for women who had had more than four children.[37]

Aided by the legalization of abortion in 1973, Tunisian women's fertility rate dropped to 4.7 by 1984, 2.9 by 1994, and 2.02 by 2004. As fertility rates went down, so did infant mortality rates, which have seen an improvement by a factor of ten since independence.[38]

Another important change in social attitudes was that it became acceptable for a woman to work before marriage—typically in an administrative government job or as a teacher. The *Code du statut personnel* and Bourguiba's overall advocacy for the liberation of women led more women to take jobs that had previously been reserved for men. A nouvelle bourgeoisie that was receptive to the notion of working women emerged. Urban attitudes concerning women in the workplace eventually trickled down to rural areas as girls started attending school and going on to university in Tunis. It also became increasingly acceptable for rural females to get jobs in urban centers, away from home but typically living with relatives. In the countryside, women took many of the new job opportunities that were created for industrial and clerical workers.

While the economic emancipation of Tunisian women did not occur immediately, it did move at a relatively fast pace, especially when considered at an Arab regional level, where women's participation in the workforce continued to lag behind.

Bourguiba pushed for the liberation of women on all fronts, and his efforts paid off. He championed women's social issues and defied accepted norms. Bourguiba was increasingly able to take charge of social affairs that had traditionally been the exclusive domain of the religious authorities. He was intent on eroding the ability of conservative *ulama* to dictate social values, and he undertook measures that would allow the state to regulate religion.

Bourguiba served a huge blow to the independence of religious authorities when he dismantled Qur'anic and rabbinical tribunals. This occurred at roughly the same time as the *Code du statut personnel* was introduced, and it was a significant step in the process of putting religion under the domain of the state.[39] By unifying the judiciary, Bourguiba also ensured that all Tunisians, regardless of faith or creed, would henceforth be subjected to the same legal process.[40]

Bourguiba's next move in bringing religion under his control was the nationalization of *habus* through two decrees issued in 1957. This had the effect of depleting the financial capacities of religious institutions, including Zaitouna, and making them dependent on, and thus controlled by, the state.[41]

The next battle was waged in the field of religious education. Bourguiba took measures that would discontinue a centuries-old tradition of the mosque. First, Bourguiba nationalized—and put under the control of his ministry of education—Zaitouna's *kuttab* schools in 1956.[42] Then, in 1958, he shut them down altogether.[43] Bourguiba also placed all of Zaitouna's postprimary education faculties under state control and began the process of secularizing the curriculum.[44] In 1961, Bourguiba closed down the mosque's faculties and integrated some of its theologians into the University of Tunis, established in 1960.[45] Others were downgraded to the status of schoolteachers, providing instruction in Arabic and Islam. By taking these steps, Bourguiba completed his task of undermining religious education and closing the gap between two divergent groups of people—the religiously and the largely secularly educated—which he saw as a threat to national unity.

A new directorate for religious affairs was subsequently established in 1967 with the prerogative of looking after both religious buildings and leaders. The directorate would appoint, train, and remunerate imams and preachers, who became public servants completely under the purview of the state. The directorate developed the curricula for religious education and controlled all manners in which religion was publicly practiced and promulgated.[46]

By pulling the rug from under religious institutions—educational, charitable, and judicial—Bourguiba secured a trajectory for Tunisia that protected it from the hegemonic role of religion that would regulate other Arab and Muslim societies. Bourguiba dared do what no other Arab leader had the courage or foresight to achieve. Bourguiba was of course aided by a tradition of progressive religious leadership, both before and during his time. He also took these steps early on in his tenure, taking advantage of a rare moment when he had the latitude to set the tone for his young nation. Bourguiba was able to impose his reforms from above, without the need for consensual debate. His leadership in this regard would prove decisive for the country.

Like Kemal Ataturk before him, Bourguiba sought his own version of a Jacobin model of state-religion relations, or *laïcité*, originating in the French revolutionary state and pursued by the French Third Republic, which subordinated religion to the state.[47] But Bourguiba wanted to be sensitive to the Tunisian context within which he was operating and was wary of inviting negative reactions. He maintained an agile and robust approach and did not go as far as Turkey or France did in his regulation of religion in the public sphere. While *laïcité* meant radical secularization for Turkey and France, it was a means for Bourguiba to moderate the role of religion in society.

Bourguiba did share with Ataturk similar attitudes toward religion and a clear vision for nation building through a "forced march to modernization."[48] But while Ataturk rejected Islam altogether and fought against religion, Bourguiba maintained a delicate balance—arguing from within Islam for moderation and assuming an Islamic persona as he brought religion under his control. Bourguiba did not present himself to the Tunisian people as a secularizing reformer, but rather as a modernist reformer of Islam. He left space for Islam, including in schools, and he allowed for Shari'a to regulate matters of inheritance in an otherwise civil state.

Bourguiba's and Ataturk's agendas had much in common, nonetheless. They both abolished Islamic institutions and courts, closed down *kuttab* schools, secularized education, and created directorates for religious affairs to control public religious activity. The abolishment of polygamy, sanctioning of adoption, and expansion of women's rights served as other important commonalities between the two leaders' programs.

To a large extent, Bourguiba followed in the footsteps of the person whom he had criticized before Tunisia's independence, when he needed Islam to galvanize the populace and to establish his credibility. In the same 1929 article in *L'Etendard tunisien* in which he scorned women for shedding the hijab, Bourguiba said—in response to comparisons that were being drawn between him and Kemal Ataturk—that he did not want to be a Tunisian version of the Turkish leader. Bourguiba reproached Ataturk for being too detached from society, too Westernized, and for not having incorporated Islam into his reforms.[49]

Ultimately, Bourguiba heeded his own cautions to Ataturk and made sure that his approach following independence was a measured and balanced one, enabling him to successfully negotiate, at least initially, opposition to his reforms and avoid the polarization that, a century after Turkey's founding, has been ripping that country apart. Bourguiba was selective in how he applied secularism. He ensured a civil state and prohibited religion from interfering in government matters, but he understood the importance of religion in a Tunisian context and preserved a role for religion—under his control.

Tunisia did not emerge as purely secular, meaning a total separation of mosque and state, no reference to religion by the state, and self-determination of religious communities without interference by the state. It also was not *laïcist* in the same fashion as France or Ataturk's Turkey, in that it subjugated religion but did not attempt to obliterate it. Bourguiba created his own version of a largely secular state that is constitutionally civil. He found common ground with Qasim Amin's advocacy for the separation of religion and state, but his was more a case of placing religion *under* the state—embracing religion as the domain of the state so that he could control it. He sought a state-sanctioned form of Islam that would strengthen his political and moral authority by dictating his version of correct religious beliefs and practices.

Tunisian state control over religious affairs extended to Tunisia's religious minorities. Jewish and Christian clerics were appointed and paid by the state. Christian organizations formed prior to independence were officially recognized by the state, as were fourteen churches that served the various Christian congregations.[50] In the same manner that he created the position of Mufti of the Republic immediately following independence, Bourguiba appointed the chief rabbi of Tunisia.

But Jews feared state monopolization of religious symbols and institutions and the evaporation of their identity. They were concerned about being subjected to Arabization policies within the judiciary system when a majority of them were French speaking. They contrasted their situation to that of Moroccan Jews, whose rabbinical tribunals and religious associations retained the same status they had enjoyed before independence.[51]

The 100,000 Tunisian Jews who lived in Tunisia at the end of the 1940s were quite heterogeneous, socioeconomically and otherwise. Many had French or Italian roots, but it tended to be the more affluent Jews who were particularly Francophone and Western in their outlook. This group feared for itself after the departure of the French, and many of its members emigrated—primarily to France. Around 20,000 Tunisians left the country shortly after the founding of the state of Israel.[52]

In an attempt to assuage the concerns of Tunisian Jews who were nostalgic for the colonial period, Bourguiba promoted dialogue with members of the Jewish community. He paid visits to important Jewish sites in Tunisia and engaged with Jewish residents. He called on the Hara neighborhood in Tunis in 1957 and paid homage to al-Ghriba Synagogue in Djerba in 1966.[53] The Jewish nationalist Albert Bessis (1885–1972) was put in charge of urban planning and housing for the state at the time of independence, and he served as a member of parliament until 1969. Sophie Bessis, the granddaughter of Albert Bessis, tells me that many families like hers chose to stay in Tunisia because they felt that the environment continued to be inclusive under Bourguiba. They felt protected by legislation such as the 1968 law that rendered illegal any discrimination on the basis of religion in the recruitment and promotion of public servants.[54]

Christians did not factor as much in Bourguiba's thinking, as they were not distinguished from colonizers—most Christians who remained in Tunisia were Europeans. The negative image in the aftermath of the 1930 Eucharist Congress in Carthage was cemented in people's minds. The Christian population had dwindled to a few thousand in the postcolonial Maghreb.[55]

In an interview with the *Christian Science Monitor* in 1962, Bourguiba pronounced that the seventh-century Muslim invasion of North Africa had wiped out the indigenous Christian population in Tunisia. He added: "Since then, I regret to say, the Christians have always been associated with colonizers. The Christians, down through our history, have always wanted to evangelize, to Christianize, and to re-Christianize North Africa." Bourguiba prophesized that "on the day when the last remnants of colonialism are gone, our relations with the Christian church will be exemplary and ideal."[56]

While Bourguiba respected personal freedoms and allowed for the practice of religion and its expression in the private sphere, he outspokenly campaigned against what he took to be backward traditions and, on occasion, curtailed freedoms to make his point and to counter currents of religiosity. The hijab served as a quintessential illustration of Bourguiba's distaste for religious symbolism. He emphatically discouraged all forms of traditional dress, claiming that "old-fashioned clothing encouraged old-fashioned modes of thinking and acting."[57] Borrowing from arguments put forth by Abdelaziz Thaalbi and Tahar Haddad, Bourguiba contended that Islamic standards of modesty did not require the wearing of a hijab. He presented the hijab as a foreign "custom" that resulted from "a misunderstanding of Qur'anic verses."[58] Bourguiba insisted that shedding the hijab was a Tunisian truism, evoking, as he often did, the Phoenician legacy when promoting his unveiling policies.

Bourguiba placed the burden of morality on both sexes, suggesting that "by the knot around the woman's neck, we pretend that we are avoiding shamelessness: however, for shamelessness to exist, there must be two people; but we refrain [ourselves] from applying the same principles to the man, the second partner."[59] Bourguiba also put the onus on parents to help rid society of the hijab. "If we understand," Bourguiba said, "that the middle-aged women are reticent about abandoning an old habit we can only deplore the stubbornness of parents who continue to oblige their children to wear a [hijab] in school. We even see civil servants going to work in that odious rag. It has nothing to do with religion."[60]

Bourguiba fell short of banning the hijab altogether, but he did forbid women to wear it to school. Monia Bouali, a middle-aged Tunis lawyer, later recounted that in 1986, when she was fifteen years old, she was jailed for two weeks for wearing a headscarf to school.[61] With the resurgence of

Islamism in the 1970s, and more specifically in 1981 when the *Mouvement de la tendance islamique* was officially constituted as an Islamist organization, the state campaign against the hijab intensified. Curbs on wearing the hijab in public spaces were imposed through government circulars in 1981; these were expanded in 1985 and reiterated under Ben Ali in 1987 and 1991.[62]

Bourguiba also tried to restrain fasting during the Muslim holy month of Ramadan. He declared in 1956 that the observance of Ramadan should be suspended because it impeded the economic development of the country. In a 1960 speech, Bourguiba said: "During Ramadan, work stops. At this moment when we are doing the impossible in order to increase production, how can we resign ourselves to seeing it slump to a value near zero?" In identifying poverty as an enemy that needed to be conquered, he used a hadith in which the Prophet is claimed to have said to his companions: "Eat! You will be stronger to tackle the enemy."[63] To drive his point home, Bourguiba drank a glass of orange juice during a television broadcast in Ramadan.

Although Bourguiba was careful to suggest that he did not outright reject fasting but proposed that it be observed only during holidays, his stance on the matter led many to view him as antireligious and brought about fierce opposition from *ulama*. Sheikh Mohamed Abdelaziz Dja'it, who had objected to the introduction of the *Code du statut personnel*, issued a *fatwa* declaring: "Fasting remains a religious duty to be excused only in cases of illness or military jihad."[64] Dja'it was consequently deposed as Mufti of the Republic.[65] Bourguiba's great ally at Zaitouna, Sheikh Tahar Ben Achour, also objected to Bourguiba's call for Muslims not to fast during Ramadan.[66]

Bourguiba was publicly critical of violent dimensions of the history of Islam and of internal divisions that were characteristic of that history. He was mindful of how "three of the four *Khulafa' Rashidun* [Rightly Guided Caliphs] were murdered," and that "Islam disintegrated into many different groups . . . an era filled with wars for the sake of authority." "Even when the Prophet died," Bourguiba declared, "we were divided amongst the *Muhajirun* [early adopters of Islam and emigrants with the Prophet from Mecca to Medina] and *Ansar* [Medina Muslims] in search of authority."[67]

Controversial positions that Bourguiba took on religious matters also brought about an international backlash, as happened when he pointed out a few supposed inconsistencies in the Qur'an in a speech he delivered in 1974 at the *Congrès international des enseignants* in Tunis. Sheikh Abdelaziz Ben Baz (1912–1999), president of the Islamic University of Medina, and later the grand mufti of Saudi Arabia, called Bourguiba an apostate and threatened to call on the Saudi government to cut diplomatic ties with Tunisia. Sheikh Youssef al-Qaradawi—a Muslim theologian, member of the Muslim Brotherhood, and former mouthpiece of *al-Jazeera* on Islam—also lodged accusations against Bourguiba, calling him an apostate and an enemy of Islam and excommunicating him from the *umma*.[68]

Bourguiba was busy performing his own excommunications at home. He punished *ulama* that opposed him and refused to comply with his directives. *Ulama* often felt humiliated and alienated, and in some cases they turned toward a fundamentalist interpretation of religious texts in reaction.[69] Islamic revival in the wider region, the rise of Islamism in neighboring Algeria, and the Islamic revolution in Iran gave strength to apprehensions toward Bourguiba's policies and to the emergence of political Islam in Tunisia.

The founding of the *Mouvement de la tendance islamique* gave voice to religious opposition and to politically charged criticisms of Bourguiba and his modernization project. Rached Ghannouchi condemned Bourguiba's religious approach, declaring that his secularization and modernization projects rested on misconceptions. He argued that Bourguiba's idea of modernity did not encourage scientific development or rationality but rather rested on the negation of Tunisia's Arab and Islamic identity.[70]

There were repercussions from the removal of religion from the public sphere and the repression of Islamic scholarship. Following the nationalization and closure of *kuttab* schools and, more important, the dismantling of Zaitouna as the main center for religious scholarship, the vacuum that was created began to be filled with reactionary ideas.

But decades of national policies also compelled Islamist actors and religious elements in civil society to innovate in their interpretations of Islam and adapt them to a modern context. Islamist groups slowly came to realize the positive impact of social and political reforms.[71] The *Mouvement de la tendance islamique* eventually accepted the *Code du statut personnel* in its entirety after having had opposed it.[72]

Building on a long history of moderation and reform, Bourguiba ensured that Tunisia averted the path that made religion and political

Islam dominant factors in shaping the societies and polities of the rest of the Arab world. Tunisia was spared the struggle for national identity that made Islam the badge of honor in societies that had little else on which to pin their newfound independence. Tunisia did not need Islam to define its identity. The state monopoly over religious affairs—for better and for worse—enabled the government to control religious discourse and to instill modern values of secularism, pluralism, gender equality, and individual freedom of belief.

Bourguiba had redefined the relationship between religion and society; his next battle would be fought in the field of education.

13

Educating a Nation

When we were in the opposition and Tunisia belonged to others, not to us, we planned and resolved that when our country was independent and the state apparatus in our hands we must treat first the problem of education.

—HABIB BOURGUIBA, JUNE 25, 1958

Intent on pulling his country out of underdevelopment and on advancing Tunisian society, *nūr al-'ilm* became Bourguiba's guiding light. He continually referred to the people's *matière grise*, in the sense of intellect: "We do not have natural resources but we do have gray matter; this is where our success lies."[1]

"We need our youth to learn the sciences that bring power [and] the knowledge that gave Europe its strength," Bourguiba would insist. In referencing the Arab Muslim world at large, he said: "Once upon a time, we used to be stronger than Europe. Then slowly, they pushed us back from Andalucía and then came to our lands in Africa and Asia. Why? Because we were too late in changing our mentality and in our growth and development."[2]

Bourguiba bemoaned the death of the renaissance of Islamic thought that had occurred further east, and he was cognizant that Arab publics were stuck in their nostalgic dreaminess of past glories. He understood Muhammad Abduh's idea that only through education could the Islamic world be restored from decay and what Tahar Ben Achour meant when he publicly argued that the Islamic *umma* had declined because of deterioration in the state of education. But Bourguiba also understood that Tunisia's modern history followed a different trajectory, one that was buoyed by continuous and cumulative reform in the domains of religion and education.

Bourguiba was an intellectually driven individual. He was a product of the best academic institutions in Tunisia and France, and he drew his inspiration both from intellectual reformers at home and from the great figures of the European Renaissance.

Bourguiba understood the value of education and of critical thinking perhaps better than any of his postcolonial Arab counterparts and nation builders. Muammar Gaddafi graduated from a military academy in Libya and was otherwise a product of traditional Islamic schooling. Algeria's Houari Boumediène (1932–1978) studied at al-Azhar Mosque-University and Zaitouna, and then joined and fought for the *Front de libération nationale.*

Gamal Abdel Nasser received a lackluster education, often switching schools as his family moved around every time his father, who worked for the Egyptian postal service, got relocated. After obtaining his high school baccalaureate in the literary section from the Nahda Secondary School in Cairo, Nasser applied to the elitist Military Academy but was rejected because of his modest academic background and political activism. He then enrolled at the faculty of law at Cairo University—then the Egyptian University—in October 1936, but he dropped out after only six months. He reapplied to the Military Academy and was accepted in late 1937, graduating shortly thereafter, in July 1938.

While other Arab leaders became preoccupied with building their military apparatus, Bourguiba's priority was education. The national budgetary allocation for education was already considerable under the protectorate, standing at 14 percent in 1950.[3] Bourguiba increased spending immediately, and by 1971 expenditures on education had reached a whopping 34.5 percent of the government's budget.[4] Significant spending on education persisted throughout Bourguiba's term and into Ben Ali's regime, sustaining a level above 20 percent of total government expenditure.[5] Even when spending slowed after the 2011 revolution, Tunisia continued to outpace other Arab countries in terms of how much of its resources it committed to education.

The comprehensive agenda that Bourguiba introduced in 1958 would establish and set in motion policies that would shape Tunisian education systems for generations to come. The program reflected Bourguiba's visionary outlook, but it was also the work of the playwright, poet, and academic Mahmoud Messaadi, Bourguiba's minister of education from 1958 to 1968 and, later, his minister of culture from 1973 to 1976. Messaadi was so closely associated with Bourguiba's plan that it was often referred to as the "Messaadi plan."

The program included a ten-year plan for primary school education. Primary education in an independent Tunisia would contribute to nation building and help galvanize public support for Bourguiba's modernization program. Textbooks made the case for his social reform, including in the spheres of health and women's suffrage.

Secondary and higher education, which would be highly selective but not elitist, would serve the economic interests of the state. Bourguiba sought to build the necessary workforce within the country to support the struggling economy of the new nation and to eliminate the void left by the departure of Europeans. He named the eradication of poverty the "second fight," as important as removing the French, and viewed policies of scale and scope—broadening breadth and providing depth in skill acquisition—as fundamental to a restructuring of the young nation's social and economic platforms.[6]

When it came to language, Bourguiba continued the reliance on French, including in education. Nearly all government officials and members of the elite class were French educated. The close association of a Western orientation with a culture of openness and progress made it easier for Bourguiba to encourage use of the French language as the key to a modern identity and high status. Ahmed Ben Salah remarked in 1956: "We have to preserve the (Arabic) language, our nation's specificities and those of the African and Arab communities . . . as well as our specificity within the Mediterranean setting. But, while preserving these characteristics, we have to remain open to the world and receptive to progress . . . the education system itself should be adapted to the economic and social structures that we want to set up in our country."[7]

With Arabic as the national language of Tunisia, but believing that the use of French would ensure the overall quality of education, Bourguiba insisted on bilingualism, reinforcing the system to which he and most of Tunisia's elites had been exposed at Sadiqi College. Teachers, including imams, were now required to be able to teach in French as well as Arabic.[8] Instruction during the first two years of primary school was mandated in Arabic, but starting in the third year, French dominated as the language of instruction. French was also to be the major language of instruction in secondary school.[9]

As it was only natural for a newly independent nation to want to reclaim its language, there was still much discussion about whether Arabization should be implemented. But unlike in Algeria and Morocco, where anticolonial sentiments pushed for quick and comprehensive Arabization across the board, language was less of a politically charged issue in Tunisia. There was, in fact, a lack of enthusiasm for adopting Arabic as the country's official language, and it remained the language of tradition and the private sphere.[10] Ultimately, because of overriding concerns with implementation and quality, and out of economic consideration, Arabization was delayed.

Bourguiba's aversion to Arabization was primarily a practical matter. Arabization would have required two conditions that could not be easily met: the replacement of French textbooks with suitable Arabic texts and of French teachers with qualified Tunisians. Bourguiba also saw in French, as a linguistic vehicle, the opportunity to expose Tunisians to modern subjects and Western thought, and to mitigate Arab Muslim influences in curricula.

But bilingualism produced some negative effects. Reliance on French as a language of instruction would later contribute to high dropout rates from primary schools, which reached 46 percent in the 1960s—also often the result of economic necessity and a strict school age policy.[11] Integration into the education system was made difficult for children who did not speak French at home—many of them rural or seminomadic. Bilingualism produced the unintended negative consequence of disadvantaging poorer sectors of society, at least during the early phases of implementation.

Ensuring a stable supply of high-quality teachers was critical for Bourguiba's timetable for school enrollment of all six-year-olds by 1966.[12] French teachers had acquired pedagogic methods based on best teaching practices that fostered active learning. A dearth of qualified Tunisian teachers at the time of independence was due to structural inequalities as well as the elite nature of education under the protectorate. Most teachers were French, and Tunisians did not have access to the same training opportunities, in Tunisia or abroad, as their French counterparts. Bourguiba chose to retain the French teaching force until a new cadre of Tunisian teachers could be trained—something that he knew could not be rushed, even with proper investment.

The Tunisification of the teaching force occurred gradually and was not fully completed until the late 1970s. The pragmatic and incremental approach, aided by a bilingual education policy, alleviated pressure on the state and ensured that the hiring and training of Tunisian teachers was not hasty. In the meantime, French aid workers, or *coopérants*, taught in Tunisian schools as part of a foreign aid deal between France and Tunisia.[13] Bourguiba's gradual approach ensured that Tunisia could eventually rely on its own well-educated, and primarily French-trained, teaching staff.

The education of girls so that they could take their place in society and contribute to economic development was paramount on Bourguiba's agenda. While education would not necessarily yield expected employment results, at least not immediately or explicitly, it was essential for girls to engage with their identities and be empowered to define their social positions. Bourguiba legislated calls for girls' education that had been made by Rifa'a Badawi Rafi' al-Tahtawi more than a century before and by Qasim Amin, Abdelaziz Thaalbi, and Tahar Haddad in the preceding decades.

Of primary concern to policymakers was the low enrollment rate for girls. In 1960, 57 percent of school-age boys attended primary school while only 27 percent of girls did;[14] only 32 percent of Tunisian primary school students were girls.[15] It took decades for enrollment figures for girls to equal those of boys in Tunisian schools and universities.

In what has endured as an essentially exceptional policy in the Arab world, schools in Tunisia—primary as well as secondary—are mixed. Girls and boys sit side by side at classroom desks and learn to respect one another as equals. Girls grow up to become women who are even partners with men who grew up accustomed to equity. To appreciate the comfortable role that women play in Tunisian society—in both the public and private spheres—is to understand the effect that mixed classroom rearing since the 1950s has had on Tunisia's cultural zeitgeist.

On a visit to a secondary school in the interior town of Gafsa, I observed a history class taught in Arabic to graduating seniors. As I sat quietly in the back of the classroom, I was immediately cognizant of how young men and women—both with and without the hijab—shared workspaces, notes, and thoughts in what seemed to be perfectly natural harmony. The scene was reminiscent of my private schooling days in a far more secular Amman of the 1970s. It stood in sharp contrast to what I later observed in public schools in Amman and other Arab capitals. The simplicity and fluidity of the interaction among the students seemed to be far healthier than in the rare instances where I have observed mixing of the sexes in similar socioeconomic settings elsewhere in the region.

One of the three students I interviewed, Omar—clearly the class jock—told me that he wanted to become Tunisia's equivalent of the legendary footballer Lionel Messi. Another boy wanted to become an English teacher and match the fluency of his cousins who lived in the United Kingdom. He spoke English best among the three, but even his was deficient—none of them felt as comfortable with the language as they did with French or Arabic. The young woman, who wore a hijab, was the most self-assured of the three, helping her would-be English teacher classmate along when he stumbled over a word or thought. She told me that she wanted to become a lawyer.

As I drove across the country, I saw boys and girls breaking out of school in small villages along routes that connected cities such as Sfax, Gafsa, and Kasserine. They walked in small groups, as pupils normally do, with backpacks in tow—boys and girls, sometimes together and at other times separate, with girls without a hijab fitting in and looking as comfortable as those wearing one. The largest building in every small town was a school. There also was always a health clinic and a mosque, which for the most part was a modest small structure, conspicuously—but not loudly—declaring itself a prayer hall, and not necessarily boasting a minaret.

Coeducation became the norm from the outset in Tunisia. The only other Arab countries where coeducation at all levels has existed and endured since independence are former French colonies: Tunisia, Morocco, Algeria, and Lebanon.

Coeducation was part of the legacy left by the French, but Tunisians took it further, faster. In France, attempts at mixing genders in schools were made over the course of almost a century and a half before coeducation firmly set in. Mixed-gender classes were first introduced in French primary schools in the 1830s, particularly in areas where there had been no schools for girls. In the years between 1833, when the Guizot law first organized primary education, and the 1848 revolution, progressive thinkers sparked debates around the institutionalization of coeducation throughout the country. But it was not until the 1920s, and in the face of fierce opposition by the Catholic Church, that mixed-gender classes in secondary schools started to emerge. Economic motivation to build fewer schools produced laws that made coeducation more common in primary schools starting in 1934 and in secondary schools in 1957. Coeducation at all levels of the education system was only codified into law in a series of legislations in the mid-1970s.[16]

The legacy of the French in the domain of education went beyond language and coeducation. In the last years of the protectorate, French administrators created a twenty-year plan for Tunisia's education system, the *Plan de développement de l'Instruction publique (1949-1969)*. The plan aimed at implementing universal primary education over the course of ten years and at creating different educational tracks in secondary school. Unsatisfactory implementation results, particularly in terms of primary school enrollment rates, cut the program short, but it still provided the foundation for Bourguiba's and Messaadi's education policies.[17]

The 1958 reform agenda differed from the French system, however, in a few respects, most notably in that the number of primary school years was decreased from seven to six.[18] Similarly, the number of class hours was reduced from the French requirement of thirty hours a week.[19] The rapid increase in student enrollment and the goal that only well-trained teachers perform the task made these cuts necessary.[20] Limiting the number of primary school years to six enabled the state to hire fewer teachers and to check the number of schools that had to be built. The downside to the decrease in the numbers of years and hours is that more teaching had to be crammed into less time and, over time, teaching quality suffered as a result.

But a commission established by Messaadi in 1967 increased the length of primary and secondary school from six to seven years each and introduced French into primary school in the second, as opposed to the third, year. These reforms, which were intended to lessen the burden on teachers and to improve overall teaching quality, occurred concurrently with the establishment of additional centers for teacher training.[21] Policies regarding education were characterized by careful monitoring and making measured adjustments when and where necessary.

The primary school curriculum was rich and diverse, consisting of Arabic, French, mathematics, history, geography, civics, drawing, singing, and physical education. Some courses were taught entirely in French or Arabic, while others were taught in both languages.[22]

Students took a national exam at the end of primary school, and a student's results helped determine her future schooling trajectory. Only about 40 percent of students who took the exam passed and got a certificate, the *certificat d'études primaires*, which, for some, signified the culmination of their schooling; for the rest, it meant that they could pursue a secondary education.[23] To improve access to secondary school, Messaadi's 1967 commission adjusted the passing grade to matriculate from primary school down to 50 percent.[24]

Upon completion of their primary school education, students had the option to enroll in a three-year course of study at a terminal intermediate school, or *collège moyen*, which offered commercial, industrial, and general training.[25] *Collèges moyens* were among the most original innovations of Bourguiba's 1958 education reforms in that they offered students who may have fallen behind opportunities for further self-development. Postprimary education now included a vocational and technical training option, which would help create a skilled workforce. The acquisition of technical skills was essential to "the future of our country," Bourguiba had asserted.[26]

Upon successful completion of the three years of study at a *collège moyen*, graduates could then enroll in a training program at one of a number of vocational training centers, *centres de formation professionnelle*, which were designed to meet the needs for middle- and higher-level skilled workers. Training was provided in industrial, construction, agricultural, and administrative skills and customarily lasted from six months to a year depending on the specific trade. Graduates of training centers would then be placed with an employer, who typically had to fill an employment quota—ranging between 20 percent and 40 percent—that was reserved for such apprentices. By 1972, more than 20,000 youth had been trained at these centers, and the number continued to grow—24,000 were trained in 1974 alone. Many of the trainees were not graduates of *collèges moyens*, but rather dropouts from primary school or graduates of primary school who did not pursue further academic education.[27]

The training centers were overseen by the *Office de la formation profes-sionnelle et de l'emploi* (OFPE), which the state set up in 1967 to administer technical and on-the-job training. The move was motivated by economic hardships, rising unemployment, and the need to ensure a better match between the skills requirements of the job market and vocational instruc-tion. The functions of OFPE were expanded in 1972 to include preparing workers for migration abroad and reintegration into the national economy upon their return.[28] For some vocationally trained graduates, emigration during difficult economic times provided the best option, especially for those with an engineering or science focus. Agricultural school graduates faced special difficulties after the fall of Ben Salah and the failure of his cooperatives plan; they did not have much in the way of options.[29]

Students who represented the crème de la crème among primary school graduates were admitted into secondary school, which encompassed what we would consider intermediate and high school. Secondary schools resembled French *lycées* and were modeled on the French *baccalauréat* sys-tem of preparation for university.

Students would all undergo the same curricular requirements during their first *lycée* year. Upon its completion, they would take an exam that would determine—along with current economic needs—the track that they would follow for the remaining years of their secondary school educa-tion: *section générale* or *section technique*. At the end of their *lycée* education, students who passed the *baccalauréat* exam would attain a *diplôme de fin d'études secondaires*, which would enable them to pursue higher education. Students who pursued the applied vocational track within *section technique* would join the workforce.

Before independence, little was offered in the way of higher education besides what Zaitouna provided in terms of instruction in Islamic studies. Graduate schools in language, literature, and law had been established in the 1920s mostly to serve *colons*. These were absorbed into the *Institut des hautes études* in 1945.[30] The new school was affiliated with the *université de Paris*, and it ultimately served as a nucleus for the University of Tunis.[31]

Inspired by the French *grandes écoles* system of a network of top-tier higher education institutes, the University of Tunis was built around a number of affiliated schools that were established between 1958 and 1964.

These included schools in professional fields such as engineering, public health, architecture, business, and journalism, as well as the fine arts.[32]

Bourguiba's education agenda proved to be quite ambitious. Officials realized that their goals of universal education could not be fully achieved, at least in the time frame they had anticipated. By 1974, primary school enrollment had reached 900,000. Enrollment in secondary school rose from a mere 3,800 students in 1958 to 50,000 in 1974, while the majority of postprimary students—close to 130,000—attended *collèges moyens*. At the higher education level, a modest number of around 13,700 students were enrolled in university in 1974, 25 percent of them women.[33]

Favoring quality over quantity, and in response to the need to adapt the education system to meet economic requirements, the state's dedication to universal enrollment was lessened. The focus then shifted to making schools more relevant to employment and expanding technical and vocational training. To address the increasing rates of unemployment of secondary and university graduates, the government directed more students to terminal technical schools, *collèges moyens*, or to the applied technical track in secondary school.[34]

School curricula ensured that all students—whatever path they ended up pursuing after primary school—received a solid, well-rounded, modern education. Secondary schools maintained high standards, both in terms of admission and in terms of qualifications to pass the *baccalauréat*. To graduate from a *lycée* having passed the *baccalauréat* was indeed to have achieved the highest quality of schooling that equipped one for a top university education and for participation in leadership positions in any number of professions. But this was not to the exclusion of the rest, who received quality technical and vocational training that qualified them to participate economically. Both paths were grounded in progressive educational approaches that enabled students to embrace and contribute to a modern society.

Most significantly, a culture that respected various modes of education, including technical, was fostered. It became well established that what is generally considered a "traditional" educational path was not necessarily for everyone. The opportunities for vocational training played a key role in serving this purpose.

Perhaps the greatest long-term accomplishment of the 1958 reform that defined Tunisia's education system was that it limited the amount of religious education in school curricula. Primary school students received only one to two hours per week of instruction in the study of Islam and the Qur'an; the course on religious and civic education delivered this basic requirement.[35] Much to the dismay of *ulama*, who protested against the closing down of Zaitouna's primary and secondary educational functions, the original 1958 education reforms did not include the teaching of religion at all in secondary school. But secularism had to give in to the introduction of some religious education—taught by theologians from Zaitouna—into secondary school curricula in 1961, albeit for only two hours a week.[36]

Religion, to the extent that it comprised part of the curriculum, was taught in a very different way than it was in other Arab countries, as the next chapter will demonstrate. Religion courses in both primary and secondary school explicitly focused on the history of Islamic thought, some of it even taught in French.[37] Special emphasis was given to ensuring that subjects were discussed within historical and sociological contexts and that students were encouraged to form their own opinions and not simply accept absolute truths.[38] Humanist values of universal solidarity and of religious diversity were included.[39]

Upon close examination of textbooks that were taught at the time, the difference in approach between what Tunisian students learned compared to what my contemporaries and I studied at some of the best schools in Jordan—a country that was more advanced in the sphere of education than most in the Arab world—was remarkable.

Tunisian second-year students in secondary school learned—analytically—from a history textbook published in French in 1959 about Islamic history and were exposed to various religious groups and faiths. The book spoke favorably of the Jews of Yathreb, who gave cover to the Prophet when he emigrated from Mecca. It offered descriptions of Shi'a and their faith and of the Shi'a Fatimid dynasty. The Tunisian book presented polygamy and slavery as negative practices, spoke of how Shari'a was not comprehensive enough to constitute the basis for a complete legislative framework, and discussed the importance of *ijtihad* and interpretations that suited changing conditions.[40]

Islamic history taught to Tunisian students explored the life of the Prophet and spoke of his leadership in restoring peace among the different warring factions of the Arabian Peninsula by establishing religious and political unity. It widened students' understanding of the Muslim world beyond Arab countries, depicting Islamic history at large, including in the non-Arab Muslim world. Of the eighth-century Umayyad conquest of Spain, students learned how Muslims delivered the local populations from oppression, but also of the mistreatment of, and revolt by, Berber elements of the Umayyad armies.[41]

By contrast, what I learned in school was a narrowly defined revisionist history that resisted any debate and lacked any discussion of religious sects other than Sunni Islam. Absolute truths were in abundance, whether in religion or history. Islamic early conquests, or *futuhat*, were glorified, as were their leaders. For the most part, relevant history was that of the "golden era of Islam."

It should be noted, however, that there were some exceptions among Tunisian textbooks—as rare as they might have been. Some textbooks, written in Arabic, echoed what students in the rest of the Arab Muslim world were exposed to—a narrow and dogmatic treatment of religion that was anything but inclusive and encouraging of critical thinking. A textbook on Tunisian history published in 1963 painted the Arab conquest of the Berbers as a positive development that brought the two peoples together under the same *umma*. It referred to non-Muslims—in the context of wars fought during the Prophet's time and after his death—as *kuffar*, or infidels.[42] But such textbooks did not remain in circulation for long, and other textbooks that fostered tolerance and mutual understanding replaced them.

When students were taught about the Arab Muslim civilization, the unique history of Tunisia within that context was underscored. As curricular content evolved and changed—particularly between 1958 and 1970, mainly under Messaadi—it continued to convey a clear departure from a traditionalist notion that modern Tunisia was born with the coming of Islam to North Africa. History textbooks, starting in primary school, showed the influence of different civilizations throughout Tunisia's history. Mahmoud Messaadi had noted early on Tunisia's participation in all forms of exchanges "between peoples and civilizations, since the Phoenicians, the Greeks, the Romans, until the Arabs, the Vandals, the Turks and the French." Messaadi reasserted in 1968 that the Tunisian people's identity was formed by both its Arab Muslim history and its pre-Islamic identity: "The young and modern Tunisia currently engaged in the nation-building process must accept [this multilayered identity]."[43]

Civics textbooks introduced in the early 1970s put forward the specific Tunisian identity that Bourguiba promoted. They included knowledge of the country's structure and state institutions as well as civil society organizations.[44] Third-year secondary students learned about the Tunisian economy and about the roles of various unions, including UGTT, and women's groups.[45]

Students were also taught about world history and the broader human community—distinct from individualist and reductionist viewpoints. Reformed history curricula stood in sharp contrast to what had been taught during the protectorate era. Instruction then had been primarily focused on European history or—as in the case of *kuttab* schools—exclusively on Islamic history. After independence, decolonization movements started to be discussed in curricula.

History books focused on liberation efforts in North Africa and on Tunisia's nationalist struggle, but the starting point was 1934 and the creation of the Neo-Destour party. The history textbook for terminal primary school students, published in 1967, gave credit for the creation of Neo-Destour only to Habib Bourguiba, who was also placed at the center of the naturalization crisis. The *Jeunes Tunisiens* were not even identified in the book, although descriptions of Abdelaziz Thaalbi and Destour were presented, but in an unfavorable light in comparison to the "better organized" Neo-Destour that "younger men" led. Nationalist movements in Maghreb countries were described, and religious and cultural ties that united Tunisia with the immediate region were emphasized. The book gave prominence to Tunisia's solidarity with other developing countries and the nonaligned movement. It painted a positive image of the Third World, whose values are those of "cohesion" and "peace," and described in detail the 1955 Bandung Conference of newly independent states in Africa and Latin America.[46]

Most important is that critical thinking was actively encouraged through the teaching of philosophy—a subject that was, and is, absent from curricula elsewhere in the Arab world. During the final year of secondary school, Tunisian students learned from a three-volume collection of philosophical essays in French that induced them to think about issues of religion, cultural relativism, and intercultural encounter and dialogue. Students were exposed to texts that examined religion's contemporary relevance. The condition of women, especially in Tunisia, and their place in society and the workplace received considerable attention. Among the almost one hundred texts that students read, however, only a few concerned Arab philosophers—four texts were dedicated to Ibn Khaldūn. There was insufficient coverage of great Arab and Muslim philosophers and reformers, including those who were part of Tunisia's modern reform movement. This contrasted with the overwhelming presence of collectivist doctrines, for instance: eight texts focused on Karl Marx's theory of alienation within the capitalist framework.[47]

But this started to change in the 1970s with the push for Arabization by Mohamed Mzali (1925–2010), who served as minister of education for three stints during the 1970s before becoming prime minister in 1980. Driss Guiga, who served as minister of education between 1973 and 1976, also contributed to the short-lived Arabization effort.

Mzali was ideologically in favor of a stronger Tunisian Arab identity; he had been the editor of a leading Tunisian Arabic literary intellectual publication, El Fikr. The Arabization process that he set into motion would be methodically applied to the education system until it was discontinued in 1982. Ironically, Mzali and other vocal supporters of an Arabization program had attended French universities and were therefore fully bilingual and heavily influenced by Western education.[48]

Advocates of Arabization rested their arguments on the first article of the 1959 constitution, which proclaimed Arabic the official language of Tunisia. Arabization was also seen as a tool that could help thwart the spread of communist thought among university students who were influenced by French-oriented groups and by the study of Marxism as part of the philosophy curriculum at school.[49] To counter leftist political opponents, political alliances were already being formed between the regime and Islamists, who favored dominance of the Arabic language.[50] It was also hoped that Arabization would bring Tunisia closer to Gulf countries and thus make much-needed investments more possible.[51] This occurred against a backdrop of the government's dropping its socialist economic agenda and adopting a policy of infitah instead.

But plans to Arabize school curricula and government transactions met serious impediments. They were impaired by the existence of very different forms of Arabic: Classical, Modern Standard, and Tounsi. Neither Classical nor Modern Standard Arabic was widely known to Tunisians, although Modern Standard was certainly more common among the educated classes. This diglossia of Tounsi as the spoken language and Modern

Standard Arabic as the official language complicated the implementation of Arabization. Also, qualified teachers who were proficient in Arabic were not abundantly available.

Bilingualism was already deeply ingrained in society, in part due to encouragement by Habib Bourguiba. Being well versed in the French language was a prerequisite for pursuing a university education. Several higher education institutions required mastery of French, but not Arabic, for admission.[52] Securing a job in government also required proficiency in French. French persisted as the working language of government; in 1989, only three of nineteen ministries—the prime ministry and the ministries of the interior and justice—had their publications produced in Arabic.[53]

Despite difficulties, some changes did take root, albeit mostly temporarily. Literary subjects and Islamic civilization were Arabized, as was philosophy, which now included a wider representation of Arab and Muslim philosophers.[54] History textbooks were also Arabized. The reformed curriculum gave more prominence to Islam, without anchoring Tunisia exclusively within the Arab or Islamic world. But this soon changed.

Emphasis on Arab and Muslim history increased as printing houses could not keep up with the need to publish texts in Arabic, and the ministry turned to printing presses in Baghdad. The civilizational syncretism that defined Tunisian identity got progressively left out of textbooks in favor of an Arab Muslim narrative. Greater emphasis was placed on the expansion of Islam and its positive contributions to people's lives in conquered lands. History textbooks became critical of nineteenth-century reformism, which they painted as having been influenced by external forces and limited. The content of textbooks became increasingly ideologically charged.[55]

During the Arabization phase and beyond, French remained the language of instruction for science courses and the primary language of instruction in institutes of higher education—except in theology and Arabic specializations, where French was taught as a second language.[56]

The Arabization program was ultimately abandoned in 1982, followed by a reversal process that started in earnest in 1986. During his significant stint as minister of education in the late 1980s and early 1990s, Mohamed Charfi (1936–2008) would take charge not only of securely reinstating ethos introduced by Bourguiba and Messaadi but of introducing unprecedented liberal and progressive principles into school curricula. Charfi's reforms would play a decisive role, as chapter 15 will illustrate, in ensuring that the Tunisian education system nurtured and graduated thinking, informed, and tolerant minds—precisely what Bourguiba had intended.

In Tunisian collective memory, Bourguiba is remembered for his dedication to his nation's intellectual and technical development. Universal access to education ensured that all Tunisians would have the opportunity to become learned human beings. Bourguiba also pragmatically underscored the vital idea that not all forms and types of education were equally suitable for everyone. Beyond a foundational primary school education, students were able to pursue tracks that matched their dispositions, competencies, and capabilities. The introduction of technical and vocational training helped mitigate chronic problems of unemployment and the stigma associated with handiwork, supporting the idea that a university education was not a prerequisite for participation in the economy—a principle that Ben Ali would catastrophically contravene in due course.

Bourguiba's education policies cemented the Tunisian identity and exposed students to the multilayered influences of various civilizations. Education reforms were part and parcel of Bourguiba's progressive reforms, and curricula became imbued with values that supported his overall agenda. Coeducation not only stressed that men and women would have an equal and mutually respectful standing in Tunisia, but it removed inane and harmful taboos that have stagnated Arab society at large.

Although the process was not immune from hiccups along the way, the gradual approach to universal education and to the Tunisification of the teaching forces ensured that a commitment to quality was preserved. The initial reliance on French teachers while Tunisian teachers were being trained reinforced this commitment.

One of the greatest contributions of the reforms was that they limited the space for religious education, both by curbing the number of hours dedicated to the subject and by insisting on a bilingual education system. A dogmatic approach to religion based on strict interpretations of Islam was eluded. The teaching of philosophy, which has been expanded to two years of secondary school, nurtured a culture of critical thinking and debate. Toleration and acceptance became deeply rooted in the Tunisian psyche, enabling the enlightened progression of the country toward democratization and freedoms not experienced elsewhere in the wider region.

14

A Different Trajectory

I mmediately following independence, mostly in the form of new nations where hitherto none had existed, Arab leaders hastened to create systems of education where for the most part there had been none. The prevalent state of education was dismal. Enrollments were low in the few schools that existed, which catered mostly to the elite, and literacy rates were commonly in the single digits.

It was widely understood that education was key to entering the modern world and participating in the global economy, and that it was the duty of a state to provide it. There was a practical imperative as well: the replacement of foreign workers in government, armed forces, and industry. Education was also to serve the purpose of fostering national unity and shaping a national identity—from scratch in most instances.

The spreading of national fervor that underscored nation building during the postcolonial era became deeply entrenched in education systems, which in turn became tools for the imposition of state-sponsored ideologies and militaristic doctrines. The classroom often became the venue for broadcasting militant rhetoric to build up state authority and national unity—galvanized against real or imagined enemies.

Instilling a national identity was predicated on patriotism to the motherland, often purely territorially defined, and a shared Arab Muslim history and belief system. "God, Homeland, and the King," or the "Party," as the case may be, became the motto adopted by regimes. Nation building meant that Arabic as a language and Islam as a religion could be depended upon as mainstays.

In Iraq, the Arab Socialist Ba'ath Party built an education system that became a focal point for Arab nationalist propaganda, promoting selective symbols and historical memories.[1] Education became the means for instilling a narrow ideal of nationalism that bolstered Sunni minority rule over a Shi'ite majority and a large Kurdish population. The state steadily pushed its political agenda through the education system; schools became one of the means of oppression as teachers and students were forcefully indoctrinated into the party and recruited as instruments of the omnipresent state intelligence service, the mukhabarat.[2]

But Iraq also served as a rare example of a state that imposed an exclusionary national identity on a religiously and ethnically diverse population while at the same time transforming the Iraqi population from an illiterate one into one of the best and most universally educated in the region—albeit in terms of knowledge and skills, but not with regard to values of toleration and inclusiveness.

As elsewhere, the main system of education in Iraq until the middle of the twentieth century was that of madrassas, or kuttab schools. Christians and Jews attended their own schools. At the time that the Ottoman Empire fell and Iraq was put under British "protection" in 1921, the population was prodigiously illiterate, with a literacy rate of less than 0.5 percent.[3]

Literacy campaigns, initiated under the British, were aggressively pursued by the Ba'ath party. In 1978, the party made it a legally binding national priority to eradicate illiteracy. Two years of literacy classes became required of all illiterate adolescents and adults between the ages of fifteen and forty-five.

Primary education was made compulsory and free after the 1958 coup that overthrew the Hashemite king, Faisal II. With the nationalization of the oil industry, free education was extended to secondary school and university students in 1974, and within two years it also became compulsory for children up to the age of fifteen. By the end of the 1970s, nearly every Iraqi child attended primary school.

The Ba'ath party also popularized women's education. Women, while restricted from entering the realm of politics, were encouraged to pursue schooling. In the 1980s, Iraqi women made up 46 percent of teachers,

29 percent of physicians, 46 percent of dentists, and 70 percent of pharmacists. Literacy rates for women became the highest among Muslim-majority countries.[4]

Jordan's Hashemite monarchy looked to education to help construct a national identity. Civics textbooks reinforced loyalty to the state and enumerated factors that validated its monarchy—from its prophetic lineage to its historical contributions, including the Great Arab Revolt that gave birth to the modern Arab world.

Complicating the creation of a national identity for the newly formed nation was that its population has always been overwhelmingly nonnative and progressively dominated by refugees—first from Palestine in 1948 and 1967 and more recently from Iraq and Syria. Identity tensions and competition between the majority Palestinian population and the indigenous "East Jordanians" have made the sustenance of a singular national identity challenging. Jordan, which has been an island of stability in an otherwise tumultuous region, has continued to find it necessary to sponsor nationalist campaigns to rally its people around a specifically Jordanian identity.

In Egypt, following the July 23, 1952, Free Officers Coup, the military's hegemony over all matters reached deep into the education system. Gamal Abdel Nasser saw in education the tool to achieve his goal of propagating an Arab and Islamic identity among Egyptians and of positioning Egypt at the center of a great Arab nation. Socialization became a prominent feature of public schools, where themes of Islam, nationalism, Arabism, and loyalty to the regime became ingrained. Islamic heroes were exalted, and anticolonial rhetoric was ample—glorifying the regime's victory over colonial reach and painting the 1952 coup as a revolution.[5]

Education in Egypt had been neglected under the Ottomans and the British, with access to primary and secondary schools and higher education almost exclusively reserved for the elite.[6] Education was otherwise consigned to the study of the Qur'an at *kuttab* schools. There had been some attempts in the nineteenth century to create secular institutions that were considered modern, but al-Azhar continued to provide the primary source of education for the mass population.

The 1923 Egyptian constitution that was drafted following the country's independence from the British in 1922 made primary school obligatory for both boys and girls, but the policy was never fully enacted. Then, in 1953,

Nasser reintroduced and enforced free and compulsory education up to the age of twelve.

Nasser was particularly focused on fixing social and regional inequalities, and he positioned education as part of his modernization project. Policies emphasized science and technical education to prepare a qualified Egyptian workforce to replace foreign technicians expelled after the nationalization of the Suez Canal in 1956; the humanities and liberal arts were downplayed, as they generally were in other budding education systems.

To achieve his goals, Nasser extended universal and free education to the postprimary level; in 1962, university tuition fees were abolished and graduates were guaranteed public sector jobs.[7] Male students were also relieved of military service.[8] But political turbulence, the outbreak of wars, and high costs put a lid on these ambitions.

As school enrollments mushroomed—more than twofold in primary schools and threefold in universities—Nasser had to drop his slogan of "every day, a new primary school."[9] Infrastructural needs and demand for qualified teachers grew with student enrollments. Schools began operating in shifts, particularly in big cities.[10] With demand for education quickly outstripping the state's ability to cope with it, and state resources becoming increasingly strained as a result of military spending—reaching 56 percent of GDP in 1974[11]—the public education system started deteriorating and being neglected.[12] Growth in the Egyptian ministry of education's budget peaked at a modest level of 5 percent of GDP in 1968, despite enormous growth in the numbers of students.[13] Universal primary education prioritized quantity over quality.

The ideological, political, and hasty approach to building systems of education meant little regard for quality or actual learning that went beyond the ability to memorize, accept, and regurgitate. Anticolonial sentiments led to the rejection of all things foreign, including language, and the adoption of parochial systems of knowledge and outdated pedagogic approaches. This was as true for Egypt as it was for other countries in the Middle East and North Africa.

With the Qur'an as an exemplar of the Arabic language, quick Arabization of curricula and the replacement of colonial teachers with a local or imported cadre—as ill prepared as they might have been for the task—became the order of the day. This quickly gave way to the infiltration of religious ideology into all subjects, including modern and ostensibly secular ones.

Immediately following Morocco's independence in 1956, King Mohammed V formed a royal commission for education reform, which made Arabization of the education system its top priority. Mohammed V declared that the type of education system needed was "Moroccan in its thinking, Arabic in its language, and Muslim in its spirit."[14]

As the process of Arabization went into effect, French was declared a secondary language but remained for the time being the language of instruction in mathematics and science. The first year of primary school was completely Arabized in 1957, just one year after independence. By 1990, instruction and educational content in both primary and secondary school curricula had been completely Arabized, except for science and technical subject matters.

The process of Arabization was interrupted briefly in 1966 when the minister of education, along with proponents of a bilingual education, argued that Arabization had failed to improve standards of Arabic and overall education levels and that the French language was necessary in school to meet the needs of modernity. During colonization, French had been imposed as the official language in public administration. The socioeconomic environment after independence, including strong political and economic ties with France, encouraged the use of French. The attempt to derail the Arabization agenda was strongly opposed, however, by traditionalist groups, such as the conservative and monarchist Istiqlal party, leading to a reversal of policy back to Arabization.[15]

Private schools and French cultural mission schools continued to be French in their orientation. Elite families—including, ironically, members of the pro-Arabization Istiqlal party—preferred to enroll their children in French schools.[16] This dual track of French and Arabic education created inequities as public school students faced obstacles in gaining access to universities, where instruction was in French.[17] This scenario was similar to Tunisia's during its Arabization phase in that access to university was limited for many who did not grow up in urban elite, bilingual households. But, unlike in Tunisia where public education continued to be superior, private schools were creating a parallel, preferred education track for Moroccans who could afford it.

The debate that took place in Morocco over Arabization was not very different from the one that emerged in Tunisia. But in Tunisia, Habib Bourguiba insisted on bilingualism, whereas his Moroccan counterpart urged for the opposite. When advocates for Arabization eventually had a say during the 1970s in Tunisia, the result was different than it was in Morocco: efforts at Arabization were limited and ultimately curtailed, and a bilingualism system continued to prevail.

Although it took more than thirty years for Arabization to be fully realized in Morocco, the process was thought to be unnecessarily hasty, especially given that there were still not enough teachers trained in Modern Standard Arabic.[18] By the early 1960s, 50 percent of Moroccan primary school teachers were themselves equipped only with a primary education.[19] Teachers were thus brought in from Middle Eastern countries to try to fill the gap created by the Arabization program.[20]

The injudicious approach to Arabization and the consequent importing of large numbers of teachers occurred as the population was growing and student enrollments were increasing rapidly. By 1985, the number of school-age children enrolled in school had increased to 85 percent—from 17 percent at the time of independence.[21]

The push for Arabization in Algeria was even stronger and more political than in Morocco.

Prior to independence, education for the local populace was limited, similar to how it was across the Arab world. Only 8.8 percent of school-age Algerian children were enrolled in school in 1944.[22] Although the French had created Franco-Arab primary schools for Algerian students as far back as 1870, these had to be shut down in 1883 because parents refused to send their children to them. *Kuttab* schools, which were regulated by the French, were the only schools in existence until private schools were established by locals in the late 1910s and early 1920s. These new schools used French pedagogic methods, but they steered away from French curricula and focused instead on instilling values of patriotism among Algerian students.[23]

Following independence in 1962, the principal objective of Algerian officials was to help the country heal itself after a long and brutal struggle for independence. Anticolonial sentiments and the rejection of the imperial power's cultural and linguistic dominance galvanized the charge for the Arabization of culture and education and the reclamation of a "lost" identity. Algerian authorities proceeded to eradicate French—the "language of colonial alienation"—from all spheres of Algerian society in what the Algerian-born academic Djamila Saadi-Mokrane calls "linguicide."[24] Independent Algeria went as far as enshrining in law, through Article Seventy-Six of the 1963 Algerian constitution, that full implementation of Arabization be achieved as soon as possible.

Arabization efforts sparked debate between proponents, whose discourse was anchored in Islam, and advocates of bilingualism—pejoratively referred to as *hizb fransa*, or the party of France. Like Morocco, Algeria continued to retain strong ties to France after independence—employing French citizens in oil exploration projects and as teachers—making it difficult to abandon the language.[25] But in the end, conservatives won and Arabization quickly took full effect. When Algeria's first president, Ahmed Ben Bella (1916–2012), was toppled in a coup in 1965, his successor, Houari Boumediène, reiterated Algeria's Muslim and Arab identity and allowed Arab Islamic values to dominate the education system.[26] Vigorous implementation of the Arabization program included Arabizing the education system, the civil service, and the public sphere.

Primary school years were Arabized in quick succession—the first primary year in 1964, the second in 1967, and the third and fourth years in 1971. One-third of middle and high school subjects were Arabized by 1971. By 1990, the process was complete, and French was taught only as a foreign language.[27]

While Arabization was taking hold at the school level during much of the first two decades following independence, Algeria relied on a dual education system. In contrast to Tunisia's integrated bilingual system, Algerian students were divided, depending on the subject matter, into either a French-oriented system that used rational and modern pedagogic methods or a Middle Eastern–oriented scheme, which was heavily infused with ideological content and depended on rote memorization.[28] French *coopérants* were relied upon to teach in the French track. For subjects that were taught in Arabic, there were very few Algerians who could perform the task. Teachers had to be imported—mainly from Egypt, but also from Syria, Iraq, and Lebanon.[29]

In 1964 alone, more than 1,000 Egyptians joined Algeria's teaching force, but they lacked proper teacher training. It was also difficult for local Arab and *Amazigh* students to understand the Egyptian dialect of their new teachers—and vice versa.[30] The need for imported teachers only height-ened with the standardization of the education system and the enforce-ment of compulsory education in 1976. Enrollment of school-age children almost tripled—to 71 percent—in 1977 from what it was at the time of inde-pendence.[31] The problem of teacher shortages persisted, and the depen-dence on foreign teachers continued. Generations of students lost out on the opportunity to gain a good education because of the understaffing and ill preparation of education workers.

Across Algeria's borders, Muammar Gaddafi saw education as a means to subjugate his people to his peculiar dogma. Gaddafi wanted to instill in students a revolutionary spirit.[32] Applying his rhetoric to education, in 1976 he launched his program of *tathwir al-manahij*, or revolutionizing the curriculum. In addition to Islamic and Arabic studies at all academic levels, several weekly hours of study were dedicated to Gaddafi's *Green Book*.[33]

The book, a comical and hypocritical manifesto of Gaddafi's "political philosophy," put forth a blueprint for how a nation should be governed, how its economy should function, and how its society should be struc-tured. It discussed "democracy," but spoke of how representative bodies like parliaments are "legal barrier[s] between the people and the exercise of authority" and how power should be totally decentralized and lie in the hands of the people—ironic given how power was centralized in *his* hands. The book elucidated that private property is only acceptable when it comes to ownership of one's home.[34] But of course this did not apply to Gaddafi, who owned a private plane and luxury homes around the world—not to mention a collection of gold and jewel-encrusted guns.

Gaddafi recruited teachers from his revolutionary council to help mold *jeel al-ghadab*, or generation of anger, predicated on anti-Americanism and anti-Zionism, and committed to pan-Arabism and the liberation of Pales-tine. School in Libya also meant mandated instruction during holidays at "ideological camps" designed to further proselytize students.[35] Gaddafi militarized schools and required army training for both male and female students, who wore army uniforms to school and participated in daily mili-tary exercises.[36]

To reinforce a sense of national identity among students, it was com-mon in countries from Turkey and Pakistan to Iraq and Egypt to promote a militaristic notion of unity against enemies—historically and at present. A narrative of victimization and values of exclusion and intolerance were propagated, whether by projecting past enemies at the time of the birth of Islam as infidels, or recent and present enemies in the form of the West and Zionism—often bringing into the discourse the relevance of jihad.[37]

Critical historical analysis has been absent, and accepted narratives, always pitting Arab or Muslim against an oppressor, usually a Western one, have been beyond reproach. Criticism of Arab and Muslim historic figures is considered sacrilegious, fostering among students beliefs that harbor a blanket absolution of responsibility and a privation of self-criticism. Students grow up to be conspiracy theorists; a sense of victimization and blame renders the most mundane of developments as couched in a Western conspiracy.

The emotionally charged clarity by which past and extant struggles have been presented cultivated uncompromising attitudes toward conflict in general. Such attitudes are most evident in textbooks, which have painted all struggles in black-and-white terms—depriving students of the opportunity or the ability to consider nuance, debate, or seek alternative narratives. The emphasis on rote memorization and on inculcating a regime narrative meant that class discussion was not encouraged. Students were not taught how to apply logic and reasoning or to write essays that took a position on a subject.

In *Pedagogy of the Oppressed*, Paulo Freire speaks of the type of education that is an act of "depositing"—the students are the "depositories" and the teacher is the "depositor." The task of the teacher becomes one of filling the minds of students with content that is often detached from reality and where the teacher knows all and the student none.[38]

In this sort of environment, which became characteristic of classrooms across the Arab world, students learned to adopt a culture of not questioning or thinking critically, and of praising the author, the teacher, and the leader. They developed a fatalistic perception of their situation, and they acquired at an early age habits of obedience and acceptance of a singular truth. Military education, with its emphasis on command and order, reinforced these habits.

The home environment has also had a bolstering effect and has become part of a vicious cycle: the cultivation of unquestioning minds in the classroom reinforced obedience at home, and vice versa. Home and classroom started forming mirror images of one another. Common methods of child rearing in rural and religiously conservative environments—rigid and suppressive of questioning, exploration, and taking initiative—coupled with the philosophies adopted by schools, reduced children's independence and undermined their self-confidence and social efficacy, fostering instead passive attitudes and hesitancy in decision making.[39]

Opportunities to foster creativity, self-expression, and openness to diverse perspectives have been chiefly absent—whether inside or outside of school. Rather than learn to love, through arts and literature, or to debate and think critically by studying philosophy, students often learned to hate through their indoctrination in an "us versus them" rhetoric.

In Jordan, despite a 1994 education law reform that explicitly stated that an educational objective is to give students a taste of aesthetics and different aspects of life in the arts, art comprises only 1 percent of the curriculum. Arts, especially theater and music, are often banned in schools that consider them *haram*, or forbidden in Islam, inciting those who consume them to lust and pleasures.[40]

The state-sponsored infiltration of religion into almost all subjects, and the insistence of monotheistic religions on an absolute truth, have had the dual effect of producing religious zeal among students and of ensuring their inability to question.

Rigid pedagogic approaches took their cues from religious education. Rote memorization is rooted in traditional Islamic learning at madrassas, which is centered almost exclusively on instruction in the recitation of the Qur'an from memory. Successful conclusion of a course of study consists of *khitm*, or completion, *hifz*, or memorization, and *tajweed*, perfecting the recitation of the Qur'an. These milestones may be achieved without necessarily acquiring a thorough understanding of the text or its language.

Strict interpretations of Islam and a dogmatic approach to religion complemented oppressive regimes' insistence on discipline and control. Acceptance of an absolute national and geopolitical truth went hand in hand with an overwhelming dominance of religious education in curricula and the use of Islam as a political tool by ruling regimes.

Morocco's King Hassan II (1929–1999, r. 1961–1999) employed religious education and further incorporated Islamic studies into curricula in the 1970s as a means to bolster his religious credentials, following failed attempts to overthrow him in 1971 and 1972. The king, after all, held the title of *amir al-mu'minin*, or commander of the faithful, given the monarchy's claim of descent from the Prophet. The role of Islam in Moroccan curricula had already been expanded in 1966, doubling the number of weekly hours dedicated to Islamic studies in middle school and adding religious topics to history, Arabic literature, and civics curricula.[41] The monarchy used Islamic education as a defensive tool to placate opposition from religious nationalists, but also as a strategic ploy to strengthen Islamists in countering leftist influences.[42]

The incorporation of Islam into education was also used as a political tool in Egypt in the 1950s and 1960s. President Gamal Abdel Nasser enlarged the nationalized al-Azhar's religious system of education in order to achieve two strategic goals. First, he needed the support of al-Azhar Mosque-University to counter the growing opposition of the Muslim Brotherhood. Second, he aimed to compete with the Saudi Islamic weight by defining Egypt as a leading Arab Muslim state.

Rather than include Islam as a subject in a modern curriculum, as Bourguiba did, Nasser incorporated modern subjects into established primary and secondary schools based on the Azharite system. Azharite institutes—ma'ahid azhariyya—proliferated as a modern alternative to traditional schools; they taught mathematics, Arabic, and natural sciences, as well as Islamic studies and history. By the beginning of the twenty-first century, 1.3 million children between the ages of five and nineteen were enrolled in separate Azharite schools for boys and girls.[43]

In no time, Islam began to dominate all subjects. Arabic language and literature textbooks became Islamized and increasingly indistinguishable from religious ones. Literary texts were replaced with Qur'anic excerpts, and Arabic exams required memorization of the Qur'an.[44] Adding modern subjects to a religiously oriented system meant that these subjects were taught from a religious perspective—a different scenario from adding religion as a subject in a modern system, as Tunisia did. This pattern has become a trend that has permeated education systems in other countries in the region where Islam has dominated.

Islam's infiltration into Egyptian education intensified under Anwar Sadat, who came to power after Nasser's death in 1970. Sadat aligned himself with the Muslim Brotherhood against Nasserists and emergent communist currents, using Islam as a source of legitimacy and calling himself the "Believing President." Sadat amended the constitution to make Shari'a the primary source of law, and he empowered Islamist organizations to influence education and civil society.[45] Sadat eventually banned the Muslim Brotherhood from university campuses near the end of his reign when they had become too powerful and increasingly extremist in their ideology and tactics. But the damage had already been done.

Islamists found their greatest opening under Mubarak's regime, when the state's investment in education dwindled, and voids—exacerbated by a boom in population growth—had to be filled by private schools. Religious groups saw an opportunity in providing education and family assistance, and Islamic schools spread. Early childhood education became almost exclusively the domain of religious charities. Qur'anic recitations replaced the national anthem at public schools, and extracurricular activities revolved around memorization of the Qur'an and recitation contests. Girls came under pressure to wear the hijab, and they were gradually excluded from any kind of sports activity. Textbooks authored by the Muslim Brotherhood cautioned that deviation from Islam would harm society. Civics books, introduced as late as 2009, defined good citizenship as synonymous with observance of the rituals of Islam and with commanding virtue and forbidding vice.[46]

Whereas Gamal Abdel Nasser increased the influence of al-Azhar and the role of Islam in the Egyptian curriculum to counter the Muslim Brotherhood, Islam's role in Jordan's education system increased due to the influence of the Muslim Brotherhood. The country's admittance of the Muslim Brotherhood, which established its Jordanian branch in 1945 under the pretext of supporting jihad in Palestine, translated into the government's offering appeasing gestures to the group while also keeping a close eye on its activities.

But the government's conciliatory approach ended up having a devastating effect on generations of Jordanians when the Brotherhood was allowed to add the ministry of education to its state spheres of influence. For much of the 1970s, a Muslim Brotherhood leader and former head, Ishaq Farhan, was put in charge of the ministry. Under Farhan, Jordan's educational policy became increasingly aligned with the Brotherhood's version of Islam. During the decades that the Muslim Brotherhood held the keys to Jordan's ministry of education, dues-paying members infiltrated the ministry and ensured permanent and utter control over curricular content. Their power has been observed in the textbooks and pedagogic approaches that dominate the educational landscape and in the visceral resistance to any attempt at progressive reform.

Primary school textbooks introduced by the ministry of education prior to 2016 described peaceful coexistence as an ethos exercised exclusively among Muslims, and presented values such as respect, justice, and tolerance as Islamic. The religious narrative pervaded textbooks for Arabic and civil and social studies—in addition to religion textbooks. Arabic curricula and textbooks taught—and continue to teach—the language through the Qur'an and Hadith.

Secondary school textbooks spoke of obedience to one's parents and of spreading and defending Islam through jihad as the duties of every Muslim, second in importance only to the worship of God. Islamic studies textbooks told students that "jihad is a must for every Muslim" and those who partake in it go straight to heaven.[47] In a high school textbook, analysis of Qur'anic text that speaks of Muslims driving out the Jews of Medina concluded that one must be "wary of hypocrites and Jews, for they are brothers in their animosity for Muslims."[48]

The textbook for eighth-grade Islamic education went so far as to prescribe a husband's authority in marital relationships and household matters. A wife, we are told, is not allowed to leave her home without her husband's permission, for her absence from the home could impede her duties toward her husband and children. Exceptions were made, however, in cases of extreme emergency such as a fire or a sick child; but even then, she should not go out wearing perfume or with her hair uncovered.[49] In Jordanian textbooks published before 2016, 90 percent of illustrations that included a woman showed her wearing a hijab.[50]

The official "philosophy" of Jordan's education system rests first and foremost on faith in an "almighty God" and in the "higher ideals of the Arab Nation." It makes it abundantly and incontrovertibly clear that Islam is the be-all and end-all source and guide for knowledge and morals; it is defined as a whole system from which consciousness is formed.[51] Education, as defined by the ministry of education on its website, rests on religion and nationalism, and has little in the way of an intellectual basis in its underpinnings.

It is no wonder, then, that Islam dominates every conceivable subject in curricula and textbooks, and that a Jordanian student is indoctrinated with religious rhetoric. In science textbooks, for example, Qur'anic verses are presented at the beginning of lessons to provide a religious context for even the most empirical of subjects.[52]

272 L'ÉCOLE, LA FEMME, ET LA "LAÏCITÉ"

Attempts by the Jordanian government in 2016 to update textbooks—fewer religious references and greater inclusiveness of Jordan's small but significant Christian minority—met staunch resistance from conservative currents, including Islamists within Jordan's teachers' union. Arguments raged between proponents of the provisional reforms and those who opposed them. Pressure mounted on the government to retract some of the changes that had been introduced. Opposition to the initial, mostly benign, changes underscored the difficulties in attempting to implement any radical reform. The state has remained committed to the reform effort, however, replacing the minister of education in early 2017 and putting in place a number of review bodies to oversee the change process.

In Saudi Arabia, the education system was from the outset entrenched in religion and in loyalty to the House of Saud. The two were presented as intertwined, with the latter as the guardian of the former. Education policy rested on ensuring that the "correct" Islamic doctrine is taught and that the legitimacy of the Saudi dynasty is understood to rest on religious foundations. To be disloyal to the regime was to be disloyal to God. Saudi textbooks are ripe with the phrase: "Obey Allah and his Prophet and those with authority."[53]

It took Saudi Arabia more than two decades after it was created as a state in 1932 to establish a ministry of education, in 1953. It was almost another two decades before the country made primary education free—but not compulsory—in 1970. Qur'anic schools were eclipsed by the creation of a public school system, but the new system was heavily comprised of religious education.

The first ever Saudi public school for girls was opened in 1960. Girls studied according to the same curriculum as boys did, but they could not avail themselves of physical education—this was replaced by home economics.[54] The education of girls was placed under the Presidency for Girls' Education, an entity separate from the ministry of education and controlled by religious authorities. The Presidency for Girls' Education was only integrated into the ministry of education after a fire at a school in Mecca in 2002 left fifteen girls dead when Saudi Arabia's religious police—the Committee for the Promotion of Virtue and the Prevention of Vice—obstructed rescue efforts because the girls were not veiled.

Islamic education, which propagates the Wahhabi ideology and teaches content that is exclusionary toward other faiths and sects, is compulsory at all levels of education in Saudi Arabia. Between 20 and 30 percent of weekly hours at the primary and secondary school levels are dedicated to this subject. This is in addition to history and Arabic classes, which are dominated by religious teachings. At the university level, one-fourth of all students were studying in Islamic institutions in the early 1990s.[55]

Unsurprisingly, coeducation is illegal in Saudi Arabia, in schools and universities—public or private. It exists only at the kindergarten level. When the Saudi monarch inaugurated the King Abdullah University of Science and Technology in 2009 as a coeducational facility, he had to establish a special economic zone for that purpose. The concept of an American-style coeducational university in an otherwise oppressively sexist and religiously dominated milieu was extraordinarily radical for Saudi Arabia. The king faced sharp criticism from conservative Saudi clerics, especially as neither gender segregation nor a dress code for women was imposed.

When male and female academics come together for workshops and conferences, they typically do so while physically separated from one another on the basis of their sex. I experienced this firsthand at an academic conference at King Abdelaziz University in Riyadh. I was, with my male colleagues, in an all-male building. Female faculty, segregated in their all-female quarters, participated by having their voices beamed into our conference room using voice teleconferencing technology. They could see us via video teleconference, but we could not see them.

On a separate occasion when I visited the president of a women's university in Jeddah, I was handed over to a woman—who was inconspicuously waiting behind a door—after I had checked in at a male-only holding area. My female escort walked in front of me in the courtyard leading to the main building. She walked faster and faster as I tried to keep pace with her. Very soon, she was running, and so I ran to try to keep step. I was completely oblivious as to why she was intent on keeping me at a distance behind her. I only understood once she hurriedly got into the building and loudly announced that a man was coming. "*Rayyal, rayyal*," she yelled, and unveiled women instinctively pulled their covers over their heads.

Ikhtilat, or mixing between the sexes, is heavily discouraged across the board in Saudi Arabia. Clerics warn that it could lead to "fornication, adultery, broken homes, children born of unmarried couples and full-blown societal collapse." When a former member of the Saudi "religious police," Ahmed Qassim al-Ghamdi, publicly challenged decisions of what constitutes right and wrong in every facet of life, including *ikhtilat*, he received anonymous death threats and was ostracized. Clerics denounced him and called for his punishment and torture.[56]

Segregation of the sexes—in school and in society at large—has reinforced the subjugation of women to an inferior status in the Arab world and to their disenfranchisement. Statistics that point to the progress of Arab women through education are misleading. While gender parity has been achieved in terms of enrollments in school and university, with females often outnumbering males, this has not translated into the advancement of the rights of women and their equal status. A major gap also persists when it comes to women's participation in the workforce. While 75 percent of eligible men between the ages of fifteen and sixty-four seek and are able to find job opportunities, only 22 percent of women do.[57]

While pressure has been mounting on Saudi Arabia to reverse the hegemony of religion in the public sphere, Turkey has been moving in the opposite direction, witnessing a deterioration of the *laïcist* education system that Ataturk introduced as an integral and defining factor of his new nation.

At the time of Turkey's founding in 1923, Ataturk declared the purpose of education as the cultivation of nationalist, republican, and secularist citizens. Ataturk firmly believed that the most important pillars of a nation were its military and the education of its people. The two often overlapped, with mandatory military courses beginning in the second year of high school for both males and females.[58]

While newly sovereign Arab countries rushed toward Arabization and often Islamization of their newly established education systems, Ataturk took Turkey in a diametrically opposite direction. The founder of modern Turkey retreated entirely from the Arab world and Islam, changing the alphabet from Arabic to Latin and restricting accessibility to religious texts, including the Qur'an.

An education unification law introduced in 1924 removed all religious teachings from Turkish public schools and resulted in the closing of 479 *kuttab* schools.[59] But Ataturk recognized that there was still a need to train religious officials. *Imam-hatip* schools were thus established for religious functionaries—under the control of the government and its *laïcité* program. *Imam-hatip* schools were to serve as Islamic vocational schools to train imams and preachers, who would spread state-sanctioned Islamic knowledge to the population in a way that did not threaten the nation's republican values.

As successive military coups and coalition governments sought stability and the appeasement of Islamists, religion reentered schools in 1953, taking hold through a series of reforms that began in the 1950s and picked up speed in the 1970s and 1980s. *Imam-hatip* schools were turned into secondary schools in 1970, enabling their graduates to enter university. When girls were admitted in 1976 and all academic disciplines within universities became open to graduates in 1980, *imam-hatip* schools essentially became an alternative track within the standard education system. By 1997, 13 percent of Turkish high school students were enrolled in *imam-hatip* schools, which were now viewed as the "backyard" of the emergent Islamist party.[60]

The number of students enrolled in *imam-hatip* schools has increased by 90 percent since Recep Tayyip Erdogan, a graduate of one himself,[61] and his Islamist Justice and Development Party (AKP) came to power in 2002. It is estimated that more than 1 million students between the ages of ten and eighteen are enrolled, and the schools have been opening at twice the rate of standard public schools. In pushing its religious agenda, AKP integrated the ministry of religious affairs, or *diyanet*, into the national education system and gradually introduced policies that mandated more Islamic education—including the teaching of children as young as five years old morals and ethics drawn solely from the Qur'an and Hadith.[62]

Erdogan has publicly stated that his dedication to expanding *imam-hatip* schools is part of his effort to nurture a "devout generation" of Turkish citizens. His government has brought under its control some 174 of the country's best schools, and it has taken over the appointment of principals and replaced thousands of long-standing teachers with a younger, government-approved cadre. Extracurricular student activities have also been affected, many replaced with religiously themed events.[63]

AKP plans call for the introduction of curricula that teach Turkey's history from a stronger national perspective, emphasizing "moral values" and presenting Sunni Islam as inseparable from Turkish identity. The growing role of religion in society, governance, and education under AKP has intensified nationalist ideals that sought to create an exclusionary identity at the time of Turkey's founding.

The removal of religion from public schools by Ataturk was accompanied by campaigns to homogenize the population and to erase the cultures, languages, and histories of minority populations. The goal was to create a distinct people who spoke a single mother tongue and held standard beliefs. The 1924 law for the unification of education also resulted in the closure of schools that had served minorities, such as Syriacs and Kurds. Teachers were employed to inculcate Turkish culture into Kurdish students and to "civilize" and assimilate them into mainstream Turkish society. Attempts at eradicating the Kurdish language were so severe that students often received beatings for speaking it in class. Kurdish children were also sent to boarding schools in order to accelerate the process of assimilation and total cultural annihilation.[64]

Exclusionary policies are not unique to Turkey. Turkey is actually a latecomer to a scene that has been played on Arab stages for decades.

The formation of a reductionist Arab identity has favored the adoption of biased, sectarian, exclusionary, and intolerant views of the "Other," or what the French Lebanese writer Amin Maalouf defines as the "tribal perception of identity."[65] The definition of who the "Other" is has been multilayered and confounded. In the broadest sense, it has been personified by Western colonial and Zionist powers. At the intraregional level, it has often been defined by national interests or along sectarian divides—most notably Sunni-Shi'ite—or both. Within national boundaries, multiplicities of ethnic, tribal, or religious affiliation have contributed to the amplification of otherness.

In Bahrain, where a Sunni regime rules over a Shi'a majority population, religious curricula are exclusively centered on Sunni Islam—Ja'fari traditions of Shi'a Islam are completely absent. Shi'a students have the opportunity to attend the one Shi'a institute in existence, which enrolls 1,200 students. While all Muslim students, regardless of sect, are required to take Islamic studies, there are no religion courses for non-Muslims in public schools, although they can elect to enroll in courses on Islam.[66]

Iraqi Shi'as were not recognized as a sect until school curricula were revised after the fall of Saddam Hussein in 2003. But textbooks had to be retracted and revised again in response to accusations that they now promoted a sectarian bias against Sunnis.[67] The valorization of Sunni heroes was a persistent feature in history textbooks, and it was often combined with narrowly defined ideals of nationalism. Primary school curricula made no acknowledgment of Iraq's multiple religious minorities. Appeals for the opening of schools and teacher training institutes in Shi'ite and Christian majority areas were rebuffed.[68]

While Sunni Islam and Christianity are both taught in Egyptian public schools—pupils are assigned to religion classes based on their father's religion—the Egyptian curriculum leaves Muslim students thinking that Sunni Islam is the only true version of Islam.[69] Students learn about their respective religions, taught dogmatically and without reference by one to the other, planting the seeds for "Otherism."

In Algeria, where native speakers of the *Amazigh* language—*Tamazight*—make up 20 percent of the population, it took thirty-three years for that identity to be formally recognized.[70] It took another twenty years for *Tamazight* to become the second official language of Algeria—in March 2016.[71]

Lebanon presents a curious case in terms of the challenges to fostering inclusivity among a diverse population with a sectarian disposition. Once independence from the French was recognized in 1943, the educational aim of the state was to build a sense of shared identity and common citizenship across sectarian divides, while countenancing religious freedom and autonomy. The state thus allowed religious communities leeway in determining their own curricula.

Various religious systems were free to devise their own faith-based curricula—one hour per week was dedicated to religious education.[72] This meant that different sects studied their own individual faith systems and historical narratives, but not others'.

In the aftermath of the sectarian civil war of 1975–1990, the state implemented, in 1997, a new, uniform curriculum that underscored values of national unity.[73] Pressure by various religious groups that felt underrepresented in the new school curriculum, however, culminated in the removal of religious education altogether—while allowing private schools, which enrolled about half of Lebanon's students, to continue to provide religious instruction in the sects of their choosing.[74] The opportunity for Lebanese children to cultivate a pluralistic ethos has thus given way to exclusionary religious education, risking resumption of old divisions among new generations.

The corollary outcome of an Arab education system dominated by exclusionary rhetoric and religious discourse has been that generations of Arabs have been deprived of the right to a good education. Around 56 percent of primary school children and 48 percent of lower secondary school students across the region are thought to have not learned rudimentary literary and numeric skills.[75]

There is also the major problem of children not having access to any kind of education. War and conflict in the region have stripped generations of children of the opportunity to even go to school. It is estimated that 21 million children and young adolescents in the Middle East–North Africa region are out of school or at risk of dropping out.[76]

The problem of poor education has been made worse by the explosive population growth over the past few decades. The region's population, which hovered around 30 million for centuries before reaching 60 million early in the twentieth century, has grown faster than in any other major region of the world—by almost fourfold in the second half of the century, from 100 million in 1950 to 380 million in the year 2000.[77] An estimated additional 7.7 million students are expected to need accommodation in primary schools by 2030. The total number of extra teachers that will be needed is just shy of half a million. In this respect, the region is surpassed only by sub-Saharan Africa.[78]

Tunisia has not been immune from some of the problems that have plagued education systems in the postcolonial Arab world. Overcrowding in schools and shortages of qualified teachers were among the challenges that faced the country during Bourguiba's reign. These problems were exacerbated in the Ben Ali era, which saw deterioration in standards and unfettered access to schools and universities, as the next chapter will reveal.

But Tunisia largely averted the major pitfalls that drove education systems elsewhere into the abyss. Bourguiba's curricular policies and the precedents they set protected Tunisian schools from the divisiveness that swept through the region.

While Bourguiba also relied on education to promote a Tunisian national identity and a nationalist narrative built around him, he had much to fall back on in terms of continuity, territorial integrity, and national historic legitimacy. He had the confidence and credibility, through decades of championing the Tunisian independence cause, that his Arab counterparts lacked. His country's colonial history had not been as acrimonious or violent as that of some of its neighbors. The push for Arabization was therefore not nearly as intense in Tunisia. Bilingualism was sustained, and it helped avoid the infiltration of religion into virtually all subjects. Bourguiba's education policies were also part and parcel of a comprehensive strategy to modernize and secularize society. The approach that Bourguiba took toward education was congruent with his *Code du statut personnel.* Ultimately, his was a subtler approach that cultivated nationalism while focusing on a broader liberal and visionary education agenda.

The trademark of Arab education elsewhere has been one of intellectual despotism—discouraging individual thinking and repressing curiosity and creativity. Students have been robbed of the opportunity to develop reasoning faculties, to acquire sociolinguistic skills, to form their own opinions, and to learn to coexist with different points of view and ways of life.

The reversal of these trends and the undoing of the grave damage that has been inflicted through exclusive religious and narrow nationalistic hegemony over education would take generations to accomplish. In the meantime, the Arab world is likely to continue its entanglement in intolerance and sectarianism, and to be ill prepared for democracy.

15

The Education Paradox

E ducation largely defined the legacy of Bourguiba, furthering Tunisia's progress on a durable and drastically different trajectory from that of other Arab countries and helping prepare Tunisians for an exceptional democratic experience.

But good education failed to translate into job prospects for many Tunisians. Problems of mass unemployment, the consequence of a challenging economic environment and policy failures—starting with Ben Salah's experiment with socialism—cast a dark shadow over Bourguiba's reign, especially toward the end.

The economic crisis that crippled Tunisia in the mid-1980s and eased Ben Ali's ascension to the presidency was marked by poor agricultural harvests, a decline in already limited oil proceeds, a devalued currency, mounting debt, and a bloated public sector. At the time, the public sector's share of the employment market was a staggering 35 percent, equivalent to Egypt's and surpassed only by Algeria's and Jordan's.[1]

So Ben Ali set out to "reform" the economy. The increasingly authoritarian president thought that if he focused his efforts on fixing economic problems, his people might be more willing to accept limited political participation and freedoms. In exchange for economic prosperity and stability, the president would be left alone to lead. "Khubzism," from khubz, or bread, became a euphemism for eating and keeping quiet.[2]

But in the end, the average Tunisian lost his freedoms, and his economic conditions did not improve—there was neither political participation nor economic prosperity.

While economic indicators did move in a positive direction, they masked serious income inequalities and regional disparities. The World Bank and the IMF used essentially misleading statistical inferences, and Ben Ali's mafia-like privatization efforts were ignored. Structural adjustments and poorly implemented economic directives, with benefits syphoned off by the powerful, ended up hurting the average Tunisian's livelihood.

Just as with his mollifying economic reforms, Ben Ali's policies on the education front produced some superficially positive results. By the mid-1990s, primary school enrollment for both boys and girls reached 100 percent.[3] Literacy rates rose to 48 percent in 1984, and to 74 percent by 2004.[4] But positive indicators concealed some serious infrastructural and organizational problems.

Ben Ali did not come into power with a grand vision like Bourguiba, nor did he possess his predecessor's charisma or political daring that enabled the country's first president to implement his reforms. Ben Ali was a product of Tunisia's police and security apparatus, having risen within army ranks to become a general and, later, head of national security and minister of the interior. He knew little about economics and, unsurprisingly, even less about education.

In populist moves meant to help address employment challenges, Ben Ali increased access to school and university. This had the dual advantage of buying the regime time as would-be job seekers stayed longer in school, while also appeasing international organizations through better enrollment metrics. But in the long run, the rapid expansion of education under Ben Ali brought down quality standards and made the problem of unemployment worse: greater numbers of university graduates, some with the illusion of a good education, started seeking and expecting employment.

In 1991, Ben Ali made school compulsory for all Tunisians until the age of sixteen. The exam that had been administered at the end of primary school and had determined admissibility into secondary school was now abandoned.

The sudden surge in student enrollment that resulted was accompanied by the elimination of the vocationally—and less academically—oriented tracks in secondary school.[5] This led to a much wider variance of aptitude among students and a higher student-to-teacher ratio. The result was extreme and growing stress on physical and human educational infrastructures, and deterioration in the quality of education at both the school and the university level.

During Messaadi's time, less than 40 percent of primary school students were admitted into secondary school, and only a portion—those who were most accomplished academically—had the opportunity to sit for the *baccalauréat* exam at the conclusion of their studies; not everyone passed the exam and obtained their *diplôme*. But with Ben Ali's populist reforms, students had unmitigated access to secondary school, and those who would have pursued the now defunct vocational track also sat for the *baccalauréat* exam and became entitled, by law, to gain admission to university upon passing the exam.[6] When many students failed the *baccalauréat* exam, the standards for passing were adjusted.

With the removal of vocational tracks from public schools, technical training was altogether dissociated from the ministry of education and put under the aegis of the *Conseil national de la formation professionnelle et de l'emploi*, created in 1993 to advise the government on matters concerning vocational training.[7] Students still could, depending on their age, opt to enroll in a two- or three-year program at *collèges techniques* that were now outside of the main system of education. Higher institutes were also set up to provide advanced vocational training, and vocational institutes were encouraged to establish partnerships with private sector companies in which students could receive professional training.[8]

But students were not inclined to pursue a nonacademic technical education when they could instead follow a general secondary school course of study and enroll in university. Before the 1991 reforms were introduced, roughly 50 percent of primary school students went on to pursue the vocational track in secondary school or enroll in vocationally oriented *collèges moyens*.[9] But as of 1998, only 12 percent of students opted for the separate technical school route.[10] Increasingly, students enrolled in vocational schools only when they had failed regular school and had few other options to pursue.[11]

The result was that, over time, there were fewer graduates equipped with the skills that the job market required and more graduates who were armed with a university degree but had not necessarily met the standards of a good education—unemployed and unemployable.

The popularization of higher education was not in and of itself a bad thing. Under Bourguiba, secondary school and university education had been to some extent elitist. But the removal of alternative tracks in vocational training, and the speed and manner in which changes were made, had three quite negative effects: employment challenges, declining standards of quality, and a cultural shift toward a sense of worthlessness if one were not equipped with a university degree. Ultimately, populism led to the failure of education to fulfill its basic objectives.

Overcrowding and shortages of teachers naturally ensued. Class sizes grew to more than thirty students in primary schools and more than forty in lower classes of secondary school. Teaching quality suffered, despite Tunisian teachers' lower than average teaching loads and higher salaries when compared to other developing countries.[12]

In response, Mohamed Charfi, Ben Ali's minister of education between 1989 and 1994, introduced new teacher training programs. A postgraduate two-year program was offered by new institutes of higher education, *instituts supérieurs de formation des maîtres*. Teachers had to undergo several months of compulsory pedagogic training and pass a national exam at the university level before they would be allowed to teach in secondary school.[13] Once they entered the teaching profession, teachers had to undergo yearly in-service training that consisted of thirty classroom hours.[14]

But Charfi was also behind the reforms that made education compulsory and eliminated vocational tracks from secondary school. His reforms reflected his ideological bent and his background as a leftist and a human rights activist. Charfi had been a student leader of the *Union générale des étudiants tunisiens* in the 1960s in Paris. He was jailed in 1968 when Bourguiba clamped down on the leftist group *Perspectives*, which Charfi had cofounded. When Ben Ali appointed him minister of education in 1989, Charfi was president of the *Ligue tunisienne pour la défense des droits de l'homme*, having cofounded the human rights organization in 1976. The education minister believed in the democratization of access to education and that education was a human right. He was also intent on removing what he saw as Islamist influence in the curriculum.

Facilitated by Mohamed Mzali's attempts at Arabization in the 1970s and early 1980s, Islamist thought entered mainstream books. According to former minister of culture Ahmed Khaled, who also worked at the ministry of education in the 1980s, Islamist rhetoric dominated philosophy textbooks.[15] The teachings of Muslim Brotherhood leaders Hassan al-Banna and Sayyid Qutb were included, but the Islamic reform movements of Jamal al-Din al-Afghani and Muhammad Abduh were left out. Western philosophy received extemporaneous and superficial attention.[16]

Contradictions, some bringing into question Tunisia's form of government, crept into curricula. Ahmed Khaled recounted to me how a fourth-year secondary school Islamic education course described a republican civil form of governance as tyrannical in its infidelity and promoted the notion of a caliphate state instead—negating what a third-year civics education textbook had taught these same students about the foundational principles of a civil state and of citizenship.

With Bourguiba's power diminishing, successive governments turned a blind eye to the collusion that was taking place with publishers and distribution houses.[17] Support for the *Mouvement de la tendance islamique* among teachers and academic leaders allowed the movement influence over the curricula.[18] This laissez-faire attitude persisted in the first years of Ben Ali's rule, during his short-lived honeymoon period with Islamists.

Charfi moved quickly to purge the curriculum of Islamism and extremist thought. He recruited respected academics to review the content of textbooks and curricula, particularly with respect to religious discourse. The reforms that Charfi subsequently introduced resulted in the removal of ideological content and the reintroduction of a more inclusive and tolerant version of Islam. Religious teaching was decoupled from civics education.

The course on Islam changed its name from *tarbiyya diniyya*, or religious education, to *tafkir islami*, or Islamic thought.[19] The textbook for the first-year secondary school course on Islamic thought, introduced later in the 1990s, discussed non-Sunni sects of Islam as well as other religions, including Zoroastrianism and Manichaeism, and did not present them as corrupt or inferior to Islam. An entire chapter was dedicated to the notion of freedom of belief, condemning hatefulness toward those who leave their religion and denouncing coercion—describing its nonviolent, subtle ways such as the denial of medical care or discrimination in employment on the basis of religious belief.[20]

The *maqasid*, or intentions and aims, of Shari'a were underscored, and the teaching of religious rituals was deemphasized. Students learned of the need for adaptation of the religion to the times and for the renewal of Islamic thought; the works of reformers and progressive thinkers were highlighted.[21] Students were also taught about the importance of *ijtihad* and of debate and acceptance of differing opinions. Textbooks spoke of the necessity for Islamic reform, citing it as an organic process that every religion must go through and drawing inspiration from the experiences and evolution of Christianity and Judaism.[22]

Science curricula were revised to incorporate Darwinian ideas of evolution and the big bang theory—unheard of in Arab curricula elsewhere.[23] The science program also included sex education for boys and girls, a first for any Arab country, where textbooks are typically censored for sexual content.[24]

The reforms ensured that a balance was struck in the history curriculum between discussions of Arab Muslim civilization and Western history and thought. An inspection of a ninth-grade history textbook revealed that it dedicated roughly half its pages to the European Renaissance, the Enlightenment era, and the Industrial Revolution.[25] Tunisia's history was framed within a Maghreb context, reflecting Ben Ali's foreign policy—strengthening ties with North African countries and joining the *Union du Maghreb arabe* in 1989. Tunisia's unique pre-Islamic history was also brought back.[26]

Charfi held a deep conviction that students ought to acquire an education that provided a balance between the humanities and the sciences, be exposed to universal values of toleration, and be prepared for a democratic society.[27] While education systems in other Arab countries at around the same time became entrenched with indoctrination into an intolerant, dogmatic, ritualistic, and ideological teaching of Islam, Charfi ensured that Tunisia persisted on a more enlightened path. Charfi understood, as did Bourguiba and Messaadi before him, that critical and analytical thinking were core tenets of an education system and that students needed to be equipped with the skills to make up their own minds.

Mohamed Charfi personally drove his reforms and ensured that any setback experienced in the 1980s was more than fully reversed. It is not surprising that, given Charfi's communist leanings and political motivations, he was quoted in a 1994 article that appeared in *Le Monde* saying: "A student who had read Voltaire would never become an Islamist."[28]

The reforms naturally attracted the ire of Islamists, who had found Charfi's appointment as minister of education objectionable in the first place. Descended from a long line of theologians and armed with a remarkable erudition, Charfi was able to confront and disarm Islamists, who vehemently opposed him and of whom he was quite distrustful. His widow, Faouzia Charfi, informs me that his life was so threatened that the family was under police protection, which was only removed in 1996 when the relationship between her husband and Ben Ali had deteriorated beyond repair.[29]

According to Ben Ali's last minister of education, Hatem Ben Salem, Charfi's termination of the vocational track in secondary school was motivated by his view that the less academically inclined students who used to enroll in these tracks became easy recruits for Islamists.[30] Hamadi Ben Jaballah, a member of Charfi's reform committee, concurred with Ben Salem's opinion on Islamist recruitment tactics, but he insisted that the decision to diminish vocational training had been made in 1985 but only implemented in 1991.[31] Faouzia Charfi was also quick to distance her late husband from the decision and to blame it on Ben Ali.[32]

To further contain and control religious education and how it was taught, one of Charfi's first acts as minister of education was to set up, in 1989, Zaitouna University as a distinct religious, coeducational institution. The move was intended both to appease Islamists and to serve as a means of curbing their influence. Faculties were organized within three institutes: theology, Islamic civilization, and Shari'a. The Shari'a institute trained imams and was placed under the jurisdiction of the ministry of religious affairs.[33] Subjects such as philosophy, sociology, history, and religious dialogue became part of the program of study at Zaitouna, and Hebrew and Latin were also taught.[34]

Charfi personally oversaw curricular design at Zaitouna, ensuring that the "universal values of Islam" were incorporated and that hints of extremist ideology were absent. Tensions grew, however, over the definition of the "correct" version of Islam, and there was strong opposition from traditionalists over Charfi's intervention.[35] To maintain tight control, the regime ensured that student enrollment at the university would remain low—reaching 833 students in the 1998–1999 academic year.[36]

More broadly, university enrollment expanded rapidly with the removal of the vocational track in high school in 1991. Until the mid-1980s, only 6 percent of Tunisians twenty to twenty-five years old enrolled in institutes of higher education.[37] But during Ben Ali's reign, universities saw a sevenfold increase in enrollment.[38] Spending on higher education did not grow at a rate nearly commensurate with this burgeoning enrollment. In 2001, higher education accounted for around 4 percent of the national budget, compared to 25 percent for primary and secondary education.[39]

Political pressures for regional expansion resulted in a number of universities popping up in rural areas without much attention paid to quality. Underqualified teachers and thousands of contract and part-time personnel were hired throughout.[40]

Universities also became highly politicized under Ben Ali. Academic freedom was compromised, and universities were exploited for the regime's political ends. The retention of students allowed for the manipulation of employment data as universities were turned into "waiting room[s] for the threshold of the job market." In order to weed out powerful faculty members who worked against the regime, the retirement age was dropped to sixty.[41]

Rising enrollment and decreasing spending brought about the dwindling of university quality standards. The situation deteriorated further when, in 2002, a reform that made it easier to gain access to university was introduced. In what has been referred to as the "25 percent rule," a cataclysmic change meant to enable more students to pass the *baccalauréat* exam and gain access to higher education was introduced.[42] The reform translated into basing 25 percent of a student's *baccalauréat* score on the average score of three less challenging exams that were administered during the final year of secondary school. Ostensibly, the move was directed by Ben Ali so that his daughter, who was due to sit for the *baccalauréat* exam in two years, could have a chance of obtaining her *diplôme*.[43] An entire one-fifth of students who sat for the *baccalauréat* in 2010 would not have passed and would not have qualified for admission to university had it not been for the 25 percent rule.[44] It became possible for almost any Tunisian to seek a university education, whether qualified or not.

The purpose of higher education, which was highly selective under Bourguiba, had been to produce well-qualified leaders. But with these reforms, universities were accepting secondary school graduates who were not adequately prepared and who might have been better able to contribute to their own well-being and to society and the economy by having pursued a vocational path. Little to no planning went into steering students toward fields of study that matched market demand. Universities were turned into factories of unemployment. They became suppliers of degrees that no longer signified the accomplishment they once had.

Private universities started appearing on the scene in 1992 to try to take advantage of the demand for higher education, but these universities were not initially recognized by the state. With mounting pressure on public universities, however, and within an economic liberalization context, private universities were admitted by virtue of a 2000 law. In 2006, there were only around 3,500 students enrolled in private universities—one-third of whom were foreigners.[45] By 2012, total enrollment had increased, but only to a modest 21,880.[46]

Elsewhere in the Arab world, the landscape has been filled with commercial private universities that have taken financial advantage of the region's population boom. The situation in Jordan is illustrative. As of the 2012–2013 academic year, eighteen of Jordan's twenty-eight universities were private, the vast majority of them for profit; private universities enrolled a full 25 percent of Jordan's university students.[47] A good education has essentially become the exclusive domain of private, nonprofit American universities, whether in the form of the American University of Beirut and the American University in Cairo or branch campuses in the Gulf.

At the pre-tertiary level of education almost anywhere in the Arab world, one would have to attend a private school—mostly nonprofit—in order to receive a good education. Parents who can afford a private school would not give any consideration to enrolling their children in public schools—known for their lesser quality. The complete opposite is true in Tunisia, where, regardless of socioeconomic status, parents want to enroll their children in public schools. For the most part, private schools cater to students who are forced out of the government system.

The foundational curricular and pedagogic legacy of a Tunisian education that Bourguiba and Mahmoud Messaadi built, and the foundations they rested it on in terms of the intellectual reforming influences that came before, has survived. Reforms introduced by Mohamed Charfi preserved curricular content that ensured that Tunisia continued to steer away from the absolutist and intolerant underpinnings of woeful Arab education systems. Under Ben Ali, the quality of education in terms of what students were exposed to in textbooks continued to be strong, progressive, modern, and inclusive—reversing harmful trends that had taken hold in the 1980s on the heels of failed attempts at Arabization.

New textbooks promoted values of political and human rights, citizenship, democratic principles, and tolerance among peoples and cultures.[48]

In a civics textbook introduced in 2009, authoritarianism is equated with tyranny. Students are asked to reflect on how their intellectual, personal, and political lives are affected by the existence of totalitarianism. Students are also taught about the responsibility of voting in elections and how exercising the right to vote is an expression of freedom.[49]

A Tunisian education is progressive, modern, largely secular, and far better than average—by regional standards, at least—despite quality standards having declined under Ben Ali. But when Tunisians are reminded of this, they are quick to quibble that their benchmark is a Western, not Arab, education.

I was quite amused when in a conversation with my friend and colleague, the political analyst Youssef Cherif, he complained about declining standards of education, citing as an example that he had not studied the likes of René Descartes the right way. I explained to Youssef that generations of Arabs have graduated, including from private schools as I did, never having heard of Descartes! Youssef took two full years of philosophy, as mandated by Tunisian secondary school education requirements, which he completed in the early 2000s.

Since the revolution, standards of quality in education have improved. The 25 percent rule has been obliterated, and there has been a push for bringing back the selectivity and academic standards that had long defined Tunisia's education system. Democratic governance has reached into universities, where presidents, deans, and department heads are elected to their positions by faculty.[50]

The government in 2015 set up the *Conseil national du dialogue social* with the aim of creating a new vision for Tunisia's school system. The committee included representatives from the ministry of education, UGTT, and the Tunisia-based Arab Institute for Human Rights. It was charged with conducting a systematic evaluation of the current education system and coming up with widespread reforms. The committee included among its priorities a focus on addressing high dropout rates among students, reorienting the education budget toward previously neglected rural areas, and giving special attention to students at risk of violence, delinquency, or suicide.[51] In July 2015, former prime minister Habib Essid announced the start of a 150 million dinar (roughly $75 million) maintenance campaign for educational institutions.[52]

Reestablishing standards of selectivity has been facilitated by a declining student population, the result of successful attempts at curbing population growth over the past few decades. While the number of teachers has nominally stayed the same, the number of students enrolled in school has declined by one-third since the year 2000.[53] Between the 1999–2000 and the 2011–2012 academic years, the number of students enrolled in primary schools alone has dropped from 1,403,729 to 1,014,836.[54] But the decline in numbers is also related to dropout rates, which have been on the rise, with more than 100,000 students reported to have left school prematurely in 2013.[55] Tunisia's youth, disenchanted by the lack of opportunities in the formal economy, are drawn to the black market, where academic degrees have little value.

The Jasmine Revolution, brought about by economic hardships, was enabled by a key role that education played—leading up to it and in its aftermath. The Tunisian public education system produced generations of critical thinkers who were not stripped of their ability to criticize, question, debate, and oppose the dominating thoughts, dogmas, ideologies, and laws of the regime. Education was the most formidable ingredient behind the conditions that caused and enabled Tunisians both to stand up against their oppressor and to consolidate the gains of the revolution. Education ensured a propensity toward democracy and consensus building, a paradox in and of itself for Bourguiba and Ben Ali, and an opportunity, especially for those educated under Bourguiba, to assume leadership positions in postrevolutionary Tunisia.

Charfi's reforms were decisive in their introduction of values of human rights, global citizenship, and toleration, and in their curbing of the Islamist tides that had taken root in the 1980s. His reforms in civics education armed the public with knowledge that helped inspire the revolution. The youth who rose up against Ben Ali had been taught in *his* schools to oppose authoritarianism and to uphold democratic values.

The celebrated American writer James A. Baldwin once posited: "The paradox of education is precisely this—that as one begins to become conscious, one begins to examine the society in which he is being educated." Education in the Arab world intended that there not be an awakening of consciences, but in the end there was—failed as the outcomes might have turned out to be. Tunisia has been the exception.

Epilogue
An Arab Anomaly

I t is a fallacy to think of the Arab world as a monolith and of Arabs as a homogeneous people, and thus of an "Arab Spring." These are countries that are historically, geographically, culturally, and politically divergent. To the extent that there are similarities that connect them—including language, religion, and recent histories—there have sadly also been parallels in terms of how they have evolved to be undemocratic, religiously oppressive, monistic, and repressive of freedoms.

Tunisia, a nation within and without the Arab world, inspired the calls for change by Arab youth who rose up in support of democracy and in defiance of corrupt authoritarianism in their countries. But with the exception of Tunisia, the particular conditions of the environments where these uprisings took place did not sustain them, and in some, they led to the brutal crushing of all potential of salvation.

Searching for hope amid a hopeless landscape, many have pointed to Tunisia as a model of what could work elsewhere. But Tunisia cannot serve as a model for the rest of the so-called Arab world.

The conditions for change in Tunisia were different. The ingredients present in Tunisia have been many generations in the making. They cannot be easily replicated. Factors that are specific to Tunisia have led the country to where it is today.

On almost every dimension, Tunisia's trajectory—over decades and centuries—has been a markedly different one than that of other Arab countries. How the country has evolved has been aided by a unique identity that is an amalgamation of different civilizations and influences and by an advantageous territorial delineation that has been essentially intact for centuries. Absent have been a resource burden, a large and politicized military, international interference, and sectarian discord.

Tunisians are cognizant of their rich identity and of the diverse aspects of their heritage—Arab Muslim and otherwise. Tribalism, which has torn apart neighboring Libya and stood in the way of a pluralistic and inclusive national construct elsewhere, has been successfully superseded by a viable and meaningful national identity—rooted in the Mediterranean, forming part of the Occident and of the Orient.

Nineteenth-century reforms that were driven by foreign influences—whether French, English, or Ottoman—which included 'Ahd al-aman, the abolishment of slavery, and the 1861 constitution, helped contextualize and give impetus to indigenous reforms that continued into the twentieth century. Khayr al-Din al-Tunisi and Ahmad Ibn Abi Diyaf inspired *Jeunes Tunisiens* and the likes of Abdelaziz Thaalbi, Salim Buhagib, and others, all of whom set Tunisia on a path of enlightened, largely secular, and Western-influenced education—building on the model of Sadiqi College and founding educational institutions such as *al-Jami'a al-khaldūniyya*.

Reformers argued from *within* Islam for modernity, the emancipation of women, and the study of the sciences and of philosophy. They promoted the practice of *ijtihad*, and they collaborated with the reforming works of *al-Nahda* that emanated from Cairo.

But whereas reform movements elsewhere were halted and gave way to regressive trends, the reforms that started in Tunisia in the nineteenth century were expansive and continuous. They produced a cumulative effect.

Intellectual reformers gave life to the nationalist movement. No other nation-building project in the Arab world was led by intellectual forces or was predicated on a profound reform movement. Bourguiba stood on the shoulders of contemporary and past reformers, and he emerged as a reforming leader who cared deeply about putting Tunisia on a modern path.

Once independent, Tunisia progressed along a postcolonial course that is remarkably different than that trailed by Arab countries. With the slight exception of Lebanon, which has been entangled for much of its history in sectarian division and geopolitical intrigue, Tunisia has been able to emerge as the lone democracy in an otherwise despairing Arab world.

Four domains have distinctively, decisively, and interrelatedly defined both Tunisia's trajectory and the opposite track that has been followed since independence by every other country that defines itself as Arab: education, women, religion, and civil society.

While *nūr al-'ilm* served as Bourguiba's mantra and Tunisians learned to learn and to coexist, education elsewhere took a nosedive into a cesspool of national fervor, reactionary dogma, exclusive religious hegemony, and narratives of victimization and hatefulness.

His orientation decidedly Western and distinct from that of other Arab leaders, Bourguiba made a modern education and the cultivation of a civilized society his top priority. He kept the military small and apolitical, and allocated the largest portion of the state's budget to education instead.

Every Tunisian child, girl and boy, was educated in mixed-gender classrooms. A progressive and tolerant bilingual curriculum, based on modern subjects and pedagogic approaches, was developed, and it endured. Hasty attempts at Arabization, meant to be a positive reclamation of language and identity but which triggered the deterioration of education in the wider region, were curtailed. Tunisian educationalists ensured that only a minimal number of hours were dedicated to religious education. The marginalization, for better and for worse, of Zaitouna at least ensured that religion did not dominate the cerebral space. While the power of religion reigns supreme throughout the wider region, it is the power of education that has defined Tunisia. Tunisia's culture of debate, consensus building, and respect for human rights and individual freedoms rests on this enlightened educational foundation.

Basing his arguments on the work of Tahar Haddad and buoyed by the support of notable Zaitouna scholars such as Tahar Ben Achour and Fadhel Ben Achour, Bourguiba achieved suffrage for women and codified into law Haddad's 1930 seminal work, *Imra'atuna fi al-Shari'a wa al-mujtama'*. Emancipated ever since Tunisia took in its first breath of independence, women have been equal partners with men and full contributors to Tunisia's development as a modern and progressive state. Alas, their counterparts in the rest of the wider region continue to struggle to assert their rightful claim to legal protection and membership in the socioeconomic and political spheres.

Tunisians are free to believe or not, protected by a constitution that guarantees their freedom of conscience. Elsewhere, imprisonment—and oftentimes death—awaits those who dare denounce Islam. As religion was put under the control of the Tunisian state, it was not purged from the public space. A "twin toleration" by religion of the state and by the state of religion endured. Tunisia is the only truly civil, largely secular Arab country—*laïcist* as it might be in the sense that religion continues to be the domain of the state.

Ennahda's decision at its May 2016 national congress to drop its Islamist label and end its religious activities, redefining itself as a party of Muslim democrats, represents a final Jeffersonian separation between institutionalized religion and politics. This move by Ennahda is a reflection of Tunisians' rejection of conservative Islam that led to the party's fall in 2013. Ennahda needed to adapt to new realities in order to compete in the democratic arena.

The timing of the move has got to be opportunistic. As with other moves and proclamations by Ennahda, however, even the most distrustful of the party admit that it is practically irrelevant and inconsequential whether Sheikh Rached Ghannouchi is being sincere or is merely maneuvering politically. The end result is that Ennahda has moved in a direction that is appealing to Tunisia's mainstream constituents.

Tunisian civil society, rooted in the *Union générale tunisienne du travail* (UGTT), saved the day when it needed saving—the Quartet serving as a prime example. The role of UGTT in organizing protests and providing logistical support cannot be underestimated. The offspring of reforming leaders like Muhammad Ali al-Hammi, Tahar Haddad, and Farhat Hached, the Tunisian labor union movement has always been intricately intertwined with the country's intellectual development.

The intersection of modern education, advanced rights of women, religious moderation, and an active civil society created a whole that was larger than the sum of its parts. Progress on each has resulted in the others' development. Reforms by Bourguiba, but with credit stretching back into Tunisia's modern and ancient histories, help explain why Tunisia has progressed toward a liberal and democratic society the way that it has.

It is no wonder, then, that while others fought for control and for the imposition of their militarism or narrowly defined religious truisms, Tunisians came together—peacefully and consensually—first to bring down authoritarianism, and then to craft their constitution and build their democracy.

Powers were handed over—peacefully—multiple times during the nascent era of democratic rule, and for the first time in the Arab world, an Islamic party, Ennahda, "voluntarily" ceded control to a secular one.

In each and every event, entity, and process during the Tunisian Spring—Kasbah, Troika, and Quartet, for inspiration—there is strong evidence of a Tunisian way, a *tunisianité*.

This is the story of Tunisia. It is a story of accommodation and moderation, of debate and consensus. It is one of erudition and of continuous and cumulative reform. It is a new story in that so little was known about Tunisia and its specificities until it became the lone success story of the Arab Spring. But it is an old story in that democratic and liberal Tunisia had been in the making for a long, long time.

Acknowledgments

W riting a book is not only an individual, and at times lonely, process but also a collaborative effort, whether by virtue of tangible assistance in the form of research, editing, and feedback, or in terms of the moral support that one receives along the way. I would not have been able to accomplish the task of authoring this book without both.

Tunisia: An Arab Anomaly simply could not have been written were it not for some magnificent colleagues and friends. I owe each and every one of them much indebtedness.

When the idea for the book had not fully manifested itself, there were a number of people who gave me the inspiration to begin to conceptualize it. My dear friend and colleague Carol Becker was one such person. My nephews Zeid and Qais Masri literally put paper and pen in my hand when they gave me a notebook to begin writing my thoughts for what was to become this book. They were my pillars of support, and Qais became my sounding board, often reviewing material and offering sage advice. Countless friends provided steadfast confidence in the endeavor, encouraging me throughout the process. I hope they will forgive me for not listing them all and that they will indulge me for singling out Ousama Ghannoum for his constant nurturing, and Meyer and Barbara Feldberg for their love and mentorship through the years.

The book benefited tremendously from those who took the time to read, with dedicated sincerity, my early synopsis chapter that turned into a proposal. Lee C. Bollinger's endorsement, along with his insistence on the value of lived experiences in telling stories such as this, has given me more encouragement than he might realize. My colleagues Rashid Khalidi and Lila Abu Lughod provided me with invaluable commentary and suggestions early on in the process. Mamadou Diouf helped me contextualize Tunisia and Islam within the Maghreb and francophone Africa. My friends Maha Kattan, Jace Schinderman, and Lillian Silver were among those who read the synopsis chapter and gave me spirited encouragement.

I am eternally grateful to the superb readers of my draft manuscript. Lisa Anderson's careful review and guidance helped me bring better focus into the analysis and to reframe arguments. Amal Ghandour challenged me with her characteristic crisp honesty and meticulous study of both the proposal chapter and the manuscript. Brinkley Messick provided me with thorough feedback and invaluable understanding of important nuance. Youssef Cherif lent his vast knowledge of Tunisia's past and present to my representation and interpretation.

The feedback I received from two sets of anonymous reviewers—for the proposal and the manuscript—was instrumental in helping me bring further rigor to the endeavor. To them, I offer my sincere gratitude.

Mark Kingdon, an individual of rare commitment to improving the state of the world, deserves special mention for his enormous friendship, counsel, and support.

I am indebted to David Ignatius for bringing the remarkable Raina Davis my way. Raina became my indispensable research assistant and collaborator. I am incredibly fortunate to have benefited from her contributions—on so many levels. The other two members of my research and editing team, Syreen Forest and Nora Bakhsh, worked extremely hard to help make this the book that it is. *Tunisia: An Arab Anomaly* is, to a large extent, the result of an effort that I simply would not have been able to complete without Raina, Syreen, and Nora. I am also grateful to Zein Jardaneh for her wonderful proofreading assistance.

The support and encouragement from home and office upon which one relies in writing a book are not insignificant. In that vein, I owe much gratitude to my family and to all of my coworkers, particularly Farrah Bdour and Rachelle Vertenten.

I could not have been more fortunate that Columbia University Press believed, from the outset, in me and in the potency of the story that I have shared in the pages of this book. Anne Routon provided me with unwavering support and sage counsel along the way. Eric Schwartz, my marvelous editor, proved to be an incredible partner in the endeavor; I am immensely grateful for his superb stewardship and steadfast confidence. I am greatly indebted to my publicist Meredith Howard for helping ensure that the book reaches its intended readers. I extend my deep appreciation to Jennifer Crewe for her leadership and to all Columbia University Press staff (Caroline Wazer, Marielle Poss, Jordan Wannemacher, and Miriam Grossman, among others) who have contributed to the project in some measure. I am also grateful to Ben Kolstad, Peggy Tropp, and their colleagues at Cenveo Publisher Services for the painstaking effort they expended in copyediting the manuscript, and to Bob Schwarz for his excellent production of the book's index.

Finally, I owe enormous gratitude to the numerous Tunisians who have educated and guided me in the process of writing this book. I am grateful to my many interviewees for their willingness to speak to me candidly and to offer their time and insights. I am also indebted to the many Tunisian friends who opened doors and provided me with rare access to individuals and information; Amel Bouchamaoui, Salah Hannachi, Ziad Oueslati, Tawfik Jelassi, and Kamel Jedidi deserve special mention in this regard.

List of Abbreviations

AL-ARIDHA: *Pétition populaire pour la liberté, la justice et le développement* (Popular Petition for Freedom, Justice, and Development)

AL-WATAD: *Mouvement des patriotes démocrates* (Movement of Democratic Patriots)

AKP: *Adalet ve kalkınma partisi* (Justice and Development Party)

CGTT: *Confédération générale des travailleurs tunisiens* (General Confederation of Tunisian Workers)

CPR: *Congrès pour la République* (Congress for the Republic)

CTRET: *Centre tunisien de recherches et d'études sur le terrorisme* (Tunisian Center for Research and Studies on Terrorism)

DESTOUR: *al-Hizb al-horr al-destouri al-tounsi* (The Constitutional Liberal Tunisian Party)

ETTAKATOL: *Forum démocratique pour le travail et les libertés* (Democratic Forum for Labor and Liberties)

ETUF: Egyptian Trade Union Federation

FLN: *Front de libération nationale* (National Liberation Front)

GDP: Gross domestic product

IFC: International Finance Commission

IMF: International Monetary Fund

LGBT: Lesbian, Gay, Bisexual, and Transgender

MTI: *Mouvement de la tendance islamique* (Islamic Tendency Movement)

NEO-DESTOUR: *al-Hizb al-horr al-destouri al-jadīd* or *Nouveau Parti libéral constitutionnel* (New Constitutional Liberal Party)

OFPE: *Office de la formation professionnelle et de l'emploi* (Office for Professional Training and Employment)

OHCHR: Office of the United Nations High Commission for Human Rights

PLO: Palestine Liberation Organization

PSD: *Parti socialiste destourien* (Socialist Destourian Party)

RCD: *Rassemblement constitutionnel démocratique* (Constitutional Democratic Rally)

SCAF: Supreme Council of the Armed Forces

UGTT: *Union générale tunisienne du travail* (General Union of Tunisian Workers)

UMFT: *Union musulmane des femmes de Tunisie* (Muslim Union of Tunisian Women)

UTICA: *Union tunisienne de l'industrie, du commerce et de l'artisanat* (Tunisian Union of Industry, Trade, and Handicrafts)

Notes

Foreword

1. "John F. Kennedy - Defining Liberal," from a speech by John F. Kennedy accepting the Liberal party nomination for president in 1960, *YouTube*, posted by NRUN65, December 1, 2012, https://www.youtube.com/watch?v=O3oY93doosg.
2. The fact that Zhou may have misunderstood the question makes the quote no less telling. See Dean Nicholas, "Zhou Enlai's Famous Saying Debunked," *History Today* (blog), June 15, 2011, http://www.historytoday.com/blog/news -blog/dean-nicholas/zhou-enlais-famous-saying-debunked.
3. Jackson Diehl, "Tunisia Boldly Embraces Democracy," *Washington Post*, October 26, 2014, https://www.washingtonpost.com/opinions/jackson-diehl-tunisia -boldly-embraces-democracy/2014/10/26/8d86b19a-5adc-11e4-b812 -38518ae74c67_story.html?utm_term=.edd06e9e7bba.
4. Norwegian Nobel Committee, "The Nobel Peace Prize for 2015," press release, October 10, 2015, https://www.nobelprize.org/nobel_prizes/peace/laureates /2015/press.html
5. Lisa Anderson, "Political Pacts, Liberalism, and Democracy—the Tunisia National Pact of 1988," *Government and Opposition 26*, no. 2 (1991): 260.

Preface

1. Christopher Hitchens, "At the Desert's Edge," *Vanity Fair*, July 2007, http:// www.vanityfair.com/news/2007/07/hitchens200707.

Introduction

1. Michael Slackman, "In Egypt, a New Battle Begins Over the Veil," *New York Times*, January 28, 2007, http://www.nytimes.com/2007/01/28/weekinreview/28slackman.html.
2. Leon Kaye, "Jordan's 6,000 Mosques to Be Powered by Solar Energy," *Triple Pundit*, February 27, 2015, http://www.triplepundit.com/2015/02/jordans-6000-mosques-powered-solar-energy/; "Health Education and Promotion," *World Health Organization: Regional Office for the Eastern Mediterranean*, accessed December 15, 2016, http://www.emro.who.int/health-education/physical-activity/king-abdullah-ii-prize-for-fitness-jordan.html.
3. Kenneth Perkins, *A History of Modern Tunisia*, 2nd ed. (Cambridge: Cambridge University Press, 2014), 6–10.
4. Central Intelligence Agency, "Tunisia," in *World Factbook*, accessed December 28, 2015, https://www.cia.gov/library/publications/the-world-factbook/geos/ts.html.
5. Norwegian Nobel Committee, "The Nobel Peace Prize for 2015," press release, October 10, 2015, http://www.nobelprize.org/nobel_prizes/peace/laureates/2015/press.html.

1. Can Tunisia Serve as a Model?

1. "Egypt Profile—Timeline," *BBC*, accessed January 14, 2016, http://www.bbc.com/news/world-africa-13315719.
2. "Tethered by History," *The Economist*, July 5, 2014, http://www.economist.com/news/briefing/21606286-failures-arab-spring-were-long-time-making-tethered-history.
3. Soumaya Ghannoushi, "Tunisia Is Showing the Arab World How to Nurture Democracy," *The Guardian*, October 24, 2014, http://www.theguardian.com/commentisfree/2014/oct/25/tunisia-arab-world-democracy-elections.
4. "Arab People," *Encyclopedia Britannica*, accessed January 12, 2015, http://www.britannica.com/topic/Arab.
5. Philip Khuri Hitti, *The Arabs: A Short History* (Washington, DC: Regnery, 1998), 7.
6. Christopher Phillips, *Everyday Arab Identity: The Daily Reproduction of the Arab World* (New York: Routledge, 2013), 10–11.
7. Lahcen Achy, *Tunisia's Economic Challenges* (Beirut: Carnegie Middle East Center, 2011), 7; "Trade (% of GDP): Tunisia (2006–2015)," World Bank, accessed July 25, 2016, http://data.worldbank.org/indicator/NE.TRD.GNFS.ZS?locations=TN&start=2006.
8. Ryo Ikeada, *The Imperialism of French Decolonisation: French Policy and the Anglo-American Response in Tunisia and Morocco* (New York: Palgrave Macmillan, 2015), 198.

9. Bénédicte Gastineau and Frédéric Sandron, *La politique de planification familiale en Tunisie (1964–2000)* (Paris: Les dossiers du CEPED, 2000), 10.

10. Elisabeth Johansson-Nogués, "Gendering the Arab Spring? Rights and (In) security of Tunisian, Egyptian and Libyan Women," *Security Dialogue* 44, no. 5–6 (2013): 393–409.

11. "School Enrollment, Secondary (Gross), Gender Parity Index (GPI): Tunisia (2000–2011)," World Bank, accessed December 15, 2016, http://data.worldbank .org/indicator/SE.ENR.SECO.FM.ZS?locations=TN&start=2000; "School Enrollment, Tertiary (Gross), Gender Parity Index (GPI): Tunisia (2000–2014)," World Bank, accessed December 15, 2016, http://data.worldbank.org/indicator/SE.ENR .TERT.FM.ZS?locations=TN&start=2000.

12. Amel Grami, "Gender Equality in Tunisia," in *Gender and Diversity in the Middle East and North Africa*, ed. Zahia Smail Salhi (New York: Routledge, 2010), 59–60.

13. Clement Henry Moore, *Tunisia Since Independence: The Dynamics of One-Party Government* (Berkeley: University of California Press, 1965), 53–54.

14. Eleanor Abdella Doumato, "Education in Saudi Arabia: Gender, Jobs, and the Price of Religion," in *Women and Globalization in the Arab Middle East: Gender, Economy, and Society*, ed. Eleanor Abdella Doumato and Marsha Pripstein Posusney (Boulder, CO: Lynne Rienner, 2003), 244–245.

15. Sharan Grewal, *A Quiet Revolution: The Tunisian Military After Ben Ali* (Beirut: Carnegie Middle East Center, 2016), 3.

16. Joel Beinin, "Workers and Revolutions in Egypt and Tunisia," a lecture at Stanford University, January 21, 2015, *YouTube*, posted by Hesham Sallam, February 4, 2015, https://www.youtube.com/watch?v=sbbrPxDyV5A.

17. John P. Entelis, "L'héritage contradictoire de Bourguiba: modernisation et intolérance politique," in *Habib Bourguiba: La trace et l'héritage*, ed. Michel Camau and Vincent Geisser (Paris: Karthala, 2004), 231.

18. Michele Penner Angrist, "Parties, Parliament and Political Dissent in Tunisia," *Journal of North African Studies* 4, no. 4 (2007): 90.

19. Joel Beinin, *Workers and Thieves: Labor Movements and Popular Uprisings in Tunisia and Egypt* (Stanford, CA: Stanford University Press, 2016), 70–73.

20. Larry Diamond and Marc F. Plattner, *Democratization and Authoritarianism in the Arab World* (Baltimore, MD: John Hopkins University Press, 2014), 225.

21. Yasmine Ryan, "Building a Tunisian Model for Arab Democracy," *Al Jazeera*, November 27, 2012, http://www.aljazeera.com/indepth/features/2012/11 /20121127143845980112.html.

22. Yadh Ben Achour (public law expert and academician, president of the *Haute Instance pour la réalisation des objectifs de la révolution, de la réforme politique et de la transition démocratique*), in discussion with Columbia University President Lee C. Bollinger, Jean Magnano Bollinger, Susan Glancy, and the author, January 2015.

23. Sharan Grewal, "Why Tunisia Didn't Follow Egypt's Path," *Washington Post*, February 4, 2015, http://www.washingtonpost.com/blogs/monkey-cage/wp /2015/02/04/why-egypt-didnt-follow-tunisias-path/.

24. Rached Ghannouchi (cofounder and president of Ennahda), in discussion with Columbia University President Lee C. Bollinger, Jean Magnano Bollinger, Susan Glancy, and the author, January 8, 2015.

25. Ahmed Nadhif, "New Study Explores Tunisia's Jihadi Movement in Numbers," *Al-Monitor*, November 8, 2016, http://www.al-monitor.com/pulse/originals/2016 /11/tunisia-center-study-terrorism-distribution.html.

26. Roundtable discussion on youth, education, and the economy, hosted by the author, Tunis, July 30, 2015.

27. Adam Shatz, "Magical Thinking About ISIS," *London Review of Books*, December 3, 2015, http://www.lrb.co.uk/v37/n23/adam-shatz/magical-thinking-about-isis.

28. Youssef Cherif, "The 3000: Why Have Some Tunisians Joined ISIL/Daesh in Syria?" *Informed Comment*, September 9, 2015, http://www.juancole.com/2015 /09/thousands-tunisians-isildaesh.html.

2. Prelude to Revolution

1. Mark Tessler, "The Origins of Popular Support for Islamic Movements: A Political Economy Analysis," in *Islam, Democracy, and the State in North Africa*, ed. John Pierre Entelis (Bloomington: Indiana University Press, 1997), 98.

2. Paul Delaney, "Tunisia's Premier Seizes Power, Declaring Bourguiba to Be Senile," *New York Times*, November 8, 1987, http://www.nytimes.com/1987/11/08/world /tunisia-s-premier-seizes-power-declaring-bourguiba-to-be-senile.html.

3. Ibid.

4. David Lea and Annamarie Rowe, *A Political Chronology of Africa* (London: Taylor & Francis, 2001), 446.

5. Minnesota International Human Rights Committee, *Tunisia: Human Rights Crisis of 1987* (Minneapolis: Minnesota International Human Rights Committee, 1988), 1–2.

6. "Population, Total: Tunisia (1960–2015)," World Bank, accessed July 13, 2016, http://data.worldbank.org/indicator/SP.POP.TOTL?locations=TN&view =chart.

7. Marion Boulby, "The Islamic Challenge: Tunisia Since Independence," *Third World Quarterly* 10, no. 2 (1988): 590–614.

8. Sophie Bessis, "Banque mondiale et FMI en Tunisie: Une évolution sur trente ans," *Annuaire de l'Afrique du Nord* 26 (1987): 140–145.

9. Lea and Rowe, *A Political Chronology of Africa*, 445–446.

10. Anthony H. Cordesman, *A Tragedy of Arms: Military and Security Developments in the Maghreb* (Westport, CT: Praeger, 2002), 174.

11. Nouri Gana, "Introduction: Collaborative Revolutionism," in *The Making of the Tunisian Revolution: Contexts, Architects, Prospects*, ed. Nouri Gana (Edinburgh: Edinburgh University Press, 2013), 13.

12. Chris Toensing, "Tunisian Labor Leaders Reflect Upon Revolt," *Middle East Research and Information Project (MERIP)—People Power* 41, no. 258 (2011), http:// www.merip.org/mer/mer258/tunisian-labor-leaders-reflect-upon-revolt-0.

13. Minnesota International Human Rights Committee, *Tunisia*, 5.
14. Paul Legg, "Ben Ali's Smooth Rise to Power in Tunisia Contrasts with Sudden Decline," *The Guardian*, January 15, 2011, http://www.theguardian.com/world/2011/jan/15/ben-ali-power-tunisia.
15. Zine al-Abidine Ben Ali, "The November 7 Declaration," radio broadcast, November 7, 1987, http://archive.wikiwix.com/cache/?url=http%3A%2F%2Ft elechargement.rfi.fr.edgesuite.net%2Frfi%2Ffrancais%2Faudio%2Fmodules%2 Factu%2FR095%2FDiscours_Ben_Ali_07_11_1987.mp3.
16. Cordesman, *A Tragedy of Arms*, 247.
17. Lucy Dean, ed., *The Middle East and North Africa 2004*, 50th ed. (London: Europa, 2004), 1073.
18. Francesco Cavatorta and Rikke Hostrup Haugbølle, "The End of Authoritarian Rule and the Mythology of Tunisia Under Ben Ali," *Mediterranean Politics* 17, no. 2 (2012): 187–190.
19. Shadi Hamid, *Temptations of Power: Islamists and Illiberal Democracy in a New Middle East* (Oxford: Oxford University Press, 2014), 191.
20. Cordesman, *A Tragedy of Arms*, 248.
21. Alfred Stepan, "Tunisia's Transition and the Twin Tolerations," *Journal of Democracy* 23, no. 2 (2012): 100.
22. Cordesman, *A Tragedy of Arms*, 247–249.
23. Michele Penner Angrist, "Parties, Parliament and Political Dissent in Tunisia," *Journal of North African Studies* 4, no. 4 (2007): 89–104.
24. Cordesman, *A Tragedy of Arms*, 249.
25. Laryssa Chomiak and John P. Entelis, "Contesting Order in Tunisia: Crafting Political Identity," in *Civil Society Activism Under Authoritarian Rule*, ed. Francesco Cavatorta (New York: Routledge, 2013), 79.
26. Laryssa Chomiak, "Spectacles of Power: Locating Resistance in Ben Ali's Tunisia," *Portal* 9, no. 2 (spring 2013), http://portal9journal.org/articles.aspx?id=102.
27. Mohamed Zayani, *Networked Publics and Digital Contention: The Politics of Everyday Life in Tunisia* (Oxford: Oxford University Press, 2015), 25–52.
28. Clement Henry, "Tunisia's 'Sweet Little' Regime," in *Worst of the Worst: Dealing with Repressive and Rogue Nations*, ed. Robert Rotberg (Washington, DC: Brookings Institution, 2007), 311.
29. Derek Lutterbeck, *Tunisia After Ben Ali: Retooling the Tools of Oppression?* (Oslo: Norwegian Peacebuilding Resource Center [NOREF], 2013), 1; Cordesman, *A Tragedy of Arms*, 255.
30. Henry, "Tunisia's 'Sweet Little' Regime," 305–306.
31. Cordesman, *A Tragedy of Arms*, 260, 250, 272.
32. Béatrice Hibou, *The Force of Obedience: The Political Economy of Repression in Tunisia* (Cambridge: Polity, 2011), 4.
33. Office of the United Nations High Commission for Human Rights (OHCHR), *Report of the OHCHR Assessment Mission to Tunisia: 26 January–2 February 2011* (Geneva: Office of the United Nations High Commission for Human Rights, 2011), 5–6.

34. Cordesman, *A Tragedy of Arms*, 271–272.
35. International Commission of Jurists, *The Independence and Accountability of the Tunisian Judicial System: Learning from the Past to Build a Better Future* (Geneva: International Commission of Jurists, 2014), 15.
36. "Tunisia: Amend Counterterrorism Law: Reforms Necessary to Protect Fundamental Rights," *Human Rights Watch*, May 29, 2013, http://www.hrw.org/news/2013/05/29/tunisia-amend-counterterrorism-law.
37. James Whidden, "Tunisia: Ben Ali, Liberalization," in *Encyclopedia of African History*, ed. Kevin Shillington (New York: Fitzroy Dearborn, 2005).
38. "GDP Growth (Annual %): Tunisia (1988–2015)," World Bank, accessed August 4, 2016, http://data.worldbank.org/indicator/NY.GDP.MKTP.KD.ZG?contextual=default&end=2015&locations=TN&start=1988&view=chart; Kenneth Perkins, *A History of Modern Tunisia*, 2nd ed. (Cambridge: Cambridge University Press, 2014), 217.
39. Perkins, *Modern Tunisia*, 234.
40. Maha Yahya, "Beyond Tunisia's Constitution: The Devil in the Details," *Carnegie Middle East Center*, April 28, 2014, http://carnegie-mec.org/publications/?fa=55398.
41. Mongi Boughzala and Mohamed Tlili Hamdi, "Promoting Inclusive Growth in Arab Countries: Rural and Regional Development and Inequality in Tunisia," Global Economy and Development Working Paper 71 (February 2014), http://www.brookings.edu/~/media/research/files/papers/2014/02/promoting-growth-arab-countries/arab-econpaper5boughzala-v3.pdf.
42. Zaibi Fakher, *Evolution du marché de l'emploi en Tunisie* (Tunis: Ministère de l'Emploi et de l'Insertion professionnelle des jeunes), 7–8; Alcinda Honwana, *Youth and Revolution in Tunisia* (New York: Zed, 2013), 25.
43. Neil MacFarquhar, "Economic Frustration Simmers Again in Tunisia," *New York Times*, December 1, 2012, http://www.nytimes.com/2012/12/02/world/africa/economic-frustration-simmers-again-in-tunisia.html?_r=0.
44. Honwana, *Youth and Revolution*, 26.
45. Abdeljalil Akkari, "The Tunisian Educational Reform: From Quantity to Quality and the Need for Monitoring and Assessment," *Prospects* 35, no. 1 (2005): 59–74.
46. United Nations, *Tunisia: National Report on Millennium Development Goals* (New York: United Nations, 2004), 13.
47. Caroline Freund, Antonio Nucifora, and Bob Rijkers, "All in the Family: State Capture in Tunisia," working paper no. 6810 (Washington, DC: World Bank, March 2014), 3, 11.
48. Peter J. Schraeder, "Tunisia's Jasmine Revolution, International Intervention, and Popular Sovereignty," *Whitehead Journal of Diplomacy and International Relations* 13, no. 1 (2012): 75–88.
49. World Bank, *The Unfinished Revolution: Bringing Opportunity, Good Jobs, and Greater Wealth to All Tunisians* (Washington, DC: World Bank, 2014), 84, 111.

50. Béatrice Hibou, Mohamed Hamdi, and Hamza Meddeb, *Tunisia After 14 January and Its Social and Political Economy* (Copenhagen: Euro-Mediterranean Human Rights Network, 2011), 14.

51. Mohammed Mossallem, *The IMF in the Arab World: Lessons Unlearnt* (London: Bretton Woods Project, 2015), 4.

52. Stephen J. King, *Liberalization Against Democracy: The Local Politics of Economic Reform in Tunisia* (Bloomington: Indiana University Press, 2003), 34.

53. Eric Gobe, "The Gafsa Mining Basin Between Riots and a Social Movement: Meaning and Significance of a Protest Movement in Ben Ali's Tunisia," working paper, IREMAM—Institut de recherches et d'études sur le monde arabe et musulman (Aix-en-Provence, France, 2010), 6–7.

3. If the People Will to Live

1. "Ben Ali Gets Refuge in Saudi Arabia," *Al Jazeera*, January 16, 2011, http://www.aljazeera.com/news/middleeast/2011/01/201111652129710582.html.

2. Joel Beinin, *Workers and Thieves: Labor Movements and Popular Uprisings in Tunisia and Egypt* (Stanford, CA: Stanford University Press, 2016), 101.

3. "Corruption in Tunisia: What's Yours Is Mine," *WikiLeaks*, June 23, 2008, https://wikileaks.org/plusd/cables/08TUNIS679_a.html.

4. Emma C. Murphy, "Under the Emperor's Neoliberal Clothes! Why the International Financial Institutions Got It Wrong in Tunisia," in *The Making of the Tunisian Revolution: Contexts, Architects, Prospects*, ed. Nouri Gana (Edinburgh: Edinburgh University Press: 2013), 46–47.

5. Cyrille Louis, "Le procès d'un réseau franco-tunisien de voleurs de yachts crée la polémique," *Le Figaro*, August 20, 2009, http://www.lefigaro.fr/actualite-france/2009/08/20/01016-20090820ARTFIG00499-le-proces-d-un-reseau-franco-tunisien-de-voleurs-de-yachts-cree-la-polemique-.php.

6. Mouldi Jendoubi (deputy secretary-general of UGTT), in discussion with the author, August 1, 2015.

7. Ibid.

8. Beinin, *Workers and Thieves*, 101–105.

9. Mark Beissinger, Amaney Jamal, and Kevin Mazur, "The Anatomy of Protest in Egypt and Tunisia," *Foreign Policy*, April 15, 2013, http://foreignpolicy.com/2013/04/15/the-anatomy-of-protest-in-egypt-and-tunisia/.

10. Eleanor Beardsley, "In Tunisia, Women Play Equal Role in Revolution," *NPR*, January 27, 2011, http://www.npr.org/2011/01/27/133248219/in-tunisia-women-play-equal-role-in-revolution.

11. Hamma Hammami (spokesperson for the Popular Front, and leader of the Workers' Party), in discussion with the author, July 31, 2015.

12. Brian Whittaker, "No Answer from Ben Ali," *Al-Bab: An Open Door to the Arab World*, December 28, 2010, http://al-bab.com/blog/2010/12/no-answer-ben-ali.

13. Peter J. Schraeder, "Tunisia's Jasmine Revolution, International Intervention, and Popular Sovereignty," *Whitehead Journal of Diplomacy and International Relations* 13, no. 1 (2012): 78.

14. Sana Barhoumi, "Facebook en Tunisie avant 2011: Vers une transition démocratique," in *Médias sociaux: enjeux pour la communication*, ed. Lorna Heaton, Mélanie Millette, and Serge Proulx (Quebec: Presses de l'Université du Québec, 2012), 177.

15. Ronald Deibert, John Palfrey, Rafal Rohozinski, and Jonathan Zittrain, eds., "Tunisia," in *Access Controlled: The Shaping of Power, Rights, and Rule in Cyberspace* (Cambridge, MA: The MIT Press, 2010): 395–399.

16. Yasmine Ryan, "Tunisia's Bitter Cyberwar," *Al Jazeera*, January 6, 2015, http://www.aljazeera.com/indepth/features/2011/01/20111614145839362.html.

17. Lina Ben Mhenni (Internet activist, blogger, and assistant lecturer in linguistics at the University of Tunis), in discussion with the author, April 18, 2016.

18. Chamseddine Mnasri, "Tunisia: The People's Revolution," *International Socialism: A Quarterly Review of Socialist Theory*, issue 130 (2011), http://isj.org.uk/tunisia-the-peoples-revolution/.

19. Andy Morgan, "From Fear to Fury: How the Arab World Found Its Voice," *The Guardian*, February 27, 2011, http://www.theguardian.com/music/2011/feb/27/egypt-tunisia-music-protests.

20. Mohamed-Salah Omri, "A Revolution of Dignity and Poetry," *Boundary 2: An International Journal of Literature and Culture* 39, no. 1 (2012): 147.

21. Nouri Gana, "Introduction: Collaborative Revolutionism," in *The Making of the Tunisian Revolution*, ed. Nouri Gana (Edinburgh: Edinburgh University Press, 2013), 19.

22. Bilal Randeree, "Tunisia President Warns Protesters," *Al Jazeera*, January 3, 2011, http://english.aljazeera.net/news/africa/2010/12/2010122823238574209.html.

23. Schraeder, "Tunisia's Jasmine Revolution," 79.

24. Derek Lutterbeck, *Arab Uprisings and the Armed Forces: Between Openness and Resistance* (Geneva: The Geneva Centre for the Democratic Control of Armed Forces, 2011), 23; Abdelaziz Ben Hassouna, "Tunisie: la véritable histoire du 14 janvier 2011," *Jeune Afrique*, January 25, 2011, http://www.jeuneafrique.com/143296/politique/tunisie-la-v-ritable-histoire-du-14-janvier-2011/.

25. Mehdi Farhat, "Yassine Ayari: «L'armée n'a jamais reçu l'ordre de tirer»," *Slate*, July 20, 2011, http://www.slateafrique.com/15009/yassine-ayari-revolution-tunisie-blogueur-rachid-ammar-armee; Yassine Ayari (blogger and political activist), in discussion with the author, March 1, 2016.

26. Schraeder, "Tunisia's Jasmine Revolution," 77.

27. Amnesty International, *La Tunisie en révolte, les violences de l'Etat pendant les manifestations antigouvernementales* (London: Amnesty International, 2011), 16.

28. Mouldi Jendoubi, in discussion with the author, August 1, 2015.

29. Schraeder, "Tunisia's Jasmine Revolution," 79.

30. Isabelle Lasserre, "Rachid Ammar, le centurion du peuple," *Le Figaro*, January 21, 2011, http://www.lefigaro.fr/international/2011/01/22/01003-20110122ARTFIG00005-rachid-ammar-le-centurion-du-peuple.php.

31. Ryan Rifai, "Timeline: Tunisia's Uprising," *Al Jazeera*, January 23, 2011, http://www .aljazeera.com/indepth/spotlight/tunisia/2011/01/201114142223827361.html.

32. Badra Gaaloul, "Back to the Barracks: The Tunisian Army Post-Revolution," *Carnegie Endowment for International Peace*, November 3, 2011, http://carnegieen dowment.org/sada/?fa=45907.

33. Schraeder, "Tunisia's Jasmine Revolution," 79.

34. "TIMELINE—Arab Spring: A Year That Shook the Arab World," *Reuters*, January 14, 2012, http://in.reuters.com/article/2012/01/13/tunisia-revolution-anniversary -idINDEE80C0IT20120113.

35. Michael J. Totten, "Arab Spring or Islamic Winter?" *World Affairs*, January –February 2012, http://www.worldaffairsjournal.org/article/arab-spring-or -islamist-winter.

36. J. Scott Carpenter, "Help Tunisia First," *Foreign Policy*, February 24, 2011, http:// foreignpolicy.com/2011/02/24/help-tunisia-first-2/.

4. A Remarkable Transition

1. Vanessa Szakal, "Four Years After the Kasbah Sit-Ins—Taking Stock of a Revolutionary Mission Confiscated," *Nawaat*, February 9, 2015, http://nawaat.org /portail/2015/02/09/four-years-after-the-kasbah-sit-ins-taking-stock-of-a -revolutionary-mission-confiscated/.

2. Alcinda Honwana, *Youth and Revolution in Tunisia* (New York: Zed, 2013), 100.

3. Alcinda Honwana, "Youth and the Tunisian Revolution," paper presented at the SSRC Conflict Prevention and Peace Forum, Geneva, September 2011, http:// webarchive.ssrc.org/pdfs/Alcinda_Honwana,_Youth_and_the_Tunisian _Revolution,_September_2011-CPPF_policy%20paper.pdf.

4. "Weekly Briefing: Tunisia: Unrest," *New Statesman*, January 27, 2011, http://www .newstatesman.com/international-politics/2011/01/italy-sex-minister-party.

5. Sami Ben Gharbia (cofounder of *Nawaat*, and director of the advocacy arm of *Global Voices Online*), in discussion with the author, November 26, 2015.

6. Carter Center, *National Constituent Assembly Elections in Tunisia: October 23, 2011— Final Report* (Atlanta, GA: Carter Center, 2012), 16.

7. Alia Gana, Gilles Van Hamme, and Maher Ben Rebbah, "Social and Socio-Territorial Electoral Base of Political Parties in Post-Revolutionary Tunisia," *Journal of North African Studies* 19, no. 5 (2014): 764.

8. Eleanor Beardsley, "Tunisia Seen as Laboratory for Arab Democracy," *NPR*, May 9, 2011, http://www.npr.org/2011/05/09/136137821/after-uprisings-tunisia-a -laboratory-for-democracy.

9. Kenneth Perkins, *A History of Modern Tunisia*, 2nd ed. (Cambridge: Cambridge University Press, 2014), 242.

10. "Tunisian Islamist Leader Rachid Ghannouchi Returns Home," *BBC*, January 30, 2011, http://www.bbc.co.uk/news/world-africa-12318824.

11. Rached Ghannouchi (cofounder and president of Ennahda), in discussion with Columbia University President Lee C. Bollinger, Jean Magnano Bollinger, Susan Glancy, and the author, January 8, 2015.

12. Ibrahim Sharqieh, "Tunisia's Lessons for the Middle East: Why the First Arab Spring Transition Worked Best," *Foreign Affairs*, September 17, 2013, http://www.foreignaffairs.com/articles/139938/ibrahim-sharqieh/tunisias-lessons-for-the-middle-east.

13. A. Gana, Van Hamme, and Ben Rebbah, "Socio-Territorial Electoral Base," 751–769.

14. Shadi Hamid, *Temptations of Power: Islamists and Illiberal Democracy in a New Middle East* (Oxford: Oxford University Press, 2014), 191.

15. Georges Fahmi (scholar on interplay between state and religion in Tunisia), in discussion with the author, November 2015.

16. Ibid.; Hamid, *Temptations of Power*, 200.

17. Yadh Ben Achour, "Religion, Revolution, and Constitution: The Case of Tunisia," lecture, Harvard University, Cambridge, MA, September 17, 2012.

18. Yadh Ben Achour (public law expert and academician, president of the *Haute Instance pour la réalisation des objectifs de la révolution, de la réforme politique et de la transition démocratique*), in discussion with the author, April 23, 2016.

19. Algerian Constitution of 1963, article 4; Algerian Constitution of 1989 (reinstated 1996, revised 2008), article 2.

20. *Laws Criminalizing Apostasy in Selected Jurisdictions* (Washington, DC: Law Library of Congress, 2014), http://www.loc.gov/law/help/apostasy/apostasy.pdf.

21. Carter Center, *The Constitution-Making Process in Tunisia: Final Report* (Atlanta, GA: Carter Center, 2011–2014), 32.

22. Monica Marks, "Women's Rights Before and After the Revolution," in *The Making of the Tunisian Revolution: Contexts, Architects, Prospects*, ed. Nouri Gana (Edinburgh: Edinburgh University Press: 2013), 236-237.

23. Hayat Al-Sayeb, "Jumla i'tiradiya: surat al-mar'a al-mushawaha" [An Objectionable Sentence: The Distorted Image of the Woman], *Assabah*, March 6, 2016.

24. Marks, "Women's Rights," 225.

25. Yasmine Ryan, "Who Killed Tunisia's Chokri Belaid?" *Al Jazeera*, September 12, 2013, http://www.aljazeera.com/indepth/%20features/2013/09/2013941833 25728267.html.

26. Ahmed el Amraoui, "Tunisia's Ghannouchi: Poverty Is a Root Cause of Terror," *Al Jazeera*, November 14, 2015, http://www.aljazeera.com/news/2015/11/tunisia-ghannouchi-terrorism-151114090804512.html.

27. Aaron Zelin, "Who Is Jabhat al-Islah?" *Carnegie Endowment for International Peace*, July 18, 2012, http://carnegieendowment.org/sada/?fa=48885.

28. Rached Ghannouchi, in discussion with the author, July 30, 2015.

29. Chris Toensing, "Tunisian Labor Leaders Reflect Upon Revolt," *Middle East Research and Information Project (MERIP)—People Power* 41, no. 258 (2011), http://www.merip.org/mer/mer258/tunisian-labor-leaders-reflect-upon-revolt-0.

30. Amel Boubekeur, "Islamists, Secularists and Old Regime Elites in Tunisia: Bargained Competition," *Mediterranean Politics* 21, no. 1 (2015): 118.

31. "Nobel Peace Prize for Tunisian National Dialogue Quartet," *BBC*, October 9, 2015, http://www.bbc.com/news/world-europe-34485865.

32. Timothy Mitchell, *Carbon Democracy: Political Power in the Age of Oil* (New York: Verso, 2011), 412.

33. Joel Beinin, *Workers and Thieves: Labor Movements and Popular Uprisings in Tunisia and Egypt* (Stanford, CA: Stanford University Press, 2016), 41–44, 73–75, 109–110, 135–137.

34. Mehdi Jomaa (prime minister of Tunisia, January 2014–February 2015), in conversation with Columbia University President Lee C. Bollinger, Jean Magnano Bollinger, Susan Glancy, and the author, January 2015.

35. Marouen Achouri, "Tough Task Ahead for Tunisia's New PM," *Al-Monitor*, December 22, 2013, http://www.al-monitor.com/pulse/politics/2013/12/tunisia-new -prime-minister-jomaa-challenges.html.

36. Kevin Sullivan, "Tunisia, After Igniting Arab Spring, Sends the Most Fighters to Islamic State in Syria," *Washington Post*, October 28, 2014, https://www .washingtonpost.com/world/national-security/tunisia-after-igniting-arab -spring-sends-the-most-fighters-to-islamic-state-in-syria/2014/10/28 /b5db4faa-5971-11e4-8264-deed989ae9a2_story.html.

37. Ghazi Jeribi (Tunisian minister of justice, August 2016–; interim Tunisian minister of religious affairs, November 2016–February 2017; Tunisian minister of national defense, January 2014–February 2015), in conversation with the author, July 2015.

38. Ahmed El Amraoui, "High Turnout in Tunisia Vote Defies Forecasts," *Al Jazeera*, October 26, 2014, http://www.aljazeera.com/news/middleeast/2014/10/high -turnout-tunisia-vote-defies-forecasts-20141026113835892666.html.

39. Ibid.

40. "Tunisian Republic," *Election Guide*, accessed October 28, 2015, http://www .electionguide.org/countries/id/217/.

5. The Morning After

1. Beji Caid Essebsi (president of Tunisia, December 2014–; prime minister of Tunisia, February–December 2011), in discussion with Columbia University President Lee C. Bollinger, Jean Magnano Bollinger, Susan Glancy, and the author, January 9, 2015.

2. Beji Caid Essebsi, in discussion with the author, July 29, 2015.

3. Yadh Ben Achour (public law expert and academician, president of the *Haute Instance pour la réalisation des objectifs de la révolution, de la réforme politique et de la transition démocratique*), in discussion with the author, November 26, 2015.

4. Rached Ghannouchi (cofounder and president of Ennahda), in discussion with Columbia University President Lee C. Bollinger, Jean Magnano Bollinger, Susan Glancy, and the author, January 8, 2015.

5. Rached Ghannouchi, in discussion with the author, July 30, 2015.

6. Amel Boubekeur, "Islamists, Secularists and Old Regime Elites in Tunisia: Bargained Competition," *Mediterranean Politics* 21, no. 1 (2015): 109.

7. Rached Ghannouchi, in discussion with the author, November 24, 2015.

8. Roundtable discussion on youth, education, and the economy, hosted by the author, Tunis, July 30, 2015.

9. Rob Prince, "Tunisia on Fire (Part 1)," *Foreign Policy in Focus*, February 25, 2016, http://fpif.org/tunisia-fire-part-1/.

10. Informal discussion with youth, initiated by author, Kasserine, April 22, 2016.

11. "Unemployment, Total (% of Total Labor Force) (Modeled ILO Estimate): Tunisia (1991–2014)," World Bank, accessed November 28, 2016, http://data .worldbank.org/indicator/SL.UEM.TOTL.ZS?locations=TN; Rouissi Chiraz and Mohamed Frioui, "The Impact of Inflation After the Revolution in Tunisia," *Procedia-Social and Behavioral Sciences* 109 (2014): 247.

12. Alexander Martin, "Despite Progress, Tunisia's Problems Go Much Deeper Than Security," *The Conversation*, July 2, 2015, http://theconversation.com/despite -progress-tunisias-problems-go-much-deeper-than-security-44051.

13. Central Intelligence Agency, "Tunisia," in *World Factbook*, accessed December 28, 2015, https://www.cia.gov/library/publications/the-world-factbook/geos/ts.html.

14. Roundtable discussion on electoral processes and democratic transitioning, hosted by Columbia University President Lee C. Bollinger, Jean Magnano Bollinger, Susan Glancy, and the author, Tunis, January 7, 2015.

15. "Tunisia: Q&A on the Trial of Ben Ali, Others for Killing Protesters," *Human Rights Watch*, June 11, 2012, https://www.hrw.org/news/2012/06/11/tunisia -qa-trial-ben-ali-others-killing-protesters#3.

16. Organization for Economic Co-operation and Development (OECD), *Examens de l'OCDE des politiques de l'investissement: Tunisie 2012* (Paris: OECD, 2012), 90–91.

17. Carlotta Gall, "In Tunisia, a Mission of Justice and a Moment of Reckoning," *New York Times*, November 6, 2015, http://www.nytimes.com/2015/11/07/world /africa/in-tunisia-a-mission-of-justice-and-a-moment-of-reckoning.html?_r=0.

18. Mohamed Salah Ben Aissa (Tunisian minister of justice, February–October 2015), in discussion with the author, April 23, 2016.

19. Ahmed Ben Amor (vice president of LGBT advocacy group Shams), in discussion with the author, April 18, 2016.

20. Max Bearak and Darla Cameron, "Here Are the Ten Countries Where Homosexuality May Be Punished by Death," *Washington Post*, June 16, 2016, https:// www.washingtonpost.com/news/worldviews/wp/2016/06/13/here-are-the -10-countries-where-homosexuality-may-be-punished-by-death-2/.

21. "Challenging Tunisia's Homophobic Taboos," *Amnesty International*, September 30, 2015, https://www.amnesty.org/en/latest/news/2015/09/challenging -tunisias-homophobic-taboos/.

22. Yadh Ben Achour, in discussion with the author, November 26, 2015.

23. Rached Ghannouchi, in discussion with the author, July 30, 2015.

24. Zied Ladhari (Tunisian minister of industry and commerce, August 2016–; Tunisian minister of vocational training and employment, February 2015–August 2016), in discussion with the author, November 27, 2015.

25. Sheikh Taieb Ghozzi (imam of the Grand Mosque of Kairouan), in discussion with the author, April 24, 2016.

26. John Champagne, "Homosexuality, Tunisian Style," *Gay & Lesbian Review Worldwide* (May–June 2009), http://www.glreview.org/article/article-534/.

27. Aziz El Massassi, "Au Caire, les homosexuels n'ont plus de bars où se retrouver," *Le Monde*, July 14, 2016, http://www.lemonde.fr/afrique/article/2016/07/14/au-caire-les-homosexuels-n-ont-plus-de-bars-ou-se-retrouver_4969508_3212.html#mIlCrpjfBIzRwQOQ.99.

28. Simon Speakman Cordall, "What It's Like to Plan a Gay-Friendly Arts Fair in a Shockingly Homophobic Country," *Washington Post*, May 23, 2016, https://www.washingtonpost.com/posteverything/wp/2016/05/23/growing-homophobia-in-tunisia-didnt-stop-this-arts-fair-for-lesbians-and-trans-women/.

29. Arch Puddington, *Freedom in the World 2014* (Washington, DC: Freedom House, 2014), 5–8.

30. "Tunisia Media Commission Resigns Over Press Freedom," *BBC*, July 5, 2012, http://www.bbc.com/news/world-africa-18717651.

31. Paul Cruickshank, "In Tunisia, Terror Attack Undercuts Arab Spring's Best Prospect," *CNN*, March 19, 2015, http://edition.cnn.com/2015/03/18/world/tunisia-terror-attacks/.

32. Tarek Amara and Patrick Markey, "After Bardo Attack, Tunisia Treads Line Between Security and Freedoms," *Reuters*, April 8, 2015, http://www.reuters.com/article/2015/04/08/us-tunisia-security-rights-idUSKBN0MZ1G620150408.

33. "Tunisia: Counterterror Law Endangers Rights," *Human Rights Watch*, July 31, 2015, https://www.hrw.org/news/2015/07/31/tunisia-counterterror-law-endangers-rights/.

34. Farah Samti, "Tunisia's New Anti-Terrorism Law Worries Activists," *Foreign Policy*, August 18, 2015, http://foreignpolicy.com/2015/08/18/tunisias-new-anti-terrorism-law-worries-activists-tunisia/.

35. Yadh Ben Achour, in discussion with the author, July 29, 2015.

36. Ghazi Jeribi (Tunisian minister of religious affairs, November 2016–; Tunisian minister of justice, August 2016–; Tunisian minister of national defense, January 2014–February 2015), in conversation with the author, July 2015.

37. Francesco Cavatorta, "Salafism, Liberalism, and Democratic Learning in Tunisia," *Journal of North African Studies* 20, no. 5 (2015): 771.

38. Rached Ghannouchi, in discussion with the author, June 28, 2016.

39. Cavatorta, "Salafism, Liberalism," 770–783.

40. Georges Fahmi and Hamza Meddeb, *Market for Jihad: Radicalization in Tunisia* (Washington, DC: Carnegie Endowment for International Peace, 2015), 5, 9.

41. Georges Fahmi (scholar on interplay between state and religion in Tunisia), in discussion with the author, November 2015.

42. Albert Hourani, *Arabic Thought in the Liberal Age: 1798–1939* (Cambridge: Cambridge University Press, 1983), 139–141.

43. Quintan Wiktorowicz, "Anatomy of the Salafi Movement," *Studies in Conflict & Terrorism* 29, no. 3 (2006): 207–209.

44. Fahmi and Meddeb, *Market for Jihad*, 5.

45. Wiktorowicz, "Salafi Movement," 207–209.

46. Nouri Gana, "Introduction: Collaborative Revolutionism," in *The Making of the Tunisian Revolution: Contexts, Architects, Prospects*, ed. Nouri Gana (Edinburgh: Edinburgh University Press: 2013), 25; Wiktorowicz, "Salafi Movement," 207–209.

47. World Travel & Tourism Council, *Travel & Tourism: Economic Impacts 2015: Tunisia* (London: World Travel & Tourism Council, 2015), 1; Marwan Muasher, Marc Pierini, and Alexander Djerassi, *Between Peril and Promise: A New Framework for Partnership with Tunisia* (Washington, DC: Carnegie Endowment for International Peace, 2016), 8.

48. Lina Ben Mhenni (Internet activist, blogger, and assistant lecturer in linguistics at the University of Tunis), in discussion with the author, April 18, 2016.

49. Yadh Ben Achour, in discussion with the author, July 29, 2015.

50. Rached Ghannouchi, in discussion with Columbia University President Lee C. Bollinger, Jean Magnano Bollinger, Susan Glancy, and the author, January 8, 2015.

51. Eileen Byrne, "Major Political Shift to Come as Tunisia Votes for New President," *National*, December 20, 2014, http://www.thenational.ae/world/20141220 /major-political-shift-to-come-as-tunisia-votes-for-new-president.

52. Roundtable discussion on youth, education, and the economy, hosted by the author, Tunis, July 30, 2015.

6. Carthage

1. John Dryden, trans., *The Aeneid of Virgil* (New York: P. F. Collier & Son, 1909), http://classics.mit.edu/Virgil/aeneid.html.

2. Simon Hawkins, "National Symbols and National Identity: Currency and Constructing Cosmopolitans in Tunisia," *Identities* 17, no. 2–3 (2010): 228–254.

3. Ramzi Rouighi, "The Berbers of the Arabs," *Studia Islamica* 106 (2011): 49.

4. Richard Miles, "Carthage: A Mediterranean Superpower," *Historically Speaking* 12, no. 4 (2011): 35–37.

5. Dexter Hoyos, *Truceless War: Carthage's Fight for Survival, 241 to 237 BC*, vol. 45 of *History of Warfare* (Boston: Brill Academic Publishers, 2006), xiii.

6. Miles, "Carthage," 35–37.

7. Richard A. Gabriel, *Hannibal: The Military Biography of Rome's Greatest Enemy* (Washington, DC: Potomac, 2011), 84.

8. Susan Raven, *Rome in Africa*, 3d ed. (New York: Routledge, 1993), 40–45.

9. Bren Kiernan, "Le premier génocide: Carthage, 146 A.C.," *Diogène* 3, no. 203 (2003): 32–48.

10. Jackson J. Spielvogel, *Western Civilization*, 9th ed. (Boston: Cengage Learning, 2013), 122.

11. Stephen Parker, *Bertolt Brecht: A Literary Life* (London: Bloomsbury, 2015).

12. Rick Gore, "Who Were the Phoenicians?" *National Geographic*, October 2004, http://ngm.nationalgeographic.com/features/world/asia/lebanon/phoenicians -text/1.

13. Robert D. Kaplan, "Roman Africa," *Atlantic*, June 2001, http://www.theatlantic .com/magazine/archive/2001/06/roman-africa/302237/.

14. "North Africa," *Encyclopedia Britannica*, accessed August 11, 2016, https://www .britannica.com/place/North-Africa.

15. Kaplan, "Roman Africa."

16. "Amphitheatre of El Jem," *United Nations Educational, Scientific, and Cultural Orga- nization*, accessed December 5, 2015, http://whc.unesco.org/en/list/38.

17. Khaled Ben-Romdhane, Abdelbaki Hermassi, Anne-Marie Driss, and Stephanie Alouache, *Arts of Tunisia* (Tunis: SIMPACT, 2004), 67.

18. Judith Evans Grubbs, *Women and the Law in the Roman Empire: A Sourcebook on Marriage, Divorce and Widowhood* (New York: Routledge, 2002), 7.

19. Kaplan, "Roman Africa."

20. Richard Edis, "The Byzantine Era in Tunisia: A Forgotten Footnote?" *Journal of North African Studies* 4, no. 1 (1999): 50.

21. Ibid., 45–61.

22. Ibid.

23. Naceur Baklouti, Aziza Ben Tanfous, Jamila Binous, Mounira Chapoitot-Remadi, Mohamed Kadri Bouteraa, Salah Jabeur, Mourad Rammah, Ahmed Saadaoui, Mohamed Tlili, and Ali Zouari, *Ifriqiya: Thirteen Centuries of Art and Architecture in Tunisia* (Tunis: Ministry of Culture, the National Institute of Heritage, Tunis, Tunisia, and Museum with No Frontiers, 2010).

24. Habib Boularès, *Histoire de la Tunisie: les grandes dates, de la préhistoire à la révolution* (Tunis: Cérès, 2012), 195.

25. Hawkins, "National Symbols," 228–254.

26. Kaplan, "Roman Africa."

27. Ibid.

28. Ibid.

29. Neji Jalloul (Tunisian minister of education, February 2015–April 2017), in dis- cussion with the author, July 30, 2015.

30. Emna Mizouni (founder and president of Carthagina, an association for the protection of Tunisia's heritage), in discussion with the author, November 24, 2015.

31. Habib Bourguiba, "Extraits du discours du Président Bourguiba prononcé le 17 avril devant les doyens des Facultés et les professeurs de l'Enseignement supérieur," *Annuaire de l'Afrique du Nord* 11 (1972): 832.

32. Lamia Ben Youssef Zayzafoon, *The Production of the Muslim Woman: Negotiating Text, History, and Ideology* (New York: Lexington, 2005), 117–118.

33. Ibid.

7. Tunisian Islam

1. Kenneth J. Perkins, *Historical Dictionary of Tunisia*, 2nd ed. (Lanham, MD: Scarecrow Press, 1997), 36; Lucy Jones, "Special Report: Tunisia's Berbers Under Threat," *Washington Report on Middle East Affairs*, August/September 2001, http://www.wrmea.org/2001-august-september/tunisia-s-berbers-under-threat.html.

2. Driss Maghraoui, "Islam in North Africa: Prehistory to 1400: Africa," in *Cultural Sociology of the Middle East, Asia, & Africa: An Encyclopedia*, vol. 4, ed. Andrea L. Stanton, Edward Ramsamy, Peter J. Seybolt, and Carolyn M. Elliott (Thousand Oaks, CA: Sage, 2012), 53.

3. Ehsan Naraghi, "The Islamic Antecedents of Western Renaissance," *Diogenes* 44, no. 173 (1996): 73–106.

4. Salah Zaimeche, *Al-Qayrawan* (Manchester: Foundation for Science, Technology, and Civilization, 2004), 1–15.

5. Jonathan E. Brockopp, "Literary Genealogies from the Mosque-Library of Kairouan," *Islamic Law and Society* 6, no. 3 (1999): 396–400; Jonathan E. Brockopp, "Rereading the History of Early Māliki Jurisprudence," *Journal of the American Oriental Society* 118, no. 2 (1998): 233–238.

6. Zaimeche, *Al-Qayrawan*, 9–11.

7. Paolo Cappabianca, Enrico de Divitiis, and Oreste de Divitiis, "The 'Schola Medica Salernitana': The Forerunner of the Modern University Medical Schools," *Neurosurgery* 55, no. 4 (2004): 726–727.

8. Haim Malka, *The Struggle for Religious Identity in Tunisia and the Maghreb* (Washington, DC: Center for Strategic & International Studies, 2014), 2.

9. Zaimeche, *Al-Qayrawan*, 4–5.

10. Ibid.; Everett Jenkins, *The Muslim Diaspora: A Comprehensive Chronology of the Spread of Islam in Asia, Africa, Europe, and the Americas, 570–1799*, vol. 1, *570–1500* (Jefferson, NC: McFarland, 2011), 129.

11. Abdallah Laroui, *The History of the Maghrib: An Interpretive Essay* (Princeton, NJ: Princeton University Press, 2015), 121.

12. Cyril Glassé, *The New Encyclopedia of Islam* (Walnut Creek, CA: Rowman & Littlefield, 2002), 62–63.

13. Muhammad Talki, "Everyday Life in the Cities of Islam," in *The Individual and Society in Islam*, ed. Abdelwahab Bouhdiba and Muḥammad Ma'rūf Dawālībī (Paris: United Nations Educational, Scientific, and Cultural Organization, 1998), 445–446.

14. Dalenda Largueche, "Monogamy in Islam: The Case of a Tunisian Marriage Contract" (paper number 39, School of Social Science, Institute of Advanced Studies, Princeton, NJ, 2010), 7.

15. Amy McKenna, ed., "From the Arab Conquest to 1830," in *The History of Northern Africa* (New York: Rosen, 2011), 46–47.

16. Ibid.

17. Paul L. Heck, "Ṣūfism—What Is It Exactly?" *Religious Compass* 1, no. 1 (2007): 151.

18. Ibid.
19. Nelly Amri, *al-Tasawwuf bi-Ifriqiya fi al-asr al-wasit* [Sufism in Africa during the Middle Ages] (Sousse: Contraste, 2009), 19.
20. Nelly Amri, *Sidi Abu Sa'id Al-Baji (1156-1231)* (Sousse: Contraste, 2015), 222.
21. Heck, "Ṣūfism," 148.
22. Amri, *al-Tasawwuf bi-Ifriqiya fi al-asr al-wasit*, 11.
23. Zied Kriechen (editor-in-chief of *Al-Maghreb*, an independent Arabic newspaper), in discussion with the author, November 26, 2015.
24. Waqās Ahmed, "Recalling the Tunisian Polymath," in *Post-Revolution Tunisia: Democracy* (Tunis: FIRST, 2012), 18.
25. Robert W. Cox and Timothy J. Sinclair, "Towards a Posthegemonic Conceptualization of World Order: Reflections on the Relevancy of Ibn Khaldūn," in *Approaches to World Order*, ed. Robert W. Cox and Timothy J. Sinclair (Cambridge: Cambridge University Press, 1992), 144–170.
26. Ibid.
27. Jenkins, *The Muslim Diaspora*, 284.
28. Jean David C. Boulakia, "Ibn Khaldûn: A Fourteenth-Century Economist," *Journal of Political Economy* 79, no. 5 (1971): 1105–1118.
29. Cox and Sinclair, "Relevancy of Ibn Khaldūn," 144–170.
30. Syed Farid Alatas, "Ibn Khaldūn on Education and Knowledge," in *Ibn Khaldūn* (Oxford: Oxford University Press, 2013), 79–99.
31. Cox and Sinclair, "Relevancy of Ibn Khaldūn," 173.
32. Javad Haghnavaz, "A Brief History of Islam (The Spread of Islam)," *International Journal of Business and Social Science* 4, no.17 (2013): 213.
33. Habib Boularès, *Histoire de la Tunisie: Les grandes dates, de la préhistoire à la révolution* (Tunis: Cérès, 2012), 13.

8. Influencing Rivalries

1. Andrew McGregor, "The Tunisian Army in the Crimean War: A Military Mystery," *MilitaryHistoryOnline.com*, accessed August 11, 2016, http://www.militaryhistory online.com/19thcentury/articles/tunisiacrimea.aspx.
2. Khalifa Chater, "L'école militaire du Bardo: l'émergence d'une élite nouvelle?" *Khalifa Chater*, accessed April 20, 2016, http://chater.khalifa.chez-alice.fr/ecole _militaire.htm.
3. Stephen Sheehi, *The Arab Imago: A Social History of Portrait Photography, 1860-1910* (Princeton, NJ: Princeton University Press, 2016), 76.
4. McGregor, "The Tunisian Army in the Crimean War."
5. James Allman, *Social Mobility, Education and Development in Tunisia* (Leiden: Brill, 1979), 29.
6. Leon Carl Brown, *The Tunisia of Ahmad Bey: 1837-1855* (Princeton, NJ: Princeton University Press, 1974), 303–304, 310.

7. McGregor, "The Tunisian Army in the Crimean War."

8. Elisabeth Cornelia van der Haven, "The Bey, the Mufti and the Scattered Pearls: Shari'a and Political Leadership in Tunisia's Age of Reform—1800–1864" (PhD diss., Leiden University, 2006), 43, https://openaccess.leidenuniv.nl/handle/1887/4968.

9. Reade to Sir Robert Stratford, 31 May 1841, Foreign Office 102/10, National Archives, Kew Gardens, quoted in Ismael M. Montana, *The Abolition of Slavery* (Gainesville: University Press of Florida, 2013), 80–81.

10. "Guide des sources de la traite négrière, de l'esclavage et de leurs abolitions XVIe–XXe siècles," *Archives Portal Europe*, accessed December 8, 2016, https://www.archivesportaleurope.net/ead-display/-/ead/pl/aicode/FR-SIAF/type/sg/id/FRDAF_esclavage001;jsessionid=443DF832545904572E2BFE22D8811D63.

11. van der Haven, "Shari'a and Political Leadership in Tunisia," 53–65.

12. Ibid., 72.

13. Ibid.; Moncef Aljazzar and Abdullatif Obaid, *Watha'iq hawl al-riqq wa ilgha'ih min al bilad al tunisiyya* [Documents on Slavery and Its Abolishment in Tunisian Lands] (Tunis: Institut Bourguiba des langues vivantes, 1997), 67.

14. van der Haven, "Shari'a and Political Leadership in Tunisia," 71.

15. Ibid., 47–48.

16. Ibid.

17. Habib Boularès, *Histoire de la Tunisie: Les grandes dates, de la Préhistoire à la Révolution* (Tunis: Cérès, 2012), 466–468.

18. van der Haven, "Shari'a and Political Leadership in Tunisia," 50.

19. Kenneth Perkins, *A History of Modern Tunisia*, 2d ed. (Cambridge: Cambridge University Press, 2014), 25.

20. Karen B. Stern, "Limitations of 'Jewish' as a Label in Roman North Africa," *Journal for the Study of Judaism* 39 (2008): 307–336.

21. Perkins, *Modern Tunisia*, 33–37, 157.

22. Elbaki Hermassi, *Leadership and National Development in North Africa: A Comparative Study* (Berkeley: University of California Press, 1972), 30.

23. Allman, *Development in Tunisia*, 28–29.

24. Boularès, *Histoire de la Tunisie*, 468.

25. Tunisian Constitution of 1861.

26. Boularès, *Histoire de la Tunisie*, 466–479.

27. Kenneth J. Perkins, *Historical Dictionary of Tunisia*, 2d ed. (Lanham, MD: Scarecrow Press, 1997), 72.

28. Arnold H. Green, *The Tunisian Ulama 1873-1915: Social Structure and Response to Ideological Currents* (Leiden: Brill, 1978), 105–106.

29. Perkins, *Modern Tunisia*, 32; Perkins, *Dictionary of Tunisia,* 52.

30. Boularès, *Histoire de la Tunisie*, 474.

31. Nathan J. Brown, *Constitutions in a Nonconstitutional World: Arab Basic Laws and the Prospects for Accountable Government* (Albany: State University of New York Press, 2001), 19.

32. Albert Hourani, *Arabic Thought in the Liberal Age: 1798–1939* (Cambridge: Cambridge University Press, 1983), 89.

33. Ibid., 88–94.

34. Green, *The Tunisian Ulama*, 107–112.

35. Boularès, *Histoire de la Tunisie*, 486.

36. Hourani, *Arabic Thought*, 90, 94.

37. Noureddine Sraïeb, "Khérédine et l'enseignement: une nouvelle conception du savoir en Tunisie," *Minorités religieuses dans l'Espagne médiévale*, no. 63–64 (1992): 203–208.

38. Alfred Stepan, "Tunisia's Transition and the Twin Tolerations," *Journal of Democracy* 23, no. 2 (2012): 98.

39. Noureddine Sraïeb, "Le collège Sadiki de Tunis et les nouvelles élites," *Revue du monde musulman et de la Méditerranée* 72, no. 1 (1994): 51.

40. Perkins, *Modern Tunisia*, 45–46.

41. Béatrice Hibou, "Le réformisme, grand récit politique de la Tunisie contemporaine," *Revue d'histoire moderne et contemporaine* 56, no. 4 (2009): 14–15.

9. The Age of Modern Reform

1. Nasrin Rahimieh, ed., *Oriental Responses to the West: Comparative Essays in Select Writers from the Muslim World* (Leiden: Brill, 1990), 17–18.

2. Ibid.

3. Rifa'a al-Tahtawi, "Takhlis al-Ibriz fi Talkhis Bariz Aw Al-Diwan al-Nafis bi-Iwan Bariz [The Extrication of Gold in Summarizing Paris, or the Valuable Collection in the Drawing Room of Paris]," in *Al-A'mal al-Kamilah li Rifa'ah al-Tahtawi* [*The Complete Works of Rifa'ah al-Tahtawi*], ed. Muhammad Imarah (Beirut: al-Mu'assassah al-Arabiyyah lil-Dirasat wa al-Nashr, 1973), 10–11.

4. Albert Hourani, *Arabic Thought in the Liberal Age: 1798–1939* (Cambridge: Cambridge University Press, 1983), 78–81.

5. Ibid., 99–102.

6. Hasan Afif El-Hasan, *Israel or Palestine? Is the Two-State Solution Already Dead?: A Political and Military History of the Palestinian-Israeli Conflict* (New York: Algora, 2010), 27.

7. Hourani, *Arabic Thought*, 103–128.

8. Shireen T. Hunter, *Reformist Voices of Islam: Mediating Islam and Modernity* (New York: Routledge, 2014), 15.

9. Hourani, *Arabic Thought*, 131–161, 253–259.

10. Charles-André Julien, "Colons français et Jeunes-Tunisiens (1882–1912)," *Revue française d'histoire d'outre-mer* 54, no. 194–197 (1967): 105–107.

11. Ibid.

12. Kenneth J. Perkins, *A History of Modern Tunisia*, 2nd ed. (Cambridge: Cambridge University Press, 2014), 70; Mohammed el-Fadhel Ben Achour, *Le mouvement*

littéraire et intellectuel en Tunisie au XIVème siècle de l'Hégire (XIX–XXe siècles) (Tunis: Alif—Les Éditions de la Méditerranée, 1998), 49.

13. Perkins, *Modern Tunisia*, 70.
14. Julien, "Jeunes-Tunisiens," 106.
15. Ibid., 108.
16. M. Ben Achour, *Mouvement littéraire et intellectuel*, 70.
17. Kenneth J. Perkins, *Historical Dictionary of Tunisia*, 2nd ed. (Lanham, MD: Scarecrow Press, 1997), 112–113; Noureddine Sraïeb, "Le collège Sadiki de Tunis et les nouvelles élites," *Revue du monde musulman et de la Méditerranée* 72, no. 1 (1994): 47–48.
18. Mary Dewhurst Lewis, *Divided Rule: Sovereignty and Empire in French Tunisia, 1881-1938* (Berkeley: University of California Press, 2014), 101.
19. Hourani, *Arabic Thought*, 363.
20. Leon Carl Brown, "Tunisia," in *Education and Political Development*, ed. James Smoot Coleman (Princeton, NJ: Princeton University Press, 1965), 146–147.
21. Ibid.
22. Ibid., 146, 150.
23. Basheer M. Nafi, "Ṭāhir ibn'Āshūr: The Career and Thought of a Modern Reformist 'ālim, with Special Reference to His Work of tafsīr," *Journal of Qur'anic Studies* 7, no. 1 (2005): 9.
24. L. Brown, "Tunisia," 144.
25. Perkins, *Modern Tunisia*, 67–68.
26. Ibid.
27. Noureddine Sraïeb, "L'idéologie de l'école en Tunisie coloniale (1881–1945)," *Revue du monde musulman et de la Méditerranée* 68, no. 1 (1993): 245.
28. Eqbal Ahmad and Stuart Schaar, "M'hamed Ali: Tunisian Labor Organizer," in *Struggle and Survival in the Modern Middle East*, ed. Edmund Burke and Nejde Yaghoubian (Berkeley: University of California Press, 2006), 166.
29. Julien, "Jeunes-Tunisiens," 110–111, 125.
30. L. Brown, "Tunisia," 150–151.
31. Julien, "Jeunes-Tunisiens," 138–139.
32. Ibid.
33. L. Brown, "Tunisia," 150.
34. Ibid., 146.
35. Sraïeb, "Collège Sadiki," 49–50.
36. M. Ben Achour, *Mouvement littéraire et intellectuel*, 90.
37. Nafi, "Ṭāhir ibn'Āshūr," 8–18.
38. Abdellatif Hermassi, "Société, Islam et islamisme en Tunisie," *Cahiers de la Méditerranée* 49, no. 1 (1994): 67.
39. Muhammad Qasim Zaman, *The Ulama in Contemporary Islam: Custodians of Change* (Princeton, NJ: Princeton University Press, 2002), 61.
40. L. Brown, "Tunisia," 145.
41. M. Ben Achour, *Mouvement littéraire et intellectuel*, 58–59.

42. Julien, "Jeunes-Tunisiens," 146–147.
43. Keith W. Martin, "Zaytuna Mosque and University (Tunisia) Chapter 9: Reforms 1932 to 1933 AD Education Reformation and Secularization," *Martin Exports* (blog), January 22, 2014, http://martinexports.blogspot.com/2014/01/zaytuna -mosque-and-university-tunisia_5696.html.
44. M. Ben Achour, *Mouvement littéraire et intellectuel*, 146–147.
45. Noureddine Sraïeb, "Université et société au Maghreb: la Qarawîyin de Fès et la Zaytûna de Tunis," *Revue de l'Occident musulman et de la Méditerranée* 38, no. 1 (1984): 71.
46. M. Ben Achour, *Mouvement littéraire et intellectuel*, 189–190.
47. Ibid., 6–7, 47.
48. Akram Fouad Khater, *Sources in the History of the Modern Middle East*, 2nd ed. (Belmont, CA: Wadsworth, 2011), 61.
49. Hourani, *Arabic Thought*, 69–83, 164–170.
50. Majdi Chakroun, "La condition de la femme en Tunisie: de l'humanitaire au partenariat," *Revue juridique Thémis* 43, no. 1 (2009): 120.
51. Khaled Ridha, *Le Capitalisme, l'Islam et le socialisme* (Saint-Denis, France: Publibook, 2011), 401–402.
52. Erik Churchill, "Tahar Haddad: A Towering Figure for Women's Rights in Tunisia," *Voices and Views: Middle East and North Africa* (blog), World Bank, August 3, 2013, http://blogs.worldbank.org/arabvoices/tahar-haddad-towering-figure -women%E2%80%99s-rights-tunisia.
53. Chakroun, "Condition de la femme," 123.
54. Amel Mili, "Exploring the Relation Between Gender Politics and Representative Government in the Maghreb: Analytical and Empirical Observations" (PhD diss., State University of New Jersey, 2009), 9.
55. Ibid., 17.
56. Joseph T. Zeidan, *Arab Women Novelists: The Formative Years and Beyond* (New York: State University of New York Press, 1995), 30; Maryam Ben Salem, "Le voile en Tunisie. De la réalisation de soi a la résistance passive," *Revue des mondes musulmans et de la Méditerranée* 128 (2010), http://remmm.revues.org/6840.
57. Hourani, *Arabic Thought*, 165.
58. Julian Weideman, "Tahar Haddad After Bourguiba and Bin 'Ali: A Reformist Between Secularists and Islamists," *International Journal of Middle East Studies* 48, no. 1 (2016): 53.
59. Lilia Labidi, "Islam and Women's Rights in Tunisia" (lecture, Austrian Oriental Society Hammer Purgstall, Vienna, 2005).
60. Noureddine Sraïeb, "Contribution à la connaissance de Tahar el-Haddad (1899–1935)," *Revue de l'Occident musulman et de la Méditerranée* 4, no. 1 (1967): 107.
61. Weideman, "Tahar Haddad," 52.
62. Martina Sabra, "A Rebel Loyal to the Koran," *Qantara.de*, November 11, 2010, https://en.qantara.de/node/327; Sraïeb, "Connaissance de Tahar el-Haddad," 108.

10. 1956

1. Kenneth Perkins, *A History of Modern Tunisia,* 2nd ed. (Cambridge: Cambridge University Press, 2014), 49, 60.

2. Kenneth J. Perkins, *Historical Dictionary of Tunisia,* 2nd ed. (Lanham, MD: Scarecrow Press, 1997), 74–75.

3. Charles-André Julien, "Colons français et Jeunes-Tunisiens (1882–1912)," *Revue française d'histoire d'outre-mer* 54, no. 194–197 (1967): 143.

4. Habib Boularès, *Histoire de la Tunisie: les grandes dates, de la préhistoire à la révolution* (Tunis: Cérès, 2012), 523–525; Perkins, *Modern Tunisia,* 74, 523–525.

5. Noureddine Sraïeb, "Le collège Sadiki de Tunis et les nouvelles élites," *Revue du monde musulman et de la Méditerranée* 72, no. 1 (1994): 49–50.

6. Perkins, *Dictionary of Tunisia,* 162–163.

7. Julien, "Jeunes-Tunisiens," 131–132.

8. Boularès, *Histoire de la Tunisie,* 533.

9. Julien, "Jeunes-Tunisiens," 134, 147, 149–150.

10. Ibid., 149.

11. Jacob Abadi, *Tunisia Since the Arab Conquest: The Saga of a Westernized Muslim State* (Reading, UK: Ithaca, 2013), 357–358.

12. Boularès, *Histoire de la Tunisie,* 540–541.

13. Leon Carl Brown, "Tunisia," in *Education and Political Development,* ed. James Smoot Coleman (Princeton, NJ: Princeton University Press, 1965), 151.

14. Benjamin Rivlin, "The Tunisian Nationalist Movement: Four Decades of Evolution," *Middle East Journal* 6, no. 2 (1952): 169.

15. Boularès, *Histoire de la Tunisie,* 545; Mary Dewhurst Lewis, *Divided Rule: Sovereignty and Empire in French Tunisia, 1881–1938* (Berkeley: University of California Press, 2014), 119–131.

16. Jamil M. Abun-Nasr, *A History of the Maghrib in the Islamic Period* (Cambridge: Cambridge University Press, 1987), 364.

17. Lamia Ben Youssef Zayzafoon, *The Production of the Muslim Woman: Negotiating Text, History, and Ideology* (Lanham, MD: Lexington, 2005), 132.

18. Joel Beinin, *Workers and Thieves: Labor Movements and Popular Uprisings in Tunisia and Egypt* (Stanford, CA: Stanford University Press, 2016), 12.

19. Ibid.

20. Emmanuel K. Akyeampong and Henry Louis Gates, eds., *Dictionary of African Biography* (Oxford: Oxford University Press, 2012), 15–16.

21. Noureddine Sraïeb, "Contribution à la connaissance de Tahar el-Haddad (1899–1935)," *Revue de l'Occident musulman et de la Méditerranée* 4, no. 1 (1967): 106, 109–110.

22. Akyeampong and Gates, *Dictionary of African Biography,* 15–16.

23. Perkins, *Dictionary of Tunisia,* 119.

24. Béchir Tlili, "La Fédération Socialiste de Tunisie (SFIO) et les questions islamique (1919–1925)," in *Mouvement ouvrier, communisme et nationalismes dans*

le monde arabe, ed. René Gallissot (Paris: Ouvrières, 1978), 76; Akyeampong and Gates, *Dictionary of African Biography*, 15–16.

25. Beinin, *Workers and Thieves*, 13.

26. Perkins, *Dictionary of Tunisia*, 38–39, 57.

27. Leon Carl Brown, "Stages in the Process of Change," in *Tunisia: The Politics of Modernization*, ed. C. A. Micaud (New York: Praeger, 1964), 41.

28. L. Brown, "Tunisia," 151–152.

29. Andrew Borowiec, *Modern Tunisia: A Democratic Apprenticeship* (Westport, CT: Praeger, 1998) 19.

30. Lewis, *Divided Rule*, 131–159.

31. "Tunisie: Hommage à Mahmoud el Materi à la Bibliothèque nationale—Le médecin, le leader, le nationaliste," *AllAfrica*, April 11, 2015, http://fr.allafrica.com /stories/201504110216.html.

32. Stephen J. King, "Economic Reform and Tunisia's Hegemonic Party: The End of the Administrative Elite," in *Beyond Colonialism and Nationalism in the Maghrib: History, Culture, and Politics*, ed. Ali Abdullatif Ahmida (New York: Palgrave Macmillan, 2009), 168–171.

33. Juliette Bessis, "Sur Moncef Bey et le moncefisme: la Tunisie de 1942 à 1948," *Revue française d'histoire d'outre-mer* 70, no. 260–261 (1983): 98.

34. King, "Tunisia's Hegemonic Party," 172.

35. Lotfi Hajji, "Pour une relecture critique de la relation de Bourguiba à l'islam," in *Habib Bourguiba: La trace et l'héritage*, ed. Michel Camau and Vincent Geisser (Paris: Karthala, 2004), 53, 59–60.

36. Haim Saadoun, "Tunisia," in *Jews of the Middle East and North Africa in Modern Times*, ed. Reeva S. Simon, Michael M. Laskier, and Sara Reguer (New York: Columbia University Press, 2003), 450–451; Perkins, *Modern Tunisia*, 104.

37. Perkins, *Modern Tunisia*, 104; Abadi, *Tunisia Since the Arab Conquest*, 370–371.

38. Perkins, *Modern Tunisia*, 104.

39. Abadi, *Tunisia Since the Arab Conquest*, 383.

40. Sami Zlitni and Zeineb Touati, "Social Networks and Women's Mobilization in Tunisia," *Journal of International Women's Studies* 13, no. 5 (2012): 47.

41. Sophie Bessis, "Bourguiba féministe: les limites du féminisme d'Etat bourguibien," in *Habib Bourguiba: La trace et l'héritage*, ed. Michel Camau and Vincent Geisser (Paris: Karthala, 2004), 103.

42. Sophie Bessis (Franco-Tunisian historian and author, associate researcher at the *Institut de relations internationales et stratégiques* [IRIS]), in discussion with the author, March 2, 2016.

43. Sophie Bessis, "Bourguiba féministe," 104; Elise Abassade, "L'Union des Femmes de Tunisie et l'Union des Jeunes Filles de Tunisie, 1944–1947," *Monde(s)* 2, no. 8 (2015): 202–203.

44. Khedija Arfaoui, "Bchira Ben Mrad," in *Des femmes écrivent l'Afrique: L'Afrique du Nord*, ed. Amira Nowaira, Azza El Kholy, and Moha Ennaji (Paris: Karthala, 2013), 239; S. Bessis, "Bourguiba féministe," 104.

45. Don Rubin, "Tunisia," in *The Arab World*, vol. 4 of *The World Encyclopedia of Contemporary Theatre* (New York: Routledge, 1999).

46. Ruth Frances Davis, *Ma'luf: Reflections on the Arab Andalusian Music of Tunisia* (Lanham, MD: Scarecrow Press, 2004), 51.

47. William Granara, "Ali al-Duaji," in *Essays in Arabic Literary Biography: 1850-1950*, ed. Roger Allen (Wiesbaden, Germany: Harrassowitz Verlag, 2010), 79–80.

48. J. C. Bürgel, "Tradition and Modernity in the Work of the Tunisian Writer al-Mas͑adī," in *Tradition and Modernity in Arabic Language and Literature*, ed. J. R. Smart (Surrey, UK: Curzon, 1996), 166–167, 169–171.

49. Nouri Gana, "Introduction," in *The Making of the Tunisian Revolution: Contexts, Architects, Prospects*, ed. Nouri Gana (Edinburgh: Edinburgh University Press, 2013), 16.

50. Mohamed-Salah Omri, "Mahmud al-Mas'adi," in *Essays in Arabic Literary Biography: 1850-1950*, ed. Roger Allen (Wiesbaden, Germany: Harrassowitz Verlag, 2010), 208.

51. Rivlin, "Nationalist Movement," 172; Lewis, *Divided Rule*, 132, 159.

52. Abadi, *Tunisia Since the Arab Conquest*, 370–371.

53. Lewis, *Divided Rule*, 161–162.

54. Leon Carl Brown, "Bourguiba and Bourguibism Revisited: Reflections and Interpretation," *Middle East Journal* 55, no. 1 (2001): 43–57.

55. Lewis, *Divided Rule*, 157–163.

56. Abadi, *Tunisia Since the Arab Conquest*, 377, 383–386.

57. Juliette Bessis, *La Méditerranée fasciste: l'Italie mussolinienne et la Tunisie* (Paris: Karthala, 1981), 329–364.

58. J. Bessis, "Moncef Bey," 102–106.

59. Andrew Hussey, *The French Intifada* (New York: Faber & Faber, 2014), 363.

60. Abadi, *Tunisia Since the Arab Conquest*, 392.

61. Ibid., 393.

62. Hussey, *The French Intifada*, 363.

63. Laszlo J. Nagy, "Les partis politiques dans le mouvement national: le cas de l'Algérie et de la Tunisie," *Cahiers de la Méditerranée* 1, no. 41 (1990): 83–84.

64. Yadh Ben Achour (public law expert and academician, president of the *Haute Instance pour la réalisation des objectifs de la révolution, de la réforme politique et de la transition démocratique*), in discussion with the author, April 23, 2016.

65. Roundtable with union leaders in Beja, regional headquarters of UGTT, April 19, 2016.

66. Beinin, *Workers and Thieves*, 4–5.

67. King, "Tunisia's Hegemonic Party," 172.

68. Beinin, *Workers and Thieves*, 4–14.

69. King, "Tunisia's Hegemonic Party," 172.

70. Abassade, "L'Union," 202–211.

71. Mounira M. Charrad, "Policy Shifts: State, Islam, and Gender in Tunisia, 1930s–1990s," *Social Politics* 4, no. 2 (1997): 293; Samar El-Masri, "Tunisian

Women at a Crossroads: Cooptation or Autonomy?" *Middle East Policy* 22, no. 2 (2015): 126.

72. Charrad, "Policy Shifts," 289, 292–295.

73. Abassade, "L'Union," 212.

74. Noureddine Sraïeb, "Le problème franco-tunisien est un problème de souveraineté," *Revue de l'Occident musulman et de la Méditerranée* 1, no. 1 (1966): 177, 206.

75. Rivlin, "Nationalist Movement," 178–180.

76. Ibid., 182.

77. Jean de Hauteclocque, *Telegram no. 959/967 to Vincent Auriol and Antoine Pinay* (Paris: French Ministry of Foreign Affairs, 1952).

78. Beinin, *Workers and Thieves*, 14–15.

79. Lisa Anderson, *The State and Social Transformation in Tunisia and Libya, 1830–1980* (Princeton, NJ: Princeton University Press, 1986), 232–233.

80. Michael J. Willis, *Politics and Power in the Maghreb: Algeria, Tunisia, and Morocco from Independence to the Arab Spring* (Oxford: Oxford University Press, 2014), 38–40.

81. Douglas Elliott Ashford, *National Development and Local Reform: Political Participation in Morocco, Tunisia and Pakistan* (Princeton, NJ: Princeton University Press, 1967), 74.

82. Ryo Ikeda, *The Imperialism of French Decolonisation: French Policy and the Anglo-American Response in Tunisia and Morocco* (Basingstoke, UK: Palgrave Macmillan, 2015), 123–131.

83. Willis, *Politics and Power*, 38–40.

84. Ibid.

85. Anderson, *State and Social Transformation*, 179–203, 251–280.

86. Hussey, *The French Intifada*, 152–155, 241.

87. Roland Oliver and Anthony Atmore, *Africa Since 1800*, 5th ed. (Cambridge: Cambridge University Press, 2005), 241–242.

88. Hussey, *The French Intifada*, 204.

11. The Father of Tunisia

1. Jacob Abadi, *Tunisia Since the Arab Conquest: The Saga of a Westernized Muslim State* (Reading, UK: Ithaca, 2013), 427.

2. John P. Entelis, "L'héritage contradictoire de Bourguiba: modernisation et intolérance politique," in *Habib Bourguiba: La trace et l'héritage*, ed. Michel Camau and Vincent Geisser (Paris: Karthala, 2004), 231.

3. Tunisian Constitution of 1959.

4. Adel Kaaniche, "La Constitution du 1er Juin 1959: une naissance difficile," *Leaders*, May 25, 2009, http://www.leaders.com.tn/article/0854-la-constitution-du-1er-juin-1959-une-naissance-difficile.

5. Ibid.

6. Tunisian Constitution of 1959, article 6.

7. Entelis, "L'héritage contradictoire de Bourguiba," 231.

8. Abadi, *Tunisia Since the Arab Conquest*, 429.

9. Werner Klaus Ruf, "The Bizerta Crisis: A Bourguibist Attempt to Resolve Tunisia's Border Problems," *Middle East Journal* 25, no. 2 (1971): 207; Abadi, *Tunisia Since the Arab Conquest*, 460–466.

10. Abadi, *Tunisia Since the Arab Conquest*, 460–466.

11. "Dars al-Palmarium wa mada 'umq thaqafat Bourguiba wa ma'rifatoh bi al-tareekh" [The Palmarium Lesson and the Depth of Bourguiba's Knowledge on History], from a speech made by Habib Bourguiba in late 1972, *YouTube*, posted by Mohamed Akacha, October 26, 2013, https://www.youtube.com/watch?v=cJG0nln1ngY&list=FLEqhvN0attu1G0Hs2uv5R9g.

12. Lotfi Ben Rejeb, "United States Policy Towards Tunisia: What New Engagement After an Expendable 'Friendship'?" in *The Making of the Tunisian Revolution: Contexts, Architects, Prospects*, ed. Nouri Gana (Edinburgh: Edinburgh University Press, 2013), 82–83.

13. Glenn A. Lehmann, *Evaluation of the U.S.-Tunisian Aid Relationship, FY 1957–1984* (Washington, DC: U.S. Agency for International Development, 1985), 2.

14. Kenneth Perkins, *A History of Modern Tunisia*, 2nd ed. (Cambridge: Cambridge University Press, 2014), 146.

15. U.S. Department of State, Telegram From the Secretary of State to the Department of State, December 19, 1959. *Foreign Relations of the United States, 1958–1960, Arab-Israeli Dispute; United Arab Republic; North Africa*, vol. 13, https://history.state.gov/historicaldocuments/frus1958-60v13/d415.

16. Kamel Labidi, "Tunisia: Independent but Not Free," *Le Monde diplomatique*, March 4, 2006, https://mondediplo.com/2006/03/04tunisia.

17. Talcott W. Seelye, "Ben Ali Visit Marks Third Stage in 200-Year-Old US-Tunisian Special Relationship," *Washington Report on Middle East Affairs*, March 4, 1990, http://www.wrmea.org/1990-march/ben-ali-visit-marks-third-stage-in-200-year-old-us-tunisian-special-relationship.html.

18. Kenneth Perkins, "Playing the Islamic Card: The Use and Abuse of Religion in Tunisian Politics," in *The Making of the Tunisian Revolution: Contexts, Architects, Prospects*, ed. Nouri Gana (Edinburgh: Edinburgh University Press: 2013), 63.

19. Peter Partner, "Bourguiba: A Different Kind of Arab," *Harper's Magazine*, October 1, 1957, 76.

20. Shaukat Ali, *Pan-Movements in the Third World: Pan-Arabism, Pan-Africanism, Pan-Islamism* (Lahore: Publishers United, 1976), 74.

21. "Dars al-Palmarium."

22. John L. Esposito and John O. Voll, *Makers of Contemporary Islam* (Oxford: Oxford University Press, 2001), 97.

23. Abadi, *Tunisia Since the Arab Conquest*, 452–454.

24. Ibid.
25. Michael M. Laskier, "Israel and the Maghreb at the Height of the Arab-Israeli Conflict: 1950s–1970s," *Middle East Review of International Affairs* 4, no. 2 (June 2000): 96–97; Abadi, *Tunisia Since the Arab Conquest*, 455–456.
26. "President Bourguiba Jericho Speech (1965)," *Bourguiba.com*, accessed March 8, 2016, http://www.bourguiba.com/pages/speeches.aspx.
27. Ibid.
28. "Laqtat archiviyya lil-za'eem al-rahil Bourguiba wa dawlat al-istiqlal" [Archival Footage of the Late Leader Bourguiba and the Independent State], *YouTube*, posted by Tunis7TV, April 6, 2013, https://www.youtube.com/watch?v=MElf6rzfGWs.
29. Laskier, "Israel and the Maghreb," 98.
30. Perkins, *Modern Tunisia*, 148–149; Abdelkrim Allagui, "Bourguiba et les Juifs: 1930–1967," in *Habib Bourguiba: La trace et l'héritage*, ed. Michel Camau and Vincent Geisser (Paris: Karthala, 2004), 121–124.
31. Perkins, *Modern Tunisia*, 148–149.
32. Myra Williamson, *Terrorism, War and International Law: The Legality of the Use of Force Against Afghanistan in 2001* (New York: Routledge, 2016), 132.
33. Leon Carl Brown, "Bourguiba and Bourguibism Revisited: Reflections and Interpretation," *Middle East Journal* 55, no. 1 (2001): 43–57.
34. "Dars al-Palmarium."
35. Seelye, "Ben Ali Visit."
36. Daniel Kawczynski, *Seeking Gaddafi: Libya, the West and the Arab Spring* (London: Biteback, 2011).
37. "Création du premier noyau de l'Armée nationale tunisienne," *Ministère de la Défense nationale, Patrimoine et histoire militaire*, accessed March 28, 2017, http://www.hmp.defense.tn/index.php/formation/formation-professionnelle/creation-du-premier-noyeau; Marie Thourson Jones, "Educating Girls in Tunisia: Issues Generated by the Drive for Universal Enrollment," in *Women's Education in the Third World: Comparative Perspectives*, ed. Gail P. Kelly and Carolyn M. Elliott (Albany: State University of New York Press, 1982), 32.
38. Rejeb, "United States Policy Towards Tunisia," 84.
39. Lisa Anderson, *The State and Social Transformation in Tunisia and Libya, 1830–1980* (Princeton, NJ: Princeton University Press, 1986), 48–49, 146, 150.
40. Ibid., 138–139.
41. Mounira M. Charrad, *States and Women's Rights: The Making of Postcolonial Tunisia, Algeria, and Morocco* (Berkeley: University of California Press, 2001), 202.
42. Ibid., 219–221.
43. Mounira M. Charrad, "Central and Local Patrimonialism: State-Building in Kin-Based Societies," *Annals of the American Academy of Political and Social Science* 636 (July 2011): 56–57.
44. Barbara K. Larson, "Local-National Integration in Tunisia," *Middle Eastern Studies* 20, no. 1 (1984): 20.

45. Clement Henry Moore, "De Bourguiba à Ben Ali: modernisation et dictature éducative," in *Habib Bourguiba: La trace et l'héritage*, ed. Michel Camau and Vincent Geisser (Paris: Karthala, 2004), 194.

46. Laurence Pierrepont-de-Cock, "Projet national bourguibien et réalités tunisiennes," in *Habib Bourguiba: La trace et l'héritage*, ed. Michel Camau and Vincent Geisser (Paris: Karthala, 2004), 34.

47. "'L'Art plastique en Tunisie,' ouvrage publié par l'Alecso," *TunisiArtGalleries*, accessed March 1, 2016, http://www.tunisiartgalleries.com/index.php?option =com_content&view=article&id=1045:lart-plastique-en-tunisie-ouvrage -publie-par-lalecso&catid=27:tagstoryhistoire-de-lart-et-de-lartiste& Itemid=21.

48. Jessica Gerschultz, "A Bourguibist Mural in the New Monastir? Zoubeïr Turki's Play on Knowledge, Power and Audience Perception," *International Journal of Islamic Architecture* 4, no. 2 (2015): 315–323, 333.

49. James Allman, *Social Mobility and Education Development in Tunisia* (Leiden: Brill, 1979), 59–60.

50. Pierrepont-de-Cock, "Projet national bourguibien," 35–37.

51. Driss Abbassi, *Entre Bourguiba et Hannibal: Identité tunisienne et histoire depuis l'indépendance* (Paris: Karthala; Aix-en-Provence: IREMAM, 2015), 73, 103.

52. Nouri Gana, "Introduction," in *The Making of the Tunisian Revolution: Contexts, Architects, Prospects*, ed. Nouri Gana (Edinburgh: Edinburgh University Press: 2013), 17.

53. Juliette Bessis, "Les contradictions d'un règne en situation défensive," in *Habib Bourguiba: La trace et l'héritage*, ed. Michel Camau and Vincent Geisser (Paris: Karthala, 2004), 262.

54. Andrew Borowiec, *Modern Tunisia: A Democratic Apprenticeship* (London: Praeger, 1998), 24.

55. L. Brown, "Bourguiba and Bourguibism," 43–57.

56. Yadh Ben Achour, "La réforme des mentalités: Bourguiba et le redressement moral," in *Tunisie au présent, une modernité au-dessus de tout soupçon?* ed. Michel Camau (Paris: CNRS, 1987), 145–159.

57. L. Brown, "Bourguiba and Bourguibism," 43–57.

58. "Dars al-Palmarium."

59. Y. Ben Achour, "La réforme des mentalités," 145–159.

60. Borowiec, *Modern Tunisia*, 24.

61. L. Brown, "Bourguiba and Bourguibism," 43–57.

62. Arnold M. Ludwig, *King of the Mountain: The Nature of Political Leadership* (Lexington: University Press of Kentucky, 2002), 171.

63. Borowiec, *Modern Tunisia*, 33–35.

64. Abdeljelil Temimi (Tunisian historian, founder of the *Fondation Temimi pour la recherche scientifique et l'information*), in discussion with the author, April 20, 2016.

65. Christopher Alexander, "Authoritarianism and Civil Society in Tunisia: Back from the Democratic Brink," *Middle East Report* 27, no. 205 (1997), http://www.merip.org/mer/mer205/authoritarianism-civil-society-tunisia.

66. Michele Penner Angrist, "The Expression of Political Dissent in the Middle East: Turkish Democratization and Authoritarian Continuity in Tunisia," *Comparative Studies in Society and History* 41, no. 4 (1999): 752.

67. Souhayr Belhassen, "Les legs bourguibiens de la répression," in *Habib Bourguiba: La trace et l'héritage*, ed. Michel Camau and Vincent Geisser (Paris: Karthala, 2004), 395–396.

68. Daniel Ritter, *The Iron Cage of Liberalism: International Politics and Unarmed Revolutions in the Middle East and North Africa* (Oxford: Oxford University Press, 2015), 73–74.

69. Larbi Chouikha, "Pluralisme politique et presse d'opposition," in *Habib Bourguiba: La trace et l'héritage*, ed. Michel Camau and Vincent Geisser (Paris: Karthala, 2004), 342; Larbi Chouikha, "Evoquer la mémoire politique dans un contexte autoritaire: 'l'extrême gauche' tunisienne entre mémoire du passé et identité présente," *L'Année du Maghreb* 6 (2010): 427–440.

70. Ahmed Ben Salah (Tunisian minister of education, October 1968–November 1969; Tunisian minister of economy, November 1961–September 1969; Tunisian minister of finance, January 1961–September 1969; Tunisian minister of planning, January 1961–September 1969; Tunisian minister of social affairs, May 1958–January 1961; Tunisian minister of public health, July 1957–January 1961), in discussion with the author, April 23, 2016.

71. Abdelessem Ben Hammida, "Pouvoir syndical et édification d'un Etat national en Tunisie," *Cahiers de la Méditerranée* 41, no. 1 (1990): 136–137.

72. Joel Beinin, *Workers and Thieves: Labor Movements and Popular Uprisings in Tunisia and Egypt* (Stanford, CA: Stanford University Press, 2016), 19.

73. Abdeljelil Temimi, in discussion with the author, April 20, 2016.

74. Stephen J. King, "Economic Reform and Tunisia's Hegemonic Party: The End of the Administrative Elite," in *Beyond Colonialism and Nationalism in the Maghrib: History, Culture, and Politics*, ed. Ali Abdullatif Ahmida (New York: Palgrave Macmillan, 2009), 174–175.

75. Anderson, *State and Social Transformation*, 237–238.

76. King, "Tunisia's Hegemonic Party," 175.

77. Abdeljelil Temimi, in discussion with the author, April 20, 2016.

78. King, "Tunisia's Hegemonic Party," 174.

79. Abadi, *Tunisia Since the Arab Conquest*, 436–441.

80. King, "Tunisia's Hegemonic Party," 177.

81. Ibid.; Abadi, *Tunisia Since the Arab Conquest*, 438.

82. Abadi, *Tunisia Since the Arab Conquest*, 436–441; Andrew Hussey, *The French Intifada* (New York: Faber & Faber, 2014), 370.

83. King, "Tunisia's Hegemonic Party," 178.

84. Anderson, *State and Social Transformation*, 244.

85. C. Moore, "De Bourguiba à Ben Ali," 196.

86. Y. Ben Achour, "La réforme des mentalités," 145–159.

87. Benoît Gaumer, *L'organisation sanitaire en Tunisie sous le Protectorat français (1881–1956): un bilan ambigu et contrasté* (Quebec City: Presses de l'Université Laval, 2006), 242–248.

88. Pablo Gottret, Geroge J. Schieber, and Hugh R. Waters, *Good Practices in Health Financing: Lessons from Reforms in Low- and Middle-Income Countries* (Washington, DC: World Bank, 2008), 390.

89. Allen James Fromherz, *Ibn Khaldūn: Life and Times* (Edinburgh: Edinburgh University Press), 151.

12. Putting Religion in Its Place

1. Marion Boulby, "The Islamic Challenge: Tunisia Since Independence," *Third World Quarterly* 10, no. 2 (1988): 592.

2. Mounira M. Charrad, *States and Women's Rights: The Making of Postcolonial Tunisia, Algeria, and Morocco* (Berkeley: University of California Press, 2001), 219–220.

3. "Laqtat archiviyya lil-za'eem al-rahil Bourguiba wa dawlat al-istiqlal" [Archival Footage of the Late Leader Bourguiba and the Independent State], *YouTube*, posted by Tunis7TV, April 6, 2013, https://www.youtube.com/watch?v=MElf6rzfGWs.

4. Franck Frégosi, "Habib Bourguiba et la régulation institutionnelle de l'islam: les contours audacieux d'un gallicanisme politique à la tunisienne," in *Habib Bourguiba: La trace et l'héritage*, ed. Michel Camau and Vincent Geisser (Paris: Karthala, 2004), 88–89; Sana Ben Achour, "Le Code tunisien du statut personnel, 50 ans après: les dimensions de l'ambivalence," *L'Année du Maghreb*, no. 2 (2005–2006): 55–70.

5. Faïza Tobich, *Les statuts personnels dans les pays arabes: De l'éclatement à l'harmonisation* (Aix-en-Provence: Presses universitaires d'Aix-Marseille, 2008), 89–126.

6. Charrad, *States and Women's Rights*, 220–222.

7. "Laqtat archiviyya."

8. Lorna Hawker Durrani, "Employment of Women and Social Change," in *Change in Tunisia: Studies in the Social Sciences*, ed. Russell A. Stone and John Simmons (Albany: State University of New York Press, 1976), 59.

9. Charrad, *States and Women's Rights*, 225.

10. Code du statut personnel (2014).

11. Rima Afifi, Jocelyn DeJong, Krishna Bose, Tanya Salem, Amr A. Awad, and Manal Benkirane, "The Health of Young People: Challenges and Opportunities," in *Public Health in the Arab World*, ed. Samer Jabbour, Rita Giacaman, Marwan Khawaja, Iman Nuwayhid, and Rouham Yamout (Cambridge: Cambridge University Press, 2012), 240.

12. "Laws Fail to Stop Child Marriage," *Aljazeera America*, January 19, 2014, http://america.aljazeera.com/articles/2014/1/19/rights-group-lawfailingtoprotect childbrides.html.
13. Code du statut personnel (1956).
14. Charrad, *States and Women's Rights*, 227–228.
15. Lamia Ben Youssef Zayzafoon, *The Production of the Muslim Woman: Negotiating Text, History and Ideology* (Landam, MD: Lexington, 2005), 103.
16. Tunisian Organic Law no. 2015–460 (2015) amending and supplementing Law no. 75–40 (1975).
17. Code de la nationalité tunisienne (2016), article 6.
18. Monia Ben Jémia, "Migration et genre, de, vers et à travers la Tunisie," *CARIM Analytic and Synthetic Notes*, no. 60 (2010): 2–3.
19. Code du statut personnel (1958), law no. 27, article 8–17.
20. Yadh Ben Achour (public law expert and academician, president of the *Haute Instance pour la réalisation des objectifs de la révolution, de la réforme politique et de la transition démocratique*), in discussion with the author, April 23, 2016.
21. Charrad, *States and Women's Rights*, 228–230.
22. Ibid., 220, 231.
23. Ibid., 223–224.
24. Lilia Labidi, "From Sexual Submission to Voluntary Commitment: The Transformation of Family Ties in Contemporary Tunisia," in *The New Arab Family*, ed. Nicholas S. Hopkins (Cairo: American University in Cairo Press, 2001), 121–122.
25. Mudawwanat al-usra al-maghribiyya (2004), article 19.
26. Siraj Sait and Hilary Lim, *Land, Law, & Islam: Property & Human Rights in the Muslim World* (New York: Zed, 2006), 170.
27. Charrad, *States and Women's Rights*, 195–196.
28. Ibid., 195–199.
29. Fati Ziai, "Personal Status Codes and Women's Rights in the Maghreb," in *Muslim Women and the Politics of Participation: Implementing the Beijing Platform*, ed. Mahnaz Afkhami and Erika Friedl (Syracuse, NY: Syracuse University Press, 1997), 79.
30. Tareq Y. Ismael, Jacqueline S. Ismael, and Glenn E. Perry, *Government and Politics of the Contemporary Middle East: Continuity and Change*, 2nd ed. (New York: Routledge, 2016), 255.
31. Seham Al-Shwayli, "Hidden Facts: Being an Iraqi Muslim Woman," in *Navigating International Academia: Research Student Narratives*, ed. Jill Brown (Rotterdam: Sense, 2014), 82.
32. "Lebanon: Laws Discriminate Against Women," *Human Rights Watch*, January 19, 2015, https://www.hrw.org/news/2015/01/19/lebanon-laws-discriminate -against-women.
33. Sajeda Amin, "Demography," in *Women and Islamic Cultures: Disciplinary Paradigms and Approaches: 2003-2013*, ed. Suad Joseph (Leiden: Brill, 2013), 69.
34. Jacob Abadi, *Tunisia Since the Arab Conquest: The Saga of a Westernized Muslim State* (Reading, UK: Ithaca, 2013), 456; Kelley Lee, Louisiana Lush, Gill Walt, and

John Cleland, "Family Planning Policies and Programmes in Eight Low-Income Countries: A Comparative Policy Analysis," *Social Science & Medicine* 47, no. 7 (1998): 949–959.

35. Kenneth Perkins, *A History of Modern Tunisia*, 2nd ed. (Cambridge: Cambridge University Press, 2014), 142–143.

36. Lee et al., "Family Planning Policies," 949–959.

37. Selma Hajri (endocrinologist, director of the *Groupe Tawhida Ben Cheikh: Recherche et action pour la santé de la femme*), in discussion with the author, April 7, 2016; "Situation Report: Women and Tunisia," *Karama: Rising for Dignity*, accessed July 31, 2016, http://www.el-karama.org/content/situation-report-women-and-tunisia.

38. Pablo Gottret, George J. Schieber, and Hugh R. Waters, *Good Practices in Health Financing: Lessons from Reforms in Low- and Middle-Income Countries* (Washington, DC: World Bank, 2008), 390–391.

39. Frégosi, "Régulation institutionnelle de l'islam," 87.

40. Abdelkrim Allagui, "Bourguiba et les Juifs: 1930–1967," in *Habib Bourguiba: La trace et l'héritage*, ed. Michel Camau and Vincent Geisser (Paris: Karthala, 2004), 118–119.

41. Frégosi, "Régulation institutionnelle de l'islam," 87.

42. Souhayma Ben Achour, "Les convictions religieuses face au droit positif tunisien," in *Convictions philosophiques et religieuses et droits positifs: textes présentés au Colloque International de Moncton (24-27 août 2008)*, ed. Marie-Claire Foblets (Brussels: Groupe de Boeck, 2010), 159.

43. Mehdi Mabrouk, "Tunisia: The Radicalisation of Religious Policy," in *Islamist Radicalisation in North Africa: Politics and Process*, ed. George Joffe (New York: Routledge, 2012), 52.

44. Michael B. Bikshu, "Kemal Atatürk and Habib Bourguiba: Brothers from Different Mothers?" in *Kurdish Issues: Essays in Honor of Robert W. Olson*, ed. Michael M. Gunter (Costa Mesa, CA: Mazda, 2016), 10–11.

45. James Allman, *Social Mobility, Education, and Development in Tunisia* (Leiden: Brill, 1979), 68.

46. Frégosi, "Régulation institutionnelle de l'islam," 83–84.

47. Edward Webb, "The 'Church' of Bourguiba: Nationalizing Islam in Tunisia," *Sociology of Islam* 1, no. 1–2 (2013): 19–22.

48. Leon Carl Brown, "Bourguiba and Bourguibism Revisited: Reflections and Interpretation," *Middle East Journal* 55, no. 1 (2001): 43–57.

49. Sophie Bessis, "Bourguiba féministe: les limites du féminisme d'Etat bourguibien," in *Habib Bourguiba: La trace et l'héritage*, ed. Michel Camau and Vincent Geisser (Paris: Karthala, 2004), 107; Habib Belaïd, "Bourguiba et la vie associative pendant la période coloniale et après l'indépendance," in *Habib Bourguiba: La trace et l'héritage*, ed. Michel Camau and Vincent Geisser (Paris: Karthala, 2004), 327; Lotfi Hajji, "Pour une relecture critique de la relation de Bourguiba

à l'islam," in *Habib Bourguiba: La trace et l'héritage*, ed. Michel Camau and Vincent Geisser (Paris: Karthala, 2004), 54.

50. Jocelyne Cesari, *The Awakening of Muslim Democracy: Religion, Modernity, and the State* (New York: Cambridge University Press, 2014), 53–55.

51. Allagui, "Bourguiba et les Juifs," 119–121.

52. Sophie Bessis (Franco-Tunisian historian and author, associate researcher at the *Institut de relations internationales et stratégiques* [IRIS]), in discussion with the author, March 2, 2016.

53. Allagui, "Bourguiba et les Juifs," 121–122.

54. Sophie Bessis in discussion with the author, March 2, 2016.

55. Andrew Borowiec, *Modern Tunisia: A Democratic Apprenticeship* (London: Praeger, 1998), 13–14.

56. Ibid.

57. Kenneth Perkins, "Playing the Islamic Card: The Use and Abuse of Religion in Tunisian Politics," in *The Making of the Tunisian Revolution: Contexts, Architects, Prospects,* ed. Nouri Gana (Edinburgh: Edinburgh University Press, 2013), 62.

58. Zayzafoon, *The Production of the Muslim Woman*, 117.

59. Ibid., 107.

60. Boulby, "The Islamic Challenge," 593.

61. Kevin Sullivan, "Tunisia, After Igniting Arab Spring, Sends the Most Fighters to Islamic State in Syria," *Washington Post*, October 28, 2014, http://www.washingtonpost.com/world/national-security/tunisia-after-igniting-arab-spring-sends-the-most-fighters-to-islamic-state-in-syria/2014/10/28/b5db4faa-5971-11e4-8264-deed989ae9a2_story.html.

62. Rory McCarthy, "Re-thinking Secularism in Post-Independence Tunisia," *Journal of North African Studies* 19, no. 5 (2014): 745.

63. Boulby, "The Islamic Challenge," 594.

64. Ibid.

65. Khaled Lasram, "Kamel Eddine Djaït, l'homme qui combattait l'hétérodoxie," *Le Temps*, January 2, 2013, http://www.turess.com/fr/letemps/72750.

66. Basheer M. Nafi, "Ṭāhir ibnʿĀshūr: The Career and Thought of a Modern Reformist ʿālim, with Special Reference to His Work of tafsīr," *Journal of Qur'anic Studies* 7, no. 1 (2005): 12.

67. "Dars al-Palmarium wa mada 'umq thaqafat Bourguiba wa ma'rifatoh bi al-tareekh" [The Palmarium Lesson and the Depth of Bourguiba's Knowledge on History], from a speech made by Habib Bourguiba in late 1972, *YouTube*, posted by Mohamed Akacha, October 26, 2013, https://www.youtube.com/watch?v=cJG0nln1ngY&list=FLEqhvN0attu1G0Hs2uv5R9g.

68. Hajji, "Relecture critique," 54–56.

69. Abdelwahab Meddeb, "Les deux fautes de Bourguiba selon Abdelwahab Meddeb," *Leaders*, February 8, 2012, http://www.leaders.com.tn/article/7631-les-deux-fautes-de-bourguiba-selon-abdelwahab-meddeb.

70. Hajji, "Relecture critique," 57.

71. Abderrahim Lamchichi, "Laïcité autoritaire en Tunisie et en Turquie," *Confluences Méditerranée*, no. 33 (2000): 36–37.

72. Alaya Allani, "The Islamists in Tunisia Between Confrontation and Participation: 1980–2008," Journal of North African Studies 14, no. 2 (2009): 263.

13. Educating a Nation

1. Nadia Dejoui, "Habib Bourguiba, 16 ans déjà," *L'Economiste Maghrébin*, April 6, 2016, http://www.leconomistemaghrebin.com/2016/04/06/habib-bourguiba-souvenir-tunisiens/.

2. "Dars al-Palmarium wa mada 'umq thaqafat Bourguiba wa ma'rifatoh bi al-tareekh" [The Palmarium Lesson and the Depth of Bourguiba's Knowledge on History], from a speech made by Habib Bourguiba in late 1972, *YouTube*, posted by Mohamed Akacha, October 26, 2013, https://www.youtube.com/watch?v=c JG0nln1ngY&list=FLEqhvN0attu1G0Hs2uv5R9g.

3. Y. G-M. Lulat, *A History of African Higher Education from Antiquity to the Present: A Critical Synthesis* (Westbrook, CT: Greenwood, 2005), 170.

4. Marie Thourson Jones, "Educating Girls in Tunisia: Issues Generated by the Drive for Universal Enrollment," in *Women's Education in the Third World: Comparative Perspectives*, ed. Gail P. Kelly and Carolyn M. Elliott (Albany: State University of New York Press, 1982), 32.

5. "Expenditure on Education as % of Total Government Expenditure: Tunisia (1997–2012)," World Bank, accessed August 11, 2016, http://data.worldbank.org/indicator/SE.XPD.TOTL.GB.ZS?locations=TN.

6. James Allman, *Social Mobility, Education and Development in Tunisia* (Leiden: Brill, 1979), 60; Ali Ben Mabrouk, "Reflecting on Bourguiba, 13 Years After His Death," *Tunisia Live*, April 9, 2016, http://www.tunisia-live.net/2013/04/09/reflecting-on-bourguiba-13-years-after-his-death/.

7. Noureddine Sraïeb, "Mutations et réformes des structures de l'enseignement en Tunisie," in *Annuaire de l'Afrique du Nord*, ed. Charles Debbasch (Paris: CNRS, 1968), 73.

8. Alfred Stepan, "Tunisia's Transition and the Twin Tolerations," *Journal of Democracy* 23, no. 2 (2012): 99–100.

9. Leon Carl Brown, "Tunisia," in *Education and Political Development*, ed. James Smoot Coleman (Princeton, NJ: Princeton University Press, 1965), 159–163.

10. Krista Moore, "Languages and Loyalties: Shaping Identity in Tunisia and the Netherlands," *Macalester International* 25, art. 12 (2010): http://digitalcommons.macalester.edu/cgi/viewcontent.cgi?article=1481&context=macintl.

11. Nancy Parkinson, *Education Aid and National Development: An International Comparison of the Past and Recommendations for the Future* (London: Macmillan, 1976),186.

12. M. Jones, "Educating Girls in Tunisia," 31.

13. Keith Walters, "Gendering French in Tunisia: language ideologies and national-ism," *International Journal of the Sociology of Language*, no. 211 (2011): 89.

14. L. Brown, "Tunisia," 159–164.

15. M. Jones, "Educating Girls in Tunisia," 34.

16. Michelle Zancarini-Fournel, "Coéducation, gémination, co-instruction, mixité: débats dans l'Éducation nationale (1882–1976)" in *La mixité dans l'éducation: Enjeux passés et présents*, ed. Rebecca Rogers (Lyon: ENS, 2004), 25–32.

17. Sraïeb, "L'enseignement en Tunisie," 62–67.

18. Allman, *Development in Tunisia*, 60–62.

19. L. Brown, "Tunisia," 159–163.

20. Allman, *Development in Tunisia*, 60–62.

21. Ibid., 73–74.

22. Sraïeb, "L'enseignement en Tunisie," 75.

23. Allman, *Development in Tunisia*, 63–64.

24. Parkinson, *Education Aid*, 171.

25. Allman, *Development in Tunisia*, 63–64.

26. L. Brown, "Tunisia," 164.

27. Allman, *Development in Tunisia*, 69–72.

28. Ibid.

29. Parkinson, *Education Aid*, 188.

30. Kmar Bendana, "Aux origines de l'enseignement supérieur tunisien," *Hypothèses*, February 2, 2012, https://hypotheses.org/21729.

31. L. Brown, "Tunisia," 159–164; Sraïeb, "L'enseignement en Tunisie," 53.

32. Parkinson, *Education Aid*, 173.

33. Allman, *Development in Tunisia*, 65–73.

34. Marie Thourson Jones, "Education of Girls in Tunisia: Policy Implications of the Drive for Universal Enrollment," *Comparative Education Review* 24, no. 2 (1980): S113.

35. L. Brown, "Tunisia," 165–166; Malika Zeghal, "Public Institutions of Religious Education in Egypt and Tunisia: Contrasting the Post-Colonial Reforms of Al-Azhar and the Zaytuna," in *Trajectories of Education in the Arab World: Legacies and Challenges*, ed. Osama Abi-Mershed (New York: Routledge, 2010), 115.

36. Clement Henry Moore, *Tunisia Since Independence: The Dynamics of One-Party Government* (Berkeley: University of California Press, 1965), 54.

37. Secrétariat d'Etat à l'Education nationale, *Histoire: Deuxième année de l'enseignement secondaire* (Tunis: Société nationale d'édition et de diffusion, 1959).

38. L. Brown, "Tunisia," 165–166.

39. Driss Abbassi, *Entre Bourguiba et Hannibal: Identité tunisienne et histoire depuis l'indépendance* (Paris: Karthala; Aix-en-Provence: IREMAM, 2015), 56–59.

40. Secrétariat d'Etat à l'Education nationale, *Histoire*, 19, 28–29, 165–169, 352–353.

41. Ibid., 9–17, 19–22, 148–149.

42. Mohammad al-Hashimi Zine al-Abidine, Hamoudeh al-Kafi, al-Nasser Hawalah, Mohammad al-Salih Karim, Mahmoud Shaaban, and Mohammad Nuqairah, *Kitab al-madrasi fi al-tareekh al-tounisi* [Schoolbook of Tunisian History] (Tunis: Maktabat al-najah, 1963), 88, 104.

43. Abbassi, *Entre Bourguiba et Hannibal*, 44, 56–59.

44. Ibid., 97–98.

45. *Al-tarbiya al-wataniyya lil talamitha al-sana al-thalitha min al-ta'leem al-thaanawi wa al-i'dadi* [Civic Education for Students in the Third Year of Secondary Education] (Tunis: Al-sharika al-tunisiyya lil tawzee', 1973), 267.

46. Jacques Grell, Mohamed Cherif, Touhami Khalfallah, and Hattab Sedkaoui, *De l'Impérialisme à la décolonisation 1881–1960: Histoire sixième année* (Tunis: Société tunisienne de diffusion, 1967), 228, 272–286, 292–299, 308.

47. Mohamed Karray, Etienne Cossement, Michel Narcy, and Pierre Ferrara, *Recueil de textes philosophiques, classe terminales* (Tunis: Société tunisienne de diffusion, 1971).

48. Mohamed Daoud, "Arabization in Tunisia: The Tug of War," *Issues in Applied Linguistics* 2, no. 1 (1991): 14–15, 19.

49. Ibid., 19–21.

50. Jocelyne Cesari, *The Awakening of Muslim Democracy: Religion, Modernity, and the State* (New York: Cambridge University Press, 2014), 128.

51. Daoud, "Arabization," 20–21.

52. Paul Stevens, "Modernism and Authenticity as Reflected in Language Attitudes: The Case of Tunisia," *Civilisations* 30, no. 1–2 (1980): 47.

53. Daoud, "Arabization," 15–18.

54. Ibid., 14; Ahmed Ben Hamida, "L'arabisation de l'administration dans les pays du Maghreb: le cas de la Tunisie," *International Review of Administrative Science* 51, no. 2 (1985): 14–20, 92.

55. Abbassi, *Entre Bourguiba et Hannibal*, 98–103, 115–120, 127, 137–141.

56. Allman, *Development in Tunisia*, 68.

14. A Different Trajectory

1. Khalil F. Osman, *Sectarianism in Iraq: The Making of State and Nation Since 1920* (New York: Routledge, 2015), 174.

2. Methal R. Mohammed-Marzouk, "Teaching and Learning in Iraq: A Brief History," *Educational Forum* 76, no. 2 (2009): 262.

3. Rakesh Kumar Ranjan and Prakash C. Jain, "The Decline of Educational System in Iraq," *Journal of Peace Studies* 16, no. 1–2 (2009), http://icpsnet.org/adm/pdf/1251368150.pdf.

4. Ibid.

5. Carrie Rosefsky Wickham, *Mobilizing Islam: Religion, Activism and Political Change in Egypt* (New York: Columbia University Press, 2002), 30.

6. Pradeep Barua, *The Military Effectiveness of Post-Colonial States* (Leiden: Brill, 2013), 148.

7. Judith Cochran, *Education in Egypt* (New York: Routledge, 2013), 46.

8. Wickham, *Mobilizing Islam*, 26.

9. Ibid., 24–25.

10. Louisa Loveluck, *Education in Egypt: Key Challenges* (London: Chatham House, 2012), 4.

11. Yasmine M. Abdelfattah, Aamer S. Abu-Qarn, J. Paul Dunne, and Shadwa Zaher, "The Demand for Military Spending in Egypt," *Defence and Peace Economics* 25, no. 3 (2014): 231–245.

12. Cochran, *Education in Egypt*, 43.

13. James B. Mayfield, *Field of Reeds: Social, Economic and Political Change in Rural Egypt: In Search of Civil Society and Good Governance* (Bloomington, IN: AuthorHouse, 2012), 144.

14. Fatima Sadiqi, "Berber and Language Politics in the Moroccan Educational System," in *Multiculturalism and Democracy in North Africa: Aftermath of the Arab Spring*, ed. Moha Ennaji (New York: Routledge, 2014), 81–91.

15. Moha Ennaji, "Language Contact, Arabization Policy and Education in Morocco," in *Language Contact and Language Conflict in Arabic,* ed. Aleya Rouchdy (New York: Routledge, 2002), 74–75.

16. Sadiqi, "Moroccan Educational System," 86.

17. Loubna Lahlou, "La réforme de l'Université marocaine entre idéal organisationnel et réalité pratique," paper presented at the université Paris 8, Vincennes-Saint-Denis, May 2009.

18. Ennaji, "Language Contact," 74–81.

19. World Bank, *The Road Not Traveled: Education Reform in the Middle East and Africa* (Washington, DC: World Bank, 2008), 143.

20. Ennaji, "Language Contact," 74.

21. Nick Clark, "Education in Morocco," *World Education News and Reviews*, April 2006, accessed May 8, 2016, https://www.wes.org/ewenr/PF/06apr/pfpractical_morocco.htm.

22. Mahfoud Bennoune, *The Making of Contemporary Algeria, 1830-1987* (Cambridge: Cambridge University Press, 2002), 219.

23. Ahmed Djebbar, "Le système éducatif algérien: miroir d'une société en crise et en mutation," in *L'Algérie face à la mondialisation*, ed. Tayeb Chenntouf (Oxford: African Books Collective, 2008), 172–174.

24. Djamila Saadi-Mokrane, "The Algerian Linguicide," in *Algeria in Others' Languages*, ed. Anne-Emmanuelle Berger (Ithaca, NY: Cornell University Press, 2002), 44–47.

25. Roland Oliver and Anthony Atmore, *Africa Since 1800,* 5th ed. (Cambridge: Cambridge University Press, 2005), 242.

26. Jonathan N. C. Hill, "Identity and Instability in Postcolonial Algeria," *Journal of North African Studies* 11, no. 1 (2006): 8.

27. Gilbert Grandguillaume, "Les débats et les enjeux linguistiques," in *Où va l'Algérie?* eds. Ahmed Mahiou and Jean-Robert Henry (Aix-en-Provence: Institut de recherches et d'études sur le monde arabe et musulman, 2001), 273–287.
28. Gilbert Grandguillaume, "Pour une histoire critique et citoyenne," in *La France et l'Algérie: leçons d'histoire*, ed. Frédéric Abécassis (Lyon: ENS, 2007), 55–64.
29. Fouad Chafiqi and Abdelhakim Alagui, "Réforme éducative au Maroc et refonte des curricula dans les disciplines scientifiques," *Carrefours de l'éducation* 3, no. 1 (2011): 29–50.
30. Grandguillaume, "Les débats et les enjeux linguistiques," 273–287.
31. Bennoune, *Making of Contemporary Algeria*, 223–224.
32. Amal Obeidi, *Political Culture in Libya* (Surrey, UK: Curzon, 2001), 52.
33. Helen Chapin Metz, ed., *Libya: A Country Study* (Washington, DC: Library of Congress, 1987), 113.
34. Muammar Gaddafi, *The Green Book* (Tripoli, 1975), 9, 13, http://openanthropology.org/libya/gaddafi-green-book.pdf.
35. Obeidi, *Political Culture in Libya*, 52–54.
36. Metz, *Libya*, 112.
37. Jocelyne Cesari, *The Awakening of Muslim Democracy: Religion, Modernity, and the State* (New York: Cambridge University Press, 2014), 87–88, 100.
38. Paulo Freire, *Pedagogy of the Oppressed: Thirtieth Anniversary Edition* (New York: Bloomsbury, 2000), 71–74.
39. United Nations Development Programme (UNDP), *The Arab Human Development Report 2003* (New York: UNDP, 2003), 3.
40. Samar Dudin, "Al-manhaj al-khafi allathi yuharrim al-funoon" [The Hidden Curriculum Banning the Arts], *Alghad*, July 29, 2015, http://www.alghad.com/articles/884244-%D8%A7%D9%84%D9%85%D9%86%D9%87%D8%AC-%D8%A7%D9%84%D8%AE%D9%81%D9%8A-%D8%A7%D9%84%D8%B0%D9%8A-%D9%8A%D8%AD%D8%B1%D9%85-%D8%A7%D9%84%D9%81%D9%86%D9%88%D9%86.
41. Sarah Feuer, "Negotiating the Nation-State: The Politics of Religious Education in Morocco and Tunisia, 1956–2010" (PhD diss., Brandeis University, 2014), 2.
42. Ann Witulski, "Islamic Education Curriculum Reform and Politics in Morocco," in *Center for African Studies: Research Report 2011* (Gainesville: University of Florida, 2011), 50.
43. Malika Zeghal, "The 'Recentering' of Religious Knowledge and Discourse: The Case of al-Azhar in Twentieth-Century Egypt," in *Schooling Islam: The Culture and Politics of Modern Muslim Education,* ed. Robert Hefner and Muhammad Qasim Zaman (Princeton, NJ: Princeton University Press, 2007), 110–124.
44. Samuel Tadros, *Motherland Lost: The Egyptian and Coptic Quest for Modernity* (Stanford, CA: Hoover Institution Press, 2013).

45. Hania Sobhy, "To Get Rid of Extremism in Egyptian Education, Understand Its Roots," *Al-Fanar Media,* November 6, 2015, http://www.al-fanarmedia.org/2015 /11/to-get-rid-of-extremism-in-egyptian-education-understand-its-roots/.

46. Ibid.

47. Thougan Obeidat, "Ashmal wa aham dirasa tahliliyya: "al-da'ishiyya" fi al-manahij wa al-kutub al-madrasiyya al-urduniyya" [A Comprehensive and Important Analytical Study: "ISIS" in the Jordanian Curriculum and Textbooks], *ArabJo,* accessed June 30, 2016, http://www.arabjo.net/index.php/2014 -12-21-16-19-16/2014-12-21-16-39-28/item/3757-2015-07-03-23-05-50.

48. Majdi Suleiman, Amina Awad Hamdan, Hassan Farhan Rababaa, Aziza Saleh Eiliwah, and Youssef Abdallah al-Sharifain, *Thaqafa Islamiyya: al-mustawa al-thani—kitab al-thanawiyya* [Islamic Culture: Part 2—Secondary Level] (Amman: Wizarat al-tarbiya wal ta'leem, 2014), 44.

49. Jameel Fakhry Janim, Arafat Rashad Yaseen, al-Mahmoud Khaza'lah, Hassan Farhan Rababaa, and Yahya Mahmoud al-Qudah, *al-Tarbiya al-Islamiyya: al-mustawa al-thani—saf thamin* [Islamic Education: Part 2—Eighth Grade] (Amman: Wizarat al-tarbiya wal ta'leem, 2014), 177.

50. Obeidat, "Ashmal wa aham dirasa tahliliyya."

51. "Education System: The Philosophy and Objectives of Education," *The Hashemite Kingdom of Jordan: Ministry of Education,* accessed May 1, 2017, http://www .moe.gov.jo/en/MenuDetails.aspx?MenuID=32.

52. Dalal Salameh, "New School Textbooks and Extremism, New Covers for Old Books," *7iber,* June 15, 2015, http://7iber.com/society/the-new-school-textbooks -and-extremism-new-covers-for-old-books/#.WAYUi-V94dV.

53. Michaela Prokop, "Saudi Arabia: The Politics of Education," *International Affairs* 79, no. 1 (2003): 79.

54. Maher Mater Abouhaseira, "Education, Political Development, and Stability in Saudi Arabia" (PhD diss., University of Southern California, 1998), 85.

55. Prokop, "The Politics of Education," 78–80.

56. Ben Hubbard, "A Saudi Morals Enforcer Called for a More Liberal Islam. Then The Death Threats Began," *New York Times,* July 10, 2016, http://www.nytimes .com/2016/07/11/world/middleeast/saudi-arabia-islam-wahhabism-religious -police.html.

57. "Labor Force Participation Rate, Female (% of Female Population Ages 15+) (Modeled ILO Estimate): Middle East & North Africa (1990–2014)," World Bank, accessed October 31, 2016, http://data.worldbank.org/indicator/SL.TLF.CACT .FE.ZS?locations=ZQ; "Labor Force Participation Rate, Male (% of Male Population Ages 15+) (Modeled ILO Estimate): Middle East & North Africa (1990–2014)," World Bank, accessed October 31, 2016, http://data.worldbank.org/indicator /SL.TLF.CACT.MA.ZS?locations=ZQ.

58. Ayşe Gül Altınay, *The Myth of the Military-Nation: Militarism, Gender, and Education in Turkey* (New York: Palgrave Macmillan, 2004), 120, 124–127.

59. Iren Ozgur, *Islamic Schools in Modern Turkey: Faith, Politics, and Education* (Cambridge: Cambridge University Press, 2012), 33.

60. Ibid., 34–37, 46, 106.

61. Sukru Kucuksahin, "Turkish Students Up in Arms Over Islamization of Education," *Al-Monitor*, June 20, 2016, http://www.al-monitor.com/pulse/originals/2016/06/turkey-high-schools-student-stand-up-against-islamism.html.

62. F. Stephen Larrabee and Angel Rabasa, *The Rise of Political Islam in Turkey* (Santa Monica, CA: RAND, 2008); Prof. Edhem Eldem (Professor of History at Boğaziçi University), Roundtable on Education, Istanbul, May 25, 2015.

63. Sukru Kucuksahin, "Turkish Students."

64. Ugur Ümit Üngör, *The Making of Modern Turkey: Nation and State in Eastern Anatolia, 1913-1950* (Oxford: Oxford University Press, 2011), 177–205.

65. Amin Maalouf, *Les identités meurtrières* (Paris: Grasset & Fasquelle, 1998), 33–46.

66. U.S. Department of State, *Bahrain: International Religious Freedom Report for 2013* (Washington, DC: U.S. Department of State, 2013), 4.

67. Cesari, *The Awakening of Muslim Democracy*, 95–96.

68. Osman, *Sectarianism in Iraq*, 178, 184–185.

69. Cesari, *The Awakening of Muslim Democracy*, 92–93.

70. Algerian Constitution of 1989 (reinstated 1996, revised 2008), preamble.

71. Algerian Constitution of 1989 (reinstated 1996, revised 2016), article 4.

72. Antoine Messarra, "La religion dans une pédagogie interculturelle," *Revue internationale d'éducation de Sèvres*, no. 36 (2004): 101–110.

73. Nemer Frayha, "Pressure Groups, Education Policy, and Curriculum Development in Lebanon: A Policy Maker's Retrospective and Introspective Standpoint," in *World Yearbook of Education 2010: Education and the Arab 'World': Political Projects, Struggles, and Geometries of Power*, ed. André E. Mazawi and Ronald G. Sultana (New York: Routledge, 2010), 104–109.

74. Huda Ayyash-Abdo, "Adolescents' Self-Image in Lebanon: Implications for Education," in *International Perspectives on Adolescence,* ed. Frank Pajeres and Timothy C. Urdan (Charlotte, NC: IAP, 2003), 178; Frayha, "Education Policy," 104–109.

75. Liesbet Steer, Hafez Ghanem, and Maysa Jalbout, *Arab Youth: Missing Educational Foundations for a Productive Life?* (Washington, DC: Brookings Institution, 2014), 9.

76. United Nations Children's Fund (UNICEF), "School Enrolment Rates Up but 21 Million Children in the Middle East & North Africa Risk Missing Out on an Education," news release, April 15, 2015, http://www.unicef.org/media/media_81564.html.

77. Farzaneh Roudi, *Population Trends and Challenges in the Middle East and North Africa* (Washington, DC: Population Reference Bureau, 2001), 1.

78. Hovig Demirjian, *Teacher Shortage in the Arab World: Policy Implications* (Doha: Arab Center for Research and Policy Studies, 2015), 2.

15. The Education Paradox

1. World Bank, *Education in the Middle East and North Africa: A Strategy Towards Learning for Development* (Washington, DC: World Bank, 1999), 6.
2. Larbi Sadiki, "Bin Ali's Tunisia: Democracy by Non-Democratic Means," *British Journal of Middle Eastern Studies* 29, no. 1 (2002): 68.
3. Ministère de l'Education, *Le développement de l'éducation en Tunisie 1996–2000* (Tunis: Ministère de l'Education, 2000), 30, 38.
4. "Adult Literacy Rate, Population 15+ Years, Both Sexes (%): Tunisia (1984–2015)," World Bank, accessed November 11, 2016, http://data.worldbank.org/indicator/SE.ADT.LITR.ZS?end=2015&locations=TN&start=1984&view=chart.
5. World Bank, *Knowledge and Skills in the MENA Region Tunisia: DIFID-WB Collaboration on Knowledge and Skills in the New Economy* (Washington, DC: World Bank, 2003), 4.
6. Chiheb Bouden (Tunisian minister of higher education and scientific research, February 2015–August 2016), in discussion with the author, July 28, 2015.
7. Tunisian Law no. 93–9 of 1993, article 7.
8. The Organization for Economic Co-operation and Development (OECD), *Investing in Youth: Tunisia; Strengthening the Employability of Youth During the Transition to a Green Economy* (Paris: OECD, 2015), 165–203; Ministère de l'Education, *L'éducation en Tunisie*, 20–26.
9. Neji Jalloul (Tunisian minister of education, February 2015–April 2017), in discussion with the author, July 30, 2015.
10. The Organization for Economic Co-operation and Development (OECD) and the United Nations Educational, Scientific and Cultural Organization (UNESCO), *Teachers for Tomorrow's Schools: Analysis of the World Education Indicators* (Paris: OECD and UNESCO, 2001), 42–43.
11. Mahmoud Yaagoubi, Salem Talbi, Sondes Laamari, Rim Ben Slimane, Fakher Zaibi, Christine Hofmann, and Paz Arancibia, *Analyse du système éducatif tunisien* (Tunis: Organisation internationale du Travail, 2013), 55.
12. OECD and UNESCO, *Teachers for Tomorrow's Schools*, 10, 86–87.
13. Ministère de l'Education, *L'éducation en Tunisie*, 45.
14. OECD and UNESCO, *Teachers for Tomorrow's Schools*, 145.
15. Ahmed Khaled (Tunisian minister of culture, March 1990–February 1991), in discussion with the author, April 21, 2016.
16. Mohamed Charfi and Patrick Camiller, *Islam and Liberty: The Historical Misunderstanding* (London: Zed, 2005), 147.
17. Abdulhalim Almasoudi, "Bazaraat al-khirab" [The Bazaars of Ruin], *AlAwan*, July 18, 2014, http://www.alawan.org/article13332.html.
18. Rollie Lal, "The Maghreb," in *The Muslim World After 9/11*, ed. Angel M. Rabasa (Santa Monica, CA: RAND, 2004), 158.
19. Malika Zeghal, "Public Institutions of Religious Education in Egypt and Tunisia: Contrasting the Post-Colonial Reforms of Al-Azhar and the Zaytuna," in

Trajectories of Education in the Arab World: Legacies and Challenges, ed. Osama Abi-Mershed (New York: Routledge, 2010), 118.

20. Kamal Imran, Mohamed al-Shteiwi, and Salem Mahjoub, *Kitab fi al-tafkir al-islami lithalameeth al-sana al-uwla min al-ta'leem al-thaanawi* [History Textbook for Students in the Third Year of Secondary School] (Tunis: Omega li al-nashr, 1998), 15, 131–132.

21. Zeghal, "Al-Azhar and the Zaytuna," 118.

22. Imran, al-Shteiwi, and Mahjoub, *Kitab fi al-tafkir al-islami,* 73, 131–132.

23. Muhammad Faour, "Religious Education and Pluralism in Egypt and Tunisia," *Midan Masr,* accessed May 30, 2016, http://www.midanmasr.com/en/article.aspx?ArticleID=216.

24. Robin Heath, "Health Education: Arab States," in *Encyclopedia of Women & Islamic Cultures,* ed. Suad Joseph (Leiden: Brill, 2005), 3.

25. Imran, al-Shteiwi, and Mahjoub, *Kitab fi al-tafkir al-islami,* 292–293.

26. Driss Abbassi, *Entre Bourguiba et Hannibal: Identité tunisienne et histoire depuis l'indépendance* (Paris: Karthala; Aix-en-Provence: IREMAM, 2015), 169–172.

27. Hamadi Ben Jaballah (professor of epistemology at the University of Gabès), in discussion with the author, June 28, 2016.

28. François Siino, *Science et pouvoir dans la Tunisie contemporaine* (Aix-en-Provence: Institut de recherches et d'études sur le monde arabe et musulman, 2004), 271–281.

29. Hmida Ennaifer (retired professor of theology at Zaitouna University, member of Ennahda), in discussion with the author, June 28, 2016.

30. Hatem Ben Salem (Tunisian minister of education, August 2008–January 2011), in discussion with the author, June 28, 2016.

31. Hamadi Ben Jaballah, in discussion with the author, June 28, 2016.

32. Faouzia Charfi (physicist and professor at the University of Tunis, widow of Mohamed Charfi), in discussion with the author, June 27, 2016.

33. Zeghal, "Al-Azhar and the Zaytuna," 117.

34. Iqbal al-Gharbi (professor at Zaitouna University), in discussion with the author, April 20, 2016.

35. Aziz Enhaili, "Tunisia," in *Guide to Islamist Movements,* ed. Barry M. Rubin (Armonk, NY: M. E. Sharpe, 2010), 2:395.

36. Zeghal, "Al-Azhar and the Zaytuna," 117.

37. Kevin Shillington, ed., *Encyclopedia of African History* (New York: Fitzroy Dearborn, 2005), 3:1606–1610.

38. Messaoud Romdhani, "A Flawed Education System Could Jeopardize Democracy," *Alternatives International Journal,* October 1, 2014, http://www.alterinter.org/spip.php?article4253.

39. Ministère de l'Education, *L'éducation en Tunisie,* 39, 79.

40. Jane Marshall, "Tunisia: Debate on Higher Education Problems and Future," *University World News,* November 20, 2011, http://www.universityworldnews

.com/article.php?story=20111120095403594&query=TUNISIA%3A+Debate+on+ Higher+Education+Problems+and+Future.

41. Abdelmajeed Charfi (scholar of civilization and Islamic thought, professor emeritus at the University of Tunis), in discussion with the author, June 28, 2016.

42. Youssef, "Bac—Le système des 25% disparaîtra en 2016," *Webdo*, April 26, 2014, http://www.webdo.tn/2014/04/26/bac-systeme-25-disparaitra-en-2016/.

43. Slim Khalbous (Tunisian minister of higher education and scientific research, August 2016–), in discussion with the author, November 29, 2016.

44. "Faut-il supprimer les 25% au Baccalauréat?" *Leaders*, June 6, 2013, http:// www.leaders.com.tn/article/14333-faut-il-supprimer-les-25-au-baccalaureat.

45. Sylvie Mazzella, "L'enseignement supérieur privé en Tunisie: La mise en place étatique d'un secteur universitaire privé," in *Les territoires productifs en question(s): Transformations occidentales et situations maghrébines* (Rabat: Institut de recherche sur le Maghreb contemporain, 2006), 231–235.

46. Ministère de l'Enseignement supérieur et de la Recherche scientifique, *L'enseignement supérieur et la recherche scientifique en chiffres, Année universitaire 2012-2013* (Tunis: Ministère de l'Enseignement supérieur et de la Recherche scientifique, 2013), 5.

47. Adnan Badran, *New Trends in Higher Education in Jordan 2014* (Amman: Arab Thought Forum, 2014), 14.

48. Ali Mahjoubi, "La réforme de l'enseignement (1989–1994)," *Attariq Aljadid*, no. 183–184 (2010).

49. Tunisian Ministry of Education, *Kitab al-tarbiya al-wataniyya litalameeth al-sana al-uwla min al-ta'leem al-thanawi* [Textbook for Civic Education for the First Year of Secondary School] (Tunis: Al-markaz al-watani al-pedagogi, 2009), 39.

50. Slim Khalbous, in discussion with the author, November 29, 2016.

51. Emna Guizani, "Education System to Face Widespread Reforms," *TunisiaLive*, April 23, 2015, http://www.tunisia-live.net/2015/04/23/education-system-in -need-of-widespread-reforms/.

52. "Tunisia: Essid Announces Start of Educational Establishments' Maintenance Campaign," *AllAfrica*, July 23, 2015, http://allafrica.com/stories/201507231518 .html.

53. Hamadi Ben Jaballah, in discussion with the author, June 28, 2016.

54. Ministère de l'Education, *Statistiques scolaires* (Tunis: Ministère de l'Education, 2012), 24.

55. Defense for Children International, *Overview of Child Rights Situation in Arab Countries* (Geneva: Defense for Children International, 2015), 46–48.

Glossary

'AHD AL-AMAN: "Security Covenant" or "Fundamental Pact," an edict issued in 1857 by Muhammad Bey granting civil and religious equality to all subjects—Muslim and non-Muslim, Tunisian and foreign.

'ASSABIYA: Ibn Khaldūn's concept of social bond and solidarity between groups of people such as clans or tribes, based on common cultural values or religion.

'ILM AL-'UMRAN: "The science of social organization," a concept first popularized by Ibn Khaldūn.

AHL AL-KITAB: "People of the book," a term for followers of any one of the three Abrahamic religions.

AL-'ULUM AL-'AQLIYYA: "The rational sciences," including theology, logic, arithmetic, and the natural sciences.

AL-LUWAT: A derogatory term for homosexuals, derived from the story of Prophet Lot and his warning to the citizens of Sodom and Gomorrah.

AL-MUJAHID AL-AKBAR: "The greatest warrior."

AL-NAHDA: The nineteenth-century renaissance movement, defined by Islamic modernism aimed at reviving Islamic thought through the reinterpretation of sacred texts.

AL-QAHIRA: The Arabic name for Cairo, the capital of Egypt.

AL-SALAFIYYA AL-'ILMIYYA: An apolitical branch of Salafism, primarily concerned with theological interpretations of scripture.

AMIR AL-MU'MININ: "Commander of the faithful."

ANCIEN RÉGIME: A historical term used to define the political regime in place before the French Revolution. By extension, the term is applied to any political regime that collapsed after a revolution.

ANSAR: A term used to refer to Muslims residing in Medina in Prophet Muhammad's time.

BA'ATHISM: Meaning "renaissance" or "resurrection," Ba'athism is a political ideology that combines strong elements of socialism and Arab nationalism. It was adopted by the ruling parties in Iraq (1968–2003) and Syria (1963–present).

BACCALAURÉAT: The national exam that students take at the end of high school in French-oriented schools, which determines their admissibility into university.

BALDIYYA: A term used during Ottoman times to refer to the merchant class of Tunis, distinct from the rural population and foreigners.

BERBER: Descendants of the indigenous population of North Africa. Today, Berber populations are present in Algeria, Morocco, Tunisia, Libya, Egypt, Mali, Niger, and Mauretania. They often refer to themselves as *Amazigh* (plural: *Imazighen*).

BEY: Governor of an Ottoman province.

COLLÈGES MOYENS: Terminal intermediate schools for vocational and technical training introduced by Bourguiba, providing an alternative track to secondary school.

COLON: European settler in French colonies. Some *colons* were also called *pieds-noirs*, a term that refers to European Christian and Jewish settlers in French colonies in North Africa, but mostly to French settlers living in Algeria during colonization.

CONTRÔLEURS CIVILS: French officials who controlled local administrative affairs at the provincial level and closely supervised tribal leaders.

COOPÉRANTS: Development aid workers dispatched by the French authorities.

DA'ESH: The transliterated Arabic acronym for the group ISIS (Islamic State in Iraq and Syria; also known as Islamic State in Iraq and the Levant (ISIL), or the Islamic State).

DAWLAH: Derived from the Arabic root "to turn" or "alternate" (*d-w-l*), *dawlah* came to mean "dynasty" or "ruler," in reference to their turn in power. The term has since evolved and in modern contexts translates as "state."

DERJA: A general term for colloquial Arabic spoken in the Maghreb.

DHIKR: The act of chanting of God's attributes, popular in Sūfism.

ÉVOLUÉS: A term used by the French during the colonial era to refer to indigenous people who had "evolved" through education and assimilation and now behaved and thought in a similar fashion to the French.

FATWA: An Islamic opinion from a learned scholar pertaining to a specific issue, usually given upon request from an individual or judge.

FELLAGHAS: Meaning "bandits," the *fellaghas* were unofficial militant resistance forces of the Tunisian and Algerian nationalist movements.

FIQH: The study and interpretation of Shari'a. *Fiqh* is also used to address questions not found in Shari'a through *ijtihad,* the opinions of *ulama,* and the issuing of *fatwas.*

FITNAH: The first Muslim civil war fought over caliphate succession.

FUQAHA': Islamic jurists who practice *fiqh.*

FUTUHAT: Early Islamic conquests as Islam spread from the Arabian Peninsula in the seventh century.

GENDARMERIE: An armed unit that fulfills the role of a second police force in France. In Tunisia, the French gendarmerie that existed during the French protectorate was replaced with the national guard and is under the jurisdiction of the ministry of interior.

GHAZI: "Raider," or one who participates in a *ghazu,* or a military expedition, usually to spread Islam.

GRAND MUFTI: The supreme authority on matters of religious law in a Sunni Muslim country, advising the state and courts.

HABUS: The term used in the Maghreb for *waqf.*

HADITH: Reports documenting the sayings of Prophet Muhammad. Hadith is an important body of knowledge in Islam, second only to the Qur'an, and is used in *fiqh* and *tafsir.*

HARAM: A term describing something forbidden or prohibited in Islam.

HASHEMITE: Members of the House of Hashim, the royal family that claims descent from the Prophet and ruled over the Hejaz in present-day Saudi Arabia from the tenth century until the conquest by the al-Saud family in 1924. Members of the Hashemite family ruled in Iraq until the mid-twentieth century and have ruled in Jordan, and before that Trans-Jordan, since the birth of the state.

HIFZ: The act of memorizing the Qur'an.

HIJAB: A headscarf that is wrapped around the head, covering the hair and neck, worn by some Muslim women.

IDDAH: The waiting period after a divorce or death of a husband during which the wife is not allowed to remarry or have contact with any male except unmarriageable kin, or *mahrams*. It allows for reconsideration of divorce and confirmation that the wife is not pregnant.

IFRIQIYA: The name given to the Roman province of Africa by Muslim Arabs upon entering North Africa in the seventh century.

IJMA': A term referring to the consensus of Islamic theologians on a certain issue in Islamic jurisprudence, or *fiqh*.

IJTIHAD: Independent reasoning practiced by an Islamic jurist to answer a legal matter in Islam. *Ijtihad* is used when a matter cannot be addressed directly by texts of the Qur'an or Hadith and there is no existing consensus (*ijma'*) on the topic.

IKHTILAT: A term that describes the intermingling of men and women in one place.

IMAM-HATIP SCHOOLS: Schools for religious functionaries, under the control of the government, that were established after the closure of *kuttab* schools in Turkey in 1924. They have since taken on a broader educational function, providing an alternative track in secondary education since 1970, and have proliferated under the patronage of Erdogan and AKP.

INFITAH: Literally meaning "opening," *infitah* signifies policies of economic liberalization.

JEUNES TUNISIENS: A group of young Tunisian intellectuals who called for greater political and economic autonomy for Tunisians within the French protectorate.

JIHAD: A term that literally translates as "struggle" or "effort." In Islam, jihad refers to the struggle to better oneself as a Muslim, whether externally (improving one's society) or internally (improving one's character). The concept also encompasses the obligations of all Muslims to inform others about Islam and, if necessary, to defend the religion by holy war.

JIZYA: Historically, a tax that was paid by Christians and Jews residing in Muslim lands.

KAFALA: "Guardianship," or the commitment of a family to raise a child that is genetically not its own.

KHITM: The act of reading the Qur'an from start to finish.

KHOUKHA: The smaller portal or entry found on large, traditional Tunisian doors through which people commonly enter and leave a house.

KHULAFA' RASHIDUN: The four Rightly Guided Caliphs who were the successors of Prophet Muhammad after his death: Abu Bakr al-Siddiq, Omar Ibn al-Khattab, Othman Ibn Affan, and Ali Ibn Abi Taleb.

KUTTAB SCHOOL: Also known as a madrassa, a *kuttab* school is exclusively dedicated to the teaching of the Qur'an and Islam.

LAÏCITÉ: The separation between church or mosque and state, establishing the state's neutrality in religious affairs. In practice, the term has come to represent the subjugation of religion to the state, in some cases to the extent of obliterating religion from the public sphere.

LYCÉE: The French term for high school in the French education system, college refers to middle school. Secondary school typically consists of middle school and high school.

MA'AHID AZHARIYYA: Institutes related to al-Azhar Mosque-University in Egypt that teach not only the curriculum prescribed by the Egyptian ministry of education but also extra subjects related to Islam and its history. These schools cater to primary, middle, and high school students.

MADHAB: A school of thought within Islamic jurisprudence or *fiqh*, such as the Hanafi, Maliki, Shafi'i, and Hanbali *madhabs* in Sunni Islam and the Ja'fari *maddhab* in Shi'a Islam.

MADRASSA: See *kuttab* school.

MAHDI: Meaning "divinely guided," the *Mahdi* is an important figure in Shi'a eschatology as a messianic deliverer of Islam.

MAHR: A gift or dowry, in the form of cash or presents, given to the wife by her husband upon marriage.

MAHRAM: The unmarriageable kin of a Muslim woman, such as her father, brother, son, or uncle.

MAJALLA: "Journal," or "code." Also appears as *majallat* and is known as *mudawwana* (or *mudawwanat*), it usually refers to an important compilation of information or record. *Majallat al-ahwal al-shakhsiyya* and *Mudawwanat al-ahwal al-shakhsiyya* mean "the personal status code."

MAJBA: A head tax imposed on all Tunisians during Ottoman rule.

MAJLIS: "Council," or representative body of expert advisers.

MAMLUK: An Ottoman slave who usually went on to become an official or a soldier, reaching high government posts in the Ottoman Empire.

MAQASID: "Intentions" or "aims." In the context of Islamic law, it refers to the principles that guide the interpretation and enactment of Shari'a.

MASLAHA: A concept in Islamic law meaning "public interest." It mandates that the greater good of society be considered when drafting legislation.

MATHALI AL-JINS: The literal translation into Arabic of "homosexuals."

MATIÈRE GRISE: Meaning "gray matter" of the brain in French, this term was used by Habib Bourguiba to encourage the Tunisian people to develop their intellectual capacities.

MUEZZIN: A designated person at the mosque who leads the call to prayer.

MUDAWWANA: see majalla.

MUFTI: An Islamic scholar with the authority to interpret Shari'a and issue *fatwas*.

MUHAJIRUN: Early adopters of Islam who emigrated from Mecca to Medina with Prophet Muhammad.

MUJTAHID: An authority capable of using reason to interpret, independently, Islamic tenets from the Qur'an and Hadith. A practitioner of *ijtihad*.

MUKHABARAT: The name for the state intelligence services in many Arab countries.

MUQADDIMAH: Ibn Khaldūn's most important work. *Muqaddimah*, meaning "Introduction," discusses the philosophy of history, Islamic theology, political theory, and science.

MUTAWASSITTIYEEN: "Mediterranean people," which is how Tunisians often refer to themselves.

NAHDAWIYAT: Female members of Ennahda.

NASSERISM: Named after Gamal Abdel Nasser, Nasserism is a socialist, pan-Arabist political ideology characterized by anti-imperialism, nationalism, and nonalignment.

NIQAB: A veil that covers the hair, face, and body, worn by some Muslim women.

NIZAMI: New Ottoman armies created around the end of the eighteenth century that mimicked European armies.

NŪR AL-'ILM: "Light of knowledge," a term used by Bourguiba to highlight the importance of education.

PASHA: Title of high-ranking officers in the Ottoman Empire.

PIEDS-NOIRS: European settlers living in French colonies in North Africa, mostly applied to French nationals who settled in Algeria during colonization.

PRÉPONDÉRANTS: A lobby of French settlers who assumed high authority and moral ground.

QADI: An Islamic judge who decides cases in accordance with Shari'a.

QIYADA: "Governorate," or province.

QIYAS: In Islamic law, *qiyas* refers to a process of analogy whereby prohibitions and teachings of both the Qur'an and Hadith are generalized to apply to novel circumstances.

RIBAT: An Islamic fort.

RIDDA: Apostasy from Islam, an action that many classical and modern jurists believe should be punishable by death. However, the definition of what constitutes *ridda* is debated. Some regard it as simply renouncing Islam, while some define it as an act accompanied by political rebellion.

SAHEL: The coastal area of eastern Tunisia that extends from Hammamet to Mahdia.

SAHW: "Sobriety," in contrast to *sukur*, "intoxication." Sūfis use these terms to describe their emotional and transformative journey in trying to be closer to God. Sūfi poetry is known for expressing joy and ecstasy in the "intoxicated" expressions of Sūfism, whereas "sober" Sūfism appeals to intellectual thought.

SALAF: "Ancestor."

SALAFISM: A conservative Islamic movement that evolved from the *Salafiyya* doctrine into three distinct, although at times overlapping, groupings: purist, political, and militant.

SALAFIYYA: An ideology attributed to Muhammad Abduh and Jamal al-Din al-Afghani that grew out of the Islamic renaissance movement, or *al-Nahda*. It called for the reassertion of Islam's rational aspects and freedom from rigidities that had inhibited the religion's development.

SHARI'A: Islamic law that is, for the most part, derived from the Qur'an and Hadith and provides the basis of Islamic jurisprudence.

SHESHIYA: Traditional Tunisian cap, usually red, worn on the head by men.

SHI'AT ALI: "Party of Ali," the supporters and descendants of Ali Ibn Abi-Taleb, cousin and son-in-law of the Prophet Muhammad and fourth of the *Khulafa' Rashidun*. Following Ali's assassination, they formed the first political, and later religious, faction of Islam known as Shi'a.

SHURA: "Consultation," encouraged in Islam between rulers and their constituents.

SHUDHŪDH: "Deviance" or "perversion," often used as a derogatory term for homosexuality.

SIYASET AL-MARAHEL: Bourguiba's "gradualism," or strategy of attaining his goals in stages.

SŪFISM: The mystical branch of Islam that seeks identification with God through love and spirituality.

SUNNAH: The reported deeds, habits, sayings, and implicit approvals of the Prophet Muhammad.

SŪF: "Wool."

TAFSIR: Qur'anic exegesis or interpretation.

TAJWEED: The art of perfecting the recitation of the Qur'an.

TAKFIR: An accusation of apostasy in Islam, making a *kafir* (unbeliever; plural: *kuffar*) of someone.

TALAQ: "Divorce."

TALFIQ: "Piecing together." *Talfiq* entails the blending of elements from different *madhabs* to create a new body of laws and was popularized by the Egyptian thinker Muhammad Abduh.

TAMAZIGHT: The most common Berber or *Amazigh* language, spoken in Algeria and Morocco.

TANZIMAT: Reforms initiated by the Ottoman Empire in the nineteenth century. They included *Gulhane hatti sherif* (Noble Edict of the Rose Chamber) and *Hatti humayun* (Imperial Edict), introduced, respectively, in 1839 and 1856.

TARIKATLAR: Sūfi brotherhoods in Turkey.

TIERS COLONIAL: A colonial practice that enabled European workers to earn one-third more than their Tunisian counterparts.

TOUNSI: Colloquial spoken Tunisian Arabic—as opposed to Classical Arabic or Modern Standard Arabic—with Berber and French influences.

TUNISIANITÉ: Tunisian specificity, which combines Western modernity with a unique national identity.

TURUQ: "Paths" (singular: *tariqa*), *turuqs* are Sūfi orders or schools. *Turuqs* have a guide who acts as a spiritual leader.

ULAMA: Muslim scholars who are knowledgeable in Islamic law and theology.

UMMA: "Community." The term usually refers to the larger Islamic community worldwide.

VAKIFLAR: Islamic foundations in Turkey that often provide needed social services.

WAHHABISM: The ideology of Muhammad Ibn Abdelwahhab that calls for a strict and puritanical interpretation of Islam.

WALAYA: A state of being achieved by Sūfi saints who have become metaphysically close to God through the abandonment of ego.

WALI: "Governor."

WAQF: A term that refers to Islamic endowments dedicated to charity. They can be in the form of cash, land, or property.

WATAN: "Homeland," "nation," or "country."

WILAYA: "Province" or "governorate." *Wilayat Ifriqiya* was the name given to the area roughly encompassing Tunisia and parts of modern-day Libya and eastern Algeria by the Arab Muslims who began their foray into North Africa in the seventh century.

YASMIN: The name of the *jasmine* flower in Arabic; also "gift from God" in Persian.

Selected Bibliography

Abadi, Jacob. *Tunisia Since the Arab Conquest: The Saga of a Westernized Muslim State*. Reading, UK: Ithaca, 2013.

Abbassi, Driss. *Entre Bourguiba et Hannibal: Identité tunisienne et histoire depuis l'indépendance*. Paris: Karthala; Aix-en-Provence: IREMAM, 2015.

Abi-Mershed, Osama, ed. *Trajectories of Education in the Arab World: Legacies and Challenges*. New York: Routledge, 2010.

Allman, James. *Social Mobility, Education and Development in Tunisia*. Leiden: Brill, 1979.

Anderson, Lisa. *The State and Social Transformation in Tunisia and Libya, 1830–1980*. Princeton, NJ: Princeton University Press, 1986.

Beinin, Joel. *Workers and Thieves: Labor Movements and Popular Uprisings in Tunisia and Egypt*. Stanford, CA: Stanford University Press, 2016.

Ben Achour, Mohammed el-Fadhel. *Le mouvement littéraire et intellectuel en Tunisie au XIVème siècle de l'Hégire (XIX-XXe siècles)*. Tunis: Alif—Les Éditions de la Méditerranée, 1998.

Borowiec, Andrew. *Modern Tunisia: A Democratic Apprenticeship*. London: Praeger, 1998.

Boularès, Habib. *Histoire de la Tunisie: Les grandes dates, de la Préhistoire à la Révolution*. Tunis: Cérès, 2012.

Boulby, Marion. "The Islamic Challenge: Tunisia Since Independence." *Third World Quarterly* 10, no. 2 (1988).

Brown, Leon Carl. "Tunisia," in *Education and Political Development*, ed. James Smoot Coleman, 144–168. Princeton, NJ: Princeton University Press, 1965.

———. *The Tunisia of Ahmad Bey: 1837-1855*. Princeton, NJ: Princeton University Press, 1974.

Camau, Michel, and Vincent Geisser, eds. *Habib Bourguiba: La trace et l'héritage*. Paris: Karthala, 2004.

Cesari, Jocelyne. *The Awakening of Muslim Democracy: Religion, Modernity, and the State*. New York: Cambridge University Press, 2014.

Charrad, Mounira M. *States and Women's Rights: The Making of Postcolonial Tunisia, Algeria, and Morocco*. Berkeley: University of California Press, 2001.

Code du statut personnel (1956).

Code du statut personnel (1958).

Code du statut personnel (2014).

Cordesman, Anthony H. *A Tragedy of Arms: Military and Security Developments in the Maghreb*. Westport, CT: Praeger, 2002.

Diamond, Larry, and Marc F. Plattner. *Democratization and Authoritarianism in the Arab World*. Baltimore, MD: Johns Hopkins University Press, 2014.

Gana, Alia, Gilles Van Hamme, and Maher Ben Rebbah. "Social and Socio-Territorial Electoral Base of Political Parties in Post-Revolutionary Tunisia." *Journal of North African Studies* 19, no. 5 (2014).

Gana, Nouri, ed. *The Making of the Tunisian Revolution: Contexts, Architects, Prospects*. Edinburgh: Edinburgh University Press, 2013.

Green, Arnold H. *The Tunisian Ulama 1873–1915: Social Structure and Response to Ideological Currents*. Leiden: Brill, 1978.

Hamid, Shadi. *Temptations of Power: Islamists and Illiberal Democracy in a New Middle East*. Oxford: Oxford University Press, 2014.

Hermassi, Abdellatif. "Société, Islam et islamisme en Tunisie," *Cahiers de la Méditerranée* 49, no. 1 (1994): 61–82.

Hermassi, Elbaki. *Leadership and National Development in North Africa: A Comparative Study*. Berkeley: University of California Press, 1972.

Hibou, Béatrice. *The Force of Obedience: The Political Economy of Repression in Tunisia*. Cambridge: Polity, 2011.

——. "Le réformisme, grand récit politique de la Tunisie contemporaine," *Revue d'histoire moderne et contemporaine* 56, no. 4 (2009): 14–39.

Honwana, Alcinda. *Youth and Revolution in Tunisia*. New York: Zed, 2013.

Hourani, Albert. *Arabic Thought in the Liberal Age: 1798–1939*. Cambridge: Cambridge University Press, 1983.

Husni, Ronak, and Daniel L. Newman, eds. *Muslim Women in Law and Society: Annotated Translation of al-Tahir al-Haddad's* Imra'tuna fi 'l-shari'a wa'l mutama', *with an Introduction*. London: Routledge, 2007.

Hussey, Andrew. *The French Intifada*. New York: Faber & Faber, 2014.

Ikeada, Ryo. *The Imperialism of French Decolonisation: French Policy and the Anglo-American Response in Tunisia and Morocco*. New York: Palgrave Macmillan, 2015.

Julien, Charles-André. "Colons français et Jeunes-Tunisiens (1882–1912)," *Revue française d'histoire d'outre-mer* 54, no. 194–197 (1967): 87–150.

King, Stephen J. "Economic Reform and Tunisia's Hegemonic Party." In *Beyond Colonialism and Nationalism in the Maghrib: History, Culture, and Politics*, ed. Ali Abdullatif Ahmida, 165–196. New York: Palgrave Macmillan, 2009.

Lewis, Mary Dewhurst. *Divided Rule: Sovereignty and Empire in French Tunisia, 1881–1938*. Berkeley: University California Press, 2014.

Lulat, Y. G.-M. *A History of African Higher Education from Antiquity to the Present: A Critical Synthesis*. Westport, CT: Greenwood, 2005.

Miles, Richard. *Carthage Must Be Destroyed: The Rise and Fall of an Ancient Civilization*. New York: Penguin, 2012.

Montana, Ismael M. *The Abolition of Slavery in Ottoman Tunisia*. Gainesville: University Press of Florida, 2013.

Moore, Clement Henry. *Tunisia Since Independence: The Dynamics of One-Party Government*. Berkeley: University of California Press, 1965.

Parkinson, Nancy. *Education Aid and National Development: An International Comparison of the Past and Recommendations for the Future*. New York: Macmillan, 1967.

Perkins, Kenneth J. *Historical Dictionary of Tunisia*. 2nd ed. Lanham, MD: Scarecrow, 1997.

———. *A History of Modern Tunisia*. 2nd ed. Cambridge: University of Cambridge, 2014.

Schraeder, Peter J. "Tunisia's Jasmine Revolution, International Intervention, and Popular Sovereignty." *Whitehead Journal of Diplomacy and International Relations* 13, no. 1 (2012).

Siino, François. *Science et pouvoir dans la Tunisie contemporaine*. Aix-en-Provence: Institut de recherches et d'études sur le monde arabe et musulman, 2004.

Sraïeb, Noureddine. "Le collège Sadiki de Tunis et les nouvelles élites." *Revue du monde musulman et de la Méditerranée* 72, no. 1 (1994): 37–52.

———. "Contribution à la connaissance de Tahar el-Haddad (1899–1935)," *Revue de l'Occident musulman et de la Méditerranée* 4, no. 1 (1967): 99–132.

———. "De la Zaytuna à l'université de Tunis: mutations d'une institution traditionnelle." In *Les institutions traditionnelles dans le monde arabe*, ed. Hervé Bleuchot, 55–70. Aix-en-Provence: Institut de recherches et d'études sur le monde arabe et musulman, 1996.

———. "L'idéologie de l'école en Tunisie coloniale (1881–1945)." *Revue du monde musulman et de la Méditerranée* 68, no. 1 (1993): 239–254.

———. "Khérédine et l'enseignement : une nouvelle conception du savoir en Tunisie," *Minorités religieuses dans l'Espagne médiévale*, no. 63–64 (1992): 203–210.

———. "Université et société au Maghreb: la Qarawîyin de Fès et la Zaytûna de Tunis," *Revue de l'Occident musulman et de la Méditerranée* 38, no. 1 (1984): 63–74.

Stepan, Alfred. "Tunisia's Transition and the Twin Tolerations," *Journal of Democracy* 23, no. 2 (2012): 89–103.

Tunisian Constitution of 1959.

Tunisian Constitution of 2014.

Van der Haven, Elisabeth Cornelia. "The Bey, the Mufti and the Scattered Pearls: Shari'a and Political Leadership in Tunisia's Age of Reform 1800–1864." PhD diss., Leiden University, 2006. https://openaccess.leidenuniv.nl/handle/1887/4968.

Willis, Michael J. *Politics and Power in the Maghreb: Algeria, Tunisia, and Morocco from Independence to the Arab Spring.* Oxford: Oxford University Press, 2014.

Zayzafoon, Lamia Ben Youssef. *The Production of the Muslim Woman: Negotiating Text, History, and Ideology.* Lanham, MD: Lexington, 2005.

Index